A FIRST COURSE IN
BUSINESS STUDIES

Stephen Danks

BSc (Hons), Dip Marketing, Cert Ed

Stephen Danks has wide experience of industry and commerce. Formerly head of business studies in a large further education college, he has also taught in schools. He is currently Chief Moderator for Pitman Examinations Institute and Senior Moderator for NVQ Business Administration. He has previously been a BTEC examiner, RSA examiner and City and Guilds Assessor.

DP PUBLICATIONS LTD.
Aldine Place, 142/144 Uxbridge Road
Shepherds Bush Green, London W12 8AW
1991

Acknowledgements

I am grateful to the following for permission to reproduce copyright material which is indicated by chapter and paragraph reference:

	Chapter/Para No.		Chapter/Para No.
Advertising Standards Authority	11/61	G-Mex	13/54
ACAS	25/54	Godfrey Hill	23/6
Alexander Howden Group Ltd	19/11	Hoverspeed Ltd	14/50
Alex Lawrie Factors	17/5	Inland Revenue Dept	22/39; 22/44;
ASDA Stores	13/16		22/46
AT & T	24/47	Lloyds International Factors	17/5
Automobile Association	14/19	Mail Order Protection Scheme	15/57
Banking Information Service	4/12; 4/37; 4/39	National and Provincial	
BBC Education	8/36	Building Society	9/39
BOTB	3/59	National Savings Dept	26/47
BP Oil Ltd	14/36; 14/50	North Sea Ferries	14/36
British Coal	7/5	Office of Fair Trading	15/23
Building Employers		Peugot/Talbot	1/14; 1/41; 9/57
Confederation	25/32	Port of London Authority	14/11
Caroline Horrigan	10/18; 21/30;	Responsive College	
	25/11	Programme	21/43
City of London	12/9	Royal Bank of Scotland plc	4/22; 4/32
Commission for Racial Equality	21/34	Royal Insurance	19/19; 19/31
Consumers Association	15/44	Sainsbury's	15/19
Crown Copyright	2/38; 2/45; 3/12;	Shell UK	14/19
	3/23; 3/45; 23/2;	Small Business Research Trust	10/18
	26/31; 25/48	W H Smith	12/40; 13/30
Andrew Danks	23/32	Sotheby's	12/25
Department of Transport	20/18	Stock Exchange	20/35; 26/40
ECGD	3/59	Jason Stott	15/11
Engineering Employers		TeleFocus: a British Telecom	
Federation	25/33	photograph	24/41
European Parliament	3/53	Tesco plc	9/39
Ford Motor Co	9/49	Trades Union Congress	25/27
Freightliners Ltd	14/11		
Forestry Commission	1/41		
GEC Transportation			
Projects Ltd	14/52		

The following Examination Boards are thanked for permission to reproduce questions:

THE NORTHERN EXAMINING
ASSOCIATION (NEA)
Associated Lancashire Schools Examining Board,
Joint Matriculation Board, North Regional Examinations Board, North West Regional Examinations
Board, Yorkshire and Humberside Regional Examinations Board

THE LONDON AND EAST ANGLIAN
GROUP (LEAG)
East Anglian Examinations Board, London Regional
Examining Board, University of London School
Examinations Board

THE MIDLAND EXAMINING GROUP (MEG)
East Midland Regional Examinations Board, Oxford
and Cambridge Schools Examination Board, Southern
Universities Joint Board for School Examinations,
The West Midlands Examinations Board, University
of Cambridge Local Examinations Syndicate

THE SOUTHERN EXAMINING GROUP (SEG)
The South-East Regional Examinations Board, The
Association Examining Board, The Southern
Regional Examinations Board, The Oxford Delegacy
of Local Examinations, The South Western Examinations Board

THE WELSH JOINT EDUCATION
COMMITTEE (WJEC)

THE NORTHERN IRELAND SCHOOLS
EXAMINATION COUNCIL (NISEC)

LONDON CHAMBER OF COMMERCE AND
INDUSTRY

PITMAN EXAMINATIONS INSTITUTE

ROYAL SOCIETY OF ARTS

I also wish to thank all the companies and newspapers for the use of other material. (Despite every effort, I have failed to trace the copyright holders for some of the illustrations.)

I am also indebted to Lynn Cross who did most of the typing and to the staff of the Bank of England, Co-operative Union Ltd. Co-operative Wholesale Society Library and Information Unit, Midland Bank, Open University Co-operative Research Unit, Stock Exchange and Trades Union Congress who kindly assisted me with the accuracy of the text.

Finally to my family without whose help, encouragement and tolerance the book would not have been possible.

ISBN 1 870941 73 x
Copyright S. Danks ©1991

Reprinted 1993

Typeset by Alphaset, Southampton

Printed in Great Britain by
The Guernsey Press Co. Ltd,
Guernsey, Channel Islands

Contents

Preface

AIM

The aim of this book is to provide a comprehensive introductory text for Business Studies courses in schools and colleges.

It is suitable for use on a range of courses including GCSE Business Studies, GCSE Business Information Studies, GCSE Commerce, GCSE Economics, BTEC First Award, TVEI, CPVE and other introductory Business Studies courses including LCCI, Pitman and RSA.

NEED

The need was seen for a complete introductory text book which:

1. provides a lively and **clear approach** to business studies
2. covers, **comprehensively**, the GCSE National Criteria and other examination board syllabuses.
3. provides a *variety of methods of assessing all abilities* e.g. structured assignments (case studies, role playing, data response and problem solving); specimen examination questions; self assessment questions and answers
4. presents Business Studies in a way which *develops other relevant skills and techniques* (numeracy, literacy, discovering, selection and the use of relevant information).

APPROACH

The text has been written in a standardised form, including chapter introductions, numbered paragraphs, summaries, self review questions and examination practice questions (including multiple choice/completion) *with answers*.

Apart from end of chapter questions with answers there are student centred *assignments* and *specimen examination questions* relevant to the text covered. *Outline answers* are provided on application to the publishers free to teachers/lecturers recommending this book as a course text.

Each chapter is illustrated, as and when appropriate, in a lively and interesting way. Cartoons, photographs and diagrams are included to support the many examples used throughout.

METHOD OF STUDY

Whilst the book has been prepared mainly as a class text, it can be used equally well by individual students. This is particularly important given the current growth of self-study learning. In both cases the summaries, review questions, examination questions and assignments will be very useful for checking understanding and assisting revision.

Although the chapters in the book can be used as and when required, it is preferable to follow the sequence laid down, as some chapters assume a knowledge of principles covered earlier.

SUGGESTIONS AND CRITICISMS

The author would welcome, via the publishers, any comments on the book. This will enable subsequent editions to be amended, if necessary, and made even more useful to students and teachers alike.

DISCRIMINATION BETWEEN THE SEXES

For reasons of textual fluency, you will find the words "he/him/her" have been used throughout this book. However, in many cases the person referred to could be of either sex.

REPRINT 1993

Reprinted 1993 with minor updates.

1. Development of Economic Activity

INTRODUCTION

1. This chapter provides a general introduction to the subject of business studies. It covers the development of economic activity and includes the division of labour, growth of trade and the factors and types of production. It provides a framework for further studies since many of the topics outlined, are discussed more fully in later chapters.

EARLY PRODUCTION

2. In primitive societies there were no shops. The simple needs of people for food, clothing and shelter were satisfied from what they could hunt, grow or make themselves, ie they were *self-sufficient*.

SPECIALISATION

3. Later men began to specialise in producing just one or a few items which they were particularly good at making. This *division of labour* as it is called, enabled men to produce more than they needed for themselves. This led to the development of *trade* (buying and selling) as they exchanged their surplus for other items that they needed.

4. **Barter**   **Money**

BARTER

5. The earliest form of trade was known as *barter*, that is the exchange of goods for goods. For example one man might exchange a boat with a neighbour who could offer him some flour or chickens. As trade increased *markets* developed in many towns providing a regular place where goods could be offered for exchange.

6. **Disadvantages of Barter**

There are three main problems with barter.

    a) It depends on a double *coincidence of wants* ie a boatbuilder who needed some flour would have to find not only someone with flour to offer, but also who wants a boat in exchange.

    b) It is difficult *to value* commodities, for example how many sacks of flour is a boat worth?

    c) Many goods are *indivisible* eg a boat owner may not need so many sacks of flour, but he may have nothing else to offer in exchange for what he needs. How then do you give change?

MONEY

7. To overcome these problems, money was introduced as a *medium of exchange*. Before the notes and coins, which we know today, earlier types of money included shells, shark's teeth and precious metals. In

fact anything which was generally acceptable. With money, the boat-builder of ancient times could not only buy his flour but also goods from other craftsmen such as weavers or blacksmiths, none of whom might want a boat.

8. Functions of Money

Money then fulfils a number of important functions. It is a:

a) MEDIUM OF EXCHANGE – which allows goods and services to be easily bought and sold
b) MEASURE OF VALUE – which is used to price goods and services
c) STORE OF VALUE – money can be saved for future use
d) MEANS OF DEFERRED PAYMENTS – for example when goods are bought on credit the amount owed is measured using money.

9. Characteristics of Money

As well as being generally accepted money also needs to be:

a) Portable – easily carried
b) Durable – will last a long time
c) Divisible – easily divided into smaller amounts – 5p, 10p, 20p coins etc
d) Easily recognized – therefore readily accepted
e) Uniform in quality – all 50p coins are of the same quality.

SPECIALISATION BY PRODUCT

10. By making exchange easier, money enabled the division of labour to develop rapidly in the nineteenth and twentieth centuries. People increasingly specialised in particular jobs, for example farmers, builders, bakers, carpenters etc, resulting in a big increase in the number of goods produced.

DIVISION OF LABOUR

11.

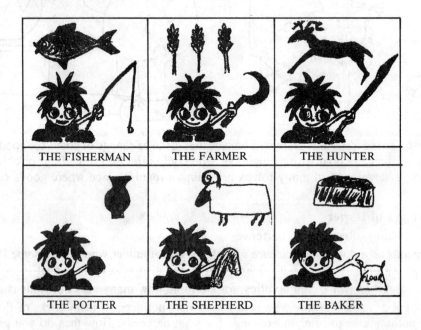

| THE FISHERMAN | THE FARMER | THE HUNTER |
| THE POTTER | THE SHEPHERD | THE BAKER |

SPECIALISATION BY PROCESS

12. The division of labour is now widely used in modern industry. Work is divided into a number of processes along a 'production' or 'assembly line' with each worker carrying out just one or two tasks.

13. This enables *mass production* to take place. Large quantities of standardised (similar) goods can be made using automatic machines and relatively few workers to operate them. Car factories are organised in this way. The shell of a car begins at one end of the 'line'; as it passes along a conveyor belt system, different parts of the car are added by each worker. By the end of the line the car is complete.

Two Stages of Mass Production

14.

15. ## Advantages of the Division of Labour
   * People can specialise in what they can do best
   * More goods are produced at a lower cost
   * Special machinery and equipment can be used
   * Practice makes perfect so each person becomes better and faster at their job
   * Time is saved because workers do not have to move from one operation to another
   * Training is much quicker because jobs are easier to learn.

16. ## Disadvantages of the Division of Labour
   * Boredom – repeating the same task can make workers dissatisfied
   * Standardised products – results in many households having similar taps, televisions, cars etc
   * Decline in crafts and skills – because work is now done by machines
   * Dependence on other people – for example absent or slow workers could disrupt the production line
   * Problems if workers lose their jobs – because they only have a few skills.

17. ## Limits to the Division of Labour
The mass production of goods is not suitable unless there is a large market in which to sell them. There would be no point in mass producing planes, ships and racing cars. However, soap powder, chocolate, toothpaste, family cars and telephones all have mass markets and therefore can be manufactured on a large scale.

NEEDS AND WANTS

18. Goods and services are produced because people need or want them. In order to survive in life, we all *need* food, clothing and shelter. These are the basic needs which must be satisfied. *Wants* on the other hand are goods and services which people seek to obtain in order to improve their standard of living, ie quality of life. When people talk about the *demand* for something, it means not just wanting it, but also being able and willing to pay for it.

SCARCITY AND CHOICE

19. We would all like to have more or better possessions than we have now – clothes, houses, furniture, holidays etc. Our wants are unlimited, ie there is always something which we would like. However, our resources are *scarce* or limited. We only have a certain amount of money and therefore must make a *choice* on how best to spend it.

20. The problems of scarcity and choice also apply to businesses and countries. A business must decide how to make the best use of its limited resources. Likewise a country cannot produce unlimited amounts of goods and services if its resources are limited.

21. One way of looking at this problem is to say that the cost of any choice is the next best alternative which we decide to do without. This is what economists call *opportunity cost*. For example, the cost to a teenager of going to the cinema is the record which could have been bought instead; a farmer may keep cattle instead of sheep, governments may spend money on hospitals instead of roads.

DEFINITIONS

22. a) The provision of goods and services is called *production*. The people who buy them are *consumers*.

b) *Goods* are tangible items which we can see and touch. For example food, make-up, motor cycles and washing machines.

c) *Services* are not goods but things which we use like the telephone, buses, education and entertainment.

GOODS AND SERVICES

23.

Some Goods **and** **Services**

ECONOMIC SYSTEMS

24. All societies in the world face this basic economic problem of scarcity and choice. Because there are limited resources, it is necessary for each to decide what goods and services it is going to produce. How this decision is made will depend on the type of economic system which operates in the country.

FREE ECONOMY

25. At one extreme, all resources could be owned by individuals who organise them to produce what people want. There is no Government intervention. This is known as a 'Free Economy'. What is produced is determined by what is called the market mechanism of supply and demand. For example, if there was no demand for wooden houses or bicycles, then an entrepreneur would not make any profit by supplying them. Therefore instead, he would use his resources to produce other goods. The USA, Canada and Japan are examples of free economies.

N.B. Free Economies are also known as Market Economies, Capitalist Systems or Free Enterprises.

26. **Advantages of a Free Economy**
   * Consumers determine demand and therefore what is produced
   * Increased competition which keeps prices down and improves efficiency and standards
   * All members of the community are free to run businesses for profit.

27. **Disadvantages of a Free Economy**
   * Successful businesses may buy up smaller ones and control a larger share of the market. This can reduce competition and lead to higher prices.
   * Some goods and services required by the community as a whole may not be produced at all, for example defence.
   * Pollution could increase because it may be difficult to contol.

CONTROLLED ECONOMY

28. At the other extreme, all resources could be owned and organised by the State. In these economies, decisions on what to produce are taken collectively by the Government on behalf of its people. Bulgaria, China and Cuba are examples of controlled economies, often called centrally planned economies or Communist states.

29. **Advantages of a Controlled Economy**
   * Resources are used to produce what the community needs which eliminates wasteful competition
   * More equal distribution of income and wealth
   * Prevents large firms controlling markets and putting up prices.

30. **Disadvantages of a Controlled Economy**
   * Lack of competition may reduce efficiency, enterprise and innovation
   * Central control may make it difficult to respond quickly to changes in needs and conditions
   * Individuals lose their freedom of choice.

MIXED ECONOMY

31. Most countries in the world, including the UK, actually have what is called a mixed economy. This means that some resources and organisations are owned and controlled by the State and others by private individuals.

5

THE FACTORS OF PRODUCTION

32. In order to produce the goods and services needed to satisfy human wants, four essential resources called factors of production are used. These are land, labour, capital and enterprise. A country's total production will depend on the quantity and quality of these resources.

Land ⟶
Labour ⟶   ⟶ PRODUCTION ⟶ Goods and Services
Capital ⟶
Enterprise ⟶

Capital
Labour
Land

LAND

34. This is needed for the building of factories, offices, shops and houses. However, land also consists of all the other natural resources which man uses, including:
   * Coal, gold, salt and all the other substances found in the ground
   * The fish in the sea
   * All the things which grow on land, such as trees, wheat, barley and fruit
   * The animals and birds like sheep and chickens which are reared for food
   * The climate which provides the air, sunshine and rain needed for life.

35. The total supply of land is fixed as is its quality. However, the quality may be improved by adding fertilisers, drainage or irrigation.

LABOUR

36. Production cannot take place without land, but it needs the skills and efforts of people to convert resources into goods and services which others want. For example, a bunch of daffodils must be cut, packed and transported to shops before we can buy them. All this requires the use of labour. Even when organisations use a lot of automatic equipment, labour is still needed to manage, control and operate it.

37. The total supply of labour is made up of many different kinds of workers, — skilled, semi-skilled and unskilled. The degree of skill is likely to depend upon the amount of education, training and experience which workers have received.

CAPITAL

38. In its broadest sense capital means anything which is owned by a business and is used to make future production easier and more efficient. It includes buildings, machinery, equipment and vehicles. For example, a window cleaner needs a ladder, bucket and wash leather. A clothing manufacturer needs a factory, machines and raw materials before anything can be made.

ENTERPRISE

39. An entrepreneur is somebody who brings together the other resources of land, labour and capital and organises them in a business. They take the risk that if the goods or services which they produce do not sell, then they might lose their money. If successful, the entrepreneur will make a profit.

40. *N.B.* Clearly not all factors of production are of the same quality. For example, barren hillsides will not grow good crops, a clumsy person will not have the skill to produce fine jewellery; capital may be new or worn, whilst some entrepreneurs will have more ability than others.

TYPES OF PRODUCTION

41.

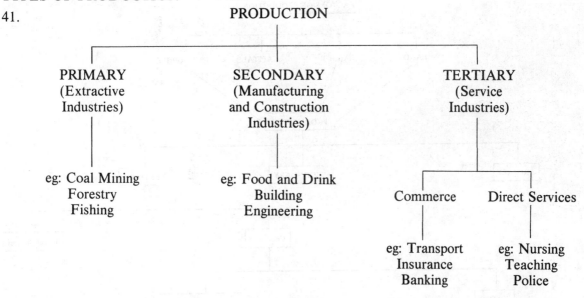

```
                            PRODUCTION
         ┌──────────────────────┼──────────────────────┐
     PRIMARY                 SECONDARY               TERTIARY
    (Extractive            (Manufacturing            (Service
    Industries)           and Construction          Industries)
                            Industries)
         │                      │              ┌────────┴────────┐
                                            Commerce      Direct Services
   eg: Coal Mining       eg: Food and Drink      │                │
       Forestry              Building       eg: Transport     eg: Nursing
       Fishing               Engineering       Insurance        Teaching
                                               Banking          Police
```

Tree Felling   Car Manufacture   Oil Delivery

PRODUCTION

42. We all consume a wide range of goods and services in life. Therefore, people work both to produce them and also to earn the money needed to buy them. Production can be considered under three main headings – primary, secondary and tertiary industries.

43. **Primary**

This consists of all the *extractive* industries, for example coal mining, quarrying, fishing, forestry and farming. Many of these primary products form the raw materials for secondary production.

44. **Secondary**

These are the *manufacturing* and *construction* industries which change the raw materials into finished products. Examples include the manufacture of chemicals, textiles and shoes, and the building of roads, houses and bridges.

45. **Tertiary**

These industries do not produce goods, but provide services. Tertiary production is often referred to as Commerce and Direct Services.

PRODUCTION AND TRADE

46.

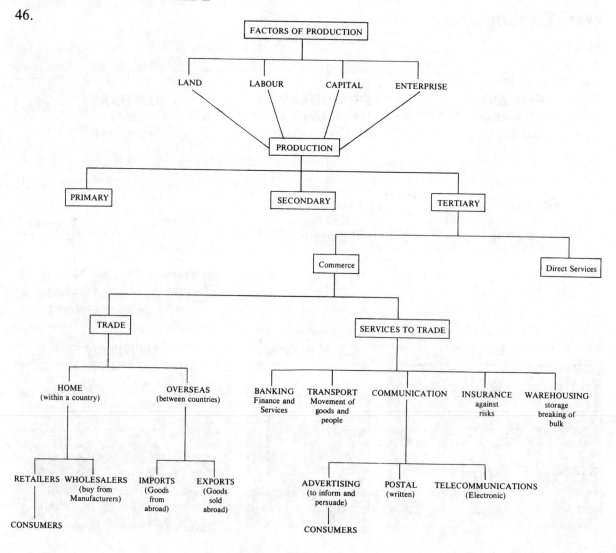

COMMERCE

47. As shown in the diagram Commerce consists of *trade* and *commercial services* which assist the process of trade. Trade can take place either within a country or between countries. In *home trade* manufacturers use wholesalers and retailers to distribute their goods. *Foreign trade* involves goods which are bought from abroad (imports) and those sold to other countries (exports).

SERVICES TO TRADE

48. The problems of getting goods from manufacturers to wholesalers, retailers and final consumers can be very complex involving many commercial services or 'aids to trade'.

Some of the more important of these services are outlined below and discussed in detail in later chapters.

BANKING

49. Banks are very important in the process of trade.
   a) They help to provide the *finance* which is needed to start or run a business.
   b) They offer a variety of *services*. For example, foreign currency for traders who import goods, information and advice, and cheques which make it safer and easier to make payments.

TRANSPORT

50. Goods cannot be easily bought and sold unless they can be moved from one place to another. Coffee, for example, which is produced in Brazil, is of little use unless it can be transported to other countries like Britain to be consumed. The *movement of goods* by road, rail, sea and air is therefore an essential aid to trade, since manufactured goods throughout the country must be moved from factories to warehouses or direct to retailers and then to final consumers. Transport is also important for *moving people*, both to their places of work and also to enable them to reach the shops in order to buy the goods produced.

COMMUNICATION

51. a) Advertising – if goods are to be produced in large quantities, then advertising is essential to ensure that they are sold. It is used both to *inform* potential customers about goods and services and also to *persuade* them to buy.
   b) Postal – letters and other *written* correspondence are an essential part of business.
   c) Telecommunications – this provides very fast methods of *electronic* communication. It includes the telephone, radio, television and the use of computerised equipment.

INSURANCE

52. Insurance companies exist to offer *protection against* the *risks* which manufacturers, wholesalers, retailers and transport firms face. The risks that goods, buildings, vehicles or money might be stolen, damaged or destroyed. Insurance companies collect small annual payments (called premiums) from large numbers of businesses. If a firm then suffers losses through fire, theft or damage, then it can be compensated out of the 'pool' of money collected.

WAREHOUSING

53. Wholesalers perform many functions which can help both manufacturers and retailers. For example, they buy goods from manufacturers and store them, whilst for retailers they keep the goods until required and then sell them in small convenient quantities.

DIRECT OR PERSONAL SERVICES

54. These are not related to trade but help to increase production by looking after people's general health and welfare. Doctors, dentists, teachers, hairdressers, policemen and entertainers all provide direct services.

DIRECT AND INDIRECT PRODUCTION

55. We noted earlier that in the past, men lived simple lives producing for themselves the few goods which they needed. Today this *direct production* is still common in under-developed countries. However, countries with developed economies, like the UK, are much more complex and highly specialised. Most of our goods and services are provided by other people, that is, by *indirect production*. Also goods and services now come from all over the world. It is the commercial services or 'aids to trade' which make this possible.

SUMMARY

56. a) The earliest form of trade was called barter.
   b) The division of labour or specialisation resulted in a big increase in the number of goods produced, leading to the need for money.
   c) Specialisation has both advantages and disadvantages and is limited by the size of the market.
   d) We all face the problems of scarcity and choice because our resources are limited.
   e) Economic systems can be free, controlled or mixed.
   f) Land, labour, capital and enterprise are the four factors of production.
   g) The three types of production consist of primary, secondary and tertiary industries.
   h) Banking, transport, communication, insurance and warehousing are some of the more important tertiary or service industries.

REVIEW QUESTIONS

Answers can be found in the paragraphs shown.

1. What is self-sufficiency? (2)
2. Using 2 examples of your own, explain the meaning of barter. (5)
3. How did money overcome the disadvantages of barter? (6-8)
4. Give 4 examples of specialisation by product. (10)
5. How does the division of labour make mass production possible? (11-14)
6. List 3 advantages and 3 disadvantages of the division of labour. (15-16)
7. In what sense is there a limit to the division of labour? (17)
8. Explain the terms scarcity, choice and opportunity cost. (19-21)
9. Outline the main features of a free economy, controlled economy and mixed economy. (24-31)
10. Briefly describe the 4 factors of production. (32-41)
11. Give 4 examples of occupations found in primary industries and 4 in secondary industries. (43-44)
12. Distinguish between commercial and direct services and say why both are important to production. (45-54)

EXAMINATION PRACTICE QUESTIONS   Marks

1. The production and exchange of goods is called . . .   1
2. The exchange of goods without the use of money is called . . .   1

Marks

3. When each of the tasks involved in the manufacture of a product is performed by a different person, this is known as the 1

4. Explain what is meant by mass production. 2

5. a) Explain the terms primary, secondary and tertiary production. Give one example of each. 9

 b) Show how the various activities of a large oil company fall into each of the 3 types of production. 9

 c) Oil is becoming a scarce resource. What does this mean and how can oil companies deal with this problem? 12

MULTIPLE CHOICE/COMPLETION

1. Basic human needs are food, clothing and
 a) Holidays
 b) Education
 c) Television
 d) Shelter

2. The basic economic problem in all countries is
 a) Over-population
 b) Scarce resources
 c) Unemployment
 d) Inflation

3. Which one of the following has a centrally planned economy?
 a) UK
 b) Cuba
 c) USA
 d) Eire

4. If a teenager buys a record he may not be able to afford to go to the cinema. This is an example of:
 a) Opportunity cost
 b) Insufficient pocket money
 c) Real cost
 d) Social cost

5. The main purpose of production is to:
 a) Make profits
 b) Provide jobs
 c) Build more factories
 d) Satisfy people's wants

6. A consumer is someone who:
 a) Owns a flat or house
 b) Owns a business
 c) Buys goods and services
 d) Pays taxes to the government

In each of the following questions, one or more of the responses is/are correct. Choose the appropriate letter which indicates the correct version.

    A   if 1 only is correct
    B   if 3 only is correct
    C   if 1 and 2 only are correct
    D   if 1, 2 and 3 are correct

7. Specialisation by product is illustrated by which of the following:
    1) Fisherman
    2) Dairy farmer
    3) Assembly line worker

8. Which of the following statements are true?
    1) Agriculture is part of primary production
    2) Advertising is a commercial service
    3) Dentistry is an example of an extractive industry.

RECENT EXAMINATION QUESTIONS

1. LCCI JUNE 1989 SSC BACKGROUND TO BUSINESS   **Marks**
   Division of labour in industry and commerce benefits everyone concerned.

   a) Explain the phrase **division of labour**.   4
   b) Give the advantages and disadvantages from the points of view of:
      i)   the owners of a business
      ii) the employees in a business
      iii) the customers of a business   14

NISEC 1988 GCSE BUSINESS STUDIES SPECIMEN PAPER II
2. "Britain is a good example of a 'mixed economy' ".
    a) State briefly what is meant by a mixed economy.   2
    b) Name 2 other kinds of national economies and give a brief description of each.   6

ASSIGNMENT

1. a) Which of the following items are needs and which are wants?
        i)   Chocolate   iv) Food
        ii) Heating   v)   Clothing
        iii) Television   vi) Car
    b) Now list 4 further items, 2 needs and 2 wants.

2. Which of the following goods could be said to be scarce?
        i)   Bread   iv) Lamp posts
        ii) Milk   v)   Greenhouses
        iii) Gas fires
    Explain your answer.

3. Match the following countries with the correct type of economy:

1	China
2	France
3	USA
4	Canada
5	UK

a	Mixed economy
b	Planned economy
c	Free economy

4. The following list contains 2 examples of each of the factors of production.

   i)   Coal
   ii) Shop till
   iii) Unemployed worker
   iv) Garage owner
   v)   Owner of an engineering business
   vi)   Apple orchard
   vii) Factory foreman
   viii) Automatic drill

   a) Name the 4 factors of production.
   b) Identify the correct examples of each factor.
   c) Which factors of production are needed to provide your education? Give examples of each.

5. Copy and complete the following diagram:

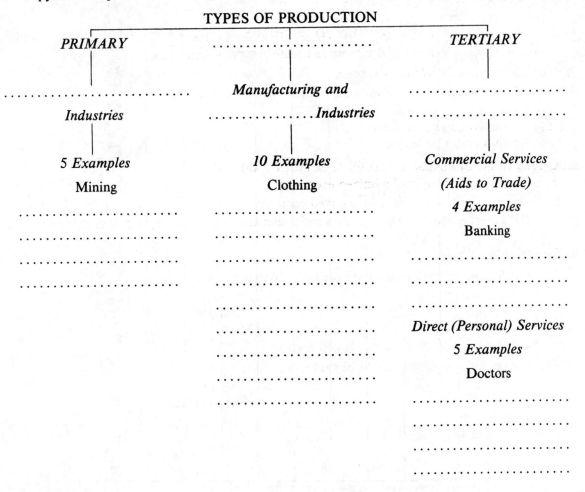

TYPES OF PRODUCTION

PRIMARY . . . . TERTIARY

. . . .   Manufacturing and   . . . .
Industries   . . . . *Industries*   . . . .

5 Examples   10 Examples   Commercial Services
Mining   Clothing   (Aids to Trade)
. . . .   4 Examples
. . . .   Banking
. . . .
. . . .

. . . .
. . . .   Direct (Personal) Services
. . . .   5 Examples
. . . .   Doctors
. . . .
. . . .
                                           . . . .

2. Population

1.   If you hear people talking about the 'population' of a place, they mean the number of people who live in it. This chapter looks at the growth of the UK's population, its age and sex structure and its geographical and occupational distribution.

CENSUS OF POPULATION

2.   The population of a country can only be accurately found by counting it. This counting is called a *census*.

3.   The questions asked at the census include the number of people who live in each house, each person's age, sex, occupation and country of birth. It also determines whether people are single, married or divorced and asks about the type of housing, number of rooms and amenities (toilets, bathrooms etc).

THE PURPOSE OF THE CENSUS

4.   The information collected is important for government planning. For example it provides facts about housing, education, transport, medical and other facilities which will be needed in the future.

5.   **UK Population Growth 1801 – 2011**

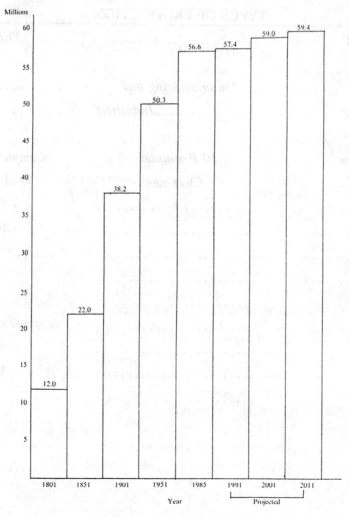

14

6. The Bar Chart shows that the UK's population increased rapidly in the nineteenth century. Although it is still growing, the rate of growth has slowed down considerably in the twentieth century.

FACTORS INFLUENCING THE SIZE OF THE POPULATION

7. Changes in the total size of the population are caused by changes in the *birth rate*, *death rate* and *rate of migration*.

8.

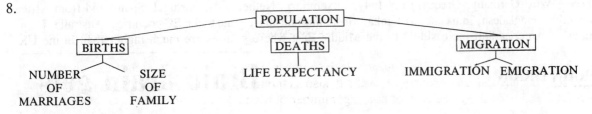

BIRTH RATE AND DEATH RATE

9. Birth and death rates are expressed as a number per thousand of the population.

10. **UK Birth and Death Rates**

Date	Birth Rate	Death Rate
1851	35.5	22.7
1901	28.7	17.3
1951	15.5	11.9
1961	17.6	12.0
1971	15.9	11.6
1981	12.8	11.7
1991	13.8	11.4

Source: Annual Abstract of Statistics/Social Trends

11. As shown in the table the birth rate was 35.5 per 1000 in 1851 when it was quite common for large families with six or more children. Nowadays the average number of children per family is only two and the birth rate has fallen to around thirteen per thousand.

12. **Reasons for the fall in the birth rate include:**
   * Improved methods and social acceptance of birth control
   * Improvements in health and food – children are less likely to die at an early age
   * Raising of school leaving age – in the nineteenth century children went to work at an early age
   * Changed status of women – many now go to work
   * Competing alternatives to children – foreign holidays, cars etc.

DEATH RATES

13. The UK death rate has fallen from 22.7 per 1000 in 1851 to a constant figure since the 1950's of about 12.0 per 1000. Over the same period *life expectancy* has increased greatly. On average men can now expect to live until the age of 73 (49 in 1901) and women to 78 (52 in 1901).

14. **Reasons for the fall in the death rate include:**
   * Improved medical knowledge, for example vaccinations, new drugs and equipment
   * Better sanitation, water supplies and waste disposal
   * Higher standards of living – better food, housing and clothing
   * Better working conditions
   * Fewer early deaths

MIGRATION

15. When people come to live in the UK they are known as 'immigrants'. People who move from the UK to other countries are called 'emigrants'. The difference between the two figures is called migration. Traditionally the UK has had a net loss of population through migration, although in the 1980's there was a net gain.

16. The majority of immigrants to the UK in the 1980's came from EC countries, (Belgium, Denmark, France, West Germany, Greece, Eire, Italy, Luxemburg, Netherlands, Portugal, Spain) and from Africa, Australia, Bangladesh, India and Sri-Lanka. Most emigrants have gone to the EC countries, Australia, United States of America and increasingly to the Middle East where salaries are much higher than in the UK.

BRAIN DRAIN

17.

Brain drain 'may force ICI abroad'

BRITAIN'S biggest industrial firm, ICI, could pull out from its base in this country because of the brain drain of top scientists to better paid overseas jobs, a former chairman believes.

This warning is to be given by Sir John Harvey-Jones in ITV's World in Action programme tonight. It underlines growing concern among many companies about the exodus of senior scientists and researchers.

The withdrawal by ICI from Britain would be a tremendous blow to the Government. Sir John says: 'The amount of capital behind each scientist in the United Kingdom is pitiful compared with other countries. And the actual funding of laboratories here is very short.

'If British science goes down the slot, or starts to lose its competitive position, then over a period of time one must question whether it is possible for a company like ICI to continue to be based in the UK.'

Brain drain gets worse as top men join exodus

THE brain drain is much worse than statistics suggest because it is the top researchers and those most difficult to replace who are flowing abroad, a report says today. The continued migration will have "long-term, deleterious consequences.

Government spending cuts in research and development have raised fears that the drain, already "a matter for serious concern," will worsen, it adds.

The report, by the Science and Engineering Policy Studies Unit of the Royal Society, is the most detailed study yet of the problem.

More scientists were leaving Britain than arriving to work here, it says. But it was the quality of scientists driven abroad which mattered most and the impact was much greater than the numbers involved might suggest.

The proportion of British Fellows of the Royal Society living abroad at the time of their election increased steadily from four per cent in 1960 to 13 per cent in 1984.

A particular worry is that an increasing percentage of Britian's brightest young scientists are joining the exodus. At 10 per cent, the figure is above average for all scientists.

salaries, and a worldwide shortage of scientists and engineers.

Those who responded to the survey suggested the following cures for the problem:
● More long-term research funding.
● A better career structure for university research staff.
● Schemes to attract "brain-drainers" back to Britain.
● More long-term posts.

According to the Save British Science campaign, the report only describes the brain drain abroad, not the "internal brain drain" of scientists away from industry and research into commerce.

The group said the drain could be reversed "for sums of money which are small compared to the long-term economic cost of the loss of so many of our best brains"

It called for an immediate infusion of £100 million-a-year to the research councils, and a long-term policy of investment in civil research and development by Government and

18. Emigration is important to the UK because the people most likely to leave are the young and well trained, for example doctors, engineers and scientists. This can result in what is called a 'brain drain' of professional and managerial workers. Whilst most immigrants tend to be manual and clerical workers who do not possess these skills.

CURRENT TRENDS IN POPULATION

19. In the 1970's and 1980's couples had slightly larger families due to:
*   Younger marriages
*   Higher standards of living
*   Increasing government help for families – maternity leave, child benefit etc
*   More facilities for women to return to work – creches, nursery schools etc.

THE CONCEPT OF AN OPTIMUM POPULATION

20. Over-Population

A country is said to be over-populated when it has more people than it can support. This can cause problems of shortages of food and water, poverty and a general lack of investment in machinery, factories and transport. Many third world countries like Ethiopia and Mozambique face these problems.

21. Under-Population

If a country does not have enough people this can also cause problems. The size of the market will be smaller because there are fewer people to buy goods and services. This may mean that resources cannot be used fully and therefore it cannot gain the benefits of economies of scale. (See Chapter 9).

22. Optimum Population

The optimum population is the ideal one which makes the most efficient use of a country's resources of land, labour and capital. At this level of population output per head is at its highest. This is illustrated in the following diagram.

Optimum Population

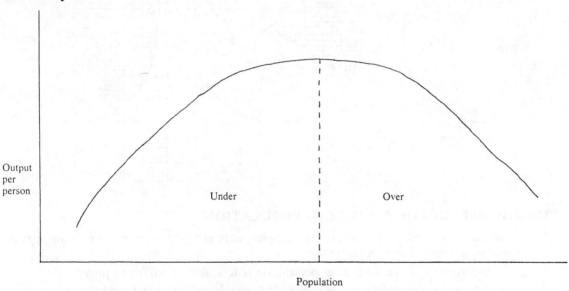

SEX AND AGE STRUCTURE OF THE POPULATION

24. Sex Distribution

This refers to the number of males and females in the population. In 1992 the UK's population was 57.6 million of which 28 million were males and 29.6 million females.

25. Throughout this century there have been more women than men in the UK's population. This is partly because many men were killed in the two world wars and also because women tend to live longer.

26. This structure is important because it affects the size of the labour force, the number of marriages and the birth rate, all of which affect the demand for different goods and services.

27. Age Distribution

The number of people of different ages in the population will depend upon the birth and death rates.

28. Age distribution is important because it influences factors such as:
    a) the size of the labour force
    b) the number of households and therefore the number of houses required

17

    c)   the size of families and therefore the type of houses required, for example two or three bedrooms

    d)   the need for schools, colleges and other facilities

    e)   the demand for goods and services which must be produced or imported

29. The present overall pattern in the UK is that of an ageing population. This is because the birth rate is low and people are living longer. As shown in the diagrams the percentage of the population over age 65 has risen from 5% in 1901 to 16% in 1991.

30. **Age Distribution of the Population**

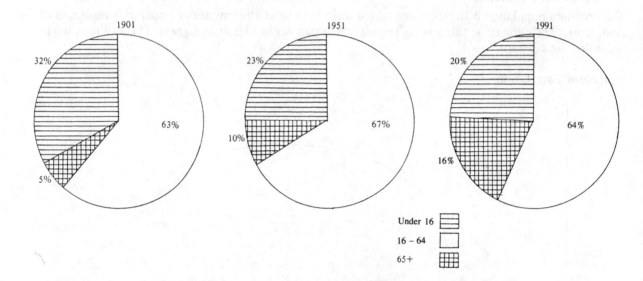

| Under 16 |
| 16 – 64 |
| 65+ |

ECONOMIC EFFECTS OF AN AGEING POPULATION

31. *   Changes in demand – for example less nappies, cots and prams but more retirement homes/bungalows, wheelchairs and false teeth

    *   Less mobile work force – an older population is less able or willing to move

    *   Less progressive – an older population may lack energy, initiative and enthusiasm for new ideas and skills

    *   Increased dependence on working population – the burden of taxation to pay pensions and provide for other facilities falls on fewer people because those of working age must support the rest.

GEOGRAPHICAL DISTRIBUTION OF POPULATION

32. There are two main trends in the geographical or regional distribution of the UK's population:

    a)   the shift of population from North to South and

    b)   the concentration of population in large conurbations.

SHIFT TO THE SOUTH AND MIDLANDS

33. As shown in the following table, since 1911 there has been a shift of population away from Northern England, Scotland, Wales and Northern Ireland. As unemployment has increased in these regions people have moved to the areas where job prospects, housing and other facilities are better, which has been mainly in the Midlands and South of England.

34.

Geographical Distribution of the Population (%)				
Area	1911	1951	1981	1991
North	6.7	6.2	5.5	5.4
Yorkshire and Humberside	9.2	9.0	8.7	8.5
East Midlands	5.4	5.7	6.8	7.0
East Anglia	2.8	2.8	3.4	3.6
South East	27.9	30.0	30.2	30.2
South West	6.4	6.4	7.8	8.3
West Midlands	7.8	8.8	9.2	9.1
North West	13.8	12.8	11.5	11.1
Wales	5.8	5.2	5.0	5.1
Scotland	11.3	10.1	9.2	8.9
Northern Ireland	2.9	3.0	2.7	2.8
	100.0	100.0	100.0	100.0

Adapted from Annual Abstract of Statistics 1993

CONCENTRATION OF POPULATION IN LARGE CONURBATIONS

35. The UK's *population density* of 237 people per square mile is one of the highest in the world. This compares with the Netherlands 359, Japan 316, West Germany 248, USSR 12 and Australia and Canada only 2. These figures are obtained by dividing a country's population by its area of land.

36. 75% of the UK's population live in urban areas (i.e. towns and cities). 30% of the population live in seven conurbations (continuous built up areas linking several towns around main cities). These seven in order of size in 1989 were:

Conurbation	Population millions	Main City
Greater London	6.7	London
West Midlands	2.6	Birmingham
Greater Manchester	2.5	Manchester
Central Clydeside	1.9	Glasgow
West Yorkshire	2.1	Leeds
Merseyside	1.4	Liverpool
Tyneside	0.8	Newcastle

Source: Office of Population Censuses & Surveys/Annual Abstract of Statistics

37. The advantages of concentration are that it can lead to better facilities, for example shops, schools, entertainment, communications (road, rail etc) and job prospects. However, it can also lead to problems of congestion, pollution and noise, and high unemployment when the main local industries decline. For example, the gradual decline since the war in the coal, cotton, shipbuilding and steel industries has had a dramatic effect on unemployment in many areas of the UK.

POPULATION DENSITY AND MAJOR URBAN AREAS

38.

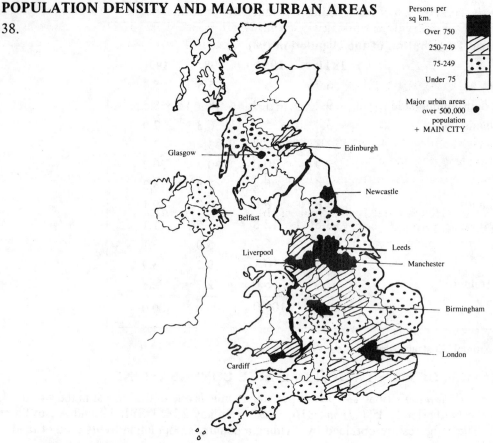

Source: Britain 1990 An Official Handbook

39. Far fewer people now choose to live in city centres but prefer instead to move outside, commuting to work by car and public transport (rail and bus). As a result many city centres have become run-down with poor houses, poor schools and high crime rates.

POPULATION AND EMPLOYMENT

Working Population

40. The working population is the number of people in work or available for work. It consists of everyone with a job, those registered as unemployed and the self-employed.

41. In the UK the total working population has gradually increased since the war and is now approximately 28 million, of which over 15 million are men. The main reason for this is the increase in the number of men and women who now work. The working population, as a proportion of the total population, has increased by 45% in 1976 to over 50% in 1993. However, approx 3 million people are unemployed.

42. The size of the working population depends upon the
   a)   size of the total population
   b)   number of people in the 16-65 age group
   c)   number of married women who return to work
   d)   number of people over 16 still in full-time education
   e)   number of people over retirement age still at work.

43. Changes in the composition of the working population are important because it affects the demand for goods and services. For example, working women have more money to spend on clothes and make-up. However, they also have less free time and therefore buy more ready prepared 'convenience' foods rather than fresh.

OCCUPATIONAL DISTRIBUTION

44. This refers to the numbers of people employed in different jobs. These occupations can be classified under three main headings:

Primary – agriculture, forestry, fishing, mining and quarrying

Secondary – manufacturing and construction

Tertiary (Services) – transport, distribution, financial services, catering and hotels, and national and local government.

45. **Changes in the Occupational Distribution of the Working Population in Britain between 1980 and 1991**

Industry or service (1980 Standard Industrial Classification)	Thousands (as at June)				Per cent (1991)
	1980	1983	1987	1991	
Primary sector	**1,099**	**998**	**820**	**703**	**3.2**
Agriculture, forestry and fishing	373	350	321	272	1.3
Energy and water supply	727	648	499	431	2.0
Manufacturing[b]	**6,937**	**5,525**	**5,167**	**4,720**	**21.7**
Construction	**1,243**	**1,044**	**1,013**	**939**	**4.3**
Services	**13,712**	**13,501**	**14,889**	**15,381**	**70.7**
Wholesale distribution and repairs	1,173	1,150	1,240	1,217	5.6
Retail distribution	2,177	2,005	2,123	2,143	9.9
Hotels and catering	972	963	1,113	1,230	5.7
Transport	1,049	912	902	913	4.2
Postal services and communications	437	433	448	415	1.9
Banking, finance and insurance	1,695	1,875	2,337	2,658	12.2
Public administration	1,980	1,918	2,046	1,923	8.8
Education	1,642	1,592	1,708	1,741	8.0
Health	1,258	1,294	1,315	1,467	6.7
Other services	1,327	1,359	1,657	1,674	7.7
Total	**22,991**	**21,067**	**21,889**	**21,743**	**100.0**

Sources: Department of Employment and Northern Ireland Department of Economic Development.

[a]Figures are not seasonally adjusted.

[b]In June 1991 employment in the main sectors of manufacturing industry included 691,000 in office machinery, electrical engineering and instruments; 678,000 in mechanical engineering; 544,000 in food, drink and tobacco; 439,000 in textiles, leather, footwear and clothing; 474,000 in paper products, printing and publishing; 497,000 in timber, wooden furniture, rubber and plastics; 303,000 in chemicals and man-made fibres; and 220,000 in motor vehicles and parts.

Note: Differences between totals and the sums of their component parts are due to rounding.

Britain '93 – An Official Handbook

46. The above table shows the main changes in the distribution of the working population between 1980 and 1991. These can be summarised as follows:

a)   A fall in the numbers employed in primary industries

b)   A fall in employment in the secondary industries

c)   An increase in employment in the tertiary sector.

47. In fact these changes have been taking place throughout the twentieth century. The main reasons for these are:

a)   The increased use of new technology and mechanisation which has improved productivity and replaced labour. For example, fertilisers and tractors have helped to increase output in agriculture, computers and robots in manufacturing industries.

b)   The general growth of the service sector in the UK, particularly insurance, banking and financial services. At the same time changes in society have led to the need for more people working in local and national government.

OCCUPATIONAL MOBILITY OF LABOUR

48. Your grandfather probably had only one or two jobs in his whole working life. However, it is now increasingly likely that the average person will change their occupation at least 3-5 times during their working life.

49. This is because as society changes so the demand for goods and services changes with it. Further developments in new computerised technology will also continue to change both what we buy and how it is made. Therefore, as some industries decline new ones, demanding different skills, will develop to take their place.

50. Increasingly this is also likely to involve more *geographical mobility* of labour. That is, people may have to move to a different area in order to find work.

SUMMARY

51. a)   An accurate count of the number of people in a country is called a census.

b)   The size of the population is affected by birth rates, death rates and migration.

c)   Both the UK's birth and death rates have fallen considerably in the twentieth century.

d)   Traditionally the UK has had a net loss of population due to migration.

e)   The concept of optimum population seeks to identify the size of population at which a country's output per head is at its highest.

f)   There are more females than males in the UK.

g)   The UK has an ageing population.

h)   The geographical distribution shows a shift of population from North to South and the concentration in large conurbations.

i)   The working population is the number of people in work or available for work.

j)   The current occupational distribution of population reflects a big change from primary and secondary industries to tertiary employment.

REVIEW QUESTIONS

Answers can be found in the paragraphs shown.

1.   What do you understand by the Census of Population? Briefly explain what information it contains and how it is used. (2-4)

2.   What is the size of the UK population? (5)

3.   What factors determine the size of a country's population? (7-18)

4.   What is meant by over-population, under-population and optimum population? (20-23)

5. Explain the terms 'sex distribution' and 'age distribution' of the population. (24-30)
6. Outline the economic effects of an ageing population. (31)
7. Explain with examples what is meant by 'population density'. (35)
8. How is the UK's population geographically distributed? (32-39)
9. What is the working population? (40)
10. Describe the main changes this century in the occupational distribution of the population. (45-47)

EXAMINATION PRACTICE QUESTIONS

	Marks

1. Besides the death rate, name 2 other factors which account for changes in the size of the population.
    2

2. State 3 possible economic effects resulting from the increasing number of old age pensioners in the population.
    3

3. Explain the following demographic terms:
   a) Life expectancy   2
   b) Death rate   2
   c) Population density   2

MULTIPLE CHOICE/COMPLETION

1. The two regions of the UK which experienced the fastest population growth between the 2 World Wars are:
   a) SE England and the Midlands
   b) SE England and SW England
   c) The Midlands and NW England
   d) Scotland and Wales

2. The potential work force of a country may change due to an alteration in all except which one of the following:
   a) The school leaving age
   b) Immigration
   c) The pensionable age of retirement
   d) The geographical distribution of the population.

3. The working population is best defined as:
   a) The number of people in the population over the age of 65
   b) All those people who are registered as unemployed
   c) All those people who are at work or are available to work
   d) The total number of school leavers in any year.

4. Which of the following is *not* true of the UK's population over the past 10 years?
   a) A fall in the numbers employed in manufacturing
   b) A fall in the size of the working population
   c) Higher unemployment
   d) An increase in the number of women employed.

In each of the following questions, one or more of the responses is/are correct. Choose the appropriate letter which indicates the correct version.

    A   if 1 only is correct

    B   if 3 only is correct

    C   if 1 and 2 only are correct

    D   if 1, 2 and 3 are correct

5. If the population of the country is said to be ageing, which of the following is likely to be true?

    1) The death rate is falling

    2) The proportion of old people in the population is increasing

    3) The proportion of old people in the population is falling.

6. Which of the following factors tend to increase the size of a country's population?

    1) An increase in the birth rate

    2) An increase in immigration

    3) A decrease in the death rate.

RECENT EXAMINATION QUESTIONS

                                                      Marks

1. **LEAG MAY 1989 GCSE BUSINESS STUDIES PAPER 2A SECTION A**

    Explain TWO effects on firms of an increasingly ageing popluation in the United Kingdom.   2

2. **RSA MAY 1990 BACKGROUND TO BUSINESS STAGE I PART II**

    Distribution of Working Population

Industry or Service	1982 (000's)	1987 (000's)
Primary Sector	1,038	818
Manufacturing	5,863	5,145
Construction	1,067	1,009
Services	13,448	14,838
TOTAL	21,416	21,810

Source: Britain '89 (HMSO)

    a) In the above table under which classification (primary, manufacturing etc) would the following be found:

        i)   Agriculture, forestry and fishing;

        ii) Banking, finance and insurance;

        iii) Textiles, leather and clothing?   3

    b) Define what is meant by the *working population*.   2

    c) Draw a simple bar chart showing the comparison of the working population between 1982 and 1987.   9

    d) Suggest TWO reasons why there has been an increase in the services sector of the working population.   6

ASSIGNMENT

The information below refers to the population and population structure of selected countries between 1971 and 2010.

Population and population structure: selected countries

	Estimates of mid-year population (millions)			Projections (millions)		Total annual rate of increase[1]	Birth rate[2]	Death rate[3]	Expectation of life at birth (years)		Population density (per sq. km)
	1971	1981	1986	2000	2010	1988	1988	1988	Males	Females	1987
United Kingdom	55.9	56.4	56.8	58.9	59.4	2.4	13.8	11.4	71.7	77.5	233
Belgium	9.7	9.8	9.9	9.9	9.7	1.5	12.1	10.6	70.0	76.8	324
Denmark	4.9	5.1	5.1	5.2	5.1	0.1	11.5	11.5	71.8	77.6	119
France	51.3	54.2	55.4	57.9	58.8	4.4	13.8	9.4	72.0	80.3	102
Germany (Fed. Rep.)	61.3	61.7	61.1	61.0	58.6	7.5	11.1	11.2	71.5	78.1	246
Greece	8.8	9.7	10.0	10.0	10.1	1.7	10.8	9.1	72.2	76.4	76
Irish Republic	3.0	3.4	3.5	3.5	3.4	− 2.5	15.4	8.9	70.1	75.6	50
Italy	54.1	56.5	57.2	57.6	56.4	1.8	10.1	9.4	71.6	78.1	191
Luxembourg	0.3	0.4	0.4	0.4	0.4	13.4	12.4	10.3	70.6	77.9	143
Netherlands	13.2	14.2	14.6	15.7	16.1	6.7	12.7	8.4	73.0	79.6	359
Portugal	8.6	9.9	10.2	11.1	11.1	3.3	11.9	9.6	70.7	77.5	111
Spain	34.2	37.8	38.7	40.7	41.2	4.2[4]	10.8[4]	8.0[3]	72.5	78.6	77
European Community	305.3	319.1	322.9	331.9	330.3	3.9	12.0	9.9	72.1	78.4	144
China	787.2	1,007.8	1,072.2	1,285.9	1,382.5	14.0	21.0	7.0	66.7	68.9	112
India	550.4	683.8	766.1	1,042.5	1,225.3	22.0	33.0	11.0	55.6	55.2	233
USSR	245.1	267.7	280.1	307.7	326.4	10.0	20.0	10.0	62.9	72.7	13
USA	207.0	229.8	241.6	266.2	281.2	7.0	16.0	9.0	71.2	78.2	26
Japan	104.7	117.6	121.5	129.1	131.7	5.0	11.0	6.0	74.8	80.5	322

[1]EEC countries; natural increase for China, India, USSR, USA and Japan.
[2]Live births per thousand population.
[3]Deaths per thousand population.
[4]1987.
Source: Social Trends 1990 Edition

Questions 1-6 are based on the information in the table.

1. What was the UK's population
    a) in 1971
    b) in 1981
    c) projected for 2010

2. Which country had the largest population
    a) in 1971
    b) projected for 2010

3. Which country had the smallest population
    a) in 1971
    b) projected for 2010

4. Where would the information about the UK have been collected from in the years 1971 and 1981?

5. How would the figures for 1986, 2000 and 2010 have been calculated?

6. a) Give the birth rates and death rates of 3 different countries in 1986.
    b) Why is this information important?

7. a) What is meant by the term 'Expectation of Life at birth?'
    b) Suggest 2 reasons why it is higher in the UK than in India or China.

8. Name 3 countries which are members of the European Community.

9. Suggest 2 reasons why the population of some countries, for example Luxemburg, Denmark, Belgium, Germany and Italy has grown very slowly compared with others like India, China and USSR.

10. Select 4 countries named in Question 9 and draw a graph to illustrate the difference in the rate of population growth.

3. International Trade

1.   In Chapter 1 we discussed the development of specialisation and the growth of trade to exchange the surplus which was produced. This chapter considers the importance of international or foreign trade, the UK's main imports and exports, the Balance of Payments, barriers to trade, the European Community, methods of selling goods abroad and sources of help for exporters.

REASONS FOR TRADE

2.   All the countries of the world are dependent upon each other to a certain extent. Very few can hope to produce everything they need because every country has a different climate, physical and geographical conditions (rivers, mountains, soil etc) and resources (raw materials, machinery, labour and capital). Therefore countries need to trade with each other. Today many goods which we buy have been made in foreign countries.

3.   All trade arises because countries can gain some benefit from it. It is clearly beneficial when a country has an *absolute advantage* in the production of a commodity. That is, it is able to produce something which other countries cannot. Britain, for example, cannot produce tropical fruits like bananas. Likewise, Jamaica has few facilities for producing motor vehicles and agricultural machinery. Thus both countries can gain from trade.

4.   But, even if a country is physically able to produce the goods which it usually imports it is nevertheless worthwhile for that country to import them from another country which can produce them more cheaply.

5.   **Trade**

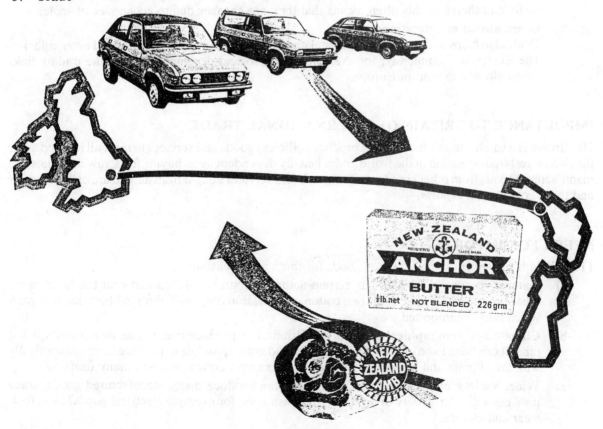

6.   Britain, for example, could grow bananas in greenhouses instead of importing them from Jamaica where they grow abundantly and cheaply. However, the cost of such production would be enormous because Britain's climate is unsuitable and therefore expensive artificial growing conditions would have to be used.

COMPARATIVE ADVANTAGE

7.   It is therefore better for Britain to concentrate on producing those goods which she can produce at relatively low cost such as chemicals, motor vehicles and agricultural machinery and use its surplus to pay for imported bananas and other fruits from Jamaica.

8.   In this way fewer economic resources are used because each country can concentrate on producing those goods in which it is relatively most efficient. More goods can be made at less cost enabling both countries to gain from trade. This basic reason for international trade is known as the *principal of comparative cost or comparative advantage*.

BENEFITS FROM TRADE

9.   *   **Higher standard of living**
         International trade is very important to a country because it enables it to have a higher standard of living. Trade widens the choice of goods in the shops because countries can buy foods, raw materials and finished goods which they cannot produce themselves.

     *   **Economies of Scale**
         Also, each country can concentrate on producing those goods which it can grow or make most easily and therefore this often means that they are cheaper due to economies of scale.

     *   **International co-operation**
         Trade also helps to develop International understanding and closer political and economic ties. The European Community, for example, was a logical development from the trading links which already existed in Europe.

IMPORTANCE TO BRITAIN OF INTERNATIONAL TRADE

10.   Britain is a small island which cannot produce sufficient goods and services to meet all its needs. It is the fifth largest trading nation in the world and is heavily dependent upon buying food, raw materials and manufactured goods from other countries. The goods and services bought from abroad are called *imports* and those sold abroad *exports*.

NEEDS FOR IMPORTS

11.   Britain is dependent upon imported goods for three main reasons:
      a)   **Natural resources**   Britain has certain natural resources, like oil and coal but lacks many other raw materials such as timber, cotton, copper, iron ore, aluminium, rubber, lead and gold, which must be imported.
      b)   **Climate and geographical conditions**   Britain can produce many of its own foodstuffs but other foods have to be imported because it would not be possible to produce them economically with the climate and soil which we have, for example coffee, tea, and many fruits.
      c)   **Wider variety of goods**   Although Britain can produce many manufactured goods, trade provides a greater variety of products for consumers, for example electrical goods, cars, footwear and clothes.

12. U.K. Imports and Exports 1991

	Exports (f.o.b.) £ million	per cent	Imports (c.i.f.)[b] £ million	per cent
Non-manufactures	**16,906**	**16·1**	**24,975**	**21·0**
Food, beverages and tobacco	7,749	7·4	12,326	10.4
Basic materials	2,013	1·9	5,065	4·3
Fuels	7,144	6·8	7,582	6·4
Manufactures	**86,058**	**82·1**	**92,103**	**77·5**
Semi-manufactures	29,358	28·0	31,494	26·5
of which: Chemicals	13,784	13·2	10,973	9·2
Textiles	2,348	2·2	3,739	3·1
Iron and steel	3,013	2·9	2,632	2·2
Non-ferrous metals	1,974	1·9	2,556	2·1
Metal manufactures	2,184	2·1	2,524	2·1
Other	6,055	5·8	9,070	7·6
Finished manufactures	56,701	54·0	60,609	51·0
of which: Machinery	29,577	28·2	29,432	24·8
Road vehicles	8,555	8·2	10,217	8·6
Clothing and footwear	2,234	2·1	5,296	4·5
Scientific instruments and photographic apparatus	4,263	4·1	4,088	3·4
Other	12,072	11·5	11,576	9·7
Miscellaneous	**1,850**	**1·8**	**1,791**	**1·4**
Total	**104,816**	**100·0**	**118,867**	**100·0**

Source: *Monthly Review of External Trade Statistics.*
[a] On an overseas trade statistics basis. This differs from a balance-of-payments basis because, for imports, it includes the cost of insurance and freight and, for both exports and imports, includes returned goods.
[b] c.i.f. = cost, insurance and freight, that is, including shipping, insurance and other expenses incurred in the delivery of goods as far as their place of importation in Britain.
Note: Differences between totals and the sums of their component parts are due to rounding.

MAIN IMPORTS

13. Britain imports about one third of its total foodstuffs, and also many raw materials. It also imports many semi-manufactured goods like chemicals and textiles and finished manufactures including machinery, vehicles, clothing and footwear.

MAIN EXPORTS

14. In order to pay for its imported goods and services Britain needs to export to other countries. Britain's main exports are machinery, vehicles, aerospace products, electrical and electronic equipment, chemicals and oil.

15. **Visible and Invisible Trade Items**

VISIBLES AND INVISIBLES

16. Imports and exports can be divided into two kinds – visibles and invisibles. These words mean exactly what they say.

17. For example a British car sold to Switzerland is a visible export, it is something which can be physically seen. Whilst if the car was insured with a British company this would represent an invisible export. That is, invisibles represent the provision of services which involve the movement of money into or out of a country.

INVISIBLE IMPORTS AND EXPORTS

18. The main invisible trade items consists of:
    Banking
    Insurance
    Tourism
    Transport
    Loans and Investments

BALANCE OF PAYMENTS

19. A country must keep a record of what it buys and sells. The annual account of a country's trade with the rest of the world is called the Balance of Payments. This consists of the Balance of Trade, Current Account, Transactions in External Assets and Liabilities and Balance for Official Financing. These terms are explained in paragraphs 20-26.

THE BALANCE OF TRADE

20. This is a record of the difference between the value of visible exports and visible imports.

21.

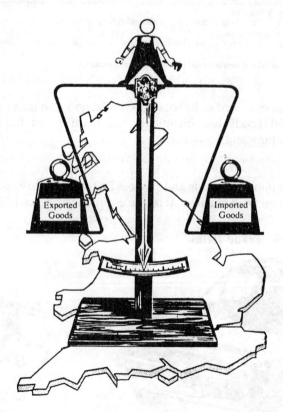

THE BALANCE ON CURRENT ACCOUNT

22. However, a country must also keep an account of all the payments which it makes and receives each year. Whereas the Balance of Trade deals only with visible imports and exports, the Balance on Current Account also includes the invisible items.

23. **Current Account of the Balance of Payments 1981-1991**

£ million	1981	1982	1983	1984	1985	1986	1987	1988	1989	1990	1991
Visible balance	3,251	1,911	−1,537	−5,336	−3,345	−9,485	−11,223	−21,078	−24,683	−18,809	−10,290
Invisibles balance	3,496	2,741	5,325	7,168	6,095	9,462	7,042	5,927	2,956	1,778	3,969
Current balance	6,748	4,649	3,787	1,832	2,750	−24	−4,182	−15,151	−21,726	−17,029	−6,321

Source: Annual Abstract of Statistics 1993

24. The ideal situation for any country is to pay for its imports by the value of goods and services which it sells abroad. Traditionally, Britain has for many years had great difficulty in doing this and usually has a deficit on its Balance of Trade. However, this deficit has been made up by a surplus on invisible trade leaving a small overall surplus on the Current Account.

TRANSACTIONS IN EXTERNAL ASSETS AND LIABILITIES

25. This account shows the movement of money into and out of a country. It lists all the lending to, borrowing from and investment between countries, for example in a factory or foreign bank account. By adding together the totals of the Current and External Assets and Liabilities Accounts we find the Balance for Official Financing.

BALANCE FOR OFFICIAL FINANCING

26. The Balance of Payments then is a record of the *total currency flow* into or out of a country and it is rather like a bank account. If the account is in deficit then the government may need to borrow or use its reserves to balance it. If it is in surplus, then it can build up its reserves or pay-off previous loans.

RATE OF EXCHANGE

27. A further term which must be understood is the rate of exchange. This expresses the value of the pound in terms of the other currencies used by the countries with which we trade. For example, £1 = 176 (Spanish) pesatas. If you have had a holiday abroad you will have bought foreign currency to spend whilst away, for example, dollars, francs, guilders or marks.

28.

July 1993	
Australia	2.12 dollars
Austria	17.50 schillings
Belgium	51.15 francs
Canada	1.84 dollars
Denmark	9.65 kroner
France	8.4 francs
Germany	2.49 marks
Greece	339 drachma
Holland	2.81 guilders
Ireland	1.03 punts
Italy	2295 lire
Japan	161 yen
New Zealand	2.65 dollars
Portugal	238 escudos
South Africa	4.9 rand
Spain	190 pesetas
Sweden	11.73 kronor
Switzerland	2.21 francs
Turkey	15670 lire
United States	1.44 dollars

29. Similarly, businessmen must also buy foreign currency to pay for imports, whilst at the same time customers abroad buy pounds to pay for the goods and services which we export to them. The rate of exchange is important because it affects the price of goods and services.

FREE TRADE

30. Trade helps to increase specialisation and achieve economies of scale through larger markets. Therefore it can be argued that it should always be free from restrictions, i.e. *free trade* should exist between all countries.

BARRIERS TO FREE TRADE

31. However, free trade can bring with it certain problems (see paragraph 36). In order to provide protection from these problems Governments may deliberately impose barriers to free trade.

TARIFFS AND QUOTAS

32. Protection usually takes place in the form of tariffs and quotas. A **tariff** (or customs duty) is a tax imposed on imported goods in order to make them more expensive, whilst a **quota** is a physical restriction on the amount of particular goods which can be imported into a country.

33. Tariffs and quotas are usually placed on imported goods which are already produced in the UK. This protects the home market and encourages us to 'Buy British'. They may also be placed on goods that we cannot produce ourselves but wish to restrict for one reason or another, (see paragraph 36).

34. **Other methods of protection** which a country might use include:
   * Embargoes – this is the complete banning of trade between one country and another
   * Subsidies – a government may provide finance to enable home goods to be sold at a lower price and thus reduce the demand for imports
   * Exchange control – a country may decide to restrict the supply of foreign currency available for imports.

35. **Barriers to Trade**

REASONS FOR PROTECTION

36. There are five main reasons why a country may decide to impose barriers to trade:
   * To correct Balance of Payment problems – a country may want to reduce imports in order to correct a trade deficit.
   * To reduce unemployment – imported goods might result in job losses in some industries.
   * To prevent dumping – this takes place when surplus foreign goods are sold abroad at a lower price than in the home market. This creates unfair competition.
   * To provide for self sufficiency – a country might wish to protect industries in case of war.
   * To protect 'Infant' industries – young industries may need protection from foreign competition to enable them to develop and grow.

37. **Infant Industries**

MOVEMENT TOWARDS FREE TRADE

38. Despite these many barriers recognition of the economic importance of *Free Trade* has been clearly illustrated since the end of the second World War. Nations throughout the world have been involved in negotiations in an attempt to reduce trade barriers and make trade easier. The result of these negotiations is shown by the International Monetary Fund (IMF) 1944, the General Agreement on Tariffs and Trade (GATT) 1948, the formation of the European Free Trade Area (EFTA) in 1959 and the European Economic Community in 1957 (now called European Community or EC) and The European Economic Area (EEA) in 1993.

39. **IMF** Most of the countries of the Western World are members of this organisation. Each member pays a contribution to the Fund (25% in gold and 75% in its own currency). The main aim is to encourage trade by using the Fund to provide short-term loans to members with a Balance of Payments deficit. It also wants to see stable (fixed) exchange rates.

40. **GATT** Over 100 countries now work together to increase trade by reducing tariffs and quotas and other barriers to trade.

41. **EFTA** This was formed to abolish tariffs on manufactured goods between its members who are Austria, Finland, Iceland, Norway, Sweden and Switzerland. Members are allowed to impose whatever restrictions they choose on non-member countries.

42. **EEA** This was formed to enable free trade between the 12 EC and 7 EFTA countries. It includes all member states except Sweden which decided not to join.

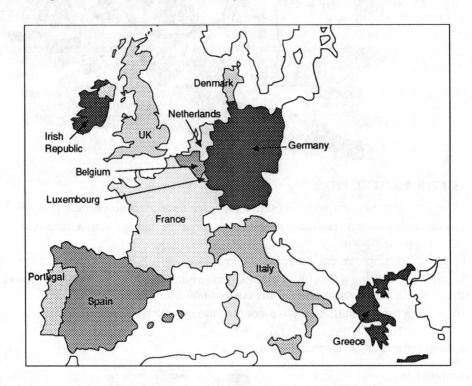

43. **EC** The EC or Common Market was originally formed in 1957 by Belgium, France, Italy, Luxembourg, the Netherlands and West Germany. The UK, Eire and Denmark joined on 1 January 1973 followed by Greece in 1981 and Portugal and Spain in 1986. The Community now has a total population of over 350 million.

44. The EC is a *customs union* in that it has:
   a) abolished virtually all tariffs between the member countries and
   b) established a common external tariff on all imported goods.

In addition to the removal of physical trade barriers the Community also aims to encourage the free movement of services, capital and people. Ultimately, European political and monetary union is planned with a single currency, Federal Central Bank and one Central Parliament.

EUROPEAN MONETARY SYSTEM

45. The EMS was set up in March 1979 with 3 aims:
    * to stabilise currency fluctuations between EC countries
    * to help keep down interest rates and
    * to control inflation.

    EMS consists of 4 elements:
    – European Currency Unit (ECU)
    – Exchange Rate Mechanism (ERM)
    – The Very Short-term Finance Facility (VSTF) and
    – European Monetary Co-operation Fund

    The *ECU* is a hypothetical exchange rate, based on a basket of EC currencies. It is used to value EC transactions, government bonds, travellers cheques and even mortgages.

    The *ERM* is a system of semi-fixed exchange rates within agreed bands. It limits how far member currencies can fluctuate against the ECU and between each other before intervention is demanded. Up to 1st August 1993 rules allowed movements of 2.25% either way, although sterling and the peseta initially had a 6% band. (Britain withdrew from the ERM in 1992 when sterling fell in value below its agreed limit). On the 1st August 1993 the movement for member countries became 15% either way.

    The *VSTF* gives ERM members unlimited credit facilities in their own currencies. This can be used to finance interventions when currencies reach their ERM margins.

Geographical Distribution of Trade 1991

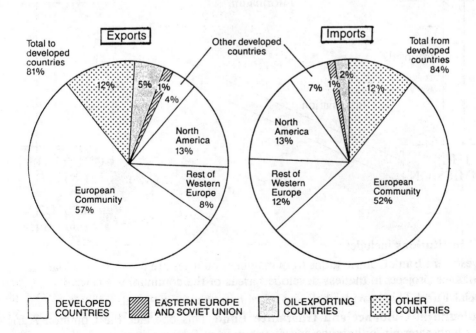

As shown above, over half the UK's trade is with EC member states.

46. **The Council of Ministers** is the decision-making body with at least one Minister appointed by each member country. Decisions are made on proposals submitted to it by the Commission. On matters of major importance, the council can only act on a unanimous vote. That is, all countries have a power of 'veto' which they can use to prevent a decision being taken.

47. **The Commission** which has 17 members plans policy and then puts forward proposals to the Council. It has members from each country who act in the interest of the whole community. This is the administrative centre of the EC based in Brussels. The Commission is responsible to the European Parliament.

48. **The European Parliament** meets once a month usually in Strasbourg (France). Member states elect representatives according to their population. Of the 518 Euro MP's Britain has 81 (England 66, Scotland 8, Wales 4, Northern Ireland 3). The Parliament debates all major aspects of policy and influences the proposals made by the Commission. It also examines and approves the EC budget.

49. **The European Court of Justice** exists to ensure that EC laws are observed by member states and to deal with any disputes. It is based in Luxembourg.

50. **Organisation of the European Community**

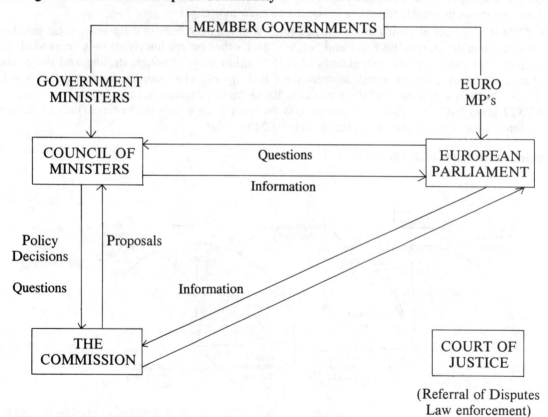

51. **Other EC Institutions** include:

European Investment Bank Contributions from member countries are used to make loans and provide assistance to finance projects in the less developed areas of the community.

European Social Fund This provides help for re-training the unemployed.

European Agricultural Guidance and Guarantee Fund This operates the Common Agricultural Policy (CAP) which determines the price and distribution of food produce.

EC BUDGET

52. All members pay a contribution to a common fund to cover the costs of running the EC. The amounts paid by each member vary as does the amount of benefit which each receives.

53. EC Parliament in Strasbourg

METHODS OF SELLING GOODS ABROAD

54. A firm can sell goods abroad in a number of different ways including:
   * DIRECT SALES FROM UK – this would involve running an export sales department and probably mean sending representatives abroad to meet foreign buyers.
   * FOREIGN DISTRIBUTORS – sometimes goods can be sold in bulk to foreign buyers who will sell and distribute them in that country.
   * OVERSEAS AGENTS – these may be appointed abroad to represent the firm and sell goods on its behalf. They are usually paid a commission on sales for the work which they do.
   * EXPORT HOUSES – these are specialist organisations which can assist a firm in three main ways:
     i) They act as merchants buying a company's products and selling them overseas on their own account.
     ii) They act as agents responsible for handling all or part of a firm's overseas sales, for example promotion, transport, distribution.
     iii) They act as agents for foreign buyers making contact with UK firms who can supply the goods required.
   * OVERSEAS SUBSIDIARIES – instead of exporting, a firm may choose to set up its own factory in a foreign country.
   * LICENCING AGREEMENT – alternatively a firm may decide to allow a foreign producer to manufacture its goods under licence. In return the licencing firm receives a special royalty payment. Coca-Cola is sold world-wide on this basis.

HELP FOR EXPORTERS

55. Exporters face a number of problems some of which also exist in home trade but require special attention when sending goods overseas. The difficulty of obtaining information and political uncertainty abroad increase these problems, examples of which include:
   * Different languages
   * Understanding the foreign market, for example different tastes and customs
   * Supplying a suitable product, for example with foreign measurements and safety standards
   * Overseas transport and packaging
   * Insurance

* Import regulations will be different in every country
* Difficulties in obtaining payment
* Fluctuations in exchange rates.

56. All of these problems increase the risks faced by firms who wish to export. In order to reduce these risks and encourage trade, help is supplied by the Department of Trade and Industry, Consular Officials, Chambers of Commerce, the Confederation of British Industry and banks.

DEPARTMENT OF TRADE AND INDUSTRY (DTI)

57. This government department runs the British Overseas Trade Board (BOTB) which aims to promote trade. It offers a wide range of advice and services for exporters. The Head Office is in London and it operates in England through seven regional offices. The Northern Ireland Department of Economic Development, Welsh Office Industry Department and Industry Department for Scotland all assist exporters in their respective areas.

58. **BOTB Services for Exporters** include:
* Assessment of overseas markets for potential exporters
* Help with market research
* Organisation of and/or support for overseas trade fairs and exhibitions
* Information on trade restrictions and regulations abroad
* Issue of export licences where required.

59. **BOTB and ECGD Logos**

EXPORT CREDITS GUARANTEE DEPARTMENT (ECGD)

60. The ECGD is a separate department within the DTI which provides insurance cover for exporters. It will also guarantee loans and overdrafts taken out to finance exports. The main risks insured against are:
* That the buyer does not pay
* That a government may take action which prevents payment, for example exchange control
* That a government may cancel an export licence
* The possible effects of war
* Rises in costs and currency fluctuations.

CONSULAR OFFICIALS

61. These are UK diplomats appointed by the government who are based in Embassies in many countries throughout the world. They can give advice and assistance to exporters and also help with import documentation.

CHAMBERS OF COMMERCE

62. These can often provide information about overseas markets and help with export procedures and documentation.

CONFEDERATION OF BRITISH INDUSTRY (CBI)

63. This provides up-to-date information about export opportunities.

BANKS

64. Banks provide information and advice, short and long-term loans and special facilities for dealing with payments from abroad including the discounting of Bills of Exchange.

BILLS OF EXCHANGE

65. Bills of Exchange are widely used for payment in foreign trade. The exporter (seller) makes out the Bill requiring the importer (buyer) to pay a stated sum of money on demand OR at some agreed future date (usually three months). The buyer then signs (to accept) the Bill and returns it to the seller. If the exporter requires money immediately, he can sell the Bill to a bank. To make a profit, banks buy Bills at a discount, ie less than their face value.

66. **Bill of Exchange**

No 490   £2,000   LONDON   20 June 199.

At 3 months after date pay to my order the sum of TWO THOUSAND pounds   Value received Drawn-under-Credit No T4175 against purchase of goods.

TO: San Ching   FOR: FRANK JONES
41 Colonial Avenue   (Signature)
HONG KONG

The Bank might discount the above Bill by buying it for £1,800. It will then receive £2,000 when it becomes due for payment on 20 September.

SUMMARY

67. a)   International or foreign trade is the buying and selling of goods and services between different countries throughout the world.

    b)   The basic reason for international trade is known as the principle of Comparative Cost or Comparative Advantage.

    c)   Specialisation and trade results in a higher standard of living, economies of scale and international co-operation.

    d)   Goods and services bought from abroad are called imports and those sold abroad exports.

    e)   The main UK imports are food, raw materials and manufactured goods.

    f)   The main exports are manufactured goods including machinery, vehicles and chemicals.

    g)   Invisible imports and exports include banking, insurance, tourism, transport, loans and investments, and other services.

    h)   The Balance of Payments Account consists of:
        i)   Visible exports – visible imports = Balance of Trade
        ii)   Balance of Trade + invisible balance = Current Balance
        iii) Current Balance + external assets and liabilities = Total Currency Flow
        iv) Total Currency Flow = Balance for Official Financing.

    i)   Protective measures include tariffs, quotas, embargoes, subsidies and exchange control.

    j)   A country may restrict trade to prevent unemployment and dumping, remain self-sufficient, to protect 'infant' industries or to solve its Balance of Payments problems.

    k)   Free Trade is encouraged by GATT, EFTA, EC, EEA and IMF.

    l)   A firm can sell goods abroad itself or through foreign distributors, agents, export houses, overseas subsidiaries or by licencing agreements.

m) Exporters face many additional problems including language and market differences, transport and packaging, documentation, insurance, import regulations, obtaining payment and fluctuations in exchange rates.

n) Exporters can obtain help from the BOTB, ECGD, Consul Officials, Chambers of Commerce, CBI and banks.

o) Bills of Exchange are widely used for payment in foreign trade.

REVIEW QUESTIONS

Answers can be found in the paragraphs shown.

1. What do you understand by International Trade? (2)

2. Explain the difference between absolute advantage and comparative advantage in International Trade. (3-8)

3. List 3 benefits from trade. (9)

4. Why is overseas trade so necessary to the UK? (10-14)

5. Give 4 examples of goods which the UK imports and 4 which it exports. (13-14)

6. What is the difference between visible and invisible trade? (15-18)

7. What is the Balance of Payments and how is it calculated and financed? (19-26)

8. Briefly explain 4 methods of protection. (32-35)

9. Give 4 reasons why a country might use protection measures. (36-37)

10. Give brief details of 3 attempts to promote 'free trade' since 1945. (38-43)

11. How is the European Community organised? (44-50)

12. Name 5 ways in which a firm can sell its goods abroad. (54)

13. What factors are likely to cause problems in International Trade? (55)

14. What sources of help are available to firms in the export trade? (56-64)

15. What is a Bill of Exchange and how does it assist exporters? (65)

EXAMINATION PRACTICE QUESTIONS

Marks

1. Briefly describe 2 methods which a country might use to restrict imports. 2

2. If the exchange rate is £1 = $2, how much would an American buyer have to pay for a £6,000 car? 2

3. The European Community is often referred to as a 'customs union'. Explain what this means and how it operates. 2

4. Explain the term 'invisible balance' in relation to the Balance of Payments. 1

5. From the following trade figures calculate the current balance for the year. Indicate clearly whether it is a surplus or deficit. 2

	Visible Trade	Invisible Trade
	£ million	£ million
Exports	12,000	6,000
Imports	14,500	7,500

MULTIPLE CHOICE/COMPLETION

1. International trade arises when countries specialise in producing these goods:
    a) In which they have the greatest comparative advantage
    b) Which are protected by tariffs
    c) Which are cheap
    d) Which they cannot obtain from abroad.

2. Which of the following imposes a common tariff on imports entering member countries from non-member countries:
    a) IMF
    b) EFTA
    c) GATT
    d) EC

3. Which of the following is concerned with reducing the barriers to world trade:
    a) IMF
    b) EFTA
    c) GATT
    d) EC

4. Which of the following is concerned with stabilising exchange rates and providing international liquidity:
    a) IMF
    b) EFTA
    c) GATT
    d) EC

5. Which of the following statements is *NOT* true?
    a) The ECGD will provide insurance cover for exporters
    b) The BOTB aims to help exporters and promote trade
    c) The government will provide long-term loans for exporters
    d) The ECGD will guarantee loans and overdrafts for exporters.

6. The balance of trade is:
    a) The balance on current account
    b) The difference in value between the import and export of goods
    c) The difference in value between income from abroad and expenditure abroad
    d) The difference in volume between the import and export of goods.

In each of the following questions, one or more of the responses is/are correct. Choose the appropriate letter which indicates the correct version.

    A   if 1 only is correct
    B   if 2 only is correct
    C   if 1 and 2 are correct
    D   if 1, 2 and 3 are correct

7. Despite the advantages of specialisation arising from the law of comparative costs, many countries 'protect' their trade and industry. Which of the following are reasons why:
   1) To correct a long-term balance of payments deficit
   2) To help maintain the level of employment in particular industries
   3) To prevent some goods entering the country for medical, moral or political reasons.

8. Which of the following are 'invisible' items in the balance of payments?
   1) Travel
   2) Insurance
   3) Goods exported.

RECENT EXAMINATION QUESTIONS

		Marks

1. NISEC SUMMER 1989 GCSE BUSINESS STUDIES PAPER 1 SECTION A   **Marks**
   State FOUR problems faced by businesses when exporting goods.   4

2. LCCI JUNE 1990 PSC STRUCTURE OF BUSINESS
   a) Explain how a Government may assist business organisations which wish to market their products abroad.   6
   b) Write *brief notes* on 6 Commercial Organisations which also give help in this way.   12

3. WJEC MAY 1988 GCSE BUSINESS STUDIES PAPER 2

Oldport Docks

Imports	'000 Tonnes	*Exports*	'000 Tonnes
Iron ore and other metals	1 900 000	Coal and coke	500 000
Timber	200 000	Iron and steel	150 000
Fruit	104 000	Chemicals	100 000
Others	55 000	Others	50 000

   a) Why does the United Kingdom import metals, timber and fruit?   5
   b) Why do we buy cars from other countries when we can produce our own?   4
   c) Draw a bar chart to show clearly the different amounts of exports from Oldport docks.   4

ASSIGNMENT

The following article is based on newspaper reports.

Trade Balance Dives Into Red

According to Department of Trade and Industry figures, in May Britain had its second worst Current Account deficit on record at £561 million. This was despite a £600 million net contribution from invisibles like banking, insurance and tourism. The visible trade gap doubled between April and May as the bill for imports leapt by £375 million to £7,450 million while export earnings fell £282 million to £6,290 million.

Demand for foreign goods rose by seven per cent across the board, with purchases of capital equipment and intermediate goods rising as fast as imports of consumer goods.

However since the country is now growing faster than almost any other major economy in the world it is hardly surprising that we are buying more from others than they are prepared to buy from us.

The set-back for exports reflects sluggish world demand but may also have something to do with the 5% rise in the price of sterling since the beginning of the year. Even so, exports are still running at levels 6.5% higher than a year ago.

Questions 1-6 are based on the information in the article.

1. How much was the deficit on the Current Account?
2. What was the net contribution from invisible trade?
3. Calculate the size of the visible trade deficit in May.
4. Give 3 examples of invisible items.
5. Explain why 'invisibles' are vital to Britain's trade.
6. Explain fully and in your own words why Britain is importing more than she is exporting.
7. Why might the Government wish to reduce the level of imports?
8. Tariffs and Quotas are 2 methods which it could use. Explain how each of these can reduce imports.
9. Briefly describe 2 other ways in which imports could be reduced.
10. Why does the Government try to encourage firms to export?

4. Commercial Banks

1. This chapter discusses the main functions of the commercial banks. It includes types of bank accounts, cheques, other methods of payments through a bank and some of the many other services which banks provide for their customers.

ORIGIN AND FUNCTIONS OF BANKS

2. In this country banking began in the 17th century with the London goldsmiths, who, because of the nature of their business, had facilities for storing valuables. They accepted DEPOSITS of cash from merchants and wealthy people who had no safe place in which to keep their money.

After a time the RECEIPTS given for these deposits began to be used as a means of payment instead of the cash itself, but these were usually for large amounts, so eventually the early 'bankers' issued 'smaller' banknotes.

A more advanced stage in the development of banking came when they began to LEND MONEY. The increasing use of banknotes meant that people no longer needed to draw out their cash and therefore the 'bankers' were able to lend out AT INTEREST, some of the money deposited with them.

3. In this brief outline of the origin of banking, there can be seen the development of the *main functions of banks* at the present day:

   a) To accept and keep safe the deposit of money from customers.
   b) To make and receive payments throughout the world.
   c) To lend money to customers.
   d) Nowadays they also provide a wide range of other services.

4. The major commercial or clearing banks are Barclays, Lloyds, Midland, National Westminster, TSB and Girobank. They are called clearing banks because they are members of the Bankers Clearing House in London which deals with the exchange and settlement of cheques (see paragraphs 53-60).

TYPES OF BANK ACCOUNT

5. Banks offer their individual or business customers a choice of two main types of account – 'current' or 'deposit'. A third type, a 'budget account', is available to individual current account holders on request (see paragraph 9).

6. **Current Account**

Customers keep funds in a current account when they are needed for *day-to-day use*. They are given a cheque book which is used to make payments to others and to withdraw cash. Interest is not usually paid on the money and bank charges may be incurred for the work done by the bank. Some current accounts do, however, pay interest, e.g. Midland's Orchard Account. The advantages of current accounts include:

   * Payments can be made by cheque (see paragraph 11)
   * Money can be withdrawn on demand
   * Regular statements from the bank showing the balance in the account
   * Overdrafts are possible (see paragraph 44)
   * Use of other bank services for payment, for example standing order and direct debit (see paragraphs 25, 26)
   * Wages and salaries can be paid directly into a current account via the credit transfer system (see paragraph 28).

7. In order to open a current account an individual customer must deposit a sum of money and complete an application form which gives:

   a) Their name and address

b) The name and address of their employer
c) The name of a referee who can vouch for their honesty
d) A specimen signature.

8. Deposit Account

This type of account is used for *savings* either by individuals or firms who may have spare cash. There are no bank charges and interest is paid on the balance in the account. Money can usually be withdrawn on demand although banks may ask for seven days notice for very large sums. However, cheques cannot be used for payments, overdrafts are not possible and other money transfer services like standing orders cannot be used.

9. Budget Account

Customers who have a current account may also open a separate budget account which enables them to pay their major bills by means of 12 equal monthly payments over a year. The customer pays bills as they become due. Thus sometimes the budget account will be in surplus and sometimes overdrawn.

10. Example

Harry Hunter has a current account with Barclay's Bank. He decides to open a budget account to pay his household bills. First of all he adds up all his bills for a year as follows:

	£
Rent	800
Poll tax	400
Gas	300
Electricity	250
Insurance	150
Telephone	100
Holiday	400
	2400

By transferring £200 per month into his budget account he will be able to cover his expenses for the year.

CHEQUES

11. A cheque is simply a written instruction by someone to a bank to pay a sum of money to another person. Cheques can be written on almost anything so long as they bear a signature. Nowadays most people use a cheque book for this purpose. This is a set of printed forms and when one of these is completed it becomes the customers instruction to their bank. There is also a counterfoil on which to record the date and amount of the cheque and to whom it is made payable. Each cheque has a serial number, sorting code and the customers account number to help the bank in identification and sorting.

12. Example of a cheque

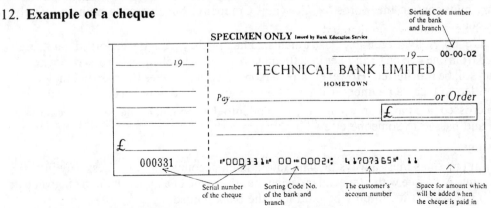

45

13. The name of the person or company to whom the money is to be paid is called the *PAYEE*. When the customer needs cash they would write 'self' or 'cash'. The *DRAWEE* is the name of the bank, whilst the customer writing and signing the cheque is called the *DRAWER*.

14. Endorsing Cheques

An important feature of cheques is that they can be endorsed and passed on to someone else. To endorse a cheque a payee signs his or her name on the back. The cheque can then be paid into another person's bank account. This is particularly helpful to someone who does not have a bank account and therefore needs to 'cash' a cheque by paying it into a friends account or a building society.

15. Open and Crossed Cheques

A crossed cheque is so called because it has 2 parallel lines across it; an open cheque (as shown on page 45) does not have them. Crossing a cheque makes it much safer because it means that it must be paid into a bank account. Thus if a crossed cheque is stolen it can be traced. On the other hand an open cheque can be cashed over the counter. It will be paid to whoever presents it at the bank branch on which it is drawn.

16. Cheque Crossings

There are two kinds of cheque crossings, either 'general' or 'special'.

Some examples of GENERAL CROSSINGS are given below:

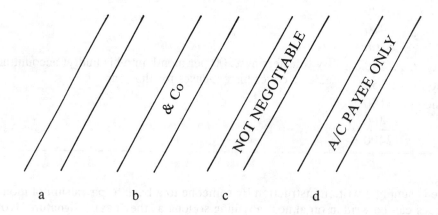

a)   This shows the general crossing which nowadays is pre-printed on most cheque books.

b)   A crossing may contain the words '& Co' (and Company) but this adds nothing effective to the cheque.

c)   Cheques are normally negotiable instruments. That is they can be endorsed and freely transferred from one person to another in settlement of a debt. If a cheque is crossed 'not negotiable' it can still be transferred. However, any person accepting it takes the risk that they would not be entitled to receive payment if it had been stolen or fraudently used.

d)   A cheque crossed 'a/c payee only' can only be paid into the account of the payee. It cannot be endorsed and passed to someone else.

17. Special Crossings

Cheques with general crossings must always be paid into a bank account but not necessarily into any particular bank account. A cheque with a 'special crossing' has the name of a particular bank between its parallel lines, which means that it can only be paid into the bank named.

18. *Some examples of SPECIAL CROSSINGS are given below:*

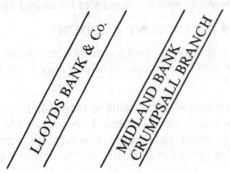

19. **Altered, Dishonoured and Post-Dated Cheques**
   a) *Alterations* to a cheque must be initialled by the drawer.
   b) *A dishonoured cheque* is one which is returned marked R/D or 'refer to drawer' because the drawer's bank has refused to make payment, i.e. it has 'bounced'. This could be because:
      *   There are *insufficient funds* in the drawers account.
      *   The drawer has *stopped payment*, i.e. asked the bank not to pay it.
      *   There is an *error or omission* on the cheque, for example it has not been signed.
      *   It is a *stale cheque* because it has not been presented for payment within six months of the date it was drawn.
      *   The *signature differs* from the specimen held at the bank.
   c) A *post-dated* cheque is one which has a future date on it. The bank will not accept it for payment before that date.

CHEQUE CARDS

20. These are issued by banks to reliable customers and guarantee that their cheques will not 'bounce' provided that:
   a) They are not made out for more than the limited printed on the card, usually £50 or £100.
   b) They are signed in the presence of the payee and the signature matches that on the card.
   c) The card number is written on the back.

21. Therefore it is not possible to 'stop payment' on any cheque given with a cheque card. Many businesses, including shops, garages, hotels and restaurants will not accept cheques unless they are backed by a cheque card.

22. **Example of a Cheque Card**

23. The use of a card also enables cheques up to £50 or £100 to be cashed at any branch of a bank. Special cheque cards can be purchased from banks to enable cheques to be cashed abroad.

OTHER WITHDRAWALS FROM A CURRENT ACCOUNT

24. In addition to the use of cheques, withdrawals from a current account can also be made by standing orders, direct debits, bank giro credits and cash cards, all which may incur bank charges.

25. Standing Orders

A customer can request their bank to make regular payments on their behalf. These are known as standing orders which the bank will carry out until they are cancelled. They are used for paying rates, mortgages, insurance premiums, hire purchase instalments and other regular bills. If the amount to be paid by standing order changes, the customer must instruct the bank to pay the new amount.

26. Direct Debits

These are similar to a standing order but instead of instructing the bank to make regular payments on their behalf, the customer gives permission for a payee to withdraw money from their account. Direct debits are used when the amount is likely to vary, for example Trade Union subscriptions (see chapter 25) which increase each year or credit payments which might alter if the interest rate changes.

27. Standing orders and direct debits avoid the need to write cheques and also mean that the account holder does not have to remember to make the payments.

28. Bank Giro or Credit Transfer

The use of this service enables money to be transferred within the banking system. Payments can be transferred directly into the bank account of a payee at a branch of any bank anywhere in the UK.

29. A Bank Giro Credit being used to pay an electricity Budget Account

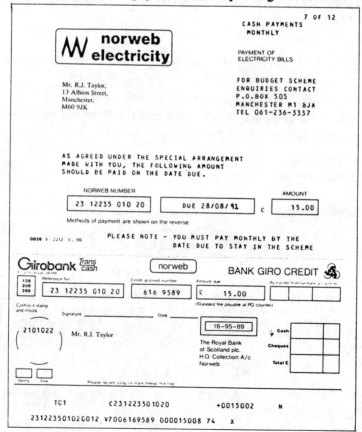

30. A form is filled in for each payment and the payer gives the bank a cheque or cash to cover the amount involved. Rent, gas, electricity and telephone bills are examples of payments which can be made by Bank Giro. People who do not have a bank account can also use the giro service.

31. Bank giro is most useful when several payments are made at the same time because it is cheaper and easier than sending lots of cheques. By writing one cheque a customer is able to have any number of payments transferred. For example, this is often used when a company pays its employees wages directly into their bank accounts. It provides a very safe and simple method of payment with less chance of a mistake since wage packets do not have to be made up.

32. **Wages to Bank Accounts**

Illustration by kind permission of the Royal Bank of Scotland.

AUTOMATIC TELLER MACHINES (ATMs)

33. Most banks now have ATMs which enable 24-hour cash withdrawal. Customers wishing to use this service are given a special cash card plus a personal identification number (PIN) which is not shown on the card but encoded into it. To obtain money the card is inserted into the machine and the number 'keyed' in. If the number is correct the machine will release the cash requested subject to a pre-arranged limit, for example £50 per day. Some machines also give customers a balance on their account, enable them to order a new cheque book or bank statement and some even accept deposits.

34. Link Machine

A national and international ATM network involving over 30 financial institutions in the U.K.

BANK CHARGES

35. Banks usually charge customers for the use of a current account. The charges will vary according to the number of cheques written, regular balance in the account, and the other services which the bank provides. The charges are shown on a bank statement (see paragraphs 38 and 39).

PAYING INTO A BANK ACCOUNT

36. To pay into a bank account a paying-in slip is completed and this is handed together with the cheques, notes and coins to the cashier. When the items have been checked, the cashier will stamp and initial the paying-in slip and the counterfoil (which acts as the customer's receipt).

37. Paying-in Slip

SPECIMEN ONLY Issued by Banking Information Service

DATE_____

CREDIT THE
ACCOUNT OF_____

£50 notes . .		
£20 notes . .		
£10 notes . .		
£5 notes . . .		
£1 · · ·		
50p · · · ·		
Silver · · ·		
Bronze · · ·		
TOTAL CASH		
Postal Orders .		
Cheques, etc. .		
TOTAL CREDIT £		

DATE_____

CREDIT

ACCOUNT_____

Paid in by_____

£50 notes . .		
£20 notes . .		
£10 notes . .		
£5 notes . . .		
£1 · · ·		
50p · · · ·		
Silver · · ·		
Bronze · · ·		
TOTAL CASH		
Postal Orders .		
Cheques, etc. .		
(listed overleaf)		

ACCOUNT NUMBER

£

Customers are advised that the Bank reserves the right at its discretion to postpone payment of cheques drawn against uncleared effects which may have been credited to the account.

THE BANK STATEMENT

38. The bank keeps a record of every payment made into and every withdrawal out of a current account. At regular intervals, or on request, it sends a bank statement to customers which lists this information. The statement can be checked against the entries on cheque and paying-in slip counterfoils.

39. Bank Statement

BiS SPECIMEN ONLY Issued by Banking Information Service

IN ACCOUNT WITH

TITLE OF ACCOUNT D K ARMSTRONG

BANK MOSS BANK LIMITED
BRANCH MANCHESTER

ACCOUNT NUMBER 22963714

STATEMENT NUMBER 4

DATE	PARTICULARS		PAYMENTS	RECEIPTS	BALANCE
	Balance Forward				
11 NOV	Balance forward				55.17
		226352	0.54		
		CD	25.00		
17 NOV		226351	6.86		22.77
		226354	8.93		
26 NOV		226350	21.50		7.66 DR
30 NOV	CITY OF MANCHESTER 321206 422631	BGC		216.97	209.31
		226356	30.00		
1 DEC	2 A/C	SO	75.00		104.31
	STANDARD LIFE MC 101062 X21	DD	15.19		
2 DEC	66917325116	SO	65.13		23.99
		226357	41.50		
		226355	60.00		
10 DEC	BGC			33.72	43.79 DR
		226358	1.89		
		226359	5.99		
19 DEC	REMITTANCE			63.10	11.43 DR
	CHS		2.84		
	INTEREST		3.12		5.47

ABBREVIATIONS

BGC	Bank Giro Credit	DIV	Dividend	O/D or DR	Overdrawn Balance
DD	Direct Debit	CHS	Charges	SO	Standing Order
CD	Cash Dispenser	ADV	Separately Advised	TFR	Inter-Account Transfer

BANK LENDING

40. Most customers who borrow from a bank will take out a loan or an overdraft. However, before deciding to lend money to customers, banks will consider a number of important factors which help to determine whether or not it is safe to do so.

* Collateral security, for example a house, stocks and shares or other items of value which could be sold if necessary to recover the banks money

* Purpose of the loan
* Amount needed and period of repayment
* Past banking record of the borrower
* Ability to repay – based on a firm's likely profit or an individuals income
* Other debts or financial commitments, for example other loans
* Government guidelines with respect to bank lending, for example restrictions on the amount of new loans or preference to certain types of borrowers like small businesses or exporters.

41. Loans

A loan is for a fixed sum of money for a stated period of time, for example £900 for three years. Each month part of the loan will be repaid plus an extra payment known as interest. Interest has to be paid on the full amount of the loan.

42. Example

	£	
Loan	900	for 3 years (36 months)
Interest 10%	270	£90 pa x 3 years
	1170	
Repayments £32.50 per month (£1170 divided by 36)		

43. When a loan is agreed the bank opens a separate loan account. This account is debited with the amount borrowed and the customers current account is credited with the same amount. Repayments are usually made by standing order and are credited monthly to the loan account.

44. Overdrafts

A bank may allow a customer to draw cheques which take more money out of their current account than they have in it. That is they are allowed to overdraw or go into the 'red'. The bank will agree a limit on how much can be overdrawn, for example £500.

45. Overdrafts are a popular way of borrowing money and are usually cheaper than having a loan. This is because the size of an overdraft is likely to fluctuate as cheques and other items are paid in and out of the account. Therefore money is only borrowed when it is needed. Interest is charged daily but only on the balance outstanding. Therefore, overdrafts tend to be used for short-term or temporary borrowing for businesses and individuals when the amount needed is uncertain or likely to vary because either income or expenses (or both) fluctuate a lot.

CREDIT CARDS

46. These are issued by most banks and some building societies e.g. ACCESS (Lloyds, Midland, National Westminster, Royal Bank of Scotland) and VISA (Barclays, TSB, Girobank, Leeds Permanent, National Provincial). Some are issued free of charge whilst others incur a small annual fee.

47. Credit cards enable the holders to buy goods or services at any shop, restaurant, garage etc which has joined the scheme. Each card holder is given an overall personal limit, for example £750, which cannot be exceeded. Each organisation in the scheme is given a 'floor limit', for example £100, beyond which it cannot accept a credit card payment without first seeking authorisation from the credit card company. This is done either by telephoning the credit card company, or by using a special machine with a direct computer link.

48. Using a Credit Card

a) The cardholder buys goods or services, presents their card and signs a 'sales voucher' which is in triplicate.

b) The customer is given one copy, the supplier keeps one and pays the third into his bank account.

c) The supplier receives payments from the credit card company. A small charge is made for this service (usually between 1 and 2%).

d) Every month the cardholder is sent a statement which shows all the transactions for that month, the total amount outstanding and the minimum payment required.

e) Part of the balance may be repaid, subject to a minimum of £5 or 5% of the total, whichever is the greater, in which case interest will be charged on the amount outstanding.

49. VISA STATEMENT

1 Account number

2 Customer's name and address

3 Balance from last month

4 Transactions this month

5 Interest charged

6 Amount repaid

7 Balance to pay

8 Maximum amount allowed outstanding

9 Minimum amount to be paid this month

10 Payment slip

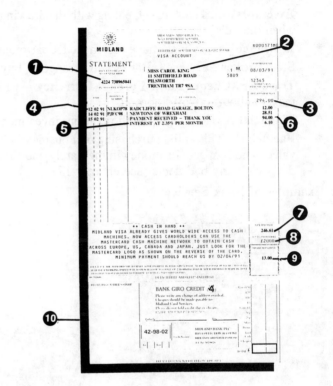

50. *N.B.* 1. Most credit cards can also be used:

a) As a cheque guarantee card (see paragraph 20)

b) To withdraw cash up to a given limit

c) As a cash card (see paragraph 33)

d) To buy goods by post or over the phone.

In the case of b) and c), interest is usually charged immediately on the amount withdrawn.

2. Retailers, if they wish, are allowed to charge customers different prices for different methods of payment i.e. higher for credit cards than cash.

SOME OTHER SERVICES PROVIDED BY BANKS

51. * **Safe Deposit Box** – A bank will store valuable items such as jewellery, store documents and house deeds.

   * **Night Safe** – This is a 'wall safe' facility which enables businesses to pay in cash after the bank has closed. The money is put into a leather wallet which the customer collects next day for paying-in.

* **Bankers Drafts** – These are cheques drawn on the bank itself and therefore as good as cash. The customer pays the bank in advance for the cheque. Traders dealing with someone for the first time may ask for a bankers draft.

* **Bills of Exchange** – These are documents used mainly in international trade, which promise to pay a specific sum of money at some future date, usually in 3 months time. To enable businesses to have their money before then, banks will buy bills, but at a discount, for example paying £950 for a £1000 bill. (see (Chapter 3).

* **Executors and Trustees** – Dealing with the drawing up of wills and handling of peoples affairs when they die.

* **Insurance** – Most banks have Insurance Departments which can arrange all types of insurance.

* **Stockbroker Services** – Banks will arrange to buy and sell shares for their customers.

* **Travellers Cheques and Foreign Currency** – which are needed by businesses or holiday-makers about to travel abroad.

* **Financial Advice** – Help with taxation, investment and general financial information.

* **Factoring** – This is the purchasing of a business's invoiced debts for a percentage of their full value. The firm gets its money immediately and the bank collects the amount outstanding and deals with any bad debts (see chapter 17).

52. Examples of Bank Services

Night Safe   Travellers Cheques

CHEQUE CLEARING

53. To clear a cheque means to pass it through the banking system so that the payees account is credited and drawers account debited with the amount concerned. This is done by either internal or general clearing.

54. Internal Clearing (within a branch)

If both payee and drawer have accounts at the same branch of the same bank then a cheque would be cleared within the branch itself.

55. Internal Clearing (within a bank)

If the payee and drawer have accounts with the same bank but at different branches then a cheque would be sent via Head Office to the appropriate branch for clearing.

56. Cheque Clearing System

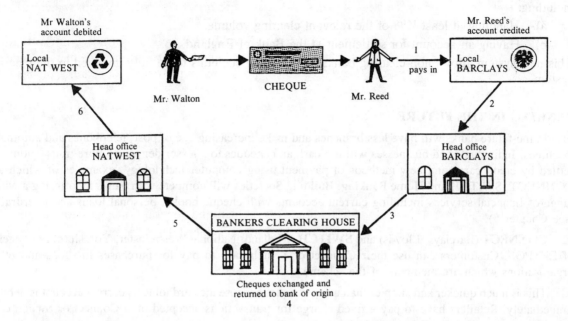

57. General Clearing (between different banks)

The above diagram shows how general clearing works. Mr Walton banks with the NatWest and Mr Reed with Barclays. Therefore cheques are cleared through the Bankers Clearing House. Each day representatives of all the clearing banks meet to *exchange* cheques which they have received from other banks. Each clearing bank has an account at the Bank of England and the difference in the value of cheques exchanged is settled by transferring funds from one bank's account to another.

58. The diagram illustrates this as follows:
    a) When Mr Reed receives his cheque he will pay it into his local branch.
    b) Barclays will then send it with all their other cheques to their Head Office.
    c) At Head Office cheques from all branches are sorted ready for clearing.
    e) Millions of cheques are exchanged daily at the Clearing House.
    f) Once exchanged, Mr Walton's cheque will be sent from NatWest's Head Office back to his local branch.
    g) At the branch Mr Walton's signature will be checked and then his account will be debited with the amount concerned.

This process usually takes two to four days.

59. The clearing system is operated by four companies set up under the control of *APACS* (The Association of Payment Clearing Services).
    a) Cheque and Credit Clearing Company to clear bulk paper items, i.e. cheques and credit transfers.
    b) CHAPS (Clearing House Automatic Payments System) and Town Clearing Company to clear high value cheques over £10,000 for settlement the same day.
    c) BACS (Bankers Automated Clearing Services) to clear small automatic payments including standing orders, direct debits and salary transfers.
    d) EFTPOS UK (Electronic Funds Transfer at the Point of Sale) to clear payments made by electronic cashless shopping.

60. Membership of APACS is given to any bank or financial institution which can meet certain criteria including:

    a)   Handling at least ½% of the relevant clearing volume.

    b)   Having an account for settlement at the Bank of England.

This new system allows non-clearing banks and building societies to be fully involved in the clearing system.

BANKING IN THE FUTURE

61. In the future banks will have less branches and make increasing use of post, telephones and automatic machines. Individuals and businesses will use cash and cheques to a lesser degree as more transactions are settled by credit cards and new methods of payment using computer technology, examples of which are CONNECT, SWITCH and Home Banking. Building Societies will compete with banks by offering a wider range of financial services including current accounts with cheque books, personal loans and overdrafts. (see Chapter 5).

62. **CONNECT** (Barclays, Lloyds) and **SWITCH** (Midland, National Westminster, Yorkshire) are systems of EFTPOS. Customers can use their Connect or Switch card to pay for purchases in shops and other organisations which are members of the scheme.

63. This is much quicker and simpler than using cheques because the cardholder's current account is debited immediately. Retailers have to pay a fixed charge for transactions accepted on a Connect or Switch card but their account is instantly credited with the money.

64. **Home Banking** involves the use of a special device which provides a link via a television set with the bank's computer. A customer can key into the computer to make transfers direct from their account to pay bills or to obtain up-to-date information. Business customers can also use this service which is currently offered by both Nottingham Building Society and the Royal Bank of Scotland.

65. **Connect card, Switch**

CONNECT   SWITCH

SUMMARY

66. a) The three main functions of commercial banks are to keep money safely, make and receive payments and to lend money.

b) The main types of bank accounts are 'current' for everyday use and 'deposit' for savings. Budget accounts are also available to spread the payment of bills over a year.

c) Most withdrawals from current accounts are made by cheque.

d) An open cheque can be cashed 'over the counter' whilst a crossed cheque must be paid into a bank account.

e) Cheque cards are issued to reliable customers and guarantee that their cheques up to £50 will not 'bounce'.

f) Withdrawals from a current account can also be made by standing order, direct debit, bank giro, credit and a cash card.

g) A bank statement is sent to customers at regular intervals giving details of all payments into and out of their account.

h) Most customers who borrow from a bank will take out a loan or an overdraft.

i) Credit cards like Access and Visa are becoming an increasingly popular method of paying for goods and services.

j) Banks provide a wide range of other services including safe deposits, night safes, bankers drafts, bills of exchange, general financial advice and factoring.

k) The general clearing of cheques takes place through **APACS**, whilst any other clearing takes place internally within a particular bank.

l) Banking in the future will make increasing use of automation and computerised technology.

REVIEW QUESTIONS

Answers can be found in the paragraphs shown.

1. Name the 'big 4' banks. (4)
2. What are the main differences between a deposit account and a current account? (5-8)
3. Briefly explain the following parties to a cheque – drawer, drawee and payee. (13)
4. What does it mean to endorse a cheque? (14)
5. How is a cheque crossed and what difference does it make? (15)
6. Distinguish between a general and a special crossing. (16, 17, 18)
7. Explain what the letters R/D written on the face of a cheque mean. (19)
8. What are the benefits to customers and businesses of having a cheque card? (20-23)
9. How does a direct debit differ from a standing order? (24-27)
10. Which bank service enables one cheque to cover many individual payments? (28-32)
11. What is the purpose of a bank statement? (38, 39)
12. What is the difference between a loan and an overdraft? (41-45)
13. Briefly describe how credit cards are used. (46-50)
14. List 6 services other than lending which a bank provides. (51, 52)
15. With the help of a diagram, explain how the Clearing House system works. (53-59)

EXAMINATION PRACTICE QUESTIONS

Marks

1. a) What services besides lending, does a bank offer to customers with a 'current' account?   4

   b) Name 3 services which are most likely to be useful to a shopkeeper. Give reasons for your answers.

   6

2. Complete the 5 sentences below with an appropriate word(s) from the following list:

   stale   post-dated   special   overdrafts   crossed

   interest   direct debit   cheque cards   commission   standing order

   a) A .... would be used to pay a fixed sum to someone at regular intervals.

   b) A cheque with 2 parallel lines across it is said to be a .... cheque.

   c) Banks lend money by granting loans and ....

   d) A customer who borrows money from a bank is charged ....

   e) A .... cheque is one which has not been presented for payment within 6 months of being drawn.

   5

3. a) Enter the following 10 transactions on the Bank Statement below. The balance b/f at 1 June was £115.50 and the account number is 07534217.   12

   b) Show the balance in the account as at 30 June.   3

i)	6.6.199.	Cheque No 117594 drawn	£4.50
ii)	8.6.199.	Cheque No 117597 drawn	£22.95
iii)	10.6.199.	Credit Transfer Received	£101.95
iv)	11.6.199.	Standing Order paid	£12.00
v)	14.6.199.	Cheque No 117596 drawn	£34.00
vi)	14.6.199.	Cash Dispenser	£50.00
vii)	18.6.199.	Direct Debit paid	£25.00
viii)	19.6.199.	Standing Order paid	£20.00
ix)	22.6.199.	Cheque No 097546 received	£13.90
x)	28.6.199.	Bank charges	£3.70

MINSTER BANK 14 High Street ASHWORTH Notts	STATEMENT OF ACCOUNT		R Jones Esq A/c No .... Date.....................	
DATE	DETAILS	DEBIT	CREDIT	BALANCE

Marks

4. What is the difference between a bank loan and an overdraft?   2

5. What is the effect of a crossing on a cheque?   2

MULTIPLE CHOICE/COMPLETION

1. A banker's draft is a:
   a) Cold reception in a bank
   b) Banks refusal to allow an overdraft
   c) Cheque issued by a bank
   d) Cheque issued by a firm

2. If you buy goods or services by cheque which of the following provides a guarantee of payment up to £50?
   a) Proof of identity
   b) Cheque card
   c) Credit transfer
   d) Crossed cheque

3. A cheque crossed with the name of a bank is:
   a) An open cheque
   b) A general crossing
   c) A special crossing
   d) A negotiable cheque

4. You buy a television on hire purchase and authorise your bank to pay the monthly instalments on your behalf. This is called a:
   a) Bank Giro
   b) Standing Order
   c) Credit transfer
   d) Cheque

5. The person who writes a cheque is called:
   a) The Drawee
   b) The Payee
   c) The Drawer
   d) The Payer

6. When a cheque is endorsed it is:
   a) Signed on the back
   b) Signed on the front
   c) Received
   d) Banked

In each of the following questions, one or more of the responses is/are correct. Choose the appropriate letter which indicates the correct version.

   A   if 1 only is correct
   B   if 3 only is correct
   C   if 1 and 2 only are correct
   D   if 1, 2 and 3 are correct

7. Which of the following information must be written on a cheque?
   1) Amount in words and figures
   2) Date
   3) Signature
8. Which of the following statements is/are correct?
   1) A bank loan is the same as an overdraft
   2) Cheque books are only issued to customers with deposit accounts
   3) Bank Giro is a system of transferring money from one bank account to another.

RECENT EXAMINATION QUESTIONS

1. NISEC SUMMER 1989 GCSE BUSINESS STUDIES PAPER 1 **SECTION B**

WESTERN BANK PLC
Mourne Street
BALLYMENA

Topline Fashions Ltd   103249954
Main Street
Ballymena   30 April 1988

Date	Details		Payments	Receipts	Balance	
1 April	Balance Forward			9102.54		
4 April	Lodgement			525.00		
	776		65.21		9562.33	
5 April	DOE Rates	SO	28.10		9534.23	
7 April	779		42.00		9492.23	
8 April	Lodgement			612.80	10105.03	
	Eagle Star	DD	80.50		10024.53	
12 April	780		12.05		10012.48	
15 April	Lodgement			354.93	10367.41	
18 April	BGC		1105.00		9262.41	
19 April	784		212.87		9049.54	
22 April	Lodgement			624.80	9674.34	
25 April	777		48.90		9625.44	
26 April	783		3756.70		5868.74	
27 April	BGC		4453.34		1415.40	
28 April	785		1894.56		479.16	DR
29 April	Lodgement			7280.00	6800.84	

		Marks
a)	What is the name given to this document?	1
b)	What is the most common method of payment used by this business?	1
c)	i) Which bank service was used to pay the Eagle Star on the 8 April?	1
	ii) Explain how this service works.	4

d) i) Topline Fashions paid a number of their suppliers on 27 April.
What bank service did they use?   1

    ii) Suggest TWO reasons why the above method may be the most suitable.   4

e) Explain what is meant by the balance on the 28 April.   2

TOPLINE FASHIONS HEAD FOR EUROPE

Mr Tony Adams, General Manager of Topline Fashions, has announced that the company is considering expanding its operations into the European market. He would not give any details at present but hoped that Germany would be the target initially.

Topline Fashions have been one of the leading fashionwear manufacturers in the UK for many years.

---

f) How might the Western Bank be able to assist Topline Fashions with their plans?   6

2. PEI 1988 SPECIMEN (212) CLERICAL & OFFICE SKILLS LEVEL 2

    You are to open a new Bank Account at a local branch.

a) Explain the main differences between a bank current account and a deposit account.

b) Describe the main advantages to the businessman of opening a bank account.

c) Explain the difference between a loan and an overdraft.

d) i) Who is the drawer of a cheque?
    ii) Who is the payee of a cheque?   25

ASSIGNMENT

You have been asked to help organise a Family Fun Run at your local Youth Club.

The aim is to raise at least £500 for a local charity which runs two homes for mentally handicapped adults.

You take on the role of treasurer to look after the 'Family Fun Run' bank account.

Money is being raised from entry fees, sponsorship by local businesses and the sale of refreshments.

Entries for the run can be made by post or in person at the Youth Club.

With one week to go to the event, you have received the following money:

- one cheque for £10 and 3 cheques for £5 each from local businesses, and the following from people who have entered to run:
- £150 in cheques (80 cheques)
- 35 x £1 coins
- 48 x 50p pieces
- silver (ie 5p and 10p pieces) worth £12.75
- bronze (ie 1p and 2p pieces) worth £2.50

As treasurer you are asked to carry out the following tasks:

1. Copy the paying-in slip shown below (or use a separate one if available) and prepare it ready to take to the bank.

SPECIMEN ONLY					bank giro credit		£50 Notes	
Date			Date _____				£20 Notes	
Credit			Cashier's stamp and initials				£10 Notes	
£50 Notes				Code No.	[- -]		£5 Notes	
£20 Notes							£1 Note/Coin	
£10 Notes				Bank _____			S. & I. Notes	
£5 Notes				Branch _____			50p	
£1 Note/Coin							20p	
S. & I. Notes				Credit _____			Silver	
50p							Bronze	
20p							Total Cash	
Silver			Fee / Number of cheques	Account No. _____			Cheques, P.O.'s etc. see over	
Bronze				Paid in by _____				
Total Cash			675-5	Address _____ Ref. No._____			£	
Cheques, P.O.'s etc. see over								
675-5 Counterfoil	£							

You will need to enter today's date, the Account Number 10540312 the bank code 40-14-21, and all the money collected so far.

2. You receive an invoice for £54.50 from Prontoprint for the cost of printing entry forms and posters.

   a) Copy the following cheque (or use a separate one if available) and complete it with all the necessary details.

```
                                            _____ 19___   40-14-21
_____19___   | TSB BANK
                |                50 High Street, ANYTOWN
_____        | Pay_____  or order
_____        |                                        ┌──────────┐
_____        |                                        │ £        │
                |                                        └──────────┘
£_____       |                                              SPECIMEN
  100151        | ⑾100151⑾ 77⑾ 0506: 0420760⑾
```

   b) Cross the cheque and say why this is important.

3. The chairman asks you to present a brief treasurer's report at the next meeting of the organising committee. He would like you to prepare the following information:

   a) At which bank is the 'Family Fun Run' account being kept?

   b) How much money has been banked to date?

   c) How much more money still has to be raised, before any expenses are paid, in order to reach the target of £500?

   d) The balance left in the bank account after the Prontoprint invoice has been paid.

5. The Government and Banking

1.   Chapter 4 looked at the services provided by banks for businesses and individuals. This chapter is about the functions of the Bank of England and the monetary policies used to control the economy. It then covers the structure of the monetary sector, role of the Post Office and building societies.

HOW CREDIT IS CREATED

2.   An important point to understand about banks is that they lend out more money than they actually have cash deposited with them. This is possible because cheques and credit cards are also used as money.

3.

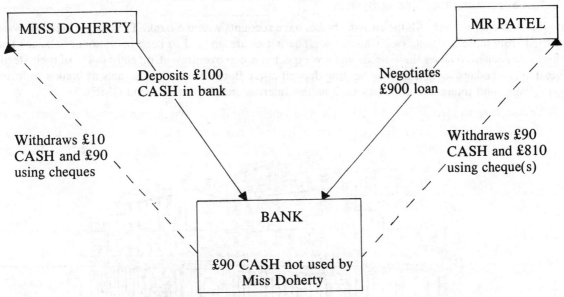

4.   Banks know from experience that if customers like Miss Doherty deposit £100 cash in a current account, then she is likely to spend £90 using her cheque book and only need £10 in cash. This 10% CASH RATIO means that banks can lend the £90 not required to other customers.

5.   If this £90 was lent out, then again only £9 would be needed in cash and £81 by cheques. Thus this £81 could be lent out and again only 10% would be needed in cash and so on. This process means that from an original deposit of £100, a bank could actually 'create credit' of £900 in loans.

6.   If Mr Patel borrows £900, again banks know that he will only need 10% in cash (£90) and the rest would be withdrawn by cheque(s). Therefore, banks are able to 'create credit' far in excess of the cash deposited with them. This enables an increased supply of money to be available for loans to both businesses and individuals, and is therefore very important to the economy.

7.   However, if too much credit is created this could lead to inflation. This is likely to happen if there are not enough goods and services available to meet the demand, causing prices to rise. Therefore, credit is controlled through the Government's monetary policy which is carried out by the Bank of England.

BANK OF ENGLAND

8.   Established in 1694 the Bank of England was originally a commercial bank which provided banking services for the Government. It gradually developed in size and scope and was nationalised in 1946. It is now the Central Bank of the UK banking system, directly linked to the Treasury, and performs a number of very important functions.

9.   Functions of the Bank of England

It is the *Government's bank* which involves:

* Keeping the Government's bank accounts.
* Receiving the income from taxation which is paid into and out of the Exchequer Account.
* Arranging Government borrowing − short-term loans through the sale of Treasury Bills, repayable three months after issue, and long-term loans by issuing gilt-edged securities on the Stock Exchange (see Chapter 20).
* Managing the National Debt which is the total amount of money owed by the Government to the public and foreign countries. Interest has to be paid and repayments arranged.
* Advising the Government and carrying out its monetary policies (see paragraph 16).
* Supervising the Banking System.

10.   It is the *bankers bank*. All the clearing banks have accounts with the Bank. The cheque clearing system is settled from these accounts (see Chapter 4). The banks are obliged to keep operational balances (cash ratio) large enough to cover these needs and are expected not to overdraw. Currently 0.4% of their sterling deposits must be kept on non-interest bearing deposit at the Bank. The Bank also acts as banker to foreign central banks and international bodies such as the International Monetary Fund (IMF).

11.

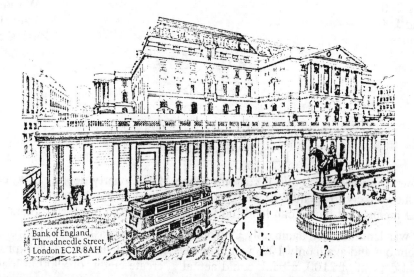

Bank of England,
Threadneedle Street,
London EC2R 8AH

12.   It is responsible for the *issue of notes* in England and Wales (coins are the responsibility of the Royal Mint). The Banks of Scotland and Northern Ireland issue a small quantity of their own banknotes. Every day large numbers of new notes are issued and worn ones withdrawn.

13. It maintains *international relations* with the central banks of other countries and monetary authorities such as the World Bank and IMF.

14. It is the *'lender of last resort'*. If the banks need cash to meet their obligations to customers they can simply call the money back which they have lent 'at call and short notice' to the Discount Houses. This leaves the Discount Houses short of funds, but they are able to borrow from the Bank as lender of last resort (see paragraph 27).

15. *N.B.* It also acts as a *commercial bank* to 10,000 private customers. It only opens new accounts for its own staff but still has some other customers whose accounts were opened before it was nationalised.

CONTROL OF THE ECONOMY

16.   The main function of the Bank of England, however, is to carry out the Government's *monetary policy* which is concerned with influencing the level of demand in the economy in order to control inflation and promote economic growth. The main instruments of U.K. monetary policy are short-term interest rates and foreign exchange market intervention.

17.   **Interest Rates**

A link between the Bank and the commercial banks is provided by the *Discount Houses*. These are banks which specialise in buying Commercial and Treasury Bills (see Chapter 20) at less than their face value (at a discount) and making a profit by keeping them until they mature. They obtain their funds mainly by short-term borrowing from the banks i.e. 'at call or short notice' which means that they can be asked for repayment at any time which is what happens if the banks need cash to meet   obligations to customers. When this happens it leaves the Discount Houses short of funds which the   e able to borrow from the Bank which acts as '*lender of last resort*'.

18.   The Bank can choose the *interest rate* at which it provides these funds. When it changes its official dealing rate the commercial banks promptly follow and change their own *base rates* for lending and borrowing. This in turn affects consumer demand, investment, output and ultimately prices.

19.   **The Exchange Rate**

Interest rates also affect the value of sterling in terms of foreign currencies. Generally, higher interest rates attract foreign funds into the U.K. and this increases the rate of exchange whilst lower interest rates have the reverse affect. To control this the Bank manages the U.K.'s gold and foreign currency reserves through the *Exchange Equalisation Account*. This is a fund which is used to buy and sell sterling and foreign exchange in order to 'smooth out' fluctuations in the exchange rate (see also Chapter 3 Exchange Rate Mechanism) known as *intervention*.

20.   **Other Policy Instruments**

Other techniques used in the past by the Bank to control the economy include:
*   Ceilings on the amount of bank lending
*   Special Deposits i.e. cash reserves which banks had to deposit with the Bank
*   Guidance on bank lending aimed at discouraging loans to consumers and
*   Open-market operations i.e. the buying and selling of Government Securities via the Stock Exchange to influence the money supply.

THE MONETARY SECTOR

21.   The 1979 and 1987 Banking Acts gave the Bank of England the powers to authorise and supervise all *deposit-taking institutions*. To become and remain authorised a 'bank' must have adequate capital; make provision against possible bad debts; have enough cash or liquidity to meet likely withdrawals and have fit and proper management.

22.   The aim of authorisation is to protect depositors against the risk of losing their money. If an authorised bank does fail depositors are entitled to limited compensation from a *Deposit Protection Fund* set up under the 1987 Act and administered by the Bank but financed by contributions levied on the institutions.

23.

```
                    ┌─────────────────────────┐
                    │   THE MONETARY SECTOR   │
                    └─────────────────────────┘
                          supervised by
                    ┌─────────────────────────┐
                    │    BANK OF ENGLAND      │
                    └─────────────────────────┘
                          which approves
                    ┌─────────────────────────┐
                    │  AUTHORISED INSTITUTIONS│
                    └─────────────────────────┘
                          which include
```

Clearing Banks		Merchant Banks		Bank of England Banking Dept		Foreign Banks
	Other Banks		Discount Houses		Finance Houses	

AUTHORISED INSTITUTIONS

24. There are some 550 institutions authorised to accept deposits by the Bank of England. These include:

* **Clearing Banks** and commercial banks which provide a wide range of services to personal and business customers (see Chapter 4).

* **Merchant Banks** and accepting houses which provide services almost exclusively for businesses. This includes accepting Bills of Exchange (see Chapter 3), acting as issuing houses for shares (see Chapter 20), providing loans and advising on business problems.

* **Banking Department of the Bank of England** which looks after the Bank's business with the exception of the issue of notes and coins.

* **Foreign Banks** – there are over 400 operating in the UK, the largest being American and Japanese.

* **Other Banks** – these include certain banks in the Channel Islands and the Isle of Man.

* **Discount Houses** – which borrow and invest short-term (see paragraph 18).

* **Finance Houses** – these make loans for hire purchase and general consumer expenditure, usually for two to three years. They also provide short-term finance for businesses.

NATIONAL SAVINGS BANK

25. This operates through Post Offices and the money deposited with it is used by the Government. It is part of the Department of National Savings and is not part of the monetary sector. There are two kinds of Savings Bank Accounts:

a) **Ordinary Accounts** which can be opened with a £1 deposit by anyone aged 7 or over. Interest is paid and deposits can be made at any Post Office. Withdrawals up to £100 can be made on demand.

b) **Investment Accounts** are intended for long-term savings and may be opened with a deposit of £5. A higher rate of interest is paid and one month's notice of withdrawal is required.

GIROBANK PLC

26. Girobank was owned by the Government until it was sold off to the Alliance & Leicester Building Society in 1990. It was started in 1968 mainly to attract the many thousands of people who did not have bank accounts. Girobank now offers a whole range of banking services for both individual and business customers. These include current and deposit accounts, loans, overdrafts, credit cards, standing orders and direct debits. It is also a member of the 5000 strong ATM 'LINK' network (see Chapter 4).

27. It differs from other commercial banks in that it operates through the network of 20,000 Post Offices where cheques can be cashed or paid in over the counter. Alternatively deposits and payments can be sent direct to the Giro Centre in Bootle using pre-paid envelopes. Girobank also offers direct banking over the phone via its 'Telecare' service and 24 hour account information through DIALOG its voice-response computer.

28.

BUILDING SOCIETIES

29. Building societies are mutual institutions owned by their savers and borrowers. They raise mainly short-term deposits from savers who are usually able to withdraw their money on demand or at short notice. The societies specialise in using these deposits to provide long-term loans for house purchase (mortgages). The rate of interest usually varies and the loan is secured against the property.

30. **Well known Building Societies**

31. The Building Societies Act 1986 allows societies to:-

i)   *diversify and offer additional services*. These include the provision of current account facilities such as cheque books; personal loans, insurance broking, estate agency and property surveys.

ii) *convert to public limited companies*, discarding their mutual status, if their savers and borrowers agree. Abbey National was the first to do this in 1989.

iii) *operate in other countries of the European Community*.

32. The 3 largest societies (Halifax, Nationwide Anglia & Woolwich) account for nearly 50% of the total assets of the movement and the twenty largest for some 90%. Building societies are supervised under the 1986 Act by the Building Societies Commission.

POST OFFICE PAYMENT FACILITIES

33. In this Chapter and Chapter 4 we have considered payment facilities provided by banks. If someone does not have a bank account, then they can make payments using one of the following Post Office services:

* **Stamps**   These may sometimes be used for small payments.
* **Registered Post**   Cash can be sent through the post using this special service.
* **Cash on Delivery (COD)**   Firms can post goods which customers pay the postman for when he delivers them. The Post Office then forwards the money to the person who sent them.

> * **Postal Orders** These can be obtained from any Post Office for amounts from 25p to £10. An additional charge called 'poundage' is made to cover the cost. Like cheques a postal order can be crossed so that it must be paid into a bank account and has a life of 6 months. If they are not crossed they can be cashed over a Post Office counter.

34. **Postal Order**

SUMMARY

35. a) Banks can create credit by lending out more money than they receive in deposits.

   b) The amount of credit in the economy is controlled by the Bank of England.

   c) The Bank is the Government's bank, bankers bank, issues bank notes and supervises the monetary sector.

   d) It also carries out the Government's monetary policy using interest rates and foreign exchange rates.

   e) The monetary sector includes commercial banks, merchant banks, foreign banks and discount houses.

   f) Girobank operates through the Post Office and provides a range of services similar to those offered by other commercial banks.

   g) Building societies are the major lenders for house purchase in Britain.

   h) Other methods of payment include the use of stamps, registered post (to send cash), cash on delivery and postal orders.

REVIEW QUESTIONS

Answers can be found in the paragraphs shown.

1. How is bank credit created? (2-6)
2. Why is it necessary to control the amount of credit in the economy? (7)
3. Outline the main functions of the Bank of England. (9-15)
4. What is monetary policy and how is it carried out? (16-20)

5. List the institutions which are authorised and supervised by the Bank of England (23-25)

6. How does Girobank differ from other commercial banks? (26-27)

7. What changes have been brought about by the 1986 Building Societies Act? (29-32)

8. Briefly describe 4 methods of payment which you could use at the Post Office. (33)

EXAMINATION PRACTICE QUESTIONS

Marks

1. a) When would a Postal Order be used as a method of payment?   1

    b) What do you have to do to make sure that a Postal Order can only be paid into a bank account?   1

    c) If you wanted to increase the value of a £1 Postal Order to £1.07, how would you do it?   1

    d) What is the fee charged for a Postal Order called?

    e) What is the name of the system of paying and receiving money by cheque through the Post Office?   1

2. Explain the difference between the National Savings Bank Ordinary and Investment Accounts.   2

3. Explain why the Bank of England is described as the 'Government's bank' and the 'banker's bank'.   4

MULTIPLE CHOICE/COMPLETION

1. Which of the following is *NOT* a function of the Bank of England?
    a) To manage the National Debt
    b) To issue bank notes
    c) To make profits for its shareholders
    d) To act as lender of last resort.

2. The main reason why higher interest rates are expected to reduce the money supply is because they:
    a) Encourage investment
    b) Increase taxation
    c) Encourage saving
    d) Discourage borrowing

3. Suppose you wish to buy a house for £25,000. You approach a Building Society which is prepared to grant you a 90% mortgage. How much will you be borrowing?
    a) £2,500
    b) £9,000
    c) £20,000
    d) £22,500

4. Which of the following is *NOT* a function of merchant banks?
    a) Acting as Banker to the Government
    b) Underwriting share issues
    c) Providing loans to businesses
    d) Accepting Bills of Exchange

5. The Alliance & Leicester Building Society runs the
   a) Bank of England
   b) Girobank
   c) Commercial Banks
   d) Post Office

In the following question, one or more of the responses is/are correct. Choose the appropriate letter which indicates the correct version.

   A if 1 only is correct
   B if 3 only is correct
   C if 1 and 2 only are correct
   D if 1, 2 and 3 are correct

6. Which of the following measures can be used by the Bank of England to increase or reduce the money supply?
   1) Special Deposits
   2) Controls of bank lending
   3) Official lending rate

RECENT EXAMINATION QUESTIONS

1. LCCI JUNE 1990 PSC STRUCTURE OF BUSINESS   **Marks**
   How may the activities of a Central Bank affect the supply of money in a country?   18

ASSIGNMENT

1. From the following list, choose the correct word(s) to complete the sentences below.

Mortgages	Discount Houses	Bank of England	Accepting Houses
Borrow	Abbey National	Accept	Government
Lend	Building Societies	Merchant Banks	Monetary

   a) The National Savings Bank is owned and controlled by the . . . .
   b) . . . . policy is implemented by the Bank of England.
   c) Merchant Banks . . . . Bills of Exchange thus insuring their owners against loss.
   d) . . . . purchase Bills of Exchange and Treasury Bills.
   e) The . . . . is the 'lender of last resort'.
   f) Building Societies lend money for . . . .
   g) Discount Houses . . . . 'money at call'.
   h) Commercial Banks . . . . 'money at call'.

2. Outline, with examples, what you understand by the monetary sector.

3. In what ways can the Bank of England control the monetary sector?

4. In what ways can action taken by the Bank of England affect businesses?

5. Collect 3 items of interest concerning finance which appear in local or national newspapers. Consider how each of these might affect businesses in your area.

6. Types of Business Organisation – Private Enterprise

1. There are many different types and sizes of businesses which have developed to supply the wide variety of goods and services which people want to buy. In this chapter we shall examine the different types of privately owned business organisations including the main features of each.

DEFINITIONS

2. As shown in the following diagram, Britain has what is known as a *mixed economy* where goods and services are supplied by both private and public sector organisations.

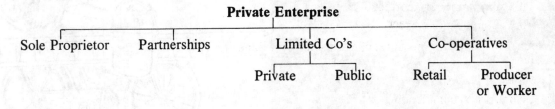

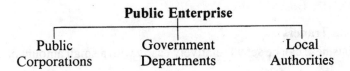

3. The *private sector* or *private enterprise* is the term used to describe all businesses which are owned by individuals or groups of individuals and run essentially for profit.

4. About three-quarters of all trading in Britain is controlled by private sector organisations. The rest, known as the *public sector* or *public enterprise* are businesses which are owned and controlled by the Government or local authorities and run for the benefit of the country (see Chapter 7).

TYPES OF PRIVATE ENTERPRISE

5. There are five main forms of business ownership in the private sector of the economy:
   a) Sole Trader
   b) Partnerships
   c) Private Limited Companies
   d) Public Limited Companies
   e) Co-operatives.

6. Franchising is another important form of private enterprise. It is a relatively new but growing form of business ownership which is considered later in this Chapter.

SOLE TRADERS (or Proprietors)

7. The oldest, simplest and therefore most common form of business unit is the sole trader or one-person concern. This is somebody who is self-employed and who usually starts a business with capital from their savings or by borrowing from friends or a bank. *Capital* is the money which every business needs to enable it to set up and operate, for example to buy premises, equipment, stock and pay wages.

8. A sole trader is not necessarily a one-person business and may have many employees or branches. However, the business is owned by only one person and it is they who receive the profits.

9. A large number of shops are owned by sole traders, for example many shoe repairers, hairdressers, cafes, laundrettes, corner shops and newsagents. Other examples include many market traders, window cleaners, farmers, lorry drivers and building workers.

10.

11. **Advantages of Sole Traders**
    *   This type of business can be set up relatively easily with a small amount of capital and few legal formalities.
    *   The owner is the 'boss' and can make decisions quickly about how the business is run.
    *   Personal contact with customers particularly where a business operates in a local area.
    *   All profits belong to the owner.
    *   Satisfaction and interest is gained from working for yourself.
    *   Business affairs can be kept private except for completing tax returns.

12. **Disadvantages of the Sole Trader**
    *   Unlimited Liability – this means that if the business fails and makes a loss, then the owner is responsible for all the debts incurred. Consequently a sole trader takes the risk that they could lose all their personal possessions including their car, house and furniture.
    *   May be unable to benefit from buying in bulk (large quantities) and thus be unable to offer competitive prices.
    *   Expansion may be limited because the owner lacks capital and may have difficulty in borrowing.
    *   Division of labour may be difficult because of the small size of the business. In a small business the owner must do most jobs themselves.
    *   Lack of continuity. If the owner dies or retires the business may go out of existence.

PARTNERSHIPS

13. As the one-person business expands, it may overcome some of its disadvantages, such as lack of capital, by changing to a larger unit. For example, a plumber whose business is growing could invite one or more of his friends to join him to form a partnership.

14. Under the *1890 Partnership Act*, a partnership is defined as 2-20 people (10 in Banking) who agree to provide capital and work together in a business with the purpose of making a profit. More than 20 partners are allowed in the case of accountants, solicitors and members of the Stock Exchange.

15. People wanting to form a partnership normally draw up a legal document called a *Partnership Deed of Agreement*. This sets out the details of the partnership including the objects of the firm, how much capital each partner will provide and how profits or losses are to be shared.

16. This Agreement is not necessary by law but is obviously very useful if a dispute arises over the terms of the partnership. If no Agreement exists then the rights and duties of the partners are determined by the 1890 Partnership Act which states, for example, that any profits or losses must be shared equally.

17. Partnerships are usually found in the professions such as Estate Agents, Insurance Brokers, Dentists, Doctors and Accountants, although they are also found in other occupations including garage proprietors, taxi drivers, small factories and workshops, and painters and decorators. Sometimes a partner may put capital into a business but not take any active part in how it is run. In this situation they are known as *sleeping partners*.

18. **Sleeping Partners**

19. **Advantages of Partnerships**
   * Easy to set up.
   * More capital can be brought into the business.
   * Division of labour is possible as partners may have different skills. For example, in a firm of solicitors one partner may specialise in the buying and selling of houses, another in divorce and another in criminal offences.
   * Responsibility for the control of the business is shared with more than one person. Therefore the problems of holidays, illness and long working hours are reduced.

20. **Disadvantages of Partnerships**
   * Partners have unlimited liability and are therefore personally liable for the debts of the business.
   * Disagreements among partners may cause problems.
   * Lack of capital may limit expansion.
   * There is no continuity of existence i.e. a partnership is dissolved (automatically ends) if one of the partners dies, resigns or becomes bankrupt.

21. Under the 1907 Partnership Act, the *ordinary partnership* described above may be changed into a *limited partnership*. This involves at least one partner agreeing to accept unlimited liability. The number of such partnerships is quite small because limited partners are not allowed to take any active part in running the business.

JOINT STOCK OR LIMITED COMPANIES

22. As businesses wish to expand they need more capital and in order to obtain this they frequently become limited companies. These are business units established under the regulations of the various *Companies Acts 1948 to 1989.*

23. Companies differ from sole traders and partnerships in 4 main ways:

    a)   **Share Capital**

        In order to raise capital, companies issue (sell) shares which means that many people are able to own a small part of the business i.e. they become shareholders. This gives the company permanent capital. If a shareholder wishes to get their money back they can sell the shares but the company's capital does not change.

    b)   **Companies have limited liability**

        This means that should the business fail the people who have invested their money in it cannot lose any of their personal possessions, i.e. their liability is limited to the amount invested. It is this important feature which gives people confidence to invest in companies without the risk of losing everything.

    c)   **Companies have a separate legal existence**

        This means that a company continues to exist in business even though the owners (shareholders) may change. Some may die, others may sell their shares but the legal existence of the company is not affected.

    d)   **Separation of ownership and control**

        The formation of a limited company enables people who cannot or do not want to take part in its management to still contribute capital and share any profits.

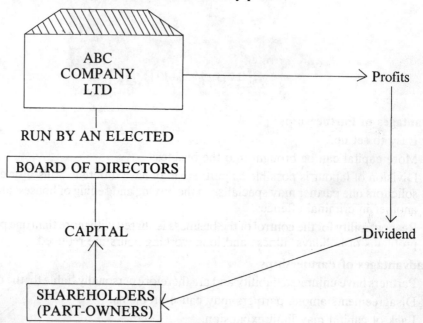

As shown on the diagram shareholders provide the capital for the company and elect a Board of Directors to run it on their behalf. In return they are entitled to share any profits made by the firm, which is commonly called a dividend. The directors make the important policy decisions on how the company is to

38. The 'Memorandum of Association' gives important information about the company including:
    a) The name with 'Limited' (Ltd) or 'Public Limited' (PLC) as the last word according to its status.
    b) Its business address.
    c) The objects of the company, for example to manufacture baked beans.
    d) Details of the company's capital, for example, £250,000 divided into 250,000 Ordinary Shares of £1 each.
    e) That the shareholders liability is limited.

39. The 'Articles of Association' are the internal rules of the company which give details of such matters as the number of directors, the voting rights of the shareholders and how profits are to be shared.

40. The 'Memorandum' and 'Articles' must be sent to the Registrar of Companies in London. When satisfied that the prospective company has met the legal requirements, he will issue a *Certificate of Incorporation*, which allows it to begin trading.

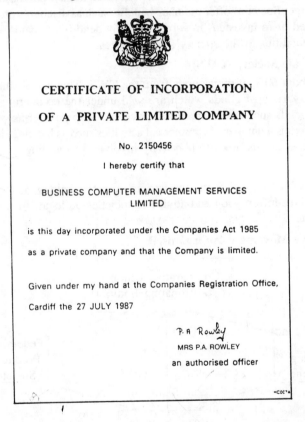

CERTIFICATE OF INCORPORATION

OF A PRIVATE LIMITED COMPANY

No. 2150456

I hereby certify that

BUSINESS COMPUTER MANAGEMENT SERVICES
LIMITED

is this day incorporated under the Companies Act 1985
as a private company and that the Company is limited.

Given under my hand at the Companies Registration Office,
Cardiff the 27 JULY 1987

P. A. Rowley
MRS P.A. ROWLEY
an authorised officer

CO-OPERATIVES

41. A further form of business organisation is that of the co-operative. The basic idea is a large number of small separate units working together in their mutual interest to achieve economies of scale. For example, the savings from bulk buying of goods and equipment, joint advertising and the use of specialist staff. There are two basic types – retail (or consumer) co-operatives and producer (or worker) co-operatives.

42. The modern Co-operative movement began in 1844 when a group of 28 working men founded the Rochdale Equitable Pioneers Society. Its aims were to supply members with pure, wholesome food (adulteration was widespread at the time), at fair prices and return any profit as a 'dividend'. This proved so successful that the movement grew rapidly throughout the U.K. and abroad, gradually widening its range of products. (see also Chapter 13).

43. The main features of retail co-operatives are:

* They are owned by their customers who can become a member (or shareholder) by purchasing £1 shares.
* They are run by a Board of Directors elected by the members.
* Each member has only one vote regardless of how many shares they hold.
* Each society operates independently under its own name (e.g. Greater Nottingham, Ipswich, Leicestershire). They are linked together through the Co-operative Union.
* The concept of a 'dividend' (see paragraph 45).

44. N.B. Societies do not operate under the same rules as limited companies. They are registered under the Industrial and Provident Societies Act and are responsible to the Registrar of Friendly Societies to whom they submit an Annual Return and financial statements.

45. Dividend

Profits have traditionally been shared among members in proportion to their purchases and some Co-operatives still pay a cash dividend. Other Societies offer member-benefits such as discounts on certain goods or dividend stamps which can be cashed or re-invested. In some cases dividend is not paid to individual members but used to fund community facilities in the society's trading area.

46. Co-operative Wholesale Society (CWS)

Retail co-operatives buy about 60% of their goods from the CWS. This was formed in 1863 and has many factories which produce a variety of goods which are sold under the co-operative brand name including foodstuffs and household goods such as 99 tea, coffee, rice and soap powder as well as clothing, furniture and bedding. The CWS also runs a number of commercial activities such as banking, insurance, travel agencies, funeral and wedding services and is now itself heavily involved in retailing.

47. Co-operative Union

This is a national body to which the CWS and the various societies belong. It represents co-operatives as a movement and also provides information and advice to societies on legal, financial, industrial relations, educational and other matters.

48. How the Co-operative Movement is Organised

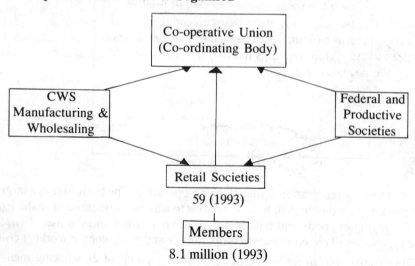

49. Producer or Worker Co-operatives

Producer co-operatives have been most successful in agriculture for example in Denmark, New Zealand and Spain where groups of small farmers have got together to share their marketing and production facilities. This enables them to gain the maximum benefit from economies of scale and therefore to operate more efficiently.

50. Except in farming, producer co-operatives were almost non-existent in Britain until the early 1970's. At this time the Government was faced with the problem of rising unemployment. Therefore it began to offer financial help to firms which were likely to close down and make their employees redundant (dismiss them because they were no longer needed). Worker co-operatives were formed where each employee bought shares in the firm and shared the profits. Through Co-operative Development Agencies they also became important for the growth of small businesses.

51. There are now over 1500 Worker Co-operatives. Examples include Suma (wholefood) wholesalers, Paper Back (paper recyclers), Scott Bader (Chemicals) and Soft Solution (Computer networks).

A stitch in time

WHEN a clothing firm shut down one of its factories, nine workers decided to pool £1,000 of their redundancy money ... and went back into business as a workers' co-operative. Now Topstitch, at Cradley Heath, West Midlands, have won £16,000 in grants and loans to help them expand. Their former employers are also lending a hand, supplying machinery and the promise of orders.

THE FRANCHISE BUSINESS

52. A comparatively new and growing form of business ownership in Britain is called *franchising*. Franchising involves an existing, usually well-known established company allowing someone the exclusive right to manufacture, service or sell its products in a particular area.

53. The franchise company also helps the person to set up and run the business by giving advice, supplying equipment and materials and assisting with the location of premises and marketing. The company charges a royalty (fee) for its services which is usually in the form of a lump sum (e.g. £10,000) and a share of the profits of the business (e.g. 10%).

54.

55. Cars, petrol, printing services, certain foods and restaurants are frequently sold like this. Examples of franchises in Britain include Burger King, Dyno Rod, Holland and Barratt, Kentucky Fried Chicken and Prontoprint.

SUMMARY

56. a) All businesses are either owned privately by individuals (or groups of individuals) or publicly by the Government.

   b) Private enterprise includes sole traders (or one-person concerns), partnerships consisting of 2-20 people, private and public limited companies which have shareholders or co-operatives which can be either retail or producer.

   c) All these different types of organisations need capital in order to pay for the costs of running the business. This capital is usually raised by sole traders and partnerships, from savings or borrowing from friends or a bank, whilst limited companies issue shares.

   d) Shareholders own part of the business and in return for lending the capital they receive a dividend each year which is a share of any profits which the firm makes.

   e) The ability of companies to raise large sums of capital has been very dependent upon limited liability. This means that if a firm is unprofitable and goes out of business then shareholders can only lose the amount of money which they have invested and not any of their personal possessions such as their house or furniture.

   f) The place where the shares, in a public limited company, are bought and sold is called the Stock Exchange.

   g) To form a limited company it is necessary for the firm to draw up A Memorandum of Association and Articles of Association giving details of the type of business and how it is to be run. These documents are sent to the Registrar of Companies who issues Certificates of Incorporation to companies who meet the legal requirements.

   h) A more recent and rapidly growing form of business organisation is franchising. This enables people to set up in business using the trade name and with the help of existing companies.

REVIEW QUESTIONS

Answers can be found in the paragraphs shown.

1. Draw a diagram to illustrate the different types of privately owned business organisations. (1, 5)
2. What do you understand by a 'mixed economy'? (2)
3. What is the oldest and simplest form of business organisation? (7)
4. Explain the need for capital in business. (8)
5. Give at least 4 examples of sole proprietors. (10)
6. Give 2 advantages and 2 disadvantages of being a sole proprietor. (11, 12)
7. Give 2 reasons why a partnership might be formed. (13, 19)
8. What is a 'sleeping' partner? (18)
9. Give 2 advantages and 2 disadvantages of forming a partnership. (19, 20)
10. Under what conditions can a limited partnership be formed? (21)
11. Explain the difference between limited and unlimited liability. (12, 20, 21, 23)
12. Draw and explain a diagram to illustrate how a limited company is run. (24)
13. Give 3 important features of private limited companies. (23-30)
14. Explain 3 features of public limited companies. (23, 31, 32, 33)

15. Briefly explain the 2 legal documents which control the affairs of limited companies. (37-40)
16. Explain with examples the meaning of 'Economies of Scale'. (29, 35, 41)
17. Why did co-operatives develop in the 19th century? (42)
18. What are the main features of retail co-operatives? (43-46)
19. How do producer or worker co-operatives differ from retail co-operatives? (49-51)
20. What is franchising? (52-55)

EXAMINATION PRACTICE QUESTIONS

Marks

The owner of a small but growing business is looking at ways of planning its future expansion. One way he is considering is to take in an active partner.

1. a) Give 2 reasons why someone may wish to run their own business.   2
   b) List 3 possible sources of finance, apart from his own funds, for a sole proprietor.   3
   c) What is an 'active' partner?   2
   d) What do you think would be 2 main advantages of a sole trader taking in a partner?   2
   e) If there is no partnership agreement, how would the profits in a partnership be divided?   1
2. a) A shareholder owns part of a business. Explain this statement.   2
   b) Explain the way in which shareholders are protected from the loss of personal wealth if the company in which they invested becomes bankrupt.   2
3. Give 2 differences between a public and a private limited company.   2
4. What is the CWS and what does it do?   3
5. The . . . . is the document which must be issued by the Registrar of Companies before a public limited company can commence business.   1

MULTIPLE CHOICE/COMPLETION

1. The maximum number of shareholders allowed in a public limited company is?
   a) 20
   b) 50
   c) 100
   d) No maximum number.
2. Which of the following types of business organisation is owned by its customers?
   a) A partnership
   b) A public limited company
   c) A retail co-operative
   d) A nationalised industry
3. One disadvantage of forming a partnership is:
   a) The number of partners is limited
   b) Specialist skills may be introduced
   c) More capital is usually available
   d) Any losses would have to be shared

4. Limited liability means that:
   a) A firm is unlikely to go bankrupt
   b) Shareholders cannot be asked to pay for company debts
   c) A firm is either a private or public company
   d) Employees are insured against accidents at work

5. A Joint Stock Company is controlled by:
   a) A Board of Directors
   b) The Personnel Manager
   c) A Board of Governors
   d) A Board of Members

6. Which of the following statements about modern retail co-operatives is incorrect?
   a) They are the fastest growing sector of the retail trade
   b) They are run by a Board of Management
   c) Profits are shared with customers in proportion to purchases
   d) The 'Rochdale Pioneers' opened the first shop in 1844

In each of the following questions, one or more of the responses is/are correct. Choose the appropriate letter which indicates the correct version.
   A   if 1 only is correct
   B   if 3 only is correct
   C   if 1 and 2 only are correct
   D   if 1, 2 and 3 are correct

7. Which of the following applies to a limited partner?
   1) His liability is limited to the amount of capital invested
   2) He is unable to take any active part in running the business
   3) Profits and losses must be shared in an agreed proportion

8. Which of the following sources of capital are available to a private limited company?
   1) Retained profits
   2) Trade Credit
   3) Shares issued to the general public

RECENT EXAMINATION QUESTIONS

1. LCCI DECEMBER 1989 PSC STRUCTURE OF BUSINESS   **Marks**
Describe how any *6* of the following are used by a large public company
   a) a bank current account
   b) Articles of Association
   c) Organisation and Method
   d) an incentive scheme
   e) a broker/dealer
   f) an organisation chart
   g) (bank giro) credit transfer
   h) a balance sheet   18

2. LEAG JUNE 1990 GCSE BUSINESS STUDIES PAPER 1

Gulshan and Pankaj own and run a residential home for 20 elderly people. They employ 5 staff to help them. The home is well run and popular and there is a long waiting list. Gulsham and Pankaj charge £300 per week for a place in the home. A local charity, however, pays a part of this charge (£100 per week for each place).

    a)   Gulshan and Pankaj run the home as a business. They have no other income.

        i)   Which type of business
            sole proprietor or
            a partnership or
            a private limited company
            is this most likely to be?

        ii) Give TWO reasons for your answer.   **2**

    b)   Explain TWO different objectives which Gulshan and Pankaj might have in running the home.   **3**

3. MEG JUNE 1990 GCSE BUSINESS STUDIES PAPER 1

> Planco is a **private limited company** located in the West Midlands. It prints diaries, calendars and year planners which it sells to businesses and individuals.
>
> Planco's printing and administrative operations are traditional. It does not yet use any **new technology** although the directors are thinking about its introduction.

    a)   i)   What is a **private limited company?**   **4**
           ii) Why is this type of organisation suitable for a small firm like Planco?   **6**

    b)   How might the introduction of new technology help Planco?   **6**

ASSIGNMENT

D. Thomas is considering setting up in business. He asks you to supply the following information to help him to decide what type of organisation would be most suitable.

1.   Who receives the profits in the following types of business organisations?

    a)   Sole Trader
    b)   Partnership
    c)   Public limited company
    d)   Co-operative society
    e)   Franchised business

2.   Why are the businesses of sole traders usually quite small?

3.   He asks your opinion as to the two main difficulties you think he might meet if he decides to enter into a partnership. What would you say?

4. To help him further copy and complete the following table:

Type of business organisation	How many owners can it have?	What type of liability has it got?	Main sources of capital	Who owns it?	Who is responsible for its day-to-day running?	How are profits or losses shared?
Sole proprietor						
Ordinary partnership						
Private limited company						
Public limited company						
Retail co-operative						
Workers co-operative						
Franchise						
Public corporation						

5. Match up the names in list A with their most likely form of organisation from List B.

A 1 J W Plumbing – a plumbing firm owned by John Williams

2 British Rail

3 Fashionwear Ltd – manufacturers of men's clothing, a firm started up by Steve and Liz Fisher, the shares are now owned by 10 members of the family.

4 Bolton Metropolitan Borough

5 Keepitt and Alwright – a firm of accountants

6 Marks and Spencer plc

B i) Sole Trader

ii) Partnership

iii) Private company

iv) Public company

v) Public corporation

vi) Local Authority

6. What type of business organisation is most likely to be set up in the following situations?

a) A man decides to open a newsagents shop

b) A group of clothing workers are resisting the closure of their factory

c) Five solicitors want to work together

d) A woman wishes to open a fast food restaurant but feels the need for the support of a larger organisation

e) A successful limited company needs more capital to enable it to expand further.

7. Look through the situations vacant columns of local newspapers and find examples of the following advertisements:

a) for a job with a private limited company

b) for a job with a large public company

c) for a job with a public corporation

d) for a job with a local authority

e) for a job which you could apply for when you have completed your present course.

8. Now write a letter of application for the job chosen in 7.e).

7. Types of Business Organisation – Public Enterprise

1. In Chapter 6 we looked at business ownerships in the private sector where goods and services are supplied by individuals, groups of individuals or companies. We now consider the public sector where the provision of goods and services has been taken over by the state, i.e. they are owned by the nation.

2. Public sector business organisations can be divided into 3 broad categories:
   a) Public Corporations or Nationalised Industries
   b) Government Departments
   c) Local Authority or Municipal Undertakings

PUBLIC CORPORATIONS

3. Public corporations are industries which are owned and controlled by the Government and therefore have no shareholders. To raise capital they can:
   * 'Plough' back profits
   * Borrow from the Government
   * Borrow from banks or
   * Issue loan stock to the public

4. When an industry which was privately owned is taken over by the government, it is said to have been 'nationalised'. When this happens the previous owners are paid compensation. Some examples and the year when they were nationalised are as follows:

   1933   London Regional Transport
   1946   British Coal
   1946   Bank of England
   1947   Electricity Council*
   1948   British Gas Corporation*
   1948   British Rail
   1948   National Water Council*
   1954   Atomic Energy Authority
   1967   British Steel Corporation*

*Now privatised (see paragraph 24)

5.

6. Although the names may be slightly confusing, whether they are called Boards, Commissions, Councils, Authorities or Corporations, all nationalised industries are in fact public corporations, set up by an Act of Parliament and run by the government on our behalf.

7. Other public corporations were set up by the government in the first place. Examples of these include:

    1927   British Broadcasting Corporation
    1969   The Post Office

8. **Organisation of Public Corporations**

9. The usual organisation and control of public corporations is outlined in the following chart:

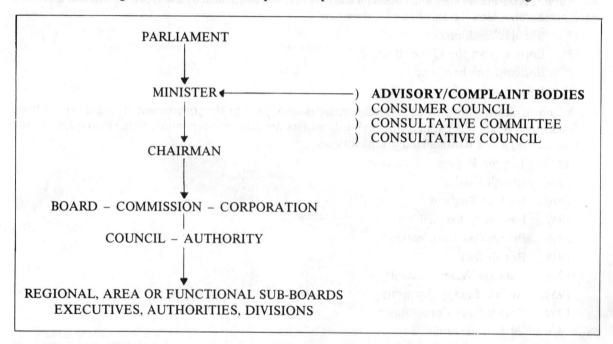

10. A Minister is put in charge of each industry to determine the general policy, and he appoints a Chairman and Board with responsibility for the day-to-day running of its affairs. An annual report has to be prepared and submitted to the Minister who may be questioned on it by Members of Parliament. In this way a public corporation is said to be made accountable (i.e. responsible) for its activities.

11. If a member of the general public has a complaint against a nationalised industry or is dissatisfied with its service then they can, if necessary, bring this to the attention of the appropriate 'watchdog' investigating body which may take the matter up with the Minister. For example, if you have a problem with the Post Office you could ask the Post Office Users National Council (POUNC) to take it up on your behalf.

12. The chief aim of a public corporation is to provide an efficient public service at a price low enough to avoid making excessive profit but high enough to cover investment costs, although sometimes other priorities may be considered as being more important than making a profit. For example, some railway lines are kept open, despite the fact that they are making a loss, in order to supply some remote areas with a transport

service. Each industry is expected to operate commercially and meet a 'required rate of return' on its assets set by the Government. Any losses are financed from taxation whilst profits are used to repay loans or finance the future development of the industry.

GOVERNMENT DEPARTMENTS

13. As well as running many industries, the government also has departments which provide a variety of services. Examples of these include the Royal Mint which supplies the country's money, Her Majesty's Stationery Office (HMSO) dealing with Government publications, the Central Office of Information which prepares Government statistics, and the Forestry Commission which controls the production and supply of timber. The Post Office was once a government department but since 1969 has been a public corporation.

LOCAL AUTHORITY OR MUNICIPAL UNDERTAKINGS

14. There are also many important services which are operated by Local Authorities for the benefit of the local community. Local Councils use money collected from rents, community charge, business rates, government grants (standard support grant) and by borrowing to provide services for the town. Examples include schools and colleges for education, health clinics and hospitals, police and fire services and recreational facilities such as parks and libraries.

15. The local authority may also receive income from trading activities. That is, many councils provide services which you pay to use, for example sports centres, entertainment facilities, public baths, and cafes in parks.

16. Council Services

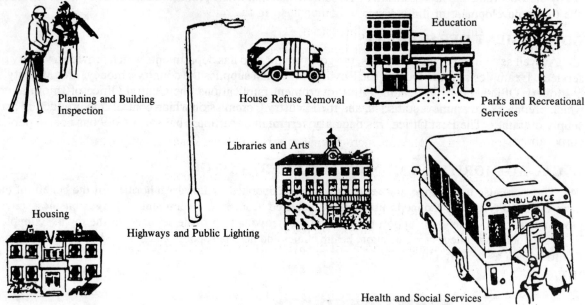

Planning and Building Inspection

House Refuse Removal

Education

Parks and Recreational Services

Libraries and Arts

Housing

Highways and Public Lighting

Health and Social Services

17. *N.B.*

    a)   **Council Tax** was introduced in April 1993 to replace the Community Charge (Poll Tax). It is based on the market value of property and takes account of the number of adults in each household, with discounts available for single adult and certain other households. Properties are allocated to one of eight broad valuation bands with associated tax rates for England and Wales. Similar provisions apply in Scotland. In Northern Ireland, the rates – local property taxes – have been retained.

    b)   **Local Authorities** are managed by a combination of employed staff and councillors elected by the local people. The councillors make the policy decisions on how the town should be run and the employees implement these and carry out the day-to-day administration.

REASONS FOR PUBLIC OWNERSHIP

18. a)   Political – to enable the nation to share the profits of industry.

    b)   Control of vital industries and commercial activities for example central banking and railways.

    c)   Control of monopolies – many nationalised industries are 'natural' monopolies i.e. they have no real competition, for example post, and therefore

    d)   Protection of national security – e.g. Atomic Energy.

    e)   Capital Costs – sometimes the capital costs of setting up or modernising an industry may be too great or unprofitable for private enterprise, for example coal and docks.

    f)   Provision of social services – which private enterprise would not wish to provide because they are unprofitable, for example railways and postal services to remote rural areas.

    g)   Survival of unprofitable industries – some industries may otherwise be forced down creating problems of unemployment, for example coal and shipbuilding.

19. Advantages of Public Ownership

    *   It enables the government to plan large sections of the economy in the public interest.

    *   Profits belong to the nation and are therefore for everyone's benefit not just a few shareholders or individuals.

* The benefits of economies of scale can be gained from operating as a large unit.
* Reduces unnecessary and wasteful duplication of resources. For example imagine the problems from competition if a number of companies ran the railways.
* Ensures survival of important industries.
* Provides capital investment for modernisation.
* Operates in the public interest in the provision of goods and services.

20. **Disadvantages of Public Ownership**
    * Lack of competition often makes it difficult to assess their efficiency. Greater possibility of waste, over-manning and poor quality service.
    * Government may delay decision-making or pursue policies which are not in the best interests of the business.
    * Government interference may make it difficult for them to operate efficiently, i.e. control of prices, or investment decisions.
    * Any losses must be paid for out of taxation.
    * May become impersonal with lots of 'red tape'.
    * National decision-making does not always work in the best interests of a local community.

PRIVATISATION

21. A lot of government control of industry has taken place in periods when the Labour Party was running the country particularly from 1946 – 1951. However, the Conservative Party does not support public ownership to the same extent and indeed in the 1980's introduced a policy of *privatisation*. That is, it has been selling off some public corporations to the private sector as public limited companies. It believes that such sales create greater competition and therefore efficiency in the industries involved. Recent examples of such privatisation include Cable and Wireless (1981), British Telecom (1986), British Gas (1986), British Airways (1987), Water (1989) and Electricity (1990).

22. *N.B.* Hence the reasons for the organisation and control of some industries may be based on political issues rather than just the business factors which affect it.

23. Some local authorities have also been encouraged by the Conservative government to increase their efficiency and cut costs by sub-contracting to privately owned firms, jobs such as refuse collecting, cleaning and maintenance. They have done this instead of employing their own staff.

SUMMARY

24. a) Public sector businesses are those which are owned and controlled by the government on behalf of the nation.

   b) There are three types – Public Corporations, Government Departments and Municipal Undertakings.

   c) Public Corporations are formed by an Act of Parliament and can be set up directly by the government as with the BBC or be the result of nationalisation for example coal and railways.

   d) Government Departments provide a variety of services examples of which are the Royal Mint and HMSO.

   e) Municipal Undertakings are the services and trading activities provided by the local council for example schools, libraries, sports centres and entertainment facilities.

   f) There are several reasons for public ownership including political arguments, to control vital industries, to control monopolies, protect national security, provide capital, provide social services and to ensure the survival of certain unprofitable industries.

   g) The degree of public ownership is a political issue and hence varies according to the Party in power. In the 1980's and 1990's the Conservative Party has pursued a policy of privatisation by selling off nationalised industries.

REVIEW QUESTIONS

Answers can be found in the paragraphs shown.

1. What is a public sector business? (1 and 2)
2. Give 4 examples of public corporations. (4-7)
3. Briefly describe how a public corporation is organised. (8-10)
4. What is the chief aim of a public corporation? (12)
5. Outline the difference between a public corporation and a Government Department. (12-13)
6. How does the local council get the money to pay for the services which it provides? (14, 15)
7. What kinds of trading activities are undertaken by a local authority? (15)
8. Give 4 reasons for public ownership. (18)
9. List 3 advantages and 3 disadvantages of the public ownership of industry. (19, 20)
10. Explain with examples the meaning of privatisation. (21, 23)

EXAMINATION PRACTICE QUESTIONS

Marks

1. Identify 3 possible sources of finance which may be used by a local council.   3
2. a)   Outline the main features of a public corporation.   6
    b)   In what ways can public corporations be said to operate in the public interest?   4
3. a)   Describe clearly how a public limited company differs from a public corporation in terms   5
    of ownership, management control, capital and size.
    b)   Is a public limited company in the public or private sector of the economy? Give reasons   3
    for your answer.

MULTIPLE CHOICE/COMPLETION

1. A public undertaking is defined as:
    a)   A public limited company
    b)   A co-operative
    c)   A publicly owned enterprise
    d)   A monopoly in the private sector

2. Nationalised industries are managed by a
    a)   Partnership
    b)   Public Corporation
    c)   Local Council
    d)   Private limited company

3. Which one of the following services is provided by a public corporation?
    a)   Telephones
    b)   Television
    c)   Defence
    d)   Education

4. Which one of the following services is provided by a central government department?
   a) Telephones
   b) Television
   c) Defence
   d) Education

5. Which one of the following services is provided by a local authority?
   a) Telephones
   b) Television
   c) Defence
   d) Education

6. A Local Authority's policy is determined by:
   a) Its local MP
   b) Its poll tax payers
   c) Central government
   d) Elected local councillors

7. The most important difference between public corporations and public companies is that public corporations:
   a) Do not offer shares to the general public
   b) Plough back some of their profits
   c) Are not primarily concerned with making a profit
   d) Are usually monopolies

In the following question, one or more of the responses is/are correct. Choose the appropriate letter which indicates the correct version.

   A   if 1 only is correct
   B   if 3 only is correct
   C   if 1 and 2 are correct
   D   if 1, 2 and 3 are correct

8. Which of the following are Government Departments?
   1) Home Office
   2) Department of Trade and Industry
   3) Atomic Energy Authority

RECENT EXAMINATION QUESTIONS

Marks

NISEC 1988 GCSE Business Studies Specimen Paper I

1. "Britain is a good example of a 'mixed economy' "
   a) State briefly what is meant by a mixed economy   2
   b) Name two other kinds of national economies and give a brief description of each.   6

2. "The private sector and the public sector are different ways of achieving the same thing".
   a) Explain the essential difference between the private sector and the public sector.   4
   b) Give an example in each case of a large organisation engaged in secondary production:

    i)   in the private sector

    ii)   in the public sector   2

c)   What is the 'same thing' that both are supposed to be achieving?   3

LCCI June 1989 PSC Structure of Business

3.   Examine the advantages and disadvantages of privatisation.   18

ASSIGNMENT

1.   Identify the public corporations in the following list:

    a)   ICI

    b)   British Petroleum

    c)   Post Office

    d)   British Rail

    e)   British Airports Authority

    f)   National Exhibition Centre

    g)   British Steel

    h)   British Coal

    i)   Department of Health and Social Security

    j)   B.T.

2.   Why might a government decide to nationalise an industry?

3.   In what sense can public corporations be made 'accountable' for the way in which the business is run?

4.   Draw up 2 lists:

    a)   to show the main services and

    b)   the main trading activities

which are provided by *your* local authority.

5.   Using your answers to question 4, list any services or activities which you feel could be provided by private sector businesses and give reasons for those which you choose.

8.   Business Organisation and Management

1.   We have seen earlier that business organisations are divided between those in the private sector and those in the public sector. In this chapter we consider the internal structure which these organisations adopt in order to meet their objectives.

2.   **Objectives** are the aims or goals which businesses seek to achieve. The specific objectives of an organisation will depend upon whether it is established in the public or private sector. However, in both sectors, to be successful, the prime objective must be to meet the needs of their customers or clients.

3.

OBJECTIVES OF PRIVATE SECTOR ORGANISATIONS

4.   Organisations in the private sector are usually created to earn *maximum profits* for their owners, i.e. to achieve the best possible return on the money which they have invested in the business. Profit is the difference between the total costs of running a business and the total income received by the business.

5.   However, whilst this will certainly be the main aim of most businesses some may have other objectives which they pursue, particularly in the short-term. For example, a new business may see *survival* as its main objective in the first year of trading, followed by consolidation and it may be some years before it reaches a position of high profit.

6.   On the other hand, established larger firms may be prepared to cut prices and accept lower profits for a short-time in order to achieve the objectives of *increasing sales* and *market share*, i.e. selling more of the total sales of a product or service than their competitors. In the longer term, if successful, this may enable the firm to expand its output or product range and enter a period of *growth*.

OBJECTIVES OF PUBLIC SECTOR ORGANISATIONS

7.   Public sector organisations are created not to maximise profit but to achieve the maximum *benefit for the nation*. In order to achieve their objectives they may be involved in operating unprofitable services because it is in the public's interest to do so. For example, the provision of rail services to country areas. Another example would be keeping an uneconomic coal mine open in an area of high unemployment to prevent the loss of further jobs.

8.   However, the government still expects public corporations to aim to at least 'break even' over a period of years and if possible to make sufficient profit to enable investment in new equipment to take place. Each one is set a profit target just like a commercial firm.

INTERNAL STRUCTURE OF ORGANISATIONS

9.   In order to achieve its objectives a business must be organised to enable it to produce the goods or services which it supplies.

10. Firms vary considerably in size and this is true even in the same industry or area of activity, for example building, retailing and farming. Hence the internal structure of a business will also vary according to its size.

SMALL FIRMS

11. Whilst an organisation is small, one man can often control it. He is able to do all of the important jobs himself e.g. ordering, accounts, VAT returns and marketing, and is very closely involved in its day-to-day running.

12. However, as a business grows one man may be too busy to perform all the jobs which he once did and he may therefore need to take in a partner or arrange for people who work for him to take on some specialist jobs, e.g. accounts and ordering.

13. If a firm continues to grow, additional skills may be required and as more staff are employed further specialisation can take place.

LARGER ORGANISATIONS

14. This process of growth and specialisation may continue as a firm develops into a private or public limited company. When this happens the shareholders will elect a Board of Directors to make the policy decisions on how the business should be organised and run in order to achieve its objectives.

15. **Organisation Chart**

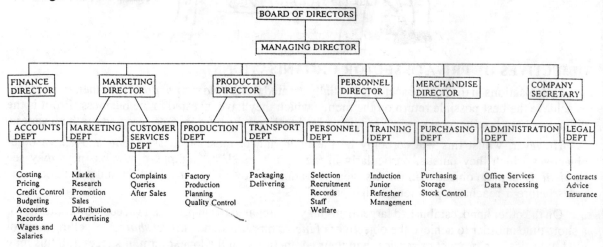

A typical organisation chart showing departments and their main functions. Businesses often use this form of diagram to illustrate the positions of staff in their organisation.

SPECIALIST DEPARTMENTS

16. As illustrated in the organisation chart the board will usually appoint a managing director or chief executive as head of the business. Specialist departments are often established, the actual number depending on the size of the firm, with a director in charge of each function, for example finance, production, marketing. The overall management and administration of the company involves the co-ordination of these different departments or parts of the business.

17. The following are examples of the departments typically found in a large organisation. They are listed in alphabetical order, not necessarily in order of importance. The number of staff employed in each will vary according to the amount of work and amount of specialisation.

18. **Administration**

Many firms have an administrative office which provides a support service to the other departments. This may include the reception area where visitors report, the switchboard which deals with telephone calls and general office facilities like typing, photocopying, filing, the handling of mail, secretarial and computing services.

19. **Customer Services**

Many manufacturing and retailing organisations have a special department to deal with customers complaints, or queries about merchandise, credit facilities, or other problems. After sales service may also be dealt with by this department which is generally concerned with maintaining customer goodwill.

20. It is important that a good relationship exists between a firm and its customers. Generally this will develop over a period of time and is particularly influenced by the service given to customers and the way in which any problems or queries are dealt with. This building up of *goodwill* is important in helping to encourage customers to buy more of a firm's goods in the future.

21. **Finance**

The finance or accounts department has a number of important functions including:

a) **Payment of suppliers** The invoices (bills) for goods purchased from suppliers must be checked and paid. Discount is usually given by firms if accounts are settled promptly.

b) **Wages of Staff** There may be a separate section dealing with the important job of paying staff wages. This also involves making income tax deductions and handling National Insurance contributions (see Chapter 22).

c) **Calculation of the selling prices** These will usually be calculated from the cost prices of the goods and the profit margin which the firm adds to make the final selling price for example, cost £2, profit margin 25%, selling price £2.50.

d) **Preparation of Company Accounts** All firms are in business to make a profit and it is the function of the accounts department to keep the financial records and calculate the annual profit or loss account. It will also prepare a Balance Sheet which is a financial summary of everything which the business owns and owes.

e) **Other functions** The preparation of company budgets, forecasts and statistics. This provides information on which future planning can be based. If a firm offers credit to its customers then credit control may be another function of the finance section.

N.B. Nowadays much of the work of the accounts department is done by computer or other mechanised equipment.

22. **Legal**

The purpose of this department is to ensure that the organisation does not break the law. The Company Secretary is usually in charge of legal matters which include contracts for goods bought and sold, guarantees and insurance.

23. **Marketing**

The overall function of this department is to enable a business to successfully sell its goods or services. Briefly this will involve:

a) Market research to find out about a firm's customers.

b) Advertising, sales and promotion to inform people about its product(s) and persuade them to buy.

c) Making sure that the product(s) are distributed to the consumer.

N.B. This activity is covered in more detail in Chapters 10-15.

24. Personnel

a) The main function of this department is to recruit the 'right' staff. This may involve advertising in the national or local newspapers, or contacting the local Careers office or Job Centre depending on the staff required. Applicants will then need to be interviewed.

b) The Personnel Department also looks after the welfare of all employees, deals with problems at work, keeps staff records and negotiates with Trade Unions (see Chapter 25). It may also be the Personnel Manager who has to dismiss unsatisfactory staff.

25. Many large firms have a separate department to look after training. However, in smaller firms it is usually organised by the Personnel department.

Training is important for all employees to enable them to perform their jobs to the best of their ability. This involves giving instruction in order to develop their knowledge and skills. The main types of training are discussed in Chapter 21.

26.

27. Production

The main function of this department is to make a firm's product(s). This involves the planning and co-ordination of work in the factory to ensure that goods of the right quality are produced on time. Quality control checks are usually performed and an examination of any goods returned as faulty is another way of checking quality.

28. **Organisation of Production**   Production can be organised in three basic ways. The method chosen will depend on the type of product and quantity required.

* **Job Production**   This is used when special or 'one-off' orders are made to customers own requirements. For example luxury goods, racing cars. Generally there is no repetition of products or jobs.

* **Flow Production**   This uses a series of repetitive processes and is common where products are mass produced along a conveyor belt or assembly line. Cars, television sets, chocolates and many tinned and packeted goods are produced by this method.

* **Batch Production**   This falls between job and flow production. Some repetition is involved so that batches or units of production can be made at any one time. For example a wallpaper firm can produce batches of different designs. Housing estates are also built by this method.

29.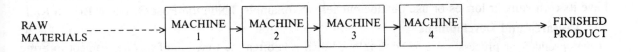

FLOW PRODUCTION

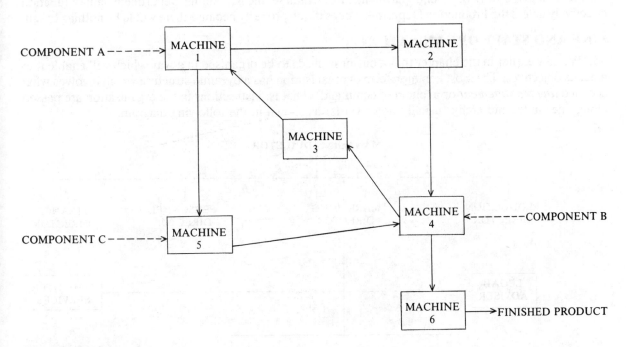

30. Purchasing

A successful buyer aims to get the right goods, at the right price, in the right place, at the right time. If this is achieved then it should lead to increased sales and profits.

The buyer, merchandise director, or purchasing manager is responsible for supervising the purchase of all supplies, materials and equipment for the organisation. This will include:

   a) Finding the best sources of supply, reliable suppliers, the 'right' quality, styles, sizes and prices with delivery when it is needed.

   b) Bulk-buying i.e. buying in large quantities to save time and money.

   c) Very large firms may employ a number of specialist buyers each dealing with different goods or materials, for example a supermarket chain might have buyers for fashion goods, hardware and food.

   d) The purchasing department may also be responsible for maintaining a store or warehouse and an efficient system of *stock control*.

31. *N.B.* **Purchase Requisitions**   These are written requests from other departments or branches to the purchasing department specifying particular items which they require for example stationery, cleaning materials or merchandise.

32. **Transport**

The function of this department is to ensure that a company's products reach its customers on time and in good condition. At the same time the Company requires this to be done as cheaply as possible. It may have its own vans or lorries or use outside carriers for example TNT, the Post Office or British Rail.

33. **Research and Development**

If new products or processes are to be developed then it is often the function of this department to bring it about. Ideas are researched to see if they are practical and then developed to the stage where they can be used or tested. For example, microwave cookers and satellite broadcasting are relatively new ideas, whereas scientists are at present still trying to discover a cure for the disease Aids.

34. *N.B.* No one department in an organisation can operate in isolation. It may depend upon or is at least related to the work of other departments. For example, the Marketing Department cannot function effectively unless the Production Department does its job properly because there would be nothing to sell.

LINE AND STAFF ORGANISATION

35. We saw earlier in the chapter that a business needs to be organised in a way which will enable it to meet its objectives. The most common form of organisation has a pyramid structure which involves what is called *line management* or a 'chain of command'. That is, instructions in the organisation are passed along lines in the hierarchy (usually downwards) as shown in the following diagram.

36.

37. Within an organisation structure there may also be specialist advisory or support services, such as legal advice or computer services which are outside the line management structure. Frequently these service several departments and therefore are referred to as *staff functions*.

AUTHORITY, RESPONSIBILITY AND DELEGATION

38. The managing director or chief executive of an organisation needs to tell his managers what is expected of them in order to enable specific tasks to be achieved. The managers in turn will also pass instructions 'down the line' to their subordinates. This is known as *delegation* and is essential because it is impossible for one manager to maintain direct control over all staff, especially in a large organisation.

39. To enable instructions to be carried out, managers must be given *authority* over their subordinates. That is, they must have the power to make decisions such as telling staff what to do and then expecting them to do it. However, a manager is still ultimately *responsible* for the actions of his subordinates. So although he may delegate the task he is still responsible to the organisation for ensuring that it is properly completed.

SPAN OF CONTROL

40. Beyond a certain size it is impossible for one person to control all the activities of a business properly. Therefore, as noted above, some tasks must be delegated. The principle of the *span of control* states that no superior can directly supervise the work of more than five or six subordinates. In practise, the span of control will vary considerably from one organisation to another. However, if it is too wide it can cause problems due to lack of proper supervision whilst too narrow a span is likely to be wasteful and costly.

41.

Narrow span of control

Wide span of control

CENTRALISATION AND DECENTRALISATION

42. Centralisation and decentralisation are terms used when referring to the way in which businesses are organised. If a business is centralised, its activities are grouped together to enable it to operate more efficiently and effectively. Purchasing, advertising, personnel, typing and other functions are all carried out centrally rather than in different parts of the organisation. Management may also be centralised so that the business is run and controlled from one place.

43. Alternatively, a business may be decentralised whereby work is carried out in a number of different places. This may mean that each department is managed separately, organising its own services such as typing, purchasing and advertising. Often firms with a number of branches or locations operate on a decentralised basis with managers in charge of each place. This enables decisions to be made faster and gives staff more responsibility.

44. *N.B.* In practise many firms often have some activities centralised and others decentralised, for example a supermarket chain may have its advertising centralised at Head Office whilst allowing each store manager to recruit his own staff.

INFORMAL ORGANISATION

45. Formal relationships between people in any organisation are those shown on an organisation chart. However, most businesses also tend to have an informal organisation which operates at the same time. This results from the relationships which exist between individuals and groups of people in one depart-

ment or several departments who have similar interests, ideas and attitudes. Such relationships are important because they can conflict with organisation's objectives. For example, if a group does not agree with a particular policy then it may deliberately try to obstruct it.

SUMMARY

46. a) The main objective of private sector organisations is usually to achieve maximum profits.

b) Public sector organisations also seek to make profits but their first concern is to operate for the benefit of the nation.

c) In order to achieve its objectives the successful running of any business, no matter how large or small, involves the co-ordination of many different departments.

d) Administration – the provision of office services to enable a business to operate efficiently.

e) Customer Services – to deal with complaints or queries and create goodwill.

f) Finance – provides the financial control for a business including paying wages.

g) Marketing – research, advertising, promotion and sales to increase the firm's profits.

h) Personnel – the selection of staff and looking after their general welfare.

i) Production – making the goods in the factory to the required standard.

j) Purchasing – buying the right goods at the right price and storing them until required.

k) Training – to improve the effectiveness of staff at all levels in the organisation.

l) Transport – arranging for goods to be delivered to customers when required.

m) Research and Development – seeking ideas for new products or to improve existing products or processes.

n) Whereas in a large organisation a different department may exist to carry out each of these functions, in a small business they may all be performed by the owner or just a few people.

o) Many businesses have a line management structure with specialist staff functions.

p) To achieve objectives, managers need to delegate work along with the appropriate authority.

REVIEW QUESTIONS

Answers can be found in the paragraphs shown.

1. What is the main objective of private sector businesses? (3)

2. Suggest 2 other objectives of private sector businesses. (4, 5)

3. With the use of an example explain the main objective of public sector organisations. (7)

4. Why do firms need to have a good internal organisation structure? (9, 10)

5. How are small firms usually organised? (11, 12)

6. What is the purpose of an organisation chart? (15)

7. How and why are large firms usually organised? (9, 10, 14-17)

8. Explain the functions of any 5 departments in an organisation. (18-32)

9. What is the difference between line management and staff functions? (35-37)

10. Briefly explain the terms 'authority', 'responsibility' and 'delegation'. (38-39)

EXAMINATION PRACTICE QUESTIONS

Marks

1. The . . . . are responsible for deciding the policy of a company and the . . . . is the executive responsible for ensuring that it is carried out.

2

Marks

2. a) Describe the functions of the following departments in a large organisation – Administration, Marketing, Purchasing, Training and Production.   10

    b) In what senses are marketing and production equally important?   6

3. What is meant by the 'span of control' in a business?   2

4. The following up of overdue accounts is part of . . . . control.   1

MULTIPLE CHOICE/COMPLETION

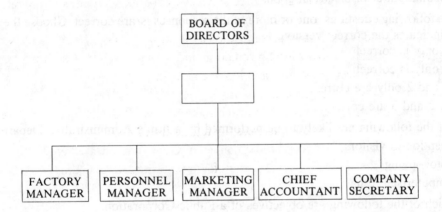

1. On the above organisation chart, which of the following is likely to be included in the blank space?
   a) General Manager
   b) Sales Representative
   c) Transport Manager
   d) Customer Services Manager

2. The Finance Department keeps information about which of the following?
   a) Wages and Salaries
   b) Faulty goods returned by customers
   c) Sales Promotions
   d) The Training needs of the company's employees

3. An organisation chart in a firm shows the:
   a) Type of work carried out by its employees
   b) Order in which work should be carried out
   c) Location of the different departments
   d) Relative positions of employees

4. Which department of a manufacturing organisation is responsible for the ordering of new materials?
   a) Accounts
   b) Customer Services
   c) Purchasing
   d) Sales

5. One of the duties of a Company Secretary is to:
   a) Organise the Finance Department
   b) Advise on legal matters
   c) Decide what goods should be produced
   d) Determine the price of goods

6. Which of the following types of business would *NOT* usually have a transport department:
   a) A meat wholesaler
   b) A department store
   c) A firm of solicitors
   d) A manufacturer of electrical goods

In each of the following questions, one or more of the responses is/are correct. Choose the appropriate letter which indicates the correct version.
   A if 1 only is correct
   B if 3 only is correct
   C if 1 and 2 only are correct
   D if 1, 2 and 3 are correct

7. Which of the following are likely to be performed by a firm's Administrative Department?
   1) Reception of visitors
   2) Photocopying
   3) Computerised filing

8. State which of the following are objectives of a Public Corporation:
   1) To 'break-even' over a period of years
   2) To operate in the public's interest
   3) To Maximise profits

RECENT EXAMINATION QUESTIONS

Marks

NISEC SUMMER 1989 GCSE BUSINESS STUDIES PAPER 1 **SECTION A**

1.   Give TWO functions of the Personnel Department in a large organisation.   4

LEAG 1988 SPECIMEN PAPER 2B **SECTION A**

2.   Finding out what consumers want and then selling it to them is called . . . .   ½

NISEC 1988 GCSE BUSINESS STUDIES SPECIMEN PAPER 2

3.   The incomplete chart shown below indicates how various work functions may be performed by specialised departments.

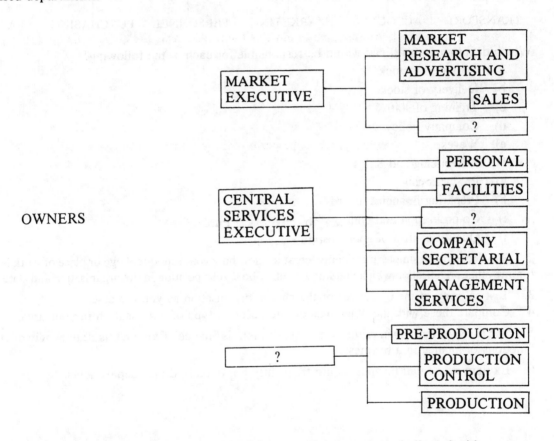

a)   Complete the chart by filling in the blank boxes which have been indicated with a
question mark.   3

b)   Give two reasons why a firm might organise itself on a departmental basis.   4

c)   Describe two functions of the marketing department of a firm.   4

d)   How and why should a sales target set by the Marketing Executive be communicated to
a production worker on the shop floor?   4

ASSIGNMENT

1. Assume that the Head Office of a local firm is organised in the following way

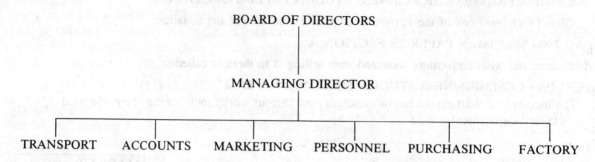

BOARD OF DIRECTORS

MANAGING DIRECTOR

| TRANSPORT | ACCOUNTS | MARKETING | PERSONNEL | PURCHASING | FACTORY |

Which department or official would be responsible for each of the following?
   a) Ordering of stock
   b) Delivery of stock
   c) Training of staff
   d) Company policy
   e) Wages
   f) Advertising and Sales
   g) Production
   h) Preparing financial records
   i) Co-ordination and control
   j) Quality control of goods produced

2. Now construct a simple organisation chart to show how your school/college or place of work is organised (or any other organisation which you know well). Show your position in the organisation and state what it is.

3. List as many of the objectives of the chosen organisation as you are able.

4. Compare these with the objectives of one different type of organisation in your area.

5. 'An essential activity in virtually all organisations is finance'. Explain this statement in relation to the functions of finance in a business.

6. Explain why small businesses are frequently not organised into departments.

9. Location and the Size of Firms

1. This chapter outlines the factors which entrepreneurs must consider before deciding where to locate their business. It then looks at the advantages which a firm can gain from either its own expansion or from the growth and concentration of an industry in a particular area. Finally after examining the ways in which firms can grow in size, it considers the impact of new technology on business today.

LOCATION OF INDUSTRY

2. There are many reasons why firms or industries are located in a particular place. A firm will usually seek a site which offers it the lowest costs of production and distribution. Some of the more important factors which will influence these costs include historical development, natural resources and raw materials, nearness to markets, transport costs, availability of labour and government intervention.

3. **Factors Influencing the Location of a Business**

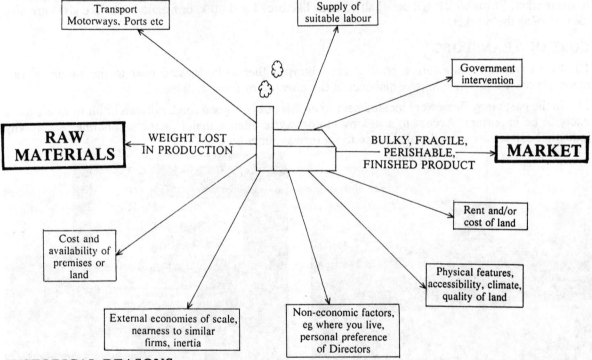

HISTORICAL REASONS

4. Many industries became established in particular areas because of the nearness of power and raw materials. This can be illustrated by the following examples:

* Wool – originally developed in Yorkshire because of the availability of sheep and water power in the Pennine valleys.
* Engineering developed in the Midlands because iron ore and coal were readily available.
* Steel production was located in Sheffield because of the availability of coal, iron ore and limestone.
* Cotton was imported from America into Lancashire where the damp atmosphere helped the spinning and weaving processes.

5. Many industries have remained in their original locations even though the initial advantages have now declined. This is known as *'industrial inertia'*.

NATURAL RESOURCES AND RAW MATERIALS

6. Primary industries have little choice in their location. Hence coal mining, quarrying and oil drilling must take place where the raw material is found. Agriculture where the land and climate is suitable and fishing near to fishing grounds and harbours.

7. The location of manufacturing industries may also be influenced by the availability of raw materials. Usually a firm will locate near to its source of raw materials if they are difficult or expensive to transport, for example bulky goods. Thus a steel firm would locate near to sources of coal, limestone and iron ore because the weight of these raw materials is far greater than that of the finished product, i.e. steel is weight reducing.

NEARNESS TO A MARKET

8. Service industries are usually located where the demand exists. Hence restaurants, hairdressers, garages, retail outlets, banks etc are all found near to centres of population.

9. If a firm manufactures bulky or heavy goods like furniture or bricks, then it is likely to be located near to the market. Firms which sell perishable goods like bread and milk, or fragile items like glass are also located near the market.

COST OF TRANSPORT

10. Firms which manufacture a product can choose either to be located near to the supply of raw materials or near to the market whichever is the cheaper or most suitable.

11. In the past many firms were located near to canals but now good road, rail, sea or air links are more likely to be important. Access to a nearby motorway is often a major factor and is one reason why industrial estates are often located close to motorway junctions.

SUPPLY OF LABOUR

12. All firms need suitably skilled workers and therefore this is an important location factor.

GOVERNMENT INFLUENCE

13. Since the 1930's depression, Governments have played an important role in influencing the location of industry. This is because the concentration of industries like coal, textiles and shipbuilding in particular areas has brought with it various problems, such as

    a) Traffic congestion, pollution, housing shortages and the strain on education, medical and social services.

    b) High unemployment as these industries have declined rapidly due to changes in demand, foreign competition and job losses from the introduction of new technology.

HOW UNEMPLOYMENT AFFECTS THE REGIONS

14.

REGION	% of all employees				
	Jan '73	Nov '78	Jan '87	Jan '91	Jan '93
South East	2.0	3.9	8.5	5.0	10.3
East Anglia	2.6	4.7	9.3	4.8	8.5
South West	3.4	6.4	10.4	5.7	9.9
West Midlands	3.0	5.4	13.8	6.7	11.5
East Midlands	2.8	4.8	11.4	5.9	9.6
Yorks and Humberside	3.8	5.8	13.8	7.6	10.5
North West	4.6	7.2	14.3	8.1	10.9
North	6.0	8.6	16.9	9.2	12.2
Wales	4.9	8.3	14.3	7.3	10.3
Scotland	6.1	7.8	15.1	8.0	9.9
Northern Ireland	7.5	10.9	19.3	14.0	14.6
Average	4.1	6.7	13.4	7.5	10.7

15. As can be seen from the table, unemployment is very high in some regions of the UK, like the North and Northern Ireland. In the South East and East Anglia it is considerably lower. It is this problem of imbalance which the Government is trying to solve. Hence governments have tried to attract new and expanding industries to so called depressed areas. That is, those with high and persistent unemployment. These are classified as assisted areas.

16. Some of the measures used to influence the location of industry include:
   * Financial incentives to firms, for example grants for buildings and equipment, loans at special low rates of interest and special tax allowances
   * Ready built factories for sale or rent on favourable terms, for example rent free for twelve months
   * Subsidies to train workers taken on
   * Prevention of industrial development in other areas
   * Building of 32 New Towns, for example Stevenage, Milton Keynes, Peterlee

17.

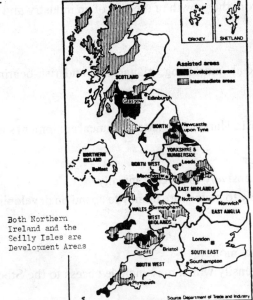

Both Northern Ireland and the Scilly Isles are Development Areas

18. Whenever possible the Government has itself set an example by moving its own departments to assisted areas. Thus the DVLC (Driver and Vehicle Licencing Centre) is located in Swansea and the DHSS (Department of Health and Social Security) in Newcastle.

19. *N.B.* **Footloose Industries** Many businesses today are referred to as being *'footloose'*. This is because the development of new and improved sources of power, transport and raw materials means that they no longer have to locate near to raw material supplies or their market. Instead they can choose to go where they like.

20. **Urban Policy Initiatives** The economic recovery of inner city areas is being encouraged by improving the environment, developing new and existing businesses and better training to improve job prospects.

This is being achieved via a number of co-ordinated Government initiatives including:

Inner Urban Programme (IUP) Grants – (Through 57 'target' local authorities e.g. Aberdeen, Newcastle, Nottingham and Leeds) to support capital investment projects for rebuilding. These are being phased out to end in 1995.

City Challenge – Introduced in 1993 whereby local authorities were invited to bid competitively for £20m of resources previously allocated within IUP. Among those successful were Bolton, Blackburn, Wigan and Sefton.

Enterprise Initiative – Which offers assistance for between 5-15 days of consultancy for small firms (less than 500 employees) in key areas of marketing, design, quality, manufacturing systems, business planning and financial and information systems.

Urban Development Corporations – 12 set up to use grants to reverse large scale urban decline e.g. London Docklands, Merseyside and Cardiff Bay.

Enterprise Zones – 27 set up offering tax incentives and easy planning permission for firms who locate there e.g. Belfast, Tyneside, Telford and Swansea Valley.

ECONOMIES OF SCALE

21. Wherever a firm is located, as it expands it can gain the advantages of operating on a large scale. That is the cost per unit falls as output increases because of what are called economies of scale. These are of two types:

a) **Internal economies** – which a firm gives directly as it increases the size of its own operations and

b) **External economies** – which arise indirectly from the growth of the size of an industry and its concentration in a particular area.

INTERNAL ECONOMIES OF SCALE

22. These are of five main kinds – production, financial, marketing, managerial and risk-bearing, examples of each are given below.

23. **Production Economies**

* Mass production makes it possible for firms to install larger and better technical equipment such as the use of computers and robots

* More use can be made of the division of labour

* Buildings and equipment can be used more intensively and economically

* Research and development – large firms are likely to have more money to spend on developing new or improved products

24. **Financial Economies**

* Large firms find it cheaper and easier to borrow money

* Large well known firms can raise capital more easily which may include access to the Stock Market for funds

25. Marketing Economies
* Bulk buying – large firms can negotiate lower prices, for materials and equipment
* Advertising and other costs can be spread over a wider range of products
* Transport – either more efficient use can be made of a firm's own vehicles or better rates obtained from outside carriers
* Packaging and administration costs – the average cost per unit will be lower for a large firm

26. An example of economies of scale – bulk buying

One packet of biscuits costs 30p

Large carton costs £18, but holds 100 packets, therefore each costs 25p

Lorry load of cartons each packet of biscuits now only costs 20p

27. Managerial Economies
* Organisation into departments and the use of specialist staff, for example purchasing, sales, accounts, marketing
* Ability to pay higher salaries to attract good staff
* Use of computers to provide management information

28. Risk-Bearing Economies
* Markets and demand – large firms can diversify and offer a wider range of products so that if demand for one falls it is possible that this can be offset by increased sales of another. For example, Walls sell both ice-cream and sausages. Therefore total demand is more stable or predictable.
* Supplies and production – as a firm increases in size it can buy from a wider range of suppliers and produce in a number of different locations. This helps to guard against the risks of raw material shortages, strikes etc.

DISECONOMIES OF SCALE
29. We have seen that as a firm expands it may be able to benefit from economies of scale. The optimum size to which it should grow being the point at which its average cost of production is at its lowest.

COSTS OF PRODUCTION
30.

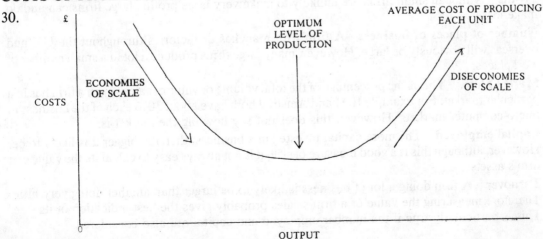

31. However, as can be seen in 30 above, it is possible for a firm to grow too large. An increase in size can bring problems as well as advantages. Problems which reduce efficiency and increase the cost per unit of output are called *diseconomies of scale*.

32. Imagine the problems of running a large secondary school or college with over seventy staff, particularly if it operates on more than one site, compared with a small primary school with perhaps four or five staff.

33. Diseconomies of scale usually result from the difficulties of managing larger organisations and include:

* Co-ordination and control – communications and management become much more complex and difficult to organise.
* Industrial relations – problems caused because workers feel unimportant or out-of-touch with management; problems of boredom because work is repetitive.
* Technical limitations – the inability to produce more with existing equipment or adapt quickly to new production methods.

EXTERNAL ECONOMIES

34. Once an industry becomes established in a particular area it can benefit from certain advantages known as external economies of scale. These are factors which keep firms in an area or attract new firms and include:

* Labour – a supply of suitably skilled labour is available
* Ancillary/Support Industry – for example firms supplying specialist machinery, collecting by-products and producing components.
* Marketing and distribution facilities – for example specialist delivery services and warehousing.
* Commercial services – for example information provided by Trade Associations, Chamber of Commerce, specialist College training courses etc.
* 'Disintegration' may take place as individual firms specialise in single processes thus reducing costs, for example specialist spinning weaving, dyeing and finishing firms in the Lancashire cotton industry.

THE SIZE OF FIRMS

35. The size of a firm can be measured in a number of different ways, each of which could give different results including:

* **The number of people employed**   However, a firm can still be 'big' without employing many people, particularly if it uses a lot of computer technology.
* **Profits**   Although small firms are unlikely to make very large profits, large firms can and do make losses.
* **Number of places of business**   A firm with branches or factories throughout the UK and overseas will obviously be large. However, many large firms produce a lot in a small number of workplaces.
* **Market Share**   This is the percentage of the total volume or value of sales which a firm has in a particular market. For example IBM and Amstrad both have about 30% each of the business in micro-computer markets. However, this does not say how big the market is.
* **Capital employed**   The more capital invested in a business, then the bigger it is likely to be. However, although this is a good measure of size, it is not always easy to calculate the value of a firm's assets.
* **Turnover**   A firm doing a lot of business is likely to be larger than another doing very little. Therefore measuring the value of a firm's sales probably gives the best indication of its size. This is particularly true if the number employed and capital are also considered.

THE GROWTH OF FIRMS

36. There are many reasons why firms wish to grow in size but at least three important ones should be noted:
    a) To achieve economies of scale and reduce costs
    b) To increase market share, possibly to gain a monopoly position
    c) To reduce risks and obtain greater security by extending the range of products, or controlling supplies of raw materials or sales outlets.

METHODS OF GROWTH

Growth can be achieved by two methods:

37. a) **Internal Growth** – that is by making more of existing products or extending the range by making new products. This may need extra capital which can be obtained by 'ploughing-back' profits, issuing further shares or by borrowing.

38. b) **Merger or Take-over** – expansion may also take place by:
    i) Merger – where two or more firms agree to amalgamate together
    or
    ii) Take-over – where one firm, not necessarily with the consent of the other, gains a controlling interest. This is possible because shares can be freely bought and sold on the stock market.

39.

Merger

Take-over

Example of a Merger
On 31 December 1982 Provincial Building Society merged with the Burnley Building Society to form a new society called National and Provincial Building Society. In August 1993 it merged with the Leeds Permanent to form the 'Leeds'.

INTEGRATION

40. When two or more firms combine together to form a larger unit it is called *integration*.

41. **Horizontal Integration**

Takes place when firms at the same stage of production combine together under the same management. For example Boots and Timothy White, National Provincial and Westminster Banks (National Westminster), Leyland Motor Company and British Motor Holdings (British Leyland).

42. **Vertical Integration**

Is the amalgamation of firms in the same industry but at different stages of production. This may take place either *'backward'* towards the source of the raw materials, or *'forward'* towards the market. For example, hop farms and public houses are all concerned at different stages with the supply of beer. Thus a brewery which acquires its own hop farms is said to be integrating backward. If it acquires its own public houses it is integrating forward.

43. **Lateral Integration**

Occurs when firms with similar, but not competing products, merge together. This enables firms to diversify and offer a wider range of related products, for example Cadbury-Schweppes (Food and Drink).

44. **Integration**

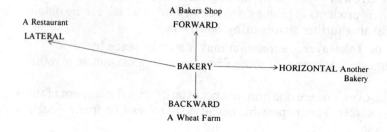

HOLDING COMPANIES

45. We noted earlier that one firm usually merges with or takes over another by buying all of the others shares. However, sometimes a firm does not actually own another completely, but still controls it by buying over 50% of its shares. A *holding company* is a company specifically formed to take a controlling interest in other firms. The firms controlled are called *subsidiaries*.

CONGLOMERATES

46. Many large companies also hold such controlling interests which enables them to diversify into a wide range of completely different product areas. Such companies are called *conglomerates*, examples of which include Great Universal Stores (which has a controlling interest in many companies including Kays, Lennards, Home Charm, Times Furnishing, Burberrys and Scotch House) and Sears (Trueform, Saxone, Selfridges, Lewis's, Olympus, William Hill and Galliford Sears Homes).

MULTI-NATIONALS

47. Some firms expand by buying foreign companies or opening divisions abroad so that they often operate throughout the world. These companies are referred to as *multi-nationals*, examples of which include the Ford Motor Company, ICI, Kodak and Gillette.

48.

FORD OPERATIONS IN EUROPE

Ford is one of Europe's leading industrial organisations, employing some 110,000 people in 15 separate national companies. Its products are sold through 2,520 main dealers and 1460 sub-dealers across Europe. In addition there are 2,150 Ford customer service and repair centres.

1 BELFAST
2 CORK
3 HALEWOOD
4 TREFOREST
5 SWANSEA
6 BRIDGEND
7 LANGLEY
8 LEAMINGTON
9 DAVENTRY
10 SOUTHAMPTON
11 DAGENHAM
   WARLEY
   AVELEY
12 ENFIELD
13 WOOLWICH
   CROYDON
14 BASILDON
   DUNTON
   BOREHAM
15 OSLO
16 STOCKHOLM
17 HELSINKI
18 COPENHAGEN
19 AMSTERDAM
20 ANTWERP
21 LOMMEL
22 BRUSSELS
23 WUELFRATH
24 COLOGNE
25 GENK
26 DUEREN
27 CHARLEVILLE
28 PARIS
29 SAARLOUIS
30 ZURICH
31 BORDEAUX
32 MADRID
33 LISBON
34 VALENCIA
35 VIENNA
36 SALZBURG
37 ROME
38 BERLIN

MONOPOLIES AND RESTRICTIVE PRACTICES

49. The growth of firms can lead to monopoly situations. If monopolies are likely to operate against the public interest, then the Director General of Fair Trading can prevent them being formed (or break-up existing ones). For example, when a firm buys up other firms because this reduces competition it may lead to higher prices.

50. The *Monopolies and Mergers Act 1965* set up the Monopolies and Mergers Commission to investigate any mergers which might be against consumers interests. If a proposed merger would result in 25% or more of a market being controlled by one supplier (or the total assets from the merger would exceed £5 million), then it must be referred to the Commission which decides whether or not it can go ahead.

51. Sometimes instead of merging, firms may come to some agreement with each other to restrict competition. For example, two large bread manufacturers may agree to restrict production in order to create a shortage of bread and therefore keep prices at a high level. Such practices can be illegal.

52. Under the *Restrictive Trade Practices Acts 1956-1976,* the Director General of Fair Trading can refer restrictive practices to the Restrictive Practices Court for investigation. Firms can be ordered to discontinue practices found to be against the public interest.

SURVIVAL OF THE SMALL FIRM

53. Despite the advantages enjoyed by large firms, small firms still predominate in most forms of businesses. Small firms are especially important in certain industries such as agriculture, building, retailing and personal and professional services. It is also important to note that even within the same industry, firms often vary considerably in size.

SIZE OF MANUFACTURING UNITS IN THE UK 1992

54.

EMPLOYEES	NUMBER OF BUSINESSES	% OF TOTAL BUSINESSES	NUMBER OF EMPLOYEES (000's)	% OF TOTAL EMPLOYED
1 - 19	118,761	77.7	585	12.7
20 - 99	24,952	16.3	1062	23.0
100 - 999	8728	5.7	2200	47.6
Over 1000	383	0.3	771	16.7
TOTAL	152,824	100	4618	100

N.B. Figures based on Annual Abstract of Statistics 1993 edition.

The above diagram shows two important features:

    a)   Small firms are typical of UK manufacturing. Nearly 94% employ less than one hundred people.

    b)   Those small units employ only a third of the total labour force.

WHY SMALL FIRMS SURVIVE

55. Below are some of the reasons why small firms are able to survive.

    a)   Professional and specialist services or products, for example accountants, solicitors, racing cars.

    b)   Sub-contracting or making components for large firms. Many small firms produce goods for other large firms.

c) Personal services, for example hairdressing, plumbing, window cleaning can be more easily supplied by small firms.

d) Limited markets, for example 'corner shops' provide a local service.

e) Banding together, for example Spar and Mace group together to gain the benefits of economies of scale such as bulk buying.

f) 'Being one's own boss'. Some entrepreneurs may accept smaller profits in order to enjoy the satisfaction of working for themselves.

TECHNOLOGICAL CHANGE

56. In recent years the introduction of new computerised technology has brought about many changes in business. The major changes and their effects are summarised below.

57. **New Technology**

Axe falls on 1,400 rail jobs

BRITISH Rail's engineering branch is to lose a further 1,400 jobs over the next 12 months. Transport Minister David Mitchell has announced.

The jobs have been lost as a direct result of new investment by BR in rolling stock which requires less maintenance.

About 1,000 of the latest job losses will come from Crewe, York and Derby.

65 jobs to go

Sixty-five jobs will be lost when modern technology replaces the operators at the telephone exchange, in Haverfordwest. Dyfed. British Telecom announced yesterday.

Newspaper jobs go

A provincial newspaper company is seeking the loss of 89 full and part-time jobs in a programme to introduce new technology and increase profitability. North of England Newspapers the Darlington based publishers of the Northern Echo, the Darlington and Stockton Times and the Advertiser series said the jobs would go mainly through voluntary redundancies and natural wastage.

Workers 'enthusiastic about new technology'

BRITISH workers are not characteristically resistant to modern technology but eager to accept change even though it may mean fewer jobs according to Mr William Daniel, director of the Policy Studies Institute.

Workers are enthusiastic because jobs using robots, computers and word processors involve more interest, skill responsibility, variety and higher pay, says Mr Daniel in his book Workplace Industrial Relations and Technical Change, published today.

"These findings turn the world upside down," said Mr Daniel, who spent a year compiling the evidence. "It is like learning that Everest is no longer the highest mountain in the world," he added.

"The stream of thinking that suggested that workers and their trade unions could be expected to be resistant to technical change has been shown to be inadequate by our results," his book states.

"In summary we found that British workers generally experience and accept a very tions of the change for employment."

Public services and nationalised industries were "very substantially" less likely to use advanced technology

Forty-three per cent of private manufacturing establishements has manual workers operating advanced technology, compared with 30 per cent of nationalised workplaces.

Managers of overseas companies operating in Britain are much more successful than British counterparts in bringing about change and using the most modern technology, says the book. It is based on interviews with more than 4,000 managers and shop stweards at 2,000 workplaces.

It makes use of surveys carried out by the Department of Employment, the Economic and Social Research Council, the Policy Studies Institute and

58. **Major Changes**

   a) **Information Technology** – the use of microcomputers and word processors to store, alter, transmit and process information on discs or tapes.

   b) **Automation** – much equipment is now controlled by computers in many cases replacing the work of people.

   c) **Robots** – have been introduced making work faster and more accurate.

   d) **New Materials** – like plastics are now used which are often lighter or stronger than those they replaced.

59. **Effects of Technological Changes**

   a) More goods can be produced and of a higher quality.

   b) Reduced production costs possibly leading to lower prices for consumers.

   c) Stock records, payrolls, accounts etc can be prepared on computers.

   d) Men have been replaced by machines leading to increased unemployment in many industries.

   e) New range of services, for example banking from home, cash-points and a general growth of tertiary industries.

   f) New technology makes jobs cleaner, easier and safer for workers.

   g) Increased leisure time because more work can be done in less time.

60. Problems Caused by New Technology

When firms introduce any form of new technology it can bring with it certain problems. The major ones include:

a) Workers resistance – because people often feel threatened and worry about losing their jobs.

b) Training – workers need to be taught how to use new equipment and this adds to the firms costs.

c) Costs of equipment – new technology is expensive to buy and install.

SUMMARY

61. a) The reasons for the location of industry include historical factors, natural resources and raw materials, nearness to markets, transport costs and the availability of labour.

b) The government tries to influence location by offering incentives to firms who move into areas of high unemployment.

c) As a firm grows in size its costs per unit of output are likely to fall because it can benefit from economies of scale.

d) Internal economies result from the growth of the firm, external economies from the growth and concentration of an industry in a particular area.

e) Internal savings include production, financial, marketing, managerial and risk-bearing economies.

f) If a firm grows too large it may encounter problems leading to diseconomies of scale.

g) External economies include the availability of labour, ancillary/support industries, marketing and distribution facilities, commercial services and 'disintegration'.

h) Firms can grow either internally by expansion or externally by integration.

i) Integration can be horizontal, vertical or lateral.

j) Despite the benefits from economies of scale, small firms continue to survive.

k) The development of new computerised technology is bringing about many changes which affect the way in which businesses operate.

REVIEW QUESTIONS

Answers can be found in the paragraphs shown.

1. List at least 5 factors which a firm is likely to consider when locating a new factory. (3-19)

2. Give 2 examples of measures which the government has used to try to influence the location of industry. (16-20)

3. Explain the difference between internal and external economies of scale. (21)

4. List and give examples of the 5 main kinds of internal economies. (22-28)

5. What are diseconomies of scale? (30-33)

6. List and give examples of 4 different external economies of scale. (34)

7. Give 3 reasons why firms may wish to expand. (35)

8. Explain the difference between a merger and a take-over. (37)

9. With the use of a diagram briefly explain the difference between horizontal, vertical and lateral integration. (39-43)

10. What is a monopoly and why might it be against the public interest? (48, 49)

11. Give 4 reasons why small firms are able to survive. (55)

12. Outline 4 major developments in new technology and for each give an example of their effects on business. (58, 59)

EXAMINATION PRACTICE QUESTIONS

Marks

1. An organisation which expands beyond its optimum size will suffer from 1

2. . . . . is the term used to describe a situation where firms are still attracted to an area even though the original reasons for location there have disappeared. 2

3. In law a monopoly exists where one firm has a total market share of at least . . . . per cent. 1

4. What is the difference between vertical, horizontal and lateral integration? 3

5. Complete the following sentences by inserting 'large' or 'small' as appropriate.
   a) Petrol companies are usually . . . . because of the benefits from economies of scale.
   b) Corner shops are usually . . . . because their owners frequently lack the capital for expansion
   c) Hairdressing firms tend to be . . . . because customers require a personal service.
   d) Chemical companies are usually . . . . because of the high capital investment required.
   e) Window cleaning businesses are usually . . . . because not much capital
   is needed to start up. 5

MULTIPLE CHOICE/COMPLETION

1. Which one of the following is *not* an internal economy of scale?
   a) Use of specialised machinery
   b) Bulk-buying
   c) Employment of specialist managers
   d) Specialist courses at local college

2. Horizontal integration takes place when a firm takes over:
   a) The transport firm which delivers its goods
   b) Another firm in the same market
   c) Its retail outlets
   d) A raw material supplier

3. Which of the following industries is *not* dispersed throughout the country?
   a) Banking
   b) Road transport
   c) Chemicals
   d) Printing

4. Which of the following is an example of vertical integration?
   a) A supermarket chain taking over its competitors
   b) A steel company increasing output
   c) A television manufacturer taking over a component supplier
   d) The merger of 2 banks

5. Diseconomies of scale in an expanding firm are most likely to be caused by
   a) Problems of organisation and control
   b) Difficulty in increasing sales
   c) Insufficient use of existing production capacity
   d) Cost of raising extra capital

6. A firm is most likely to introduce new technology into its factories if:
   a) It will increase the labour force
   b) It is expensive to buy and install
   c) It will increase production
   d) Its workers need training in new skills

In each of the following questions, one or more of the responses is/are correct. Choose the appropriate letter which indicates the correct version.
   A   if 1 only is correct
   B   if 3 only is correct
   C   if 1 and 2 only are correct
   D   if 1, 2 and 3 are correct

7. Which of the following would be true of a 'foot-loose' industry?
   1) Relies heavily on raw materials which are expensive to transport
   2) Requires a large pool of unskilled labour
   3) Sells its products in many different markets

8. Which of the following measures have been used by UK governments to try to influence the location of industry?
   1) Prevention of industrial development in some areas
   2) Grants for buildings and equipment
   3) Provision of ready built factories at low cost

RECENT EXAMINATION QUESTIONS

Marks

SEG JUNE 1990 GCSE BUSINESS STUDIES A PAPER I

1. Industrial robots are a form of automation.

   a) What benefits do manufacturers gain from automation?   3

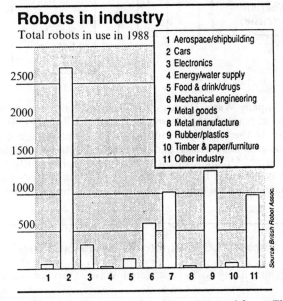

Robots in industry

Total robots in use in 1988

1 Aerospace/shipbuilding
2 Cars
3 Electronics
4 Energy/water supply
5 Food & drink/drugs
6 Mechanical engineering
7 Metal goods
8 Metal manufacture
9 Rubber/plastics
10 Timber & paper/furniture
11 Other industry

Source: British Robot Assoc.

Adapted from: *The Guardian*, May 1989

b)   i)   Which industry employs most robots?   1

      ii)   Why do you think this industry uses more robots than aerospace/shipbuilding?   3

c)   A food manufacturing company is considering the use of robots for the first time.

      i)   What factors are the directors likely to consider before making their decision?   4

      ii)   What are the advantages and disadvantages to the employees?   10

d)   How could the government encourage firms to invest more in robots?   4

NEA MAY 1989 GCSE BUSINESS STUDIES PAPER I SYLLABUS A   **Marks**

a)

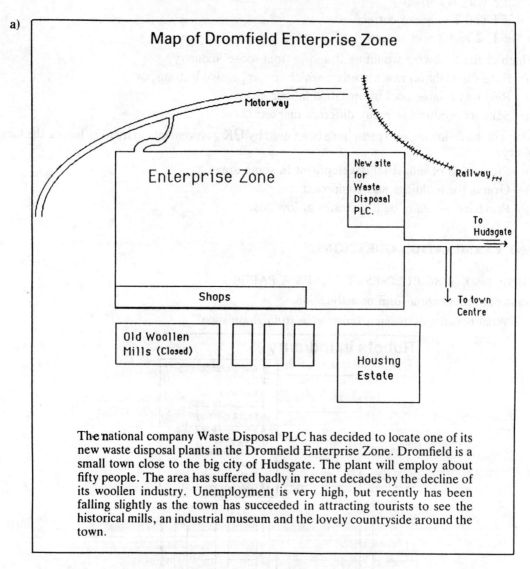

Map of Dromfield Enterprise Zone

The national company Waste Disposal PLC has decided to locate one of its new waste disposal plants in the Dromfield Enterprise Zone. Dromfield is a small town close to the big city of Hudsgate. The plant will employ about fifty people. The area has suffered badly in recent decades by the decline of its woollen industry. Unemployment is very high, but recently has been falling slightly as the town has succeeded in attracting tourists to see the historical mills, an industrial museum and the lovely countryside around the town.

   i)   Why might Waste Disposal PLC be attracted to an Enterprise Zone?   8

   ii)   What other things are likely to have affected Waste Disposal's decision to locate in Dromfield?   10

ASSIGNMENT

1.

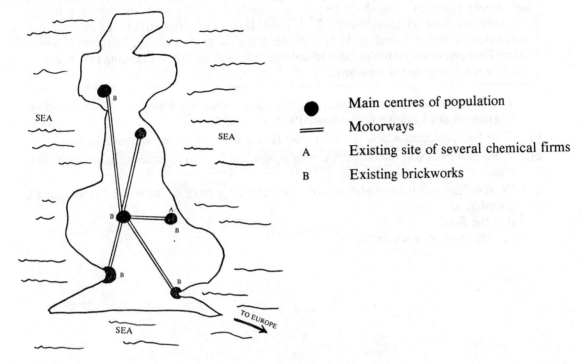

●   Main centres of population

═   Motorways

A   Existing site of several chemical firms

B   Existing brickworks

On the above map, mark the best location for the following firms. Briefly give the main reason for the site you have chosen.

   a) A brickworks
   b) A firm in the chemical industry
   c) A firm producing goods mainly for export to Europe
   d) An engineering firm
   e) A soft drinks manufacturer

2. Match the different types of economies shown in column A with their associated features shown in B.

A	B
a) Marketing	i) Centralising company records
b) Technical	ii) Bulk buying
c) Risk-bearing	iii) Machinery being fully utilised
d) Managerial	iv) Borrowing money at low cost
e) Financial	v) Supply of skilled labour
f) External economy	vi) Manufacturing a wider range of products

3. State whether the method of growth in each of the following is by horizontal, vertical (backward), vertical (forward) or lateral integration.

   a) A brewery takes over the public houses which it supplies with beer
   b) A chocolate company takes over a soft drinks manufacturer
   c) A weaving firm takes over a spinning company
   d) Two retail jewellery chains join together

4.

> A small manufacturing company in Birmingham is considering moving its business to new larger premises some 50 miles further south. The proposed location is a new industrial estate on the outskirts of a major town. If the move goes ahead the firm plan to develop an automatic production system using the latest technology. Computers and Word Processors would be introduced into the offices. The firm is planning to move its existing workforce to the new site.

a) What are the main points which the company would need to consider in deciding whether or not to move to the new site?

b) Give two problems which the firm may face if it moves its present workforce.

c) What problems will the introduction of computers lead to for management and office staff?

d) What effects will the introduction of new technology have on the overall employment situation in:
    i)   the firm?
    ii) the area as a whole?

10.   Marketing

1.   The next four chapters are all about marketing. This chapter looks at what is meant by the marketing activities of a firm. This is followed by chapters on advertising and sales promotion, markets and middlemen, and retailing.

DEFINITION

2.   Marketing is not just another word for selling, although the selling of goods and services is what it aims to achieve. The term marketing is used to describe a whole group of business activities which are concerned with obtaining and keeping customers. It involves:

   a)   Finding out which goods and services people want
   b)   Providing them
   c)   Pricing them
   d)   Promotion and advertising to sell them and then
   e)   Distributing them to the final consumer.

3.   Marketing begins with the customer. Instead of a firm saying "We only make two sizes of soap powder (or television, trousers or whatever), take it or leave it!", they now ask consumers "What size and type do you require?" Operating this way enables firms to sell more and make more profit.

DIFFERENT TYPES OF MARKETING

4.   There are three broad categories into which marketing can be divided – consumer, industrial and services.

5.   **Consumer Marketing**
Where products are sold directly to the general public mainly through the retail trade, i.e. shops etc. This includes:

   a)   **Consumer Goods** such as food and cosmetics, i.e. items which are bought frequently and are relatively cheap
   b)   **Consumer Durables** such as cars, furniture and washing machines which are expected to last several years and are relatively expensive to buy.

6.   **Industrial Marketing**
Where products are sold to companies and manufacturers who use them to produce other goods and services. Examples include chemicals, nuts and bolts, raw materials and machinery.

7.   **Marketing in Service Industries**
Services such as banking, insurance, plant hire, office cleaning, travel and transport can include either consumer or industrial marketing. For example, banks advertise their services to both the general public and businesses, whilst cars can also be hired by both individuals and companies.

8.   **Types of Marketing**

Consumer Goods

Consumable Durables

Industrial Marketing

Packaging

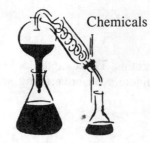

Chemicals

Timber

Marketing in Service Industries

Insurance

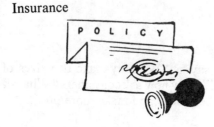

Shipping

Restaurants

MARKETING RESEARCH

9. The aim of good marketing is that firms should produce goods and services which consumers *want*. Therefore market research is used to find out what this is.

10. **Market Research** involves collecting, recording and analysing information about products or markets. The more a firm can find out about the people who buy or may buy their products the easier it becomes both to produce what they want and then to persuade them to buy.

11. For example, information about consumers age, sex, income, jobs, habits, likes and dislikes, where they live, which newspapers they read or when they watch television, can all be used to improve the way in which goods and services are marketed.

12. Market Research then is used to find the answers to a number of questions. For example:

> a)   Who might buy a product? – anyone, teenagers, parents.
> b)   Who actually buys it?
> c)   How often do they buy it? – weekly, monthly.
> d)   Why they buy it? – like smell, colour, sound etc.
> e)   How did they find out about it? – TV, newspapers, friends.
> f)   Where did they buy it from? – supermarket, mail order catalogue.

13. Based on this type of information it is possible for firms to *forecast* (estimate) the likely sales of their products or services. They can then make the important marketing decisions which are necessary to achieve these sales including:

*   What and how much to produce
*   What price to charge
*   The best place to advertise
*   Which method of distribution to use.

14. Market research can usually be carried out by either:
    a)   A firm's own market research department
    b)   A specialist market research company, for example AGB, Mori or Gallop
    c)   An advertising agency, for example Saatchi and Saatchi, J Walter Thompson

MARKET RESEARCH METHODS

15. Market research information can be obtained in two main ways – using Desk Research or Field Research.

16. **Desk Research** or secondary data.

This involves studying *existing information* which can be found either:
    a)   within an organisation i.e. a firm's own records, for example sales, stock or accounting records, customer complaints and salesmen's reports OR
    b)   outside an organisation i.e. published by someone else, for example by banks, newspapers or governments.

Some examples of the many UK Government publications which a firm could study include:	
Annual Abstract of Statistics	Monthly Digest of Statistics
Population Trends	Social Trends

17. **Field Research** or primary data.

This involves the collection of *new information* about a firm's products and markets.

18. **Example of a Questionnaire**

SMALL BUSINESS RESEARCH TRUST: QUARTERLY SURVEY NO. 10

Please circle the appropriate numbers or fill in the blanks. Your answers will remain confidential.

1 Please indicate the location of your business:

1.01 North	1.04 East Midlands	1.07 South East
1.02 Yorkshire & Humberside	1.05 West Midlands	1.08 South West
1.03 North West	1.06 East Anglia	1.09 Wales
		1.10 Scotland
		1.11 Northern Ireland

What is your Postal Code?

2 What is the legal form of your organisation?
2.01 Sole Proprietor 2.02 Partnership 2.03 Ltd Co 2.04 Other ....
(please specify)

3 3.01 How many years have you personally been in business?

3.02 How many years has your present business been trading?

4 Please classify your business activity by circling one or more of these categories: –

4.01 Agricultural, Forestry, Fishing	4.06 Wholesale Trade
4.02 Mining	4.07 Retail Trade
4.03 Construction	4.08 Finance, Insurance, Estate Agents
4.04 Manufacturing & Processing	4.09 Other Services
4.05 Transportation & Public Utilities	4.10 Other, not classified in one of above

(please specify)

Please describe in a few words the precise nature of your business (e.g. manufacturing electronic equipment, hairdressing, etc.). If you are involved in more than one field, please state that which constitutes the major proportion of your turnover –

5 What is the approximate annual turnover of the business excluding VAT?

5.01 Less than £10,000	5.04 £50,000-£99,999	5.06 £250,000-£999,999
5.02 £10,000-£24,999	5.05 £100,000-£249,999	5.07 More than £1 million
5.03 £25,000-£49,999		

6 Please enter in the appropriate boxes below, the total number of people (including yourself) who worked in the business at the end of December 1986 and a year earlier and how many of these worked part-time. Also give an estimate of the number of employees you expect at the end of March 1987.

	End December 1985	End December 1986	End March 1987
Total number of employees			
Of which: part-time			

7 What is the **single** most important reason preventing you from hiring more employees. Please tick one: –

7.01 Finance and interest rates	7.06 High rates of pay
7.02 Lack of skilled/trained employees	7.07 Do not wish to expand
7.03 Total tax burden	7.08 Other (please specify)
7.04 Low turnover — lack of business	
7.05 Government regs. and paperwork	

Thank you for completing this confidential questionnaire.

19. A common method for the collection of new information is the use of *questionnaires*, i.e. a list of questions which are used to ask the opinions of existing or potential consumers. For example, you or your parents may have been stopped in the street and interviewed about a particular product or asked which television programmes you watch. Sometimes these surveys are also carried out on the telephone or by post.

20. Another method of field research is the use of *consumer panels*. This involves selecting groups of consumers to use a particular product and then asking them what they think about it.

21. Sometimes manufacturers may introduce a new product or promotion in a particular town or area before deciding whether or not to sell it throughout the country. This type of field research is known as *test marketing*.

22. *N.B.* **Sampling**

Obviously it is not possible to ask all consumers what they think about a particular product or service. Therefore market research surveys usually select a 'representative' cross section, or sample of people and ask them. The answers from this sample should be very similar to asking everyone.

MARKETING ACTIVITIES

23. The main activities involved in marketing a product or service are known as the 4 P's – product, price, promotion and place.

24. **Product**

Using the findings from market research firms can develop new products or improve existing ones. This includes considering the design of goods, the product mix (assortment) offered and how they are packaged. For example, the size(s), shape(s), colour(s), label(s) and brand name of a product are all very important in attracting customers.

25. Marketing a Product

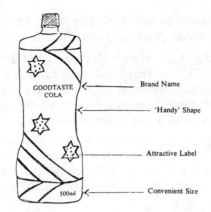

GOODTASTE COLA ← Brand Name

← 'Handy' Shape

← Attractive Label

500ml ← Convenient Size

26. Price

Deciding how much to charge for goods or services is also very important. A price must be set which:

a)   is attractive to customers so that they will buy the goods and

b)   covers the cost of production and provides a profit for the firm.

The price will also be affected by competition, special promotions and pricing psychology, for example £1.99 sounds a lot cheaper than £2.03.

27. Promotion

This includes advertising, selling and public relations which together are often referred to as *'marketing communications'*. The aim of promotion is:

a)   to tell potential customers about the benefits of a company's goods or services and

b)   encourage them to buy or use them. (see Chapter 11)

28. Place

This involves:

a)   choosing the channels of distribution through which goods or services are sold. For example a manufacturer may use wholesalers or retailers or he may decide to sell his goods direct to consumers. (see Chapters 12 and 13)

29. Example

> The 4 P's can be illustrated by considering the marketing of video recorders.
> What facilities and services does the consumer require? (the product), for example remote control, 7 day timer, 12 month's guarantee.
> How much is the consumer prepared to pay and what profit does the manufacturer require? (the price), for example £399.
> How and when should the manufacturer inform potential customers about his product? (the promotion), for example television and newspaper advertising.
> Where and how should the recorders be offered for sale? (the place), for example shops, mail order.

30.   If a firm is to be successful in providing what consumers want at a profit then it is important that its market research and the 4 P's are carefully planned and co-ordinated to achieve this.

31. Marketing Mix

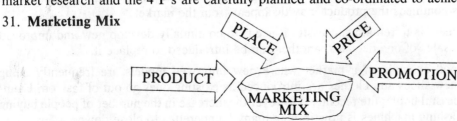

PLACE   PRICE

PRODUCT   PROMOTION

MARKETING MIX

32. The 4 P's together are known as the *'marketing mix'*. The particular mix used at anytime will vary depending upon the type of goods or services and the circumstances.

33. For example, fashion clothing is always changing and therefore will require considerable product development and promotion. On the other hand, manufacturers of some goods such as basic foodstuffs like tea and sugar will be more concerned with price and place, i.e. making the goods available to consumers at the right price. Whilst an increase in competition might mean that a firm must alter its prices or increase its promotion if it is to avoid a fall in sales.

PRODUCT LIFE CYCLE

34. Just as we are born, grow up, mature and eventually become old and die, so the sales of many products have a similar life cycle. This involves six important stages which are illustrated below:

35. **Stages in the Product Life Cycle**

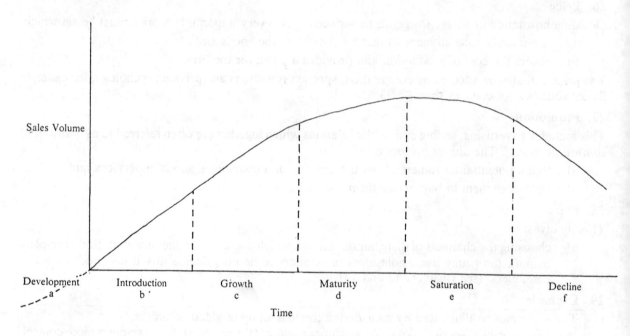

36. a) **Development** – with the help of market research new products are designed.

    b) **Introduction** – once it has been developed, the product is advertised and brought to the market for sale.

    c) **Growth** – if the product is successful sales will increase rapidly.

    d) **Maturity** – once established in a market the sales of a product do not grow so rapidly. A main reason for this is likely to be increased competition as other firms introduce similar products.

    e) **Saturation** – in time sales stop increasing, leading to

    f) **Decline** – eventually competition and other new products are likely to result in falling sales and profits. If this continues the product may disappear from the market.

37. Therefore if a business is to remain successful it needs to continually develop new and improved products so that as the sales of one declines, another can be introduced to replace it.

38. Cars provide a good example of a market where new improved models are frequently being introduced. Likewise, new shoes and clothes are introduced as existing ones go out of fashion. Launderettes were very successful until quite recently. However the increase in the number of people buying their own automatic washing machines is now forcing many launderettes to close down.

39. New and Improved Products

SUMMARY

40. a) Marketing begins with consumers and what they want.

b) It is concerned with the way in which a business operates and includes all aspects of selling goods and services from initial market research to distribution to the final consumer.

c) The three main types are Consumer Marketing, Industrial Marketing and Marketing in Service Industries.

d) Market research is used to provide information to firms about consumers.

e) This can be obtained through desk or field research.

f) Field research is based on a 'sample' of consumers and uses questionnaires, consumer panels and test marketing.

g) The marketing activities of the 4 P's – product, price, promotion and place are together known as the marketing mix.

h) Most products have a life cycle of sales covering their development, introduction, growth, maturity, saturation and decline.

REVIEW QUESTIONS

Answers can be found in the paragraphs shown.

1. What is marketing? (2)

2. List the 3 different types of marketing. (4-7)

3. What is market research and why do firms use it? (9-13)

4. Name the 2 main methods of market research and give examples of each. (15-21)

5. Why is it necessary to use sampling in market research? (22)
6. Describe the 4 P's and give examples of each? (23-30)
7. What is the 'marketing mix?' (32)
8. Explain what is meant by the 'product life cycle'. (34-38)

EXAMINATION PRACTICE QUESTIONS

Marks

1. Match the marketing terms in List A with the appropriate example in List B

    LIST A   LIST B

    a) Consumer durable   i)   Insurance
    b) Service Industry   ii)   Sales records
    c) Consumer good   iii) Test Marketing
    d) Secondary data   iv)   Coffee
    e) Field research   v)   Electric kettle

    5

2. The collection and analysis of data about problems relating to a firm's goods or services is called . . . .

    1

3. a) What do you understand by the term 'product life cycle?'

    2

    b) Why should it concern a successful manufacturer of home computers?

    2

MULTIPLE CHOICE/COMPLETION

1. The diagram below includes three of the four elements of the marketing mix

PLACE	PROMOTION
PRODUCT	?

Which is the missing element?
    a) Price
    b) Publicity
    c) Competition
    d) Consumer Protection

2. The sales graph opposite is for:
    a) Christmas Trees
    b) Fireworks
    c) Easter Cards
    d) Suntan lotion

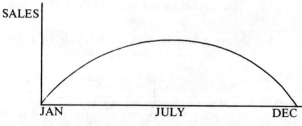

3. Which of the following would provide secondary data in respect of a firm's sales?
    a) Interviews with customers
    b) Questionnaires completed by customers
    c) Consumer panel
    d) Analysis of orders placed

4. What is meant by the term product mix?
   a) The combination of products offered by a firm
   b) The number of items in a product line
   c) The variety of products purchased
   d) The number of different product lines offered

5. The following graph shows the stages in the product life cycle. What is the name given to stage 3?

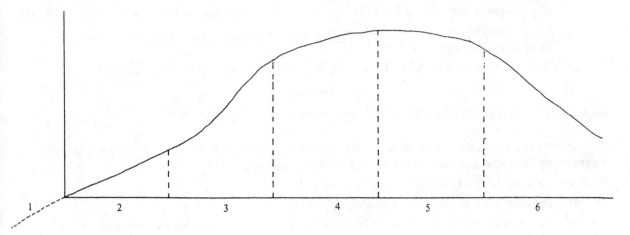

   a) Maturity
   b) Decline
   c) Growth
   d) Introduction

In the following question, one or more of the responses is/are correct. Choose the appropriate letter which indicates the correct version.
   A if 1 only is correct
   B if 3 only is correct
   C if 1 and 2 only are correct
   D if 1, 2 and 3 are correct

6. From a marketing point of view, product price depends upon which of the following:
   1) Competition
   2) Psychology
   3) Special Promotions

RECENT EXAMINATION QUESTIONS

SEG JUNE 1990 GCSE BUSINESS STUDIES B PAPER I

1. Hobbs & James plc are a long-established manufacturer of sweets. Although they are a public limited company the majority of the shares are owned by members of the James family. The James family hold the main positions on the company's Board. The firm produces a range of well-known products but sales have declined in recent years as newer products have entered the market. For many years the firm's best seller has been 'Fruit Ovals' a very popular variety of hard sweet. It is this brand which has suffered the largest fall in sales.

Marks

As a result, younger members of the family have put pressure on the Chairman, Sir Harold James, to react to changes in the sweet market and, at last, he has accepted their advice.

a)   Why do you think the James family wish to own over half the company's shares?   2

b)   Draw a diagram to illustrate the life cycle of a typical product and clearly illustrate the point of the cycle which 'Fruit Ovals' may have reached.   4

c)   Before introducing new products Hobbs & James have to research their market.

   i)   List **three** ways by which Hobbs & James may carry out market research.   3

   ii)   Researching a market to discover customer's opinions is expensive. Why, then, do firms spend money on such research?   3

d)   What evidence would show that a company was, perhaps, being badly managed?   4

RSA JUNE 1990 BACKGROUND TO BUSINESS STAGE II PART II

2.   Select TWO examples of a good or service. One of your examples should be of a product in the early stages of its life cycle and one should be of a product in decline.

With reference to the TWO examples you have selected:

a)   Describe what is meant by a product life cycle.   4

b)   Compare how firms might use advertising as part of the marketing mix for each of the products you have selected.   6

In order to develop and advertise products in the early stages of their life cycle, firms require finance. Firms will also require finance to prevent a product from declining.

With reference to the TWO examples you have selected:

c)   i)   compare the alternative sources of finance available to firms to develop and advertise their products.   6

   ii)   Which source of finance would be most appropriate for each of the products you have selected? Give ONE reason for each of your answers.   4

ASSIGNMENT

1.   Working in small groups you are to conduct a market research survey and produce an *individual report* at the end.

2.   Each group must decide what to research into, for example pop records, school/college meals, homework, television viewing.

3. Now prepare a short questionnaire with no more than 10 questions. The following example will help you.

```
                          SHOPPING SURVEY

        Please tick or circle the appropriate response.

        AGE GROUP

        16 - 25    □                       M    □

        26 - 35    □                       F    □

        36 - 45    □
                                        TIME: _____
        46 - 60    □

        61 +       □

        1.  How did you travel to town?
               Car □    Bus □    Train □    Foot □    Other ........
                                                        (please state)

        2.  Where have you come from? .................................

        3.  How long are you staying in the shopping area? ...............
               0 - 15 mins □    16 - 30 mins □    31 - 45 mins □

               46 - 60 mins □    60 - 90 mins □    91 - 120 mins □

               121 mins + □

        4.  What shops are you going to visit/have visited? ..............

        5.  Did you make a purchase?  YES/NO

        6.  If not, why not? ...........................................

        7.  Which shop do you like shopping at the most? ................

        8.  Why?  Prices □    Choice □    Service □    Other ........
                                                        (please state)

        9.  Do you ever look in the windows before going into a shop?  YES/NO

        10. If you do why? .............................................
```

4. The group will have to decide how to organise the survey. Including:
    a) How many people are to be interviewed both male and female, so that you obtain a good cross section of the 'public'
    b) How many copies of the questionnaire you will need and how you are to get them produced
    c) Where, when and how the interviews are to take place, for example, town centre, school, college etc.

5. Once the survey has been completed, you will have to collect all the information and sort and count the answers.

6. Next prepare tables, charts and diagrams and write a brief summary on the answers given to each question.

7. Now write a conclusion which might include suggestions for improvement, new ideas or any other comments which you want to make.

8. Finally present your findings in the form of a report. This should give details of *YOUR* contribution(s) to the assignment and a summary of the work of the other group members.

11. Advertising and Sales Promotion

1.   This chapter considers another aspect of marketing, the importance and main methods of sales promotion. It then looks at advertising including why firms advertise, advertising media, the arguments for and against it, and how it is controlled.

DEFINITION

2.   Sales promotion is an essential feature of modern business. It consists of all the various activities used by firms to maintain and increase their sales. If firms are to be successful, then they must make potential customers aware of what they sell. They must also provide reasons for customers to buy from them rather than from their competitors.

METHODS OF SALES PROMOTION

3.   Sales promotion involves many carefully planned events which take place throughout the year to attract customers. For example retailers use 'January Sales', 'Easter', 'Holiday Wear', 'Back to School' and 'Christmas' promotions. Some other methods of sales promotion used by businesses are described below.

4.   'Sales' Promotion

5. Price Promotions

This involves reducing the price of goods or services to appeal to customers. This may be regular monthly promotions like those run by grocery firms, for example Safeway, Kwik Save, Tesco, or regular annual events such as the sales 'Sales'.

6. Trading Stamps

There are two main types of trading stamps, those of the Green Shield Company, and the Co-op, which nowadays pays its dividend in the form of stamps. Completed books of stamps can be exchanged for cash or goods.

7. Loss Leaders

Often retailers will feature a promotion which involves selling one or two items at very low prices, sometimes less than cost, in order to attract customers into their store. For example, supermarkets often use sugar, bread, tea and other everyday items for this type of promotion.

8. Personality Promotions

The use of famous people, for example footballers or television stars, either in advertising or for personal visits to stores can be a big attraction for customers. Authors often visit bookshops to sign copies of their books.

9. Free Gifts

The appeal of 'something for nothing' is a strong promotional offer, for example *free* underfelt or fitting with carpets, plugs with electrical appliances, pillows with beds, saucepans with cookers, buy 2 get 1 free.

10. Shows and Demonstrations

The Ideal Home Exhibition, Motor Show and Boat Show are examples of exhibitions used by manufacturers to promote their products. Whilst free samples and special cooking demonstrations are often used in shops.

11. Coupons

Coupons may be given out in shops or delivered to homes, although nowadays they are often used as part of an advertisement in the press which customers cut-out themselves. They are also used as an 'on-pack' promotion by manufacturers offering money off your next purchase of the same or some other product.

12. Coupons/Free Gifts

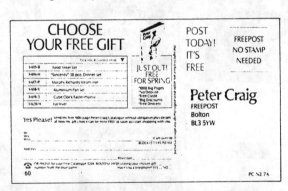

13. Prize Competitions

These are used by both manufacturers and retailers, sometimes as a joint promotion. Customers are given the opportunity to win attractive prizes, like cars or holidays, by entering a simple competition. Some proof of purchase of either a product or in a particular store is usually a condition of entry, for example a label or till receipt.

ADVERTISING

14. Almost £7,600 million was spent on advertising in 1991 and it is an essential part of any business if firms are not to lose out to their competitors. It is through advertising that sales promotions are communicated to the general public.

15. Two parts to Consumer Advertising

   a)   Advertising by *stores* who want to persuade as many customers as possible into their shops to make purchases, for example MFI, Dixons and ASDA.

   b)   A massive volume of advertising is carried out by *manufacturers* to encourage consumers to buy their products. For example Heinz, Proctor & Gamble (Fairy Liquid and Bold) and Kelloggs.

16. *N.B.* Brand Names

   a)   Most goods which are sold are branded, that is they are given trade marks or brand names to distinguish them from similar products. Brand names are registered so that they cannot be used by anyone else. This enables manufacturers to advertise the qualities of their products so that very often when we go into shops we ask for a product by name. For example Sony, Weetabix, Hoover or Levi.

   b)   Many retailers also sell goods which are specially made for them under their *own brand* name. For example St Michael (Marks and Spencers), Boots, Tesco and Winfield (Woolworths).

17. Branded Goods

18. Why Firms Advertise?

a) **To inform**

Advertising is used by firms to tell potential customers about goods and services which they sell.

b) **To persuade**

However, the main object of advertising is to increase sales by persuading people to buy a certain brand of goods or buy at a particular shop.

19. What are the Main Advertising Media

The term media is given to the various methods which firms can use to advertise their goods and services. If a firm wants its advertising to be seen throughout the country, then it may well use the *mass media* such as television and newspapers which can very quickly reach millions of people everywhere.

20. Newspapers

Press advertising can take place in Daily, Sunday, Weekly and Evening newspapers, and is the most popular media for retailers. This is because it is possible to give detailed information about the variety of goods which they sell, and use illustrations. It is also the cheapest way of reaching a large number of people.

21. Two Main Kinds of Newspapers

a) **National** – which cover the whole country, for example Daily Mirror, The Sun, Daily Mail.

b) **Local** – serving a particular town or area, for example Yorkshire Post, Newcastle Journal, Glasgow Herald, Nottingham Evening Post.

22. Press Advertising

Display Advertising

Classified Advertising

23. Two Forms of Press Advertising

a) **Classified** – small advertisements which appear under 'classified' headings, costing so much per line or word and basically giving information, for example Articles for Sale, Wanted, Business Services and Situations Vacant.

b) **Display** – larger advertisements, ranging from a few column inches, to a half, or even a full page. These advertisements often contain illustrations and are designed to persuade people to buy.

24. Magazines

Magazines usually cater for particular groups, or people with special interests, for example women, teenagers, gardeners and motor cycle enthusiasts.

25. The importance to advertisers is that they can more easily reach the consumers who form the main part of their market. This is shown by a study of women's magazines, such as Family Circle, Woman or Woman's Own, which reveals many advertisements selling cosmetics, foods, fashions and articles for the home. Whilst a Gardening magazine is likely to advertise plants, seeds, greenhouses or lawn mowers.

26.

27. Trade Magazines, for example The Grocer, National Newsagent, Nursing Times and Computer News may be used by manufacturers to inform potential customers about new products or special promotions.

28. Television

Television advertising is broadcast on The Independent Broadcasting Authority's channels since 'commercials' are not allowed on the BBC.

29. Although expensive, the appeal of TV advertising is that it usually produces good results and reaches a vast number of people of all ages. One of its other big advantages is that it brings sound, colour and movement into advertisements.

30. Peak Viewing hours, that is when most people watch television, are between 7-10 pm, and consequently advertising is dearer during these times. Sometimes, the same advertisement is shown several times in one evening and this is called *saturation* advertising.

31. Cinema

Cinema advertising has become less popular with the growth of commercial television. However, it is still a useful means of reaching young people in the 16-34 age group who are the most frequent cinema goers, accounting for about 75% of total audiences.

32. Commercial Radio

Advertising on radio can be heard on local radio or on Luxembourg. Radio Luxembourg operates only in the evening and concentrates on 'pop' programmes. It is listened to mainly by young people and consequently much of the advertising is aimed at them. Local radio stations broadcast throughout the day to audiences in particular areas, for example Radio Trent, Capital Radio, Radio Leicester, Radio Newcastle. These stations are a popular media with local businesses as they are a relatively cheap means of advertising to potential customers.

OUTDOOR ADVERTISING – Hoardings, Posters and Neon Signs

33. **Hoardings** are sited in main streets, or along main roads, and although they are only seen for a few seconds they may remain in position for several weeks, or months, catching peoples' attention. They usually contain a very short and simple advertising slogan.

34.

35. Many **poster** advertisements can be seen in shop windows, on buses and trains, as well as being common sights on 'underground' walls, escalators and staircases. A poster on the side of a firm's van is also a cheap and effective way to advertise.

36. **Neon or illuminated signs** are best known in Piccadilly Circus, London, which is lit up at night by many advertising signs. A shop's sign may be illuminated so that its name can always be clearly seen.

37. **Promotional Leaflets**

 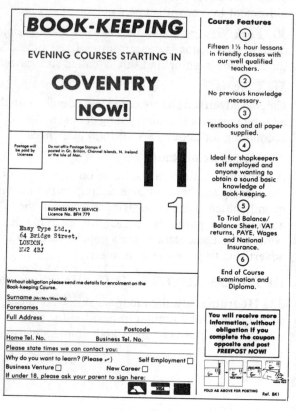

CATALOGUES, CIRCULARS AND LEAFLETS

38. These may be handed out, placed on cars or delivered door-to-door by people specially employed to distribute them. They may also be sent by post, which is known as *direct mail* advertising.

SPONSORSHIPS

39. Many manufacturers pay towards the cost of sporting and other events as a way of promoting their name. For example, Barclays Bank and B&Q sponsor football, John Players sponsor motor racing and Colgate-Palmolive sponsors golf.

OTHER METHODS OF ADVERTISING

40. These include the advertising on beer mats, sandwich boards, bags and wrapping paper, the back of bus tickets, names on key rings, pens and calendars, and the use of the Yellow Pages telephone directory. An important type of advertising used by shops are special displays of goods for sale.

41. How many different methods of advertising can you spot in the 3 pictures?

42. No firm is likely to use all of the above methods of advertising, but will usually concentrate on what is considered to be the most effective combination of media for them.

COST OF ADVERTISING

43. This depends on the media used and the size, or length, of the advertisement. As a general rule, the bigger or longer, the advertisement the more it will cost. But the cost also depends upon the number of people who are likely to see it. For example, a television advertisement is most expensive at peak viewing times because the potential audience is greater; a full page in a national newspaper costs considerably more than a full page in a local newspaper, because the larger circulation means that more people will read it.

44. Some Typical Examples of Advertising Costs – March 1993

Regional Television	£40,000 for 60 seconds (peak viewing)
Local Radio	£500 for 30 seconds
National Daily Newspaper	(10cm x 2 columns) £2,500 per day
Local Evening Newspaper	(10cm x 2 columns) £200 per evening
Local 'Free' Newspaper	(10cm x 2 columns) £100 per issue
Teletex	£1,000 per page per week
Stands at Major Exhibition	£1,000 per day
Panel on side of Bus	£70 per space per month

N.B. Rates vary depending on size/time/position/frequency of advertisement.

Expenditure on Advertising 1991

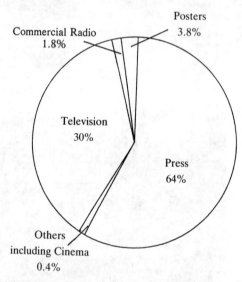

WHICH MEDIA SHOULD BE USED?

45. Where firms advertise will depend on the cost involved, the type of goods or services being promoted, the size of the firm, the market aimed at, and the results expected. The aim is to find the most effective media, at the lowest cost and with the most persuasive message possible.

46. Since advertising is expensive, to be effective it must be done where the maximum number of people can see it, and be done well to attract the greatest number of buyers. When choosing a media, advertisers will always take into account the type of people they wish to reach, for example will they be male, female, young, old, rich or poor? It is the type of people who are likely to buy the product which determines how an advertisement is designed and where it is to be placed.

WHEN AND WHY FIRMS ADVERTISE

47. A firm should advertise whenever it has an opportunity to promote its goods and services. Advertising usually takes place for the following reasons:

    a) **Promotional Campaigns** – regular weekly or monthly special offers or features, which should coincide with seasonal demand, a national or local event, or a manufacturers promotion.

    b) **Awareness Campaigns** – frequent advertising is used to keep the name of a product or store before the public in order to maintain sales.

c) **New Lines** – It is important to advertise new products or additional services.

d) **Public Relations** – to create goodwill with its customers, a firm will often ensure that the public is kept informed of its trading activities. This may take the form of a special *press release* about the opening of a new shop or factory, or a change of management.

e) **Government Advertising** – the government uses advertising not to sell goods, but to put across 'social' messages to the public. For example, 'Clunk-Click', 'Don't Drink and Drive', 'Don't Die of Ignorance'.

48. **Awareness Advertising**

Public Relations

Coundon shop top

MASTER BUTCHER Geoffrey Saunders, manager of Dewhurst, 76 Barker Butts Lane, Coundon, Coventry, and his staff are celebrating success in a national Best Kept Shop competition.

Geoffrey and his team are Coventry district winners in the Dewhurst Group's 1987 Best Kept Shop competition, open to 1,400 shops throughout England, Scotland and Wales.

MOTIVES TO WHICH ADVERTISERS APPEAL

49. Advertisers try to persuade people that there is something particularly attractive about their brand of goods that will not be found in any of its rivals. In so doing the advertiser appeals to certain motives. A few examples are:

50. **Ambition and Success**

Many advertisements appeal to people's desire to succeed in life. The successful person in the advertisement uses the product. For example, if the consumer buys a particular brand of clothing they could get a better job.

51. **Romance**

This type of advertising is widely used and is particularly aimed at young people. In them, success with the opposite sex and the product advertised are put together. One usual form is a picture of a good looking young man and a pretty girl walking hand in hand by a riverside setting.

52. **Hero Worship**

Advertisers pay famous personalities to praise and recommend particular products. Because consumers admire the celebrity featured in the advertisement, they want to use the same product. For example Henry Cooper and Brut, Twiggy and Oil of Ulay.

53. **The Desire for an 'Easy' Life**

These advertisements usually provide a picture of a life made easier and simpler through the use of labour-saving devices. Domestic appliances like washing machines and vacuum cleaners are advertised in this way.

ADVERTISING AGENCIES

55. Firms can either arrange their own advertising or instead may use an advertising agency, for example Saachi and Saachi, J Walter Thompson. These are specialist firms who employ experts to find the most

effective way of advertising. An agency will plan and carry out an advertising campaign for which they charge a fee.

56. Agencies carry out five main functions:

a) **Market Research** is used to discover information on which to base the advertising. The success of a campaign can also be monitored through research.

b) **Media Planning** – involves selecting the most suitable media and booking it. For example the time on television or space in the press.

c) **Creating the Advertisement** – i.e. designing the advertisement and writing what is called the copy often with 'catchy' slogans. For example, 'The answer's yes at TSB', 'Mr Kipling makes exceedingly good cakes'.

d) **Producing the advertisement** – for example making a film for television or drawing an illustration for the press.

e) **Account Management** – agencies will look after a firms advertising budget and advise them on future campaigns.

ADVANTAGES OF ADVERTISING

57. a) Consumers receive *information* about new and existing products, enabling them to make comparisons.

b) If firms sell more than mass production is possible. Producing in larger quantities is cheaper and therefore leads to *lower prices*.

c) Advertising promotes *competition* between firms and this results in lower prices and better quality products.

d) Advertising *pays for ITV* and *Commercial radio*, and keeps down the cost of *newspapers and magazines*.

DISADVANTAGES OF ADVERTISING

58. a) Initially it can lead to *higher prices*, for example if a product costs 10p to make and 2p to advertise, then this will mean a higher selling price.

b) People may be persuaded to *buy goods which they cannot afford* and do not really want.

c) Some products may be *harmful*, for example medicines, alcohol and tobacco. The advertising of cigarettes on television was banned in 1965 because it was felt that they were harmful to health.

d) Advertising *can make people dissatisfied* by appealing to their ambitions, desires and emotions. For example, 'keeping up with Joneses', success with the opposite sex, or in a job; it encourages greed, or an easier life with more leisure. Advertising leads us to believe that we can only achieve these by buying a particular product.

THE CONTROL OF ADVERTISING

59. Manufacturers and retailers cannot say anything they like in advertisements, otherwise this might lead to all sorts of misleading claims to entice customers. Therefore advertising is carefully controlled to protect consumers. This control takes two forms, voluntary control consisting of a list of rules drawn up by the industry itself and which advertisers have agreed to follow, and legal control enforced by laws passed by the government.

Voluntary Control

60. **The Advertising Standards Authority**   This is financed by the industry and issues the 'British Code of Advertising Practice' which is a list of guidelines aimed at ensuring that all advertising is 'legal, decent, honest and truthful'.

61.

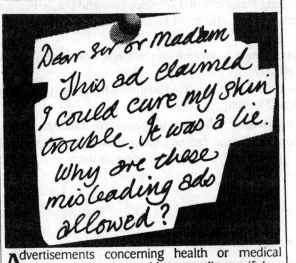

A dvertisements concerning health or medical matters can cause real harm or distress if they make false claims or encourage unnecessary fears. We keep a close eye on such advertisements and always investigate complaints about them.

If you'd like to know more about the rules governing advertisements containing health claims, please send for a copy of the Code of Advertising Practice. It's free.

The Advertising Standards Authority.
We're here to put it right. ✓

ASA Ltd., Dept H. Brook House. Torrington Place. London WC1E 7HN

LEGAL CONTROL

62. **The Broadcasting Act (1990).** This was introduced to provide for the regulation of both independent television (ITV) and radio. It set up an **ITV Commission** which controls the issue of licences and generally regulates ITV including local cable and satellite services. The Commission has a Code of Practice which includes advertising standards and methods. It also has the power to investigate complaints and ban advertisements which do not comply with the Code. A **Radio Authority** was also set up to issue licences and oversee all independent radio services again including advertising.

63. **The Trade Descriptions Act 1968** This aims to ensure that traders tell the truth about goods and services. The descriptions used in advertisements must be accurate and truthful. If the law is broken, traders may be fined or imprisoned (see Chapter 15). Altogether about 60 laws have been passed which affect advertising in some way.

64. **The Consumer Credit Act 1974** This states that advertisements for goods sold on credit must include the cash price, the credit price and the true rate of interest. (see Chapter 15)

SUMMARY

65. a) Sales promotion involves all the activities used by businesses to maintain and increase their sales.

b) Some of the many methods of sales promotion include: cut-price offers, trading stamps, 'loss' leaders, the use of personalities, free gifts, trade fairs, exhibitions, demonstrations, coupons, competitions and advertising.

c) Advertising is very important because it is used to tell potential customers about goods and services and to persuade them to buy.

d) Methods of advertising include: press (newspapers and magazines), television, cinema, radio, outdoor (hoardings, posters and neon signs), direct mail (catalogues, circulars and leaflets) and sponsorship.

e) Other methods may include names on carrier bags, key rings, pens and in the Yellow Pages of the telephone directory.

f) Because advertising is a very specialised business, firms frequently use an advertising agency to carry out campaigns for them.

g) There are many arguments both for and against advertising.

h) There is careful control of what can be said or shown in advertisements. This consists of both voluntary control by the firms in the advertising industry and legal control such as the Trade Descriptions Act.

REVIEW QUESTIONS

Answers can be found in the paragraphs shown.

1. What do you understand by sales promotion? (2-3)
2. Give 6 ways of promoting sales. (4-13)
3. Why do both manufacturers and retailers advertise? (14-15)
4. How do branded goods help advertisers? (16-17)
5. What are the 2 main purposes of advertising? (18)
6. What do you understand by 'mass media'? Give 2 examples. (19-32)
7. Which national and which local newspapers do you read? (21)
8. Why is television the most expensive form of advertising? (29)
9. What is 'saturation' advertising? (30)
10. At which group of people are cinema and radio advertisements aimed? Why is this? (31, 32)
11. Is advertising harmful, or does it benefit consumers? (57-58)
12. In which 2 main ways are consumers protected from false or mis-leading advertising? (59-64)

EXAMINATION PRACTICE QUESTIONS

	Marks
1. With examples explain what is meant by the following terms:	
a) 'loss leader'	2
b) 'brand name'	2
2. In what sense can advertising lead to:	
a) Higher prices	2
b) Lower prices	2
3. Give 2 examples of how advertising is controlled.	2
4. If a person buys goods on the spur of the moment, this is referred to as	1

5. A manufacturer is planning to introduce a new range of male and female deodrants aimed at the teenage market.

    a)   Suggest, with reasons, 3 forms of advertising which you consider to be most suitable for this purpose.   3

    b)   Give 2 motives to which the advertising could appeal.   2

    c)   Explain, with examples, the difference between informative and persuasive advertising.   4

    d)   Describe 2 methods of collecting information for market research before the launching of a new product.   2

    e)   Explain why you think the deodorant manufacturer should carry out market research before introducing the new product range.   4

MULTIPLE CHOICE/COMPLETION

1. A manufacturer of textile machinery is most likely to advertise:
    a) In National newspapers
    b) In trade magazines
    c) In cinemas
    d) On television

2. Press advertisements in small type and grouped under suitable headings are called:
    a) Display
    b) National
    c) Informative
    d) Classified

3. Which one of the following is *not* a method of mass media advertising:
    a) Television
    b) Sunday Newspapers
    c) Shop Window displays
    d) Commercial Radio

4. Three of the following are examples of sales promotions, which is the odd one out?
    a) Special Price reduction
    b) Free Gift offer
    c) Two for the price of one
    d) Sponsorship of sporting events

5. The name given by a manufacturer to a product to enable it to be easily identified is known as:
    a) Advertising
    b) Marketing
    c) Distribution
    d) Branding

6. 'Loss Leaders' are used by retailers to attract customers. They are best described as:
    a) Any sale item
    b) A product which is sold below cost
    c) A special weekend bargain
    d) Any supermarket special offer

In the following questions, one or more of the responses is/are correct. Choose the appropriate letter which indicates the correct version.

    A   if 1 only is correct

    B   if 3 only is correct

    C   if 1 and 2 only are correct

    D   if 1, 2 and 3 are correct

7. The most suitable advertising media for a small fish and chip shop would be:

    1)   Local Newspaper

    2)   Sunday Newspaper

    3)   Trade Magazine

8. Which of the following is/are examples of own label branding of baked beans:

    1)   Tesco

    2)   ASDA

    3)   Heinz

RECENT EXAMINATION QUESTIONS

Marks

RSA MAY 1989 BACKGROUND TO BUSINESS STAGE I PART II

1. Following a market research survey, a soft drinks manufacturer is planning to market a new canned drink.

    a)   List TWO *sources* of information that would be useful for market research into the product launch.   4

    b)   Explain in detail what is meant by the term 'marketing'.   6

    c)   Select TWO appropriate advertising media for the new product, giving reasons for your choice.   6

    d)   Show diagrammatically *or* describe a distribution system which could be used for the canned-drink nationally.   4

MEG MAY 1988 GCSE BUSINESS STUDIES PAPER 2

2.

> Busy Bee Bus PLC was set up when bus services were opened to competition two years ago. It operates on dozens of routes in South Manchester. The company has been successful so far because it offers good service to its customers.

    a)   What image do you think the company wanted to give by choosing the name 'Busy Bee'?   2

    b)   The company is said to offer good service to its customers. Suggest THREE things which you as a customer would want in the way of good service from a bus company.   3

    c)   What name is given to an economy where some services are provided by private firms like Busy Bee and others by the state?   1

ASSIGNMENT

Your local newsagent has decided to advertise to try and clear some of his old stock. The main items to be sold are:

   i)   Paperback books reduced from £2.95 and £1.95 to £1.50 and £1.25.

   ii) Greetings cards all at 30p.

   iii) 10% off all toys originally priced from £10 to £1.

   iv) Assorted pens and pencils priced from 10p to £3.

   v)   Two large wooden shop display cabinets @ £25 each.

From your knowledge of advertising:

1.   List any 10 different methods of advertising.

2.   Suggest 5 which would be most suitable for use by your local newsagent.

3.   Which methods of advertising would you suggest are most suitable to sell the items in iii) and v) above? Explain your answer.

4.   Prepare an advertisement (using one of the methods of advertising you have listed in Question 1), to help sell one of the items above. Alternatively choose a product which you feel would appeal to a teenage market.

5.   A quick stock check reveals that your newsagent has 200 greetings cards which he wants to clear. On average the cards cost 24p each. They usually retail for 60p each.

   a)   How much did this stock cost to buy?

   b)   What is its retail value?

   c)   What percentage profit does he usually make on cards?

   d)   What percentage profit will he make if the average selling price is now 30p?

   e)   What would be his total profit if all the cards were sold at 30p?

6.   Apart from reducing his prices, suggest one other method of sales promotion which your newsagent could use to help him clear his stock.

12. Markets and Middlemen

1.   This chapter is about the 'middlemen' who provide an important link in the chain of distribution. It outlines the different types of markets in which they work and moves onto a more detailed look at the middlemen who operate as wholesalers, describing the services which they offer for manufacturers and retailers. Finally it examines how supply and demand can influence market prices.

DEFINITIONS

2.   The term *'middlemen'* is used to refer to anyone who comes between the producer of goods or services and the final consumers. They are specialists in the work which they do and may be involved in the distribution of raw materials, foodstuffs or manufactured goods. Middlemen are also important in other areas including shipping, insurance, financial and foreign exchange markets.

3.   A *market* is defined as any situation where buyers and sellers are brought together. It may be located in a specific place or building or merely involve the use of the telephone or some other means of communication. There are many types of markets ranging from you selling something to one of your friends, to highly complex financial markets dealing in millions of pounds worth of goods and services.

4. **Retail Market**

TYPES OF MARKETS

5.   The main types of markets are retail, wholesale, produce, commodity, shipping, insurance, financial and foreign exchange.

6. **Retailing** – goods and services are sold to the final consumer usually through shops. (see Chapter 13)

7. **Wholesaling** – wholesalers buy goods from manufacturers which they then sell to retailers.

8. **Wholesale Produce Markets** – Perishable goods are supplied to shops, hotels and restaurants etc through large wholesale markets. For example, in London:

a) Billingsgate is famous for fish
b) Smithfield for meat and
c) New Convent Garden for fruit and vegetables

Most large towns have similar wholesale produce markets.

9. 'Smithfield' Market

10. Commodity Markets or Exchanges

These are markets where manufacturers throughout the world can buy their raw materials. London is the centre for many of these important markets including: ple:

a) Metal Exchange (aluminium, tin, zinc, silver, lead etc)
b) Diamond Market (Hatton Garden)
c) Baltic Exchange (grain, seeds and vegetable oils, air transport and shipping)
d) Commodity Exchange (rubber, cocoa, jute and sugar etc)
e) Fur Market (Beaver House)

11. Other markets also exist outside London, for example the Liverpool Cotton Exchange and the Bradford Wool Exchange.

12. Shipping and Insurance Markets

Britain is a world centre for both of these markets which are based on Lloyds of London. Shipping freight services are also sold on the Baltic Exchange.

13. Financial Markets

London also has many national and international financial markets. A financial market is one which deals in money, examples of which are given below.

14. The Money Market

This market consists of institutions which borrow and lend money usually for *short periods*. The price which has to be paid is the rate of interest which is charged.

15. The main institutions which deal in the money market include:

Commercial Banks	–	who provide loans and overdrafts to businesses and individuals
Merchant Banks	–	who provide loans for businesses
Government	–	which borrows money by issuing Treasury Bills repayable usually in three month's time. (See Chapter 20).
Discount Houses	–	who specialise in borrowing from banks in order to buy Government Treasury Bills and Bills of Exchange. This enables businesses to get money quickly when required rather than having to wait for payment.
Finance Houses	–	who provide the money required for people to buy goods on hire purchase.

16. The Capital Market

This market deals with the provision of *longer-term* finance for the Government, businesses and individuals. This market includes Institutional Investors, The Stock Exchange and Issuing Houses.

17. Institutional Investors

These are organisations which use other people's money to invest in shares or to provide loans:

a) **Insurance Companies** – use some of the premiums which they collect.

b) **Pension Funds** – use the contributions which people make towards their future retirement.

c) **Unit Trusts** – are set up with the purpose of investing in the shares of different companies. The money is provided by the public who are invited to buy 'units' in the Trust.

d) **Investment Trusts** – operate in a similar way to Unit Trusts, except that the investors are shareholders of the investment company.

e) **Building Societies** – these are non-profit making institutions who specialise in using the savings from investors to provide loans (called mortgages) for house purchase. They also invest surplus funds in the capital market. (See Chapter 5).

f) **Trade Unions** – use the subscriptions which are paid by their members.

18. Examples

FULCRUM
INVESTMENT TRUST
P.L.C.

FRAMLINGTON
UNIT TRUST

19. Stock Exchange

This provides a market where 'second-hand' shares can be bought and sold. (see Chapter 20)

20. Issuing Houses

These organisations specialise in the issue of new shares. For example the sale (issue) of shares in British Gas was organised by Rothschilds and TSB shares were issued by Lazard Bros.

21. The Foreign Exchange Market

This market deals in the buying and selling of foreign currencies, for example dollars, pesetas and francs. Most of the business in this market takes place on the telephone between banks and foreign exchange dealers both in the UK and overseas.

22.

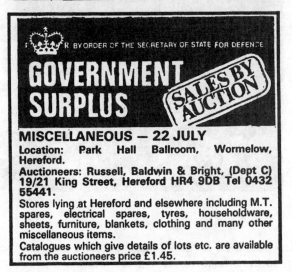

Sales by Auction

BY ORDER OF THE SECRETARY OF STATE FOR DEFENCE

GOVERNMENT SURPLUS *SALES BY AUCTION*

MISCELLANEOUS — 22 JULY
Location: Park Hall Ballroom, Wormelow, Hereford.
Auctioneers: Russell, Baldwin & Bright, (Dept C) 19/21 King Street, Hereford HR4 9DB Tel 0432 55441.
Stores lying at Hereford and elsewhere including M.T. spares, electrical spares, tyres, householdware, sheets, furniture, blankets, clothing and many other miscellaneous items.
Catalogues which give details of lots etc. are available from the auctioneers price £1.45.

METHODS OF MARKET DEALING

23. Trading in the markets outlined may take place in a number of different ways, some of which are listed below.

24. **Auctions** – require people to make a bid for the commodity offered with the highest bidder 'winning'. Tea, grain and wool are sold in this way.

25. **Ring Trading** – is used, for example, on the London Metal Exchange. The dealers gather in a circle and shout out the price at which they are prepared to buy or sell a particular metal. Each metal is traded for only a few minutes during which time a market price is agreed.

26. **Private Dealing** – takes place when a broker approaches several sellers to obtain the best deal for their client. The Stock Exchange, Baltic Exchange and Foreign Exchange Markets use this method of trading.

27. **'Sights' Market** – the seller shows his commodity and asks a certain price for it. If no-one offers the price the goods are withdrawn from sale. Diamonds are usually sold in this way.

28. **'Spot' Market** – this is where goods could have been sold by any of the above methods but at a cash price for immediate delivery. Examples might include tea, coffee, wool, gold and oil.

29. **'Futures' Market** – it is also possible to buy goods which are not yet available. The price is agreed now and the goods delivered at some future date perhaps 3 or 6 months later. Examples of commodities often bought in this way include metals, grains and sugar. Foreign Exchange is also frequently bought in this way.

30. **An Auction at Sotheby's**

WHOLESALERS

31. Wholesalers are often described as 'middlemen' because they are the middle link in the chain of distribution coming between the manufacturer and the retailer.

32. Essentially a wholesaler purchases goods in bulk (large quantities) from a number of manufacturers and makes them available in smaller quantities to retailers. The goods are stored in a warehouse until required.

MAIN TYPES OF WHOLESALER

33. Traditional

These wholesalers send their representatives out to shops to collect orders which are then delivered from the warehouse. The retailer will be sent an invoice which he usually settles at the end of each month. However, this type of wholesaler has been declining in the past 20-30 years particularly since the development of supermarkets who order their goods direct from the manufacturers.

34. Cash and Carry (Trademarkets)

To make their prices more competitive by reducing selling and delivery costs, cash and carry wholesalers have developed where retailers go to the warehouse themselves, collect their goods on a trolley and pay cash for them at the exit. In many ways they resemble a large supermarket but with goods displayed in boxes instead of open on fixtures. For example, Booker, Nurdin and Peacock, Makro and Holmes (Northern Ireland).

35. Wholesaling Groups (Symbol or Voluntary Groups)

The growth of supermarkets has made it increasingly difficult for small independent shops to compete in terms of price and variety therefore they have joined together to form bulk-organised buying groups. That is, a wholesaler will gather round him a group of retailers who agree to pool their orders and buy a regular amount of goods from him.

36. This enables the wholesaler to buy in bulk from manufacturers and pass on the saving to the retailers who in turn can offer lower prices to their customers. Voluntary groups are usually limited to a local area as few wholesalers operate nationally.

37. **Voluntary chains** are an extension of voluntary groups where a number of wholesalers join together throughout the country to pool their resources. In this way symbol chains such as VG, Spar and Mace and Wavy Line have been able to compete with the larger supermarkets.

38. Both voluntary groups and chains offer special services to their retail members. For example newspaper and television advertising, window posters and information and advice.

39. Co-operative Wholesale Society (CWS)

As mentioned in Chapter 6, the CWS supplies goods for the co-operative retail societies. It is the largest wholesaler in the UK and obtains many of its goods from its own farms and factories.

40. W.H. Smith Wholesale

Examples of 'Symbol' Wholesalers

FUNCTIONS OF WHOLESALERS

41. For Manufacturers

a) They provide an *outlet* where manufacturers can sell their products.

b) They carry *stocks* which would otherwise have to be held by the manufacturer.

c) They provide *economy* in distribution of goods – a manufacturer can deliver to one place in bulk instead of too many smaller outlets. This helps to reduce the costs of selling, delivery and administration.

d) They pay promptly for goods when received and in this way the wholesaler saves the manufacturer from having *capital* 'tied-up' in stock for long periods.

e) They take the *risk* that the goods might not sell (or not sell as well as expected) which could result in heavy losses.

42. Economy in the distribution of goods is clearly illustrated by the following two diagrams:

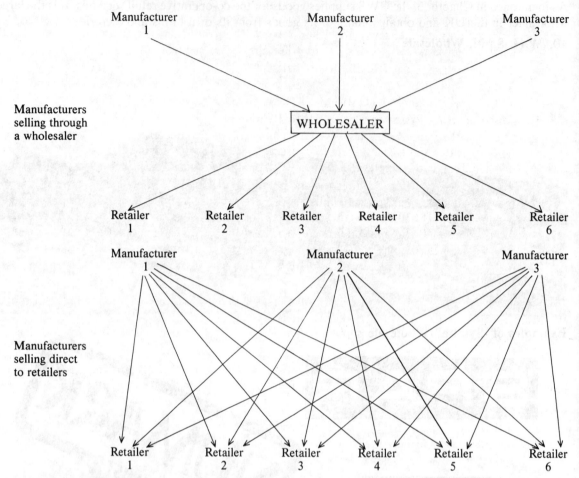

In the above example it can be seen that many extra deliveries are necessary if a manufacturer sells direct to retailers rather than through a wholesaler.

43. For Retailers

a) The *breaking of bulk* i.e. wholesalers sell goods in small convenient quantities.

b) They *store* goods in large quantities – so that a retailer can usually be certain of getting what he needs quite quickly.

c) They stock a *variety of goods* and different makes – thus offering a wide choice to the retailer.

d) They reduce the *risk* of a retailer carrying large stocks of unsaleable goods because stock can be bought in small quantities as when required.

e) They may provide *credit* i.e. with traditional and symbol wholesalers the retailer settles his account at the end of the month.

f) They may *deliver* the goods to the retailer.

TENDENCY FOR THE WHOLESALER TO BE ELIMINATED

44. Wholesalers today are less important than in the past, the main reasons for this are as follows:

a) **The Decline in the Number of Small Independent Retailers**
    Means that less wholesalers are needed.

b) **The Development of Improved Transport and Communications**

This enables retailers to restock quickly, direct from manufacturers. Modern transport, in particular the growth of motorways, means that goods can now be delivered within days of an order being placed. Previously, when restocking took longer, a retailer would rely on the wholesaler having the goods in stock when they were needed.

c) **The Growth of Large Retail Organisations**

Such as department stores, chain stores, multiples and more recently superstores and hyper-markets, which can buy goods in bulk themselves direct from the manufacturers.

d) **Manufacturers Prefer to Sell Direct to Retailers**

There has been a strong tendency in recent years for manufacturers to sell goods directly to retailers and in some cases direct to consumers, (for example double glazing, encyclopaedias) thus eliminating the wholesaler. This gives them closer control over the sale of their products.

e) **The Increase in Mass Production and Branding of Goods**

Nowadays large quantities of similar goods are produced and then given a brand name, for example Heinz Baked Beans, Ty-phoo tea, Sony televisions, Suzuki motor-bikes. Manufacturers then spend vast sums of money on advertising to persuade people to buy their products. Since a wholesaler may not 'push' a particular manufacturers range, many again prefer to distribute their products direct to retailers as this ensures that they reach as many shops as possible.

45. Despite the above exceptions, wholesaling is still very important in the distribution of certain goods. Wholesalers serve the needs of independent retailers, particularly in the grocery, fish, fruit and vegetable and clothing trades. They are also important in many other trades, for example newspapers and electrical goods.

46. When the wholesaler is eliminated someone else has to do the work. For example, large retailers who buy direct from manufacturers have to provide their own financing and storage for the goods.

47. *N.B.*

a) 'Middlemen' are sometimes called merchants, agents, brokers, factors or wholesalers depending on which type of trade they work in. For example, Corn Merchant, Insurance Agent, Stockbroker, Coal factor, electrical wholesaler etc.

b) Thus some of these 'middlemen' make a profit by selling actual goods whilst others are paid commission or a fee for the work they do.

MARKETING BOARDS

48. These are set up by the Government to handle all the sales of particular types of agricultural products. The Board fixes prices and controls all aspects of marketing including the amount which farmers are allowed to produce. Examples in Britain include the Marketing Boards for Milk, Hops, Potatoes and Wool.

SUPPLY AND DEMAND

49. We noted earlier that a market is any situation where buyers and sellers are brought into contact with each other. All markets which have many buyers and sellers operate according to the laws of supply and demand which are explained below. Many of the markets mentioned in this chapter operate this way.

50. **Supply**

This is the total amount of a particular commodity which suppliers are prepared to offer for sale, at a given price, over a period of time. For example, the supply of commodity x at a price of £2 is 4,000 units per week.

51. For each price the supply will usually be different. Normally the higher the price the greater the amount supplied, the lower the price the less the supply. This can be shown on the following diagram of a *supply curve* for shoe laces.

52. Supply of Shoelaces

Price Per Unit (pence)	Quantity Supplied (000's per week)
25	250
20	200
15	140
10	100
5	40

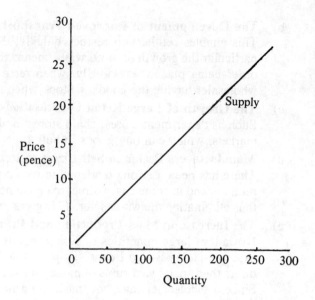

53. Demand

This is the total amount of a particular commodity which consumers with to buy (and have the money to do so), at a given price, over a period of time. For example, the demand for commodity x at a price of £2 is 5,000 units per month.

54. For the great majority of goods if the price falls, consumers will buy more of it, if it rises then they will buy less. This is shown on the following diagram of a *demand curve* for shoe laces.

55. Demand for Shoelaces

Price Per Unit (pence)	Quantity Demanded (000's per week)
25	50
20	100
15	140
10	170
5	300

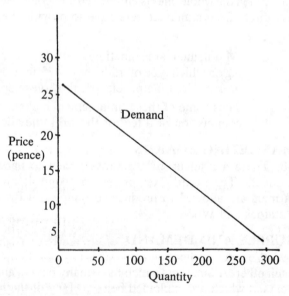

56. Changes in Demand

In addition to price, demand is influenced by many other factors including:

* CHANGES IN THE SIZE AND COMPOSITION OF THE POPULATION – for example whether it is increasing or decreasing, getting younger or older.
* CONSUMER INCOME – if people have more money to spend then this is likely to increase demand
* CONSUMER TASTES AND PREFERENCES – changes brought about by advertising, climate etc. For example fashion is often a reason for purchasing new clothes.

* NEW IMPROVED PRODUCTS – for example the introduction of colour television led to a big fall in the demand for black and white models
* PRICES OF OTHER PRODUCTS – for example an increase in the price of butter often leads to higher sales of margarine and vice versa.
* TAXATION – the Government can influence demand by altering either the price of goods (for example VAT) or the level of people's income (for example income tax and allowances).

57. Interaction of Supply and Demand

As shown in the following diagram the *equilibrium price* is given by the interaction of the supply and demand curves i.e. 15p. At this price the amount brought to the market by suppliers exactly matches the amount demanded by the buyers.

58. Interaction of Supply and Demand

Price Per Unit (pence)	Quantity Demanded	Quantity Supplied
25	50	250
20	100	200
15	140	140
10	170	100
5	300	40

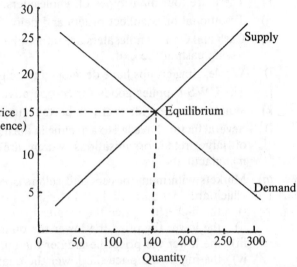

59. Above the equilibrium price supply is greater than demand. Therefore the price must be reduced to attract more buyers. Below this price, demand is greater than supply. This will result in an increase in price.

60. Everyday, this operation of the laws of supply and demand can be seen in many markets. For example, the price of surplus package holidays is often reduced at the last minute. The prices of stocks and shares move up and down in response to changes in demand; whilst a market trader selling fruit and vegetables will often lower his prices to clear stock at the end of the day.

61. Example of the Operation of Supply and Demand

STOCK MARKET PRICES

MAJOR PRICE CHANGES	RISES		FALLS	
	British Aerospace	420p +15p	Central TV	1978p −52p
	Brown & Tawse	53p +9p	Lambert Howarth	355p −28p
	Essex Furniture	126p +8p	Kwik Save	691p −16p
	Stanley Leisure	224p +7p	Anglia TV	320p −15p
	Spring Ram	54p +5½p	Mirror Group	153p −14p
	Rolls-Royce	142½p +5½p	Tiphook	274p −14p
	FNFC	78p +4p	Dalepak Foods	193p −12p
			Dixons	193p −7p
			Reject Shop	49p −6p

SUMMARY

62. a) The term 'middlemen' is used to describe anyone who comes between producers and final consumers.

b) A market is any situation where buyers and sellers come together.

c) The main types of markets are retail, wholesale, produce, commodity, shipping, insurance, financial and foreign exchange.

d) Some of the different methods of trading include auctions, ring trading, private deals, and 'sights', 'spots' and 'futures' markets.

e) Wholesalers provide the link between manufacturers and retailers. They buy goods in bulk and sell them in smaller quantities as required by retailers.

f) There are four main types of wholesalers.

g) Traditional ones collect orders and deliver goods to the retailer.

h) Cash and Carry wholesalers are rather like supermarkets where retailers go to buy their goods, paying cash at the exit.

i) Wholesaling groups have developed to help small retailers to compete with the large retailers.

j) The CWS supplies goods for co-operative stores.

k) Wholesalers provide many important functions for both manufacturers and retailers.

l) Several factors have led to a decline in the number of wholesalers, in particular the development of large retail organisations which are able to buy goods themselves directly from manufacturers.

m) Markets with many buyers and sellers operate according to the laws of supply and demand which are:
   i)   the higher the price the greater the quantity supplied
   ii)   the lower the price the lower the quantity supplied
   iii) the lower the price the greater the quantity demanded
   iv)   the higher the price the lower the quantity demanded.

REVIEW QUESTIONS

Answers can be found in the paragraphs shown.

1. What is a market? (3)

2. Briefly describe and give examples of at least 4 different types of markets. (4-22)

3. What is the main difference between the money market and the capital market? (14, 16)

4. Explain any 2 methods of market dealing. (23-30)

5. Why are wholesalers often described as 'middlemen'? (2, 31)

6. How do middlemen make their profit? (32, 48)

7. Describe 4 main types of wholesaler. (33-39)

8. List and briefly explain 3 functions which a wholesaler may provide for a manufacturer. (42)

9. List and briefly explain 4 functions which a wholesaler may provide for retailers. (43)

10. Why are wholesalers generally less important today than they used to be? (44-46)

11. Outline 6 factors which may cause demand for a particular product to change. (56)

12. With the use of a simple diagram explain how prices are determined by the interaction of supply and demand. (57-60)

EXAMINATION PRACTICE QUESTIONS

Marks

1. From the following list of words select the most appropriate and complete the summary below. Use each word once only.

cost	consumers	wholesaler	size
manufacturers	goods	retailers	middleman

The . . . . (a) . . . . is often described as the . . . . (b) . . . . It is sometimes

argued that this adds to the . . . . (c) . . . . of goods and that if . . . . (d) . . . .

bought directly from . . . . (e) . . . . then this would result in lower prices for . . . .

(f)   6

2. a) Explain the following functions of a wholesaler:
        i)   the breaking of bulk   2
        ii) the provision of credit   2
    b) Why are the services of wholesalers not required by large supermarket chains?   2

3. Hatton Garden is a wholesale market for   1

4. a) What is meant by dealing in 'futures?'   2
    b) Give 2 examples to illustrate your answer   2

5. What are institutional investors? Use examples to illustrate your answer.   2

MULTIPLE CHOICE/COMPLETION

1. Which of the following services is not provided by cash and carry wholesalers?
    a) Storage
    b) Credit
    c) Breaking of Bulk
    d) Variety of goods

2. Which of the following is *not* a voluntary chain?
    a) VG
    b) Mace
    c) Comet
    d) Spar

3. A sweet manufacturer might choose to use wholesalers rather than deliver to retailers because:
    a) It means that he will sell more
    b) It reduces his costs of delivery
    c) He will not need to advertise
    d) There will be less complaints to deal with

4. A wholesaler:
    a) Buys goods from manufacturers
    b) Only sells goods in large quantities
    c) Buys goods from retailers
    d) Is a store with 10 or more branches

5. The capital market is essentially a market for
   a) Commodities
   b) Foreign currencies
   c) Short-term loans
   d) Long-term loans

6. The sale of commodities to the highest bidder is known as:
   a) A 'spot' market
   b) An auction
   c) Ring Trading
   d) A 'futures' market

In each of the following questions, one or more of the responses is/are correct. Choose the appropriate letter which indicates the correct version.

   A   if 1 only is correct
   B   if 3 only is correct
   C   if 1 and 2 are correct
   D   if 1, 2 and 3 are correct

7. Which of the following factors have resulted in wholesalers being less important today than they used to be?
   1. Improved transport and communications
   2. Decline in the number of independent traders
   3. Growth of multiples

8. Which of the following is/are markets?
   1. Stock Exchange
   2. London Commodity Exchange
   3. Lloyd's of London

RECENT EXAMINATION QUESTIONS

Marks

RSA MARCH 1990 BACKGROUND TO BUSINESS STAGE I PART II

1. a) Give FOUR reasons why small retail outlets still rely on the services of a Cash and Carry wholesaler.   12
   b) Give TWO reasons why there has been a decline in the importance of wholesalers in recent years.   8

ASSIGNMENT

Working in small groups carry out the following:

1. Make a study of the area in which you live. Draw a plan to show the location of the following:
   a) **Wholesalers** – cash and carry, traditional, symbol. Include groceries, electrical goods, newspapers etc.
   b) **Voluntary Chain Shops** – for example Mace, Spar, VG.
   c) **Wholesale Produce Markets** – for example meat, fish fruit and vegetables.

N.B. The Yellow Pages Telephone Directory will help you with this study and you will probably need a local map.

2. Each member of the group should take one example from a, b or c above and try to discover as much information as possible about it. Make notes including:

   a) How long it has been located in the area.
   b) The type of goods which it sells and where they come from, for example names of manufacturers.
   c) The methods of sales promotion and advertising.
   d) Where the majority of their customers come from, for example from a local housing estate, up to 30 miles away, within a few miles. Name the places concerned.

N.B. You will need to visit the wholesaler, shop or produce market which you choose.

3. Write up your findings including any overall comments or conclusions which you feel are interesting or important.

4. As a group prepare a 5-10 minute presentation of your findings. Use displays, handouts and overhead projector slides if you think they will help.

5. Now deliver your presentation to the rest of the class.

13. Retailing

1. This chapter is about the last link in the chain of distribution, the retail trade, which brings goods and services to the final consumer. It covers the many different kinds of shops, including the advantages and disadvantages of each, and ends with a look at retailing without shops.

FUNCTIONS OF RETAILERS

2. Retailers provide important outlets where manufacturers and/or wholesalers can sell their goods. In addition they also perform a number of valuable functions which are essential in encouraging consumers to purchase goods. These functions include:

   a) **Breaking of bulk**   To 'retail' means to sell in small quantities, for example a consumer expects to be able to buy one tin of baked beans not a whole case of 24 tins.

   b) **Choice of goods** – retailers usually stock goods from a variety of different manufacturers.

   c) **Stock** – a supply of goods when needed.

   d) **Information and advice** – retailers have expert knowledge about the goods which they sell.

   e) **After sales service, credit facilities** and **delivery** are all important particularly for anyone buying consumer durables such as cars, televisions and video recorders.

INDEPENDENT TRADERS

3. Usually small counter service shops are run by the person who owns them, particularly many newsagents, tobacconists, and 'corner shops'. These are called independent, or sole traders, and despite competition from larger retailers, which keeps forcing some to close down, many still manage to survive. The main reasons for this can be seen in the advantages which they offer to their customers.

4. **Advantages**
   *   Friendly, personal service – get to know customers
   *   Convenience – situated locally, may open long hours including Sunday
   *   Some allow customers credit
   *   Orders can be made up and delivered – important where groceries are sold.

5. **Disadvantages**
   *   Higher prices – because unable to buy in bulk
   *   Limited range of goods – because they are only small shops
   *   Counter service makes it difficult for customers to see all the merchandise.
   *   Waiting may be involved, particularly if staff are 'chatty'.

6.

A 'Corner' Shop

SELF-SERVICE

7.   A self-service shop is designed to allow customers to select goods themselves. By definition it has a selling area of less than 200 square metres (2,500 square feet) and frequently these stores are run by people who belong to symbol groups. That is, small independent retailers who agree to buy from a group wholesaler, to obtain lower prices, for example Spar, Mace or VG.

8.   **Advantages**
   * Able to offer cut prices
   * Wider choice of goods
   * Seeing goods displayed openly reminds you of your needs.

Plus the usual advantages offered by small independent traders such as personal service, convenient location and the longer opening hours.

9.   **Disadvantages**
   * Lack of space
   * Relatively limited choice of goods
   * Possible delays at the checkout
   * Slightly higher prices than supermarkets, but cheaper than 'corner shops'
   * Pre-packed goods, for example meat, bacon, cheese cannot be easily examined.

SUPERMARKETS

10.   A supermarket has a minimum of 2,000 square feet of selling area and operates principally on a self service basis with 3 or more checkouts, for example Tesco, Safeway, Sainsbury's and ASDA. They sell a broad range of grocery items and usually some non-food items all at cut prices. Goods are displayed in sections so that related products are together, for example dairy produce, meats, groceries, hardware. Most goods are pre-packed, for example coffee, tea, sugar, dried fruit and butter, all of which were once sold loose.

11.   **Advantages**
   * Cut prices/special offers – because they buy in large quantities.
   * Wider choice of goods
   * 'One-stop-shopping' – fetching a week's groceries at once makes shopping quicker and more convenient. This is helped by most supermarkets having late night opening on one or two days per week.
   * Seeing goods displayed reminds you of your needs
   * Pleasant atmosphere – often with music playing in the background

12.   **Disadvantages**
   * Impulse buying, i.e. buying goods which you see but did not go into the store for
   * Possible delays at the check-outs – particularly at busy times
   * Location – usually in towns
   * Impersonal
   * Have to pay cash, although many stores, for example ASDA and Tesco now accept Access and Visa Credit Cards.

13.   Retailers prefer self-service and supermarkets because they result in:
   * Increased sales
   * Lower running costs leading to higher profits
   * Bigger and better displays of stock – more stock in the shop and less in the storeroom
   * Less staff are needed
   * Economies of scale (generally it is cheaper to operate on a larger scale.)

SUPERSTORES AND HYPERMARKETS

14. Superstores and hypermarkets are self-service stores which sell groceries and a very wide range of other goods from handkerchiefs to colour televisions, all at discount prices, and all on one floor. A range of over 30,000 different items is common. The idea being that of 'one shop' for virtually everything.

15. Superstores are usually defined as having a selling area of over 2,500 square metres (25,000 square feet), whilst hypermarkets have over 5,000 square metres (50,000 square feet). Both types of store are located away from town centres (in places where rent and rates are cheaper), always have large car parks and often a garage selling cut price petrol as well.

16. **ASDA's Superstore at Nuneaton**

17. Examples of hypermarkets include Carrefour with stores at Eastleigh (Hants), Telford (Staffs), and Caerphilly (South Wales), Tesco at Irlam (Lancs), and Pitsea (Essex) and the Co-op at Westwood (Kent).

18. **Advantages**
   * Low prices on all types of merchandise, including such items as furniture and household durable goods, for example televisions, irons and kettles.
   * Quick and convenient way to shop for a very wide range and choice of goods.
   * Attractive locations away from congested town centres.
   * Usually late opening hours on most evenings.

19. **Disadvantages**
   * They rely on people having cars to get to them, although some also run local free bus services, for example ASDA.
   * Extra large and impersonal.
   * May be difficult to find some items from the vast range in stock.

DEPARTMENT STORES

20. A department store is a collection of different departments, each specialising in one type of merchandise, under one roof, for example hardware, men's clothing, electrical goods, food. The aim being to provide everything a customer might need in one building, which usually has four or more floors.

21. Department stores often have many additional features, including carpets, lifts, a hairdressing salon, restaurant, travel bureau and toilets, and some even have a bank. Well known examples include Harrods, Debenhams and Lewis's. (also Grace Brother's in the television series "Are you being served?")

22. **Advantages**
   * Comfortable shopping under one roof with a wide choice of quality goods.
   * Self selection of most merchandise with assistants to help when required.
   * Usually credit facilities are available, for example Debenham's Budget Account.
   * Often free delivery of goods.

23. **Disadvantages**
   * Usually only in large towns or cities – due to the heavy overheads (costs of running them) they need to be where a lot of people shop.
   * Big and impersonal.
   * Slightly higher prices – to cover the cost of comfort and services.

MULTIPLE STORES

24. A multiple is defined as a group of shops with 10 or more branches which usually sell only one type of merchandise. Many multiples are well known in High Streets throughout the country and are easily recognised by their name and similar shop fronts. Inside, the layout, design and merchandise are also very similar.

25. For example:

Mothercare	–	Baby goods (with over 250 branches)
Curry's	–	Electrical domestic appliances (over 480 branches)
Ratners	–	Jewellers (over 250 branches)
Chelsea Girl	–	Fashion clothing (over 100 branches)
Tesco	–	Supermarkets (over 380 branches)
Peter Dominic	–	Wine shops (over 360 branches)

26.

27. Advantages

* Similar standards throughout the country.
* Competitive prices – because of bulk buying.
* Good range of stock – often specially made for the multiple or possibly manufactured in its own factories.
* Modern shops often situated in convenient and attractive shopping centres, and easily recognised by their familiar name and shop front.

28. Disadvantages

* Similar items in all stores – 'seen one, seen the lot'.
* Double transport costs add to the cost of the goods. That is, goods are delivered from the manufacturers to a central warehouse and then from there sent to branches.
* Less personal service.

VARIETY CHAIN STORES

29. Variety chain stores are multiples which instead of specialising in one type of merchandise sell a range of goods. The idea is to offer variety under one roof. These stores are divided into sections, and the merchandise is displayed on open counters or racks (self-selection). Nowadays many operate on self-service principles with cash and wrap points situated throughout the store. Well known examples include Marks & Spencer, F W Woolworth, Boots, British Home Stores, Littlewoods and W H Smith.

30.

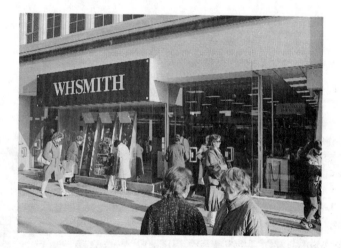

31. Advantages

* Branches in most large towns and cities.
* Own brands – which are usually cheaper than manufacturers brands, for example Winfields (Woolworth's), Prova (British Home Stores).
* The same advantages as other multiples, i.e. competitive prices, quality merchandise, modern shops, good range of stock and similar standards in all stores.

32. Disadvantages

* Impersonal
* Similar items in all stores.
* May be unable to 'try on' goods like clothing.
* Usually they do not offer credit, although this has begun to change as the range of merchandise is extended, for example Woolworth's now sell more expensive items like televisions and furni-

ture, on which they offer credit. Littlewood's and Mark's & Spencer have also recently introduced their own credit cards.

DISCOUNT STORES

33. Discount stores are multiples which basically sell durable household equipment (electrical goods and furniture) at greatly reduced prices. They operate on a low profit margin but high turnover (sales). Usually, but not always, they are found on the outskirts of towns and cities and have their own car parks. Well known examples of discount stores are Comet (electrical equipment), MFI (furniture) and Argos who sell a wide range of items.

34.

ORGANISATION AND GROWTH OF MULTIPLES

35. Multiple stores are becoming increasingly important in the retail trade. The main reason for this is because they can take advantage of economies of scale. For example:

   a) They are run from a central Head Office where they can employ specialists to manage the business including experts in buying, accounting, advertising and display etc.

   b) They can miss out the wholesaler by buying direct from manufacturers or producing goods in their own factories.

   c) They can buy in bulk and hence more cheaply.

   d) They can control stock by distributing goods from a central warehouse often using their own vehicles.

   e) They can use a single advertisement to attract customers to all branches throughout the country.

CO-OPERATIVE STORES

36. From its beginnings in Rochdale, Lancashire, in 1844 up until the 1950's, the Co-operative movement grew rapidly, but since then it has gradually declined in terms of its share of the retail trade. In 1993 there were 59 Co-operative societies throughout the country operating some 4,600 shops with 8.1 million members. They sell many types of merchandise including, groceries, clothing, footwear and furniture. The main feature of Co-operative retail stores is the 'dividend', that is, profits are shared with customers based on how much they spend. (See Chapter 6).

37. Number of Co-operative Societies

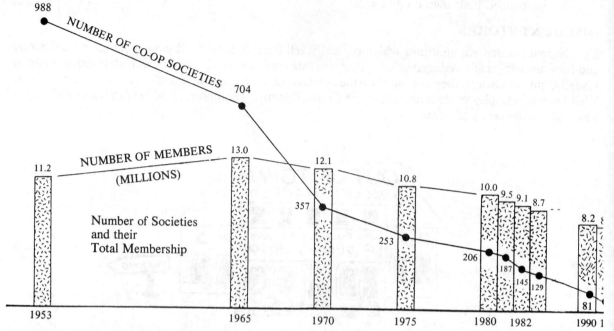

RECENT TRENDS IN RETAILING

38.   Retailing is always changing as you will certainly have observed yourself. Some recent and/or current trends include the following:-

*   The growth of multiples which now account for over 60% of retail turnover.
*   The growth of superstores selling an increasing variety of goods.
*   The development of large specially designed shopping precincts.
*   The development of out-of-town regional shopping centres e.g. Metro Centre, Gateshead.
*   The growth of shops selling computers, software, videos and video cassettes.
*   An increasing emphasis on price competition and quality to promote sales.
*   Increased use of credit cards (e.g. Access, Visa) and retailers own cards (e.g. Debenhams, Comet) to pay for goods.
*   The increasing use of new technology including laser-scanning electronic check-outs which make stock control and pricing more efficient.
*   The development of computerised shopping services from home.
*   The establishment of an EFTPOS system including Switch and Connect (See Chapter 4).

RETAILING WITHOUT SHOPS

39.   So far we have considered the main types of retail outlets or shops. However, it is also possible to sell goods to consumers without shops, using one or more of the following ways.

40.   Markets

Nearly every town has a market on one or more days each week and they prove to be a great attraction to shoppers. Usually the market stalls, which are hired for the day, are set up outside in the main street or the market square, but some large towns have permanent covered markets. The traders have low operating costs which enables them to charge lower prices.

41. Automatic Vending

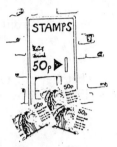

A mobile 'shop'

42. Street Traders

Street Traders display their goods on the pavement in suitcases or on barrows and usually offer very low prices. They require a licence from the local authority which states where they are allowed to stand. Barrow boys are a common sight in large cities like London, Newcastle and Glasgow. Newspapers, flowers and fruit and vegetables are often sold this way.

43. Mail Order

Mail Order means buying goods through the post and is a rapidly growing section of the retail trade. This type of business is usually carried out in one of two main ways.

44. Direct to Customers

This is done by advertising in newspapers, (particularly on Saturdays and Sundays) in magazines and on television or radio.

45. Part-time Agents

Many housewives take on this role using a mail order catalogue. Most catalogues are very expensive to produce, often containing over 20,000 different items, ranging from socks to car insurance. The agents collect orders for the firms and payment from the customers, for which they are normally paid a commission of about 10p, for every pounds worth of goods sold. Well known examples include Grattan's, Kays, Littlewoods and Avon cosmetics.

46.

47. Mail order shopping provides the advantage of buying at leisure in the comfort of your own home. Usually goods can be returned if unsatisfactory and free credit is often given.

48. Against this you must wait for delivery and prices may be higher than in the shops. It is also difficult to judge the quality and features of goods from an advertisement or catalogue.

49. Mobile Shops

We do not usually think of the milkman, baker, or coalman as retailers, but that is what they are. Other familiar examples of mobile 'shops', i.e. which go to the customer, include traders selling fish, ice-cream, fruit and vegetables and groceries.

50. Door-To-Door Sales

Door-to-door selling takes place when a salesman calls at someone's home and invites them to buy their goods. Examples include encyclopaedia firms (such as Encyclopaedia Britannica), double glazing companies (such as Everest, Alpine and Cold Shield) and charity organisations offering toiletries and stationery.

51. Automatic Vending Machines

The sale of goods through automatic slot machines is another growing form of retailing. They are common sights nowadays in schools, clubs, motorway service stations, outside shops and in launderettes. They have the advantage of being open for 24 hours a day and sell a wide range of goods, including drinks, chocolates, milk and cigarettes.

52. Party Selling

Party selling involves housewives who are asked to hold coffee parties to which friends, neighbours and relatives are invited. In return they receive commission on sales, or free gifts, from the firm. Well known examples of party selling firms include Tupperware (polythene goods), Sarah Coventry (jewellery), Pippa Dee (women's clothing) and Dee Minor (children's clothing).

53. Trade Fairs and Exhibitions

Trade Fairs and Exhibitions are huge market places for the display and sale of goods which take place throughout the world and are very important, particularly for manufacturers. They usually take place in special halls or centres like Olympia in London, or the National Exhibition Centre near Birmingham. Examples include annual events like the Daily Mail Ideal Home Exhibition, the Motor Show, International Boat Show and the Royal Agricultural Show.

54. GMEX Exhibition Centre in Manchester

SUMMARY

55. a) The main function of retailers is the breaking of bulk. They also provide choice, stock, information and advice, after sales service, credit and delivery.

b) There are many different types of retailers each providing particular services for customers.

c) Independent traders offer personal counter service but their prices are often higher than other shops.

d) Self-service retailers are also often independent but frequently join group wholesalers like Spar or VG to enable them to compete with larger shops.

e) Supermarkets offer cut prices and a wider choice of goods.

f) Superstores and Hypermarkets are very large stores usually located away from town centres, which sell a vast range of merchandise.

g) Department stores are found in the centre of large towns or cities and offer a large range of goods and facilities.

h) Multiple retailers (those with more than 10 branches) specialise in selling a wide variety of one particular type of merchandise.

i) Variety Chain stores are multiples which sell a variety of goods.

j) Discount stores concentrate on selling durable household goods at cut prices.

k) Co-operative stores are best known for the dividend which they give to customers.

l) There are many current trends which are shaping the future of retailing.

m) There are also many methods of retailing without shops including market stalls, mail order, mobile shops, door-to-door, party selling, vending machines and trade fairs and exhibitions.

REVIEW QUESTIONS

Answers can be found in the paragraphs shown.

1. List 5 functions of a retailer. (2)

2. Why are many independent traders being forced to close down? (3, 5)

3. What is the difference between self-service stores and supermarkets? (7-12)

4. Give 2 distinguishing features of a hypermarket. (14-19)

5. Give 2 advantages and 2 disadvantages of department stores. (22, 23)

6. Give 2 examples of both multiples and variety chain stores. (25, 26, 30)

7. Outline some of the recent trends in retailing. (35-38).

8. List 8 methods of retailing without shops. (39-53)

9. Describe 2 advantages and 2 disadvantages for customers of buying by mail order. (47, 48)

10. Why are Trade Fairs and Exhibitions important for manufacturers? (53)

EXAMINATION PRACTICE QUESTIONS

Marks

1. Read the following 5 statements carefully. From the list of words a-j select one which you think is the most suitable to complete each statement. Each word may be used once only.

    i)   An example of a multiple chain is   1

    ii)   A major advantage of a small local shop is that it offers   1

    iii) The selling of goods through the post is called   1

    iv) The main function of a retailer is to   1

    v)   . . . . is a well known variety chain store.   1

a)	Personal Service	f)	Harrods
b)	Mail Order	g)	Marks & Spencers
c)	Tesco	h)	Break Bulk
d)	Automatic Vending	i)	Offer Credit
e)	Door to Door	j)	Lower Prices

2. Give 2 distinguishing features of:

    a)   Variety chain stores   2

    b)   Department Stores   2

    c)   Hypermarkets   2

    d)   Discount Stores   2

3. Give 2 reasons why multiple shops can operate at lower costs than small independent retailers.   2

4. Give one main *advantage* and one main *disadvantage* from the customers point of view of each of the following:

    a)   Small local retailer   2

    b)   Supermarket   2

    c)   Department Store   2

    d)   Multiple Store   2

    e)   Discount Store   2

5. What is the main difference between the Co-operative and all other types of retailers?   2

6. a)   List 4 types of goods which you would expect to buy from a vending machine.   2

    b)   With examples, explain why this sort of retailing would not be suitable for all goods.   3

MULTIPLE CHOICE/COMPLETION

1. British Home Stores is an example of a:

    a)   Variety Chain Store

    b)   Multiple shop

    c)   Mobile shop

    d)   Department Store

2. The main difference between a mail order business and most other forms of retailing is that:

    a)   Credit is usually allowed

    b)   The buyer and seller never meet

    c)   Branded goods are sold

    d)   Goods are delivered to the customer

3. The newest and largest type of retail outlet is known as a:
   a) Co-operative Society
   b) Supermarket
   c) Department Store
   d) Hypermarket

4. Which of the following statements is incorrect?
   a) Spar is an example of a voluntary chain
   b) Mail Order shopping is becoming less popular
   c) A multiple is a retail group with 10 or more branches
   d) Department Stores are located in town centres

5. A supermarket is usually cheaper than a small shop because it:
   a) Is found in city centres
   b) Pays lower wages
   c) Sells poorer quality goods
   d) Buys in bulk

6. A shop which specialises mainly in one type of merchandise and has more than 10 branches is known as a:
   a) Department Store
   b) Multiple
   c) Sole Trader
   d) Superstore

In each of the following questions, one or more of the responses is/are correct. Choose the appropriate letter which indicates the correct version.
   A   if 1 only is correct
   B   if 3 only is correct
   C   if 1 and 2 are correct
   D   if 1, 2 and 3 are correct

7. Which of the following features are usually associated with hypermarkets?
   1) Out of town location
   2) Plenty of car parking space
   3) Limited range of goods

8. The main difference(s) between the Co-operative and all other types of retailer is/are:
   1) They usually give dividend stamps on purchases
   2) They usually open 6 days a week
   3) They obtain some of their goods from the CWS

RECENT EXAMINATION QUESTIONS   **Marks**

RSA JUNE 1990 BACKGROUND TO BUSINESS STAGE I PART II SECTION A

1. a) Describe, giving examples, TWO advantages for retailers and TWO advantages for customers of the use of self-service.   8
   b) Explain, giving TWO examples, why some goods are sold using counter service in retail outlets   6

c) Explain, giving examples, TWO reasons why some goods are delivered direct from manufacturers to consumers using mail order.

6

ASSIGNMENT

1. Match each multiple with the right merchandise:

   a) Granada   Butchers

   b) B & Q   Furniture

   c) W H Smith   Electrical Appliances

   d) Little Chef   Shoes

   e) Halfords   Restaurants

   f) Burtons   Motorist's and Cyclist's goods

   g) Saxone   Men's clothing

   h) Rumblelows   Newspapers, Books and Stationery

   i) Cantors   DIY Products

   j) Dewhurst   Television Rental

2. Give 3 reasons why the 'corner shop' manages to survive when multiples and variety chains can sell goods at much cheaper prices.

3. Name 2 costs, besides advertising, which would be heavy in a mail order business, which are not normally incurred by a shop retailer.

4. Look at a mail order catalogue and answer the following questions:

   a) What happens if mail order goods are found to be unsuitable when delivered?

   b) Why do you think that mail order is one of the fastest growing sections of the retail trade?

   c) How are the housewives who run mail order agencies paid?

   d) Are they full-time employees of the firms they represent?

   e) Do you have to pay for goods in cash or can they be bought on credit?

5. Assume that a new department store with 5 floors is opening in your town in the near future. You are asked to decide on which floors the following goods and services should be put, giving reasons for your arrangement. Use a simple sketch if you find this helpful.

   a) Toys

   b) Cosmetics

   c) Ladies and Gents Hairdressing

   d) Accounts

   e) Furniture

   f) Ladies' and Men's clothing

   g) Offices

   h) Jewellery

   i) Radio and Television

   j) Toilets

   k) Food Hall

   l) Staff Canteen

   m) Restaurant

   n) Staff Rooms

   o) Travel Agency

   p) Coffee Bar

14. Transport

1. This chapter begins by discussing the importance of transport and the factors which firms consider in deciding which method to use. It then outlines the key features of the United Kingdom's road, rail, sea and air transport systems and the main advantages and disadvantages of each. Finally it looks at some possible future transport developments.

THE IMPORTANCE OF TRANSPORT

2. Transport is concerned with the movement of materials, goods or people from one place to another and is therefore an essential part of marketing and trade.

    a) Raw materials must be transported to factories, often between one country and another.

    b) Goods need to be distributed from factories to wholesalers, retailers and consumers.

    c) People must be transported both to and from work and also for leisure and other activities like shopping and holidays.

3.

4. An efficient transport system also helps to increase a country's standard of living. Good transport enables more people to be reached thereby increasing the size of a firm's market. This in turn encourages the mass production of goods and allows greater use to be made of the division of labour. This increases the amount of goods which we can all enjoy.

5. Efficient transport also reduces the amount of finance and storage space needed by manufacturers, wholesalers and retailers. If deliveries can be made regularly and quickly then smaller stocks are needed.

6. Transport is also a major cost of production and the location of modern industry is often determined by the availability of an efficient system.

CHOICE OF TRANSPORT

7.   A business has a choice of using road, rail, sea or air transport. However, not all methods are suitable for the movement of all freight (goods and materials). Therefore, the form of transport used by any particular firm will in general depend upon the relative importance of a number of key factors.

*   **Type of goods** – clearly fragile items like pottery and perishables cannot be transported in the same way as petrol, bricks or coal.

*   **Value** of the goods – valuable items like jewellery will probably be sent in the quickest, safest way to reduce the risks of loss, theft or damage.

*   **Size and Weight** of the goods – bulky products like coal can be sent by rail, whereas small packages might be better sent by road.

*   **Cost** – is it better to purchase, lease or hire transport?

*   **Speed** – the urgency with which goods must be delivered.

*   **Frequency** – how often the transport is needed.

*   **Convenience** – road and postal services offer regular door-to-door delivery which is important for many firms. A nearby airport, station, port or freight depot may be other considerations.

*   **Distance** involved – road transport is often best for short distances but rail preferable for longer journeys.

THE RELATIVE IMPORTANCE OF THE DIFFERENT TRANSPORT SYSTEMS

8.

a) Share of Goods Transport By Value	1979 (%)	1991 (%)
Road	79.0	80.7
Rail	9.0	6.8
Water – Coastwise Oil	2.8	2.2
Water – Other	4.7	5.0
Pipeline	4.5	5.3

N.B.   Oil comprises crude oil and all petroleum products.
'Coastwise' includes all sea traffic within the UK, Isle of Man and Channel Islands.
'Other' means all Coastwise plus inland watereway traffic and one-port traffic (largely crude oil direct from rigs).
Source: Adapted from Annual Abstract of Statistics 1993.

b) **Share of Goods Transport To and From Britain**				
	1975 (%)		1991 (%)	
	Imports	Exports	Imports	Exports
Shipping	83	86	82	80
Air Freight	17	14	18	20
	100	100	100.0	100.0

Source: Great Britain Handbook

9.   As can be seen from the above tables, road transport is by far the most important for inland transport, and shipping for the movement of goods to and from other countries.

CONTAINERS

10. Probably the most important development in recent years in the field of freight transport has been the introduction of *containers*. These are like large metal packing cases which can be used to transport goods by road, rail, sea or air.

Loading Containers

Freightliner Terminal

12. Goods are packed into containers at the factory and delivered direct to their destinations as a unit load. The containers are transported on specially designed lorries and transferred by special cranes onto trains or ships which:

*   Saves time
*   Reduces handling costs
*   Reduces the risks of loss, theft or damage

Therefore the use of containers provides firms with a fast, cheap and reliable method of transporting large quantities of goods.

13. Containers are now used extensively in the **UK** particularly for goods going to and from abroad. Overseas containers save time because they can be quickly checked and sealed by Customs and documents prepared in advance. Containers can now be shipped throughout the world, for example from Liverpool to Budapest or Istanbul, or from Tilbury or Felixstowe to New York, Montreal, Rotterdam or Sydney.

ROAD TRANSPORT

14. This is the core method on which all other transport relies. Since the 1950's road transport has increased rapidly, particularly with the development of motorways. These were built because of the need for fast roads which by-passed towns and villages, linking the main centres of population. At the same time a reduction in the number of railway lines has meant that road transport has become essential in many areas. Consequently, road haulage is now by far the most popular and important internal method of transport.

15. **Britain's Motorways and Major Roads**

16. The costs of building and maintaining roads are paid for out of local authority revenue and government taxes. However, road users have to pay a road fund licence plus VAT on the purchase of vehicles, fuel and parts and a special tax on fuel.

17. **Advantages of Road Transport**
   * Door-to-door service
   * Flexibility – goods can be moved when ready and on any route
   * Quick – particularly since the development of motorways and because of the relatively short distances involved in the UK
   * Cheaper – strong competition between road hauliers keeps costs down
   * Can reach areas not accessible by rail or water
   * No transhipments – which reduces risks of theft, damage or delays because less handling is involved
   * Firms can buy their own vehicles for greater convenience. They can also advertise on the sides.

18. **Disadvantages of Road Transport**
   * Can be slow over long distances
   * Cost of road fund licence and fuel
   * Delay may be caused by bad weather or breakdowns
   * There may be no return load, making journeys more expensive
   * Not suitable for all goods, for example large quantities of bulky goods such as coal and cement
   * Legal controls, for example speed limits, weight limits, type of vehicle, driving hours
   * Social costs – road maintenance, police patrols, hospital services for accidents, pollution, noise etc.
   * Road congestion – particularly in large towns and cities

19. **Problems of Road Transport**

RAIL TRANSPORT

20. The railways developed rapidly in the nineteenth century. This enabled a great variety of foods and other goods to be transported throughout the country. Railways were nationalised in 1948 giving British Rail a monopoly of rail transport. British Rail also operates some ferry services and a freightliner service. In Northern Ireland the railway service is operated by the Northern Ireland Railways Company Ltd.

21. Since the 1960's, following the Beeching Report, the railways have undergone vast changes with many uneconomic lines being closed down. A large modernisation programme has been undertaken including the introduction of electrification on many lines, more comfortable trains and faster more reliable passenger and freight services.

22. Over 90% of rail freight is obtained from bulk commodities, most of it in full trainloads. The most important freight goods handled are coal, coke, iron, steel, building materials and petroleum. The freight traffic is now concentrated in fewer but better-equipped terminals and a network of express services (speedlink and freightliner) have been introduced connecting the main ports and industrial areas.

23. **Speedlink**   About 130 high speed trains, consisting of specially constructed wagons, run daily on regular timetables and guaranteeing next day arrival.

24. **Freightliner**   This is a high speed container service linking rail transport to special road and sea terminals. Freightliner terminals are located in large towns and centres of industry. Freightliner lorries collect and deliver the containers at each end of the rail journey.

25. **Computerisation**   The daily movement of all British Rail freight trains is monitored by an advanced computerised information system called *Total Operations Processing System* (TOPS). This reduces costs and improves the use and efficiency of goods wagons.

26. **Parcels Service**   British Rail also offers the Red Star parcel service which guarantees same day or overnight delivery on specified routes. Parcels travel on passenger trains and must be delivered to and collected from the railway stations.

27. BR's Advanced Passenger Train

British Rail

28. Because of increased competition from road transport the future of the railways is likely to lie in fast inter-city passenger services and the carrying of heavy or bulky goods like coal, cement and cars which would otherwise cause congestion on the roads.

29. **Advantages of Rail Transport**
   * Can take large quantities of heavy and bulky goods, for example coal, iron ore, china clay.
   * Faster than road, particularly for distances over 200 miles
   * Special trains can be chartered (hired) for example to carry mail, cars, cement and coal
   * Direct routes to the centres of towns and cities
   * Cheap for container traffic
   * Offers both passenger and goods services, for example commuters who travel to and from London rely heavily on rail transport thus relieving road congestion.

30. **Disadvantages**
   * Can be expensive for small loads or short journeys
   * Routes are fixed by railway lines and stations, therefore other forms of transport are also needed
   * Fixed timetables may be inconvenient
   * High costs of equipment and maintenance lead to higher prices
   * Extra loading and unloading increases risks of damage or loss, and may cause delays
   * Impractical for high or wide loads

31. **Other Public Rail Services**

The London Underground, Glasgow Underground and Tyne and Wear Metro are very important for the transport of people in the crowded cities which they serve.

INLAND WATERWAYS (Rivers and Canals)

32. Water is one of the cheapest forms of transport. Before the development of roads and railways, rivers and canals were widely used in Britain and still are for some heavy and bulky goods like coal, sand, cement and timber.

33. However, water is also a slow means of transport and only available on limited routes. Therefore it is unsuitable for many of the vast range of goods which we buy today. Consequently, many rivers and canals are now used only for leisure and not for trade.

SEA TRANSPORT

34. Britain is an island inhabited by over 57 million people. We could not possibly produce enough food and other goods for our needs and we have insufficient supplies of most raw materials. Therefore we need to import these from other countries and in order to pay for them we must export (sell) all sorts of finished goods and services. Sea transport is very important in enabling much of this trade to take place.

35. There are several different types of sea transport available:

a) **Coastal shipping**   These are ships which are used for carrying cargo when it is more economical or convenient to send goods by sea instead of by road or rail. In the UK they move between major ports like Newcastle, Southampton and London, carrying coal, clay, timber etc.

b) **Tramp Ships**   These travel anywhere in the world and operate rather like taxis. That is they have no regular route but can be hired to go where required. The arrangements are made at the *Baltic Exchange* in London using a document called a 'Charter Party' agreement. Charges are based on the space available on board, the bulk or weight of the cargo and its destination.

c) **Liners**   These carry passengers and/or cargo operating on regular timetables like trains. They travel to main ports throughout the world.

d) **Bulk Carriers**   Many cargos are carried in purpose built vessels. Examples include oil tankers, container ships, refrigerated ships and bulk carriers for wheat and other grains. Some have special decks for carrying containers.

e) **Roll-on/Roll-off Ferries**   These are used to enable cars and lorries to drive onto a ship at one port and drive off at their destination without the need for any loading or unloading of their goods. These are very important for trade with Europe.

36.

A North Sea Ferry

A BP Oil Tanker

37. Advantages of Sea Transport
* Cheap means of transport
* Use of container facilities throughout the world keeps costs to a minimum
* Access to all parts of the world
* Can transport very heavy and bulky goods

38. Disadvantages of Sea Transport
* Slow and therefore unsuitable for goods required quickly
* Requires other forms of transport to take goods to and from ports
* Cargoes can be damaged by salt air and bad weather

39. The chief ports in the UK are London, Tilbury, Liverpool, Hull, Southampton, Glasgow, Leith, Grangemouth, Bristol and Belfast. There are also many other smaller ports including Felixstowe, Dover, Immingham and Shoreham.

40. Chief Ports and Shipping Routes

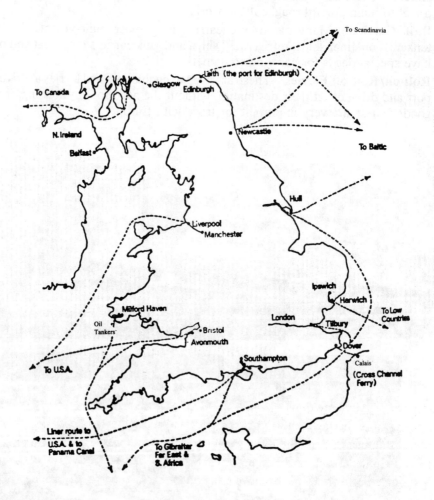

41. Lloyd's Register of Shipping   All ships are examined and classified according to their safety and efficiency on what is called *Lloyd's Register*. It is from this that the expression 'A1 at Lloyd's' comes. Lloyd's underwriters who insure ships (see Chapter 19) use this classification to obtain information about the condition of ships and therefore the risks involved.

AIR TRANSPORT

42. Air transport has developed rapidly in the twentieth century helped partly by the two world wars. Air cargo services now operate to most parts of the world from all the main airports in Britain. Goods may be sent on regular scheduled services or charter flights.

43. The major part of air transport is concerned with carrying passengers (56 million on international flights in 1988) but in recent years there has also been a big increase in air cargo traffic. This has been made possible by the development of larger aircraft and better storage facilities at airports.

44. Charges for air freight are based on the value, bulk and destination of the goods. The arrangements for chartering aircrafts are made at the Air Freight Market in the Baltic Exchange.

45. There are some 40 airports in the UK, the most important being Heathrow and Gatwick, both near London. Stanstead in Essex is London's third airport. Most large cities such as Manchester, Birmingham and Liverpool have their own airports as well as smaller places like Luton, Southend and Blackpool. Prestwick is the main airport in Scotland and Belfast (Aldergrove) in Northern Ireland.

46. **Loading Air Freight**

47. **Advantages of Air Transport**
   * Speed – it is the fastest form of transport and particularly effective over long distances
   * Increasing use of containers for freight traffic
   * Less documentation than for sea transport
   * Insurance costs are lower because risks of theft and damage are reduced by shorter travelling times
   * Reduced packaging costs compared with sea transport because special protection from the elements is not needed
   * Particularly suitable for small, light, valuable items such as gold, diamonds, medicines, machine parts and mail, or the fast movement of perishable goods like fruit and flowers.

48. Disadvantages of Air Transport
* Cost – high operating and maintenance costs make it the most expensive form of transport
* Occasional problems due to bad weather
* Not suitable for short distances
* Limits on the weight which can be carried therefore certain heavy and bulky products could not be accepted
* Airports are situated on the outskirts of towns and cities therefore requiring other forms of transport and time to reach them.

OTHER FORMS OF TRANSPORT

49. **Hovercraft**   These are crafts which can carry passengers or cargo over land or sea. They skim along close to the surface on a cushion of air. Hovercrafts do not have to use harbours or airfields and can go anywhere if the surface is not too rough. They can travel faster than ships but are expensive to build and operate, are noisy and cannot be used in rough seas. The hovercraft is a popular alternative way of crossing the English Channel to the ports of Europe.

50.

A Cross-Channel Hovercraft

A BP Oil Pipeline at Grangemouth

51. Pipelines Pipelines are generally used for transporting liquids such as water, gas and oil. They are expensive to install and can only be used for a limited range of products. However, maintenance costs are low and pipelines provide a safe and speedy method of transport which can be used for 24 hours a day. They have been particularly important in the development of North Sea Oil and Gas.

52. The Light Rail Transit System for London Docklands

TRANSPORT IN THE FUTURE

53. There are a number of interesting ideas for improving transport in the future. Some of these are still being developed whilst others you may already have seen. The following are some examples of transport developments which are likely to be introduced or improved in the near future:

a) **Electric Road Vehicles** are little used at present because they can only travel short distances before needing to be re-charged. This problem will eventually be overcome.

b) **Conveyor Belts** could be used to carry people from one place to another rather like an escalator carries people up and down. Moving pavements are already used at several airports and at the Bank underground station in London.

c) **Hovertrains** are currently being tested at speeds of up to 300 mph.

d) **Vertical take-off and landing Aircraft** which, at present, are only used for military purposes are likely to be available in main towns and cities just as trains and buses are now.

e) **Monorails** could be built on concrete pillars above existing streets. Japan already has a monorail system and they are being considered in several other large cities throughout the world.

f) The **Channel Tunnel** between England and France when completed will mean that trains will be able to carry cars, passengers and freight direct to Europe.

SUMMARY

54. a) Transport is concerned with the movement of materials, goods and people by road, rail, sea or air.

b) An efficient transport system is essential to enable trade to take place throughout the world thus improving standards of living.

c)   The form of transport used by a business will depend upon the relative importance of a number of factors including the type of goods, their value, size and weight, the cost, speed, frequency and convenience of the method of transport and the distance involved.

d)   The use of containers has made the transport of goods much cheaper and more efficient.

e)   In the UK most inland transport of goods and people takes place by road, the main advantage of which is its door-to-door service over a wide area.

f)   The railways which are state owned are particularly suited to moving large quantities of bulk freight over long distances.

g)   Speedlink and freightliner are two high speed rail freight services.

h)   Inland waterways (rivers and canals) are a slow means of transport available on only limited routes.

i)   Sea transport is very important for the import and export of goods.

j)   The main types of sea transport are coastal ships, tramps, passenger and cargo liners, bulk carriers and roll-on/roll-off ferries.

k)   Sea transport is slow but cheap and provides access to countries throughout the world.

l)   Air freight traffic is growing steadily and provides the quickest means of transport particularly over long distances.

m)   Hovercrafts on cross-channel routes and pipelines in the North Sea are examples of other types of transport.

n)   Future developments could include wider use of electric vehicles, conveyor belts, hovertrains, vertical take-off and landing aircraft, monorails and the building of the Channel Tunnel.

REVIEW QUESTIONS

Answers can be found in the paragraphs shown.

1.   Why is transport important? (2-6)

2.   List at least 4 factors which a firm would consider in deciding how to transport its goods. (7)

3.   What are containers and why is their use so important? (10-13)

4.   What are the advantages and disadvantages of road transport? (17-19)

5.   Briefly describe British Rail's 2 high speed freight services. (22-24)

6.   Outline the main advantages and disadvantages of rail transport. (29-30)

7.   Why is sea transport so important to the UK?.(34)

8.   What is meant by 'roll-on/roll-off'? (35)

9.   What are the advantages and disadvantages of transporting goods by sea? (37-38)

10. Why is air cargo traffic increasing? (42-43)

11. What are the advantages and disadvantages of air transport? (47-48)

12. Outline some possible future developments in transport. (52-53)

EXAMINATION PRACTICE QUESTIONS

Marks

1.   The place where air and sea transport can be bought and sold is called the   1

2.   Explain with examples what is meant by the term 'social costs' in respect of road transport.   3

3.   What would be the advantages and disadvantages for a business which formerly used road and rail transport deciding to deliver goods in its own vehicles.   6

MULTIPLE CHOICE/COMPLETION

1. A ship which can be chartered to travel anywhere is called a:
   a) Bulk carrier
   b) Ferry
   c) Tramp
   d) Liner

2. Canals are unsuitable for the transport of:
   a) Sand
   b) Milk
   c) Coal
   d) Timber

3. Which of the following is not an advantage of sending goods by rail?
   a) Can use containers
   b) Door-to-door service
   c) Can take unlimited loads
   d) Fast over long distances

4. Which methods of transport will be most suitable for a UK manufacturer of home computers exporting to Canada?
   a) Road and sea
   b) Rail and air
   c) Road and rail
   d) Road and air

5. Pipelines can be used to transport all except which one of the following?
   a) Salt
   b) Water
   c) Oil
   d) Gas

6. Which of the following is not an advantage of sea transport?
   a) Access to all parts of the world
   b) Suitable for bulky goods
   c) Fast delivery
   d) Relatively cheap

In each of the following questions, one or more of the responses is/are correct. Choose the appropriate letter which indicates the correct version.
   A   if 1 only is correct
   B   if 3 only is correct
   C   if 1 and 2 are correct
   D   if 1, 2 and 3 are correct

7. Which of the following are reasons for the increase in the commercial use of air transport in recent years?
   1) Advantage of speed
   2) Lower packaging and insurance costs
   3) Development in planes and airport facilities

8. In which of the following methods of transport are containers widely used?
   1) Sea
   2) Rail
   3) Canals

RECENT EXAMINATION QUESTIONS

Marks

NISEC 1988 GCSE BUSINESS STUDIES SPECIMEN PAPER I
1. Name 3 advantages of transporting goods by container.   3

LEAG 1988 GCSE BUSINESS STUDIES SPECIMEN PAPER I
2. A brick manufacturer wishes to assess road and rail transport as means of delivering loads of bricks to customers nation-wide. Use the graph below and your own knowledge to answer the following matters raised by the manufacturer.
   a) i)   Which is the cheaper method of transport for a 100 mile journey, A or B?   1
      ii) Which is the cheaper method of transport for journeys over 250 miles, A or B?   1
      iii) At what distance does it cost the same by A and B?   1
   b) What is the difference in *total* cost between A and B for a journey of 200 miles?   2
   c) Identify the form of transport called A and state your reasons.   3
   d) Identify the form of transport called B and state your reasons.   3

The graph shows the cost per mile for various journeys up to 350 miles, by two forms of transport, A and B. The costs refer to the transportation of bulky and very heavy loads.

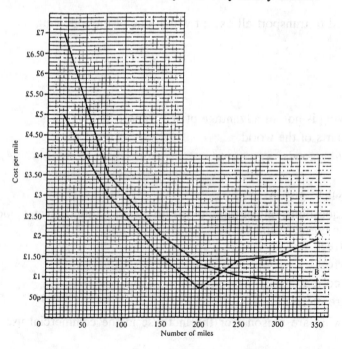

ASSIGNMENT

1. Why might a business send goods by air despite the fact that it is most expensive?

2. How do containers reduce the cost of transporting goods?

3. Give reasons as to which form of transport a business is likely to use for each of the following:
   a) Expensive jewellery from Glasgow to Bristol
   b) Coal from Newcastle to an electrical power station near London
   c) 200 gallons of milk from Leicester to Coventry

4. Assume that you want to transport the following from London. Using each method once only, choose the most appropriate method of transport for the following items:

Article/Item		Destination
a)	Book	Edinburgh
b)	50 school pupils	Calais
c)	Wardrobe	Oxford
d)	Cheque	Belfast
e)	Heavy steel ingots	Manchester
f)	Urgent medical supplies	Paris
g)	Small packet of jewellery	Hawaii
h)	Consignment of tomatoes	Birmingham
i)	2 large heavy machines	Rotterdam
j)	250 cruise passengers	Mediterranean

Method of Transport		Most appropriate for Article/Item
1)	Letter post	....
2)	Parcel post	....
3)	British Rail	....
4)	Roll-on/Roll-off Ferry	....
5)	Furniture removers	....
6)	Chartered Aircraft	....
7)	Scheduled Airline	....
8)	Liner	....
9)	Tramp	....
10)	Road Haulier	....

5. A small computer company has successfully negotiated its first export order for a quantity of high value components for an engineering firm. Identify the delivery problems faced by the company and explain how these can be overcome.

15. Consumer Protection

1.   We have seen in earlier chapters that there are many methods which businesses may use to increase the sale of their goods or services. In this chapter we shall look at how these methods can affect consumers and the various ways in which they are protected from unfair trading practices.

DEFINITION

2.   Consumer protection is the term used to describe all the efforts on the part of the Government and consumer organisations to protect consumers against inferior goods and services, and misleading advertising.

THE NEED FOR CONSUMER PROTECTION

3.   The vast majority of businesses are run honestly and do not attempt to deceive or mislead consumers. Their goods work properly and if problems arise they offer a service to put them right with the minimum of fuss and bother. However, unfortunately, some traders are dishonest. These people will often mislead consumers about the goods or services which they provide and some even sell faulty or dangerous products. Others may give incorrect weight or quantity or falsely describe goods in advertising or on labels. Therefore, some form of consumer protection is necessary in these situations.

FORMS OF CONSUMER PROTECTION

4.   This protection is provided in four main ways through:
   a)   Government legislation
   b)   Consumer bodies and organisations
   c)   Labelling and standards
   d)   Professional and Trade Associations – Codes of Practice

GOVERNMENT LEGISLATION

5.   The Government has passed many laws to protect consumers from unfair trading. The following is an outline of the main ones.

6.   **Sale of Goods Act 1979**

When customers buy something in a shop they enter into a legal <u>contract</u> and the retailer by law has to fulfil certain obligations. The goods sold must:

   *   Be FIT FOR THE PURPOSE for which they are generally used. For example, glue sold to mend china must do just that.

   *   Be of MERCHANTABLE QUALITY, considering the price and description. For example, someone buying a new pair of shoes would obviously not expect the soles to come away from the uppers soon after they started wearing them. Whilst on the other hand, a pair of shoes costing £29 would be expected to wear better than a pair costing £9.99.

   *   MEET THE DESCRIPTION applied to them. For example, a '1986 1300 cc car' must be a car of that year and capacity.

7.   If any of these conditions are not met then the retailer has broken the contract and customers have the right to return goods and receive compensation. This may be a part or full cash refund, repair or exchange.

8.   *N.B.* Although many retailers offer credit notes when faulty goods are returned, customers do not have to accept them. They are entitled to their money back.

9.   This Act further states that a customer's rights cannot be taken away by any guarantee they sign or by any notices in a shop saying 'No money refunded'. It is the responsibility of the retailer (not the manufac-

turer) to ensure that any problems with faulty goods are put right. The law applies to both new and secondhand goods but does not cover private sales.

10. *N.B.*
   a) This Act replaced the earlier Sale of Goods Act 1893 and Supply of Goods (Implied Terms) Act 1973.
   b) The Supply of Goods and Services Act 1982 extended the provisions of The Sale of Goods Act to include services such as the work carried out by a plumber, builder or television repairer.

11.

"Yes madam I know I said it was unbreakable but . . ."

12. Food Safety Act 1990

This Act consolidated and enhanced earlier legislation which make it an offence to sell food which is unfit for human consumption.

13. Key points:

* Most pre-packed foods must have a label listing the *ingredients in descending order* of weight i.e. what there is most of at the top and least at the bottom.
* Certain foods must have *minimum contents* before they can be sold by that name e.g. jam must contain at least 20% of the named fruit; sausage at least 50% meat.
* Protection against the use of harmful *additives, flavourings and colourings* in food.
* Minimum standards for food *hygiene* and cleanliness.

14. Weights and Measures (Consolidation) Act 1985

This Act updates several others which go back to 1878.

15. Key points:

* *Inspectors* to check that weights and measures are accurate and standardised. They visit trade premises like shops, dairies, public houses and garages to check the equipment used, e.g. scales and petrol pumps.
* *Penalties* for traders who give short weight or measure.

* Certain goods must be sold in '*prescribed quantities*', e.g. milk can only be sold in ⅓ pint, ½ pint or multiples of 1/2 pint containers.
* All pre-packed foods must have the *net weight* (i.e. weight of contents) clearly marked on the label.

16. **Prices Acts 1974 and 1975**

These Acts enable the Government to control the price of food and other household necessities.

17. **Key points:**

* Certain goods must have *prices clearly displayed* e.g. price lists in public houses and cafeterias.
* *Unit pricing* was introduced for certain food products to enable consumers to compare prices i.e. prices expressed by reference to some specified weight e.g. meat £1.78lb, this piece 94p.
* All pre-packed foods must be stamped with a latest '*sell-by*' date.

18.

Unit Pricing

Sell-by Date

19. **Trade Descriptions Acts 1968 and 1972**

These Acts make it an offence to falsely describe goods or services offered for sale e.g. if a retailer says that a jumper is 'made of wool', 'unshrinkable', or 'handmade' or cutlery is made from 'Sheffield stainless steel' then these statements must be true.

20. **Key points:**

* *Fines or imprisonment* for law breakers.
* Applies to *verbal or written descriptions*, including advertisements.
* Includes *secondhand* goods and *private sales*.
* Under the 1972 Act most imported goods must be marked with their *country of origin* e.g. Made in Hong Kong, Made in Taiwan, etc.
* Some kinds of *false price reductions* are also an offence e.g. if a retailer crosses out £2.99 on a price ticket and adds £2.50 as the new price, then the goods must have been sold at the higher price for at least 28 consecutive days during the previous 6 months. If not, then this must be made clear.

21.

22. Unsolicited Goods and Services Act 1971

This makes it an offence for any trader to demand payment for goods which people have not ordered, for example records, books or Christmas Cards, which are sent through the post. If someone receives such goods, then he may write to the sender asking for them to be collected within thirty days. If not collected then legally they can be kept. Alternatively, he can do nothing and if they are not collected after 6 months keep them.

23. Fair Trading Act 1973

This Act set up an *Office of Fair Trading* (OFT), run by a Director General to continuously review consumer affairs and consumer credit.

24. The OFT aids consumers by:

* Publishing all kinds of *information*, most of which is issued free of charge, advising people of their rights and where they can go for help if problems arise.

* Encouraging Trade Associations to establish voluntary *Codes of Practice* to safeguard and promote the interests of consumers. (See 56).

* Enforcing the law by *prosecuting traders* who persistently commit offences.

* *Issuing credit licences* to approved traders who wish to offer this facility to their customers.

* *Encouraging competition* in business and closely monitoring the formation of monopolies, mergers and restrictive practices.

25.

Your rights as a shopper

The law says a shop must sell goods which are:

1 Of merchantable quality – that means reasonably fit for their normal purpose. Bear in mind the price and how the item was described. Goods should not be broken, or damaged, and should work properly.

2 Fit for any particular purpose you make known to the shop – they should do what you were told they would.

3 As described – on the package, or by the salesman or on a sign.

What happens next?

If goods are faulty you can claim compensation from the shop – the law says it should be money. How much will depend on how serious the fault is and how soon you tell the shop. If you've had the item some time and had considerable use from it, you can hardly expect all your money back. The shop doesn't have to offer anything except cash compensation, but if you and the shop agree, you may accept a replacement or a free repair.

A credit note does not have to be accepted as a form of compensation.

"No Refund" notices cannot take away your legal rights, even in sales.

Customer note

If something's wrong –

* Tell the shop at once.
* Ask for the manager.
* Be polite and calm – shops are usually willing to help.
* Take along your bill or receipt – it's not essential, but it helps.

Be Fair!

Customers must play fair with the shopkeeper – he has rights too!

You are not entitled to anything if you:

* simply change your mind about the purchase.
* buy clothes, try them for size in the shop and later decide they don't fit.
* damage the item – by not following the instructions, or using it for a purpose it wasn't meant for.
* were told about a fault, or were able to examine the item yourself and you should have seen it.
* did not buy the item yourself.

If you and the shop can't solve the problem, get help from a Citizens Advice Bureau or a Trading Standards Department.

"The above is an extract from the Office of Fair Trading leaflet 'Shops and Shoppers'. The leaflet is no longer available but 'How to put things right' (England and Wales), 'Dear Shopper in Scotland' and 'Dear Shopper in Northern Ireland' look at shopping law in a little more detail."

26. Consumer Credit Acts 1974, 1980, 1985.

These Acts, which incorporate the earlier Hire Purchase and Money Lenders Acts, aim to protect consumers by ensuring 'truth in lending' and preventing mis-leading advertising about interest rates.

27. Key points:

* *All businesses concerned with credit or hire transactions must be licenced by the OFT.* This includes not only money lenders, finance houses and equipment hire companies, but also organisations such as employment agencies concerned with the hiring of temporary staff.

* *Borrowers must be advised of the true cost of interest on any loan known as the annual percentage rate (APR).* This enables consumers to compare the interest rate charged by different lenders. For example, a credit offer with an APR of 26% is cheaper than another with an APR of 32%.

* *The borrower must be given an agreement to sign for all forms of credit*, which must show the cash price, credit charges, repayments and the terms for cancelling the agreement.

* Consumers are entitled to a *'cooling-off'* period in which to change their mind and cancel any credit agreement which is signed off trade premises, for example in their own home. Credit agreements signed on trade premises such as a shop or garage cannot usually be cancelled.

* *Individuals are entitled to know what information credit reference agencies give to credit companies about their financial position.* These agencies keep records of consumers who have failed to pay their debts or defaulted on credit agreements and are thus considered bad risks.

* *Protection for consumers who fail to keep up their payments.* Provided that at least one-third of the total price has been paid then the goods can only be taken back by an Order of a County Court which will only be made after a consumer has been given a reasonable chance to pay.

28. *N.B.* Credit actions *not* covered by the Acts include:

a) House mortgages
b) Transactions of less than £50 or more £15,000
c) Credit given to companies

29. **Comparing the cost of credit.**

MONTEGO 1.3			
Cash price	£5932.95	Final Payment	£2875.00
Deposit	£567.39	*(Not payable if car returned)*	
24 Monthly Payments *(Weekly Equivalent)*	£189.13 *£43.65)*	Total Amount Payable*	£7981.51
APR 26.2%			

30. **Unfair Contract Terms Act 1977**

This Act prevents traders from refusing to accept responsibility for specific events by using 'small-print' exclusion clauses or notices. It allows consumers to claim compensation for negligence or breach of contract, for example, if a garage scratches your car or a dry cleaner damages your clothing.

31.

> **LOOK SMART CLEANERS**
> All goods are cleaned
> at your own risk. No
> responsibility accepted
> for loss or damage
> however caused.

Under the Act this notice has no effect.

32. This Act applies to a wide variety of trades including laundries, dry cleaners, carpet cleaners, television repairers, central heating installers, burglar alarm renters, car hire firms, garages, car parks, cloakrooms, warehouses, cinemas, theatres, sports grounds, holiday camps and holiday package tour operators.

33. **Consumer Protection Act 1987**

This Act consolidated and enhanced previous legislation concerned with the sale of dangerous goods.

34. **Key points:**

* Certain goods (e.g. bleach, toilet cleaners, medicines) must be marked with *warnings* (including symbols) and safety *advice* (e.g. first aid).

* *Safety regulations* covering many goods including heaters, toys, nightwear and cooking utensils.

* *Damages* can be claimed against the suppliers of defective products which cause death or injury.

* The Act also made it an offence to give misleading *price indications*.

35.

Saabs recalled

Saab 9000 Turbo 16 cars are being recalled for re-designed bonnet-retaining catches to be fitted, the company said today. Some 720 right-hand-drive models are affected, up to and including chassis number CG 1007702.

Blanket warning

TRADERS are being urged to take 'Lynnat' baby blankets off the market after safety experts warned that fluff from them could choke a small child.

Timely warning

WRIST-WATCH lighters which throw off a four-inch flame have been condemned by Manchester's trading standards officer.

CONSUMER BODIES AND ORGANISATIONS

36. The Office of Fair Trading itself cannot take up individual consumer complaints about unfair trading practices. Instead it provides information and advice for consumers and issues many publications which are available free from Local Authority Trading Standards Departments, Consumer Advice Centres, Citizens Advice Bureaux and Nationalised Industry Consumer Councils. It is the role of these bodies and other organisations to help to make the consumer protection laws effective.

37.

MR CONSUMER

goes back to the shop with a complaint

if still dissatisfied he can go to

| LOCAL AUTHORITY TRADING STANDARDS DEPARTMENT | CONSUMER ADVICE CENTRE (where these exist) | CITIZENS ADVICE BUREAUX | NATIONALISED INDUSTRY CONSUMER COUNCIL |

38. **Local Authority Consumer Departments**

All Local Councils have a Trading Standards or Consumer Protection Department. This will deal with consumer complaints about faulty goods or services and enforce the consumer protection laws when necessary. Complaints about food which is unfit to eat or the cleanliness of places where it is sold, such as shops or restaurants, are dealt with by the Environmental Health Department.

39. Some Local Authorities have opened **Consumer Advice Centres** to help consumers to decide what to buy and to deal with complaints. In Northern Ireland consumer complaints are handled by the Area Trading Standards Office of the Department of Commerce.

40. Citizens Advice Bureaux (CAB)

There are at least 700 CAB's throughout the country. These are voluntary agencies financed mainly by Local Authority grants. They give free, confidential advice on any sort of problem – personal, health, legal and social, including consumer complaints.

Nationalised Industry Consumer Councils

41. If a consumer has a complaint about goods or services supplied by a nationalised industry, and it is not settled satisfactorily, then he can go to the appropriate consumer council about it. For example:

Coal (Domestic Coal Consumers Council – DCCC)

Post Office (Post Office Users National Council – POUNC)

These councils also make recommendations to the Government on any matters which affect consumers, for example POUNC is campaigning for the return of Sunday postal collections and a special 'cheap' rate for Christmas post.

OTHER CONSUMER ORGANISATIONS AND PRESSURE GROUPS

42. There are several other independent bodies which also provide help to consumers and therefore help to maintain and improve trading standards. They act as pressure groups, so called because they can represent a point of view to the Government to try and influence its policies. Some well known pressure groups include the Consumers Association, National Consumer Council and local Consumer groups.

43. Consumers Association

This is a non-profit making organisation which was set up in 1957. It aims to help consumers to get a fair deal by testing products and providing reports comparing the standards, performance and value of different brands and therefore helping people to decide which is the best buy. This information is published in the monthly 'WHICH' magazine or its satellites. The satellites – 'Holiday Which?' and 'Gardening from Which?' are published quarterly.

The Consumers Association receives its income solely from members subscriptions (ie money paid for the magazines) and from the sale of its other publications. Examples include the 'Which? Way to Complain', 'The Good Food Guide' and the 'Which? Software Guide'.

44.

45. National Consumer Council

This was set up in 1975, and although financed by the Government, it operates as an independent body to represent consumers. Its main function is to put forward consumer views to the Government, Office of Fair Trading, or Industry. The Government may also consult it on policies or proposals affecting consumers, transport, education and housing as well as goods and services. The Council also represents consumers on various Government and other bodies, including international organisations, and makes studies of various consumer issues.

46. Local Consumer Groups

The first of these voluntary groups was formed in Oxford in 1961 and there are now well over fifty throughout the country. Each group promotes consumer interests by carrying out surveys of goods and services in its area with the aim of maintaining and improving standards. Groups publish their reports and campaign for improvements where necessary.

47. The *National Federation of Consumer Groups* was founded in 1963 to co-ordinate local groups by circulating information and advice between them.

LABELLING AND STANDARDS

48. In addition to the legal protection and consumer organisations which provide information and advisory services, there are also many other bodies which help consumers in particular ways, for example, about the design, safety or efficiency of products. Most of these are financed and run by the industries themselves. Some of the main organisations are as follows.

49. British Standards Institution (BSI)

The BSI is an independent body, financed by the Government, which tests the safety, quality and reliability of goods. Products which reach the specifications laid down are awarded the BSI Kitemark or Safety Mark which manufacturers usually display on the goods.

50. British Electrotechnical Approvals Board (BEAB)

BEAB tests domestic electrical appliances (like hair dryers, washing machines, vacuum cleaners) and approves them, if they meet the standards of safety which it lays down. The seal of approval is not a guarantee of quality or performance but merely confirms that the product meets certain safety standards.

51. Gas Council's Kitemark

All appliances bought from the gas showrooms bear this mark which shows that each article has been thoroughly tested for safety, performance and durability, for example cookers and fires.

52. Teltags

These are the result of the National Consumer Council's recommendation to manufacturers to label their products, for example electric kettles and carpets, with factual and useful information. The scheme started in 1967 and the information given includes details of a products composition and performance and how it stood up to an impartial test carried out by the BSI.

53. Design Council

This is a Government sponsored body set up to promote the improvement of design in the products made by British firms. The Design Council selects products for display in its centres in London and other major cities on the grounds of their fitness for purpose, appearance, quality, ease of maintenance and value for money. The maker of an article selected may display the Design Council label on its products.

54. Standards Labels

| Design Council | British Electrotechnical Approvals Board | BSI Kitemark | BSI Safety Mark | |

PROFESSIONAL AND TRADE ASSOCIATIONS – CODES OF PRACTICE

55. Professional and trade associations are formed when firms in the same industry join together to protect their interests and deal with common problems. Associations may establish common standards in an industry and represent members by acting as a spokesman to the Government when new legislation, taxation or matters which affect them are being considered.

56. As mentioned earlier, the Office of Fair Trading encourages these various associations to draw up voluntary Codes of Practice aimed at improving the standards of goods and services. One well known example is the *Association of British Travel Agents (ABTA)*, which operates a Code of Practice covering booking conditions and surcharges for holidays. It has also established a fund to compensate consumers if they book a holiday through an ABTA member firm which goes out of business. Other examples include the *Motor Agents Association*, which represents car dealers and handles consumer problems about buying cars, servicing or repairs, the *Advertising Standards Authority* which issues a Code of Practice for advertising: and the *Retail Trading Standards Association (RTSA)* whose members include all types of retailers, manufacturers, advertising agencies and newspaper publishers.

57. The symbols of some well-known associations.

Mail Order Protection

Holidays and Travel

Motor Cars

Shopping by post?
Play it safe MOPS

If you reply to a cash with order advertisement in a national newspaper or colour supplement your money may be safeguarded by our Mail Order Protection Scheme. All participating advertisers display our symbol in their advertisements, or the initials MOPS.
 MOPS guarantees that you will get your money back if a member advertiser stops trading and does not deliver your order or refund your payment.
 Some categories of advertising are not covered by the scheme. For full details please send a stamped and addressed envelope to:
**The National Newspaper
Mail Order Protection Scheme (MOPS)
16 Tooks Court, London EC4A 1LB**
Play it safe – look for the symbol

Hotels and Catering

Shoe Repairs

SUMMARY

58. a) Consumers need to be protected against unfair trading practices.

b) This protection is provided through Government legislation, consumer bodies and organisations, labelling and standards, and professional and trade associations.

c) The most important laws which have been passed are the Sale of Goods Act 1979, Food Safety Act 1990, Weights and Measures Act 1985, Prices Acts 1974 and 1975, Trade Descriptions Acts 1968 and 1972, Fair Trading Act 1973 (which set up the Office of Fair Trading), Consumer Credit Act 1974, Unfair Contract Terms Act 1977 and the Consumer Protection Act 1987.

d) All these laws are enforced by Local Authority Trading Standards Departments or Environmental Health Department in the case of food complaints.

e) If a consumer needs help or advice he can also go to a Consumer Advice Centre, Citizens Advice Bureau or Consumer Council of a Nationalised Industry. Alternatively, he could contact the Consumers Association, National Consumer Council, a local Consumers Group or relevant professional or trade association.

f) Consumers can also help to protect themselves by buying goods which carry recognised safety standard labels including the BSI Kitemark, BEAB Seal of Approval, Gas Council Kitemark, Teltags or the Design Council label.

REVIEW QUESTIONS

Answers can be found in the paragraphs shown.

1. What is meant by consumer protection? (2)

2. Why is it necessary? (3)

3. List the 4 main types of consumer protection. (4)

4. Briefly outline the main provisions of the:
    a) Sale of Goods Act 1979 (6-10)
    b) Trade Descriptions Act 1968 (19-21)
    c) Consumer Credit Act 1974 (26-29)

5. If you look at the list of ingredients on a tin of mixed vegetables, how would you know which was the main ingredient? (13)

6. What are the main functions of the Office of Fair Trading? (23-25)

7. Explain what you understand by:
    a) Unsolicited Goods (22)
    b) Unit Pricing (17)

8. Which body is responsible locally for enforcing consumer protection? (38)

9. Outline briefly the work of a Citizens Advice Bureau. (40)

10. If you could not resolve a problem over your electricity bill, to which organisation could you go for help and advice? (41)

11. From what source does the Consumers Association get its funds? (43)

12. Name 3 organisations which exist to help shoppers choose the best value for money when buying goods or services. (42-47)

13. In what ways are manufacturers encouraged to produce well-designed goods? (48-53)

14. What are Codes of Practice? (24,56)

15. What do the following initials stand for? (23,27,41,49,56)
    OFT   APR   POUNC   BSI   ABTA

EXAMINATION PRACTICE QUESTIONS

	Marks

1. If a customer buys something in a sale is he still protected by the Sale of Goods Act if the goods are faulty? Explain your answer. **3**

2. What, by law, must a trader do before offering credit to his customers? **1**

3. a) Choose any 3 Acts of Parliament which have been passed to protect consumers and outline the importance of each. **6**
    b) Name one other way in which the state provides protection for consumers. **2**

4. Which organisation was set up in 1973 to look after consumer affairs and consumer credit? **1**

MULTIPLE CHOICE/COMPLETION

1. Which of the following can the Director General of the Office of Fair Trading *NOT* do?
    a) Encourage trade associations to issue Codes of Practice
    b) Recommend changes in the law to protect consumers
    c) Control the prices at which goods are sold
    d) Prosecute traders who persistently commit offences

2. The Trade Descriptions Act 1968 requires that retailers:
    a) Offer goods for sale at the lowest possible prices
    b) Advertise their goods on a regular basis
    c) Offer customers a wide choice of goods
    d) Provide accurate information about goods, prices and services

3. Which of the following is *NOT* able to help with consumer problems?
    a) Department of Health and Social Security
    b) Trading Standards Department
    c) Environmental Health Department
    d) Citizen's Advice Bureau

4. The Association of British Travel Agents is an example of a:
    a) Trade Association
    b) Nationalised Industry
    c) Chamber of Commerce
    d) Public Company

In each of the following questions, one or more of the responses is/are correct. Choose the appropriate letter which indicates the correct version.

    A   if 1 only is correct
    B   if 3 only is correct
    C   if 1 and 2 are correct
    D   if 1, 2 and 3 are correct

5. The 5 day 'cooling off' period applies to credit agreements where goods
    1) Are ordered through the post
    2) Are purchased in a shop
    3) Are purchased in someone's own home

6. The Consumer Credit Act 1974 requires that:
    1) Consumers must be advised of the true annual percentage rate of interest
    2) Approved lenders must be licenced by the Office of Fair Trading
    3) Consumers are allowed to borrow any amount which they require

RECENT EXAMINATION QUESTIONS

NEA JUNE 1990 GCSE COMMERCE

1. You are considering buying a Hi-Fi. Study the two advertisements shown below.

CREDIT SALE

instant credit
STORE CARD

APR
33.7% available
variable

Hi-Fi
£400
cash price

**You could
own this today using
our instant credit store card.**

**HI FI — pay just £17 a
month for 36 months**

HIRE PURCHASE

HIRE PURCHASE

100 WEEK CREDIT TERMS
AVAILABLE TO PERSONS
OVER THE AGE OF 18

APR
24.9%

Hi-Fi
£400
(CASH PRICE)

1st payment of £19.27
then 99 weekly payments of
£4.75

Total amount payable:
£489.52

Marks

a) Compare the two methods of buying on credit and explain which of the two you would choose to buy the Hi-Fi.

12

b) The Hi-Fi system which you buy turns out to be faulty and will only play your LP's, not your singles. Describe the action you would take when dealing with the faulty Hi-Fi.

4

c) Giving reasons, explain how you would reply to a shopkeeper who says:
   i) 'You will have to take it back to the manufacturer.'

2

   ii) 'Look at the notice in the window — it says "No Refunds".'

2

   iii) 'That Hi-Fi was in the Sale, you will just have to keep it.'

2

d) Name the following label and describe how it might be useful when buying goods.

4

e) Explain how the work of the Consumers' Association could help you to make a choice between different Hi-Fi systems.

6

ASSIGNMENT

1. State which law is being broken in each of the following situations:
   a) A company demands payment for Christmas cards sent through the post but not ordered by the customer.
   b) A coat which the salesman claimed was made of wool but is in fact polyester.
   c) A customer purchases 2 lb of carrots but on weighing them at home finds she has only received 1 lb 14 ozs.
   d) A customer buys a 'King size' continental quilt which only fits a double bed.
   e) You agree to buy Central Heating on credit from a salesman who calls at your home but the company refuses to let you cancel the agreement the following day.

2. Nita Patel has recently purchased a cassette player from a local store. However, after just one week it does not work properly but unfortunately she has lost her receipt.
Advise Nita on what action she should take and what her legal rights are in this situation.

3. John Williams saw the following advertisement in a shop window.

'Reconditioned bicycles for sale'.

Bargain prices from £25 – £30

Sold as seen

John needed a bike and he could not resist a bargain. Therefore he withdrew his savings from the Post Office and purchased a nice looking model for £30. On the way home the brake cable broke causing John to fall off and tear his trousers. What legal rights, if any, does John have? What should he do in this situation?

16. Business Documents

1. The buying and selling of goods between firms is called a transaction. This often involves considerable paperwork. Therefore special documents are frequently used in order to make the process quicker and more efficient. Each of these documents has a particular purpose in passing information between buyers and sellers and although they may vary in style and layout from firm to firm, the basic principles are the same. This chapter explains the purpose of each of these documents and when they are used. Finally it outlines the documents used in overseas trade.

DOCUMENTS USED IN A BUSINESS TRANSACTION

2. Enquiry

When a business wishes to buy goods it will frequently send an enquiry to several firms asking them if they can supply the goods and requesting details of the price, quality and delivery dates.

3. The enquiry may be by letter or on a specially printed form, verbally to a sales representative when he calls, over the telephone or at a trade exhibition.

4. Names and addresses of suppliers may be obtained from:
  * Catalogues
  * Price Lists
  * Telephone Directory – Yellow Pages
  * Trade Directories
  * Trade Journals, for example 'The Grocer', 'The Hardware Trade Journal', 'Retail Confectioner', 'Shoe and Leather News' etc.

5.

```
                          ENQUIRY

                      R Fisher & Company
                          'Pet Place'
                          Martin Street
                    SHEFFIELD    S30 5AP

   Tel:  56353                    Directors:  R Fisher
                                              M E White
   Ref:  RSW/AED                              L Taylor

   TO:  The Albion Supply Co Ltd   Date:      21 July 199
        Ashfield Avenue
        West Street Corner
        MIDDLESBROUGH
        MR16 3AL

   Dear Sirs
   ENQUIRY NO 76139/S
   We are interested in purchasing the following and would be pleased to receive your best price
   and delivery:

   100 Cases 'Happy Pet' Dog Food      400 gm size
    25 Cases 'Contented' Cat Food      400 gm size
    50 Cases 'Purr' Cat Food           400 gm size
   Yours faithfully


      R.S. Warren.

   R S Warren
   Office Manager
```

6. Quotation

The firms approached will usually reply by giving a quotation for the goods required and these are then compared to see which is the most favourable.

7.   The quotation will give details of the price, any **TRADE** or **CASH** discount allowed, when delivery can be made, and any *terms* or special conditions under which the goods will be sold. (see paragraph 10)

8.

QUOTATION

Directors:

K Jones
K Moore
S Wickstead

Telephone 88226

THE ALBION SUPPLY CO LTD
Ashfield Avenue
West Street Corner
MIDDLESBROUGH
Cleveland   MR16 3AL

Your Ref: RSW/AED
Our Ref: DC/BA

23 July 199

Messrs R Fisher & Co
'Pet Place'
Martin Street
SHEFFIELD
S30 5AP

Dear Sirs

Quotation No 48973

Thank you for your enquiry no 76139/B dated 21 July for dog and cat food. We have pleasure in quoting as follows:

100 Cases 'Happy Pet' Dog Food   400 gm   – £5.45 per case delivered
 25 Cases 'Contented' Cat Food   400 gm   – £5.75 per case delivered
 50 Cases 'Purr' Cat Food   400 gm   – £6.00 per case delivered

Less 20% Trade Discount
Plus 15% VAT

Delivery – by our own van 2 weeks after receipt of order

Terms – 5% Cash Discount for payment within 28 days

We trust our offer will be of interest to you and look forward to receiving your order.

Yours faithfully

D. Coyne

D Coyne
Sales Manager

---

9.   General enquiries, not about a specific item, might be dealt with by sending a price list, some descriptive leaflets, or a general catalogue instead of a quotation.

10. *N.B.* A firms buyer or purchasing officer must be familiar with certain terms and conditions used by a supplier which affect delivery and packing costs. These can include:

   a)   Carriage Paid – the price includes the cost of delivery
   b)   Carriage Forward/ex Works – the price quoted does not include the cost of delivery
   c)   Returnable Empties – firms who supply goods in expensive packing or containers, for example wooden crates, often make a charge for them. This is refunded if the containers are returned in good condition.

11. Trade Discount

This is a form of discount given by one firm to another for goods which are to be re-sold. For example, retailers usually receive trade discount from manufacturers and wholesalers. The amount of trade discount is deducted from the invoice for the goods and may vary with the quantity bought so that bigger discounts are often given for larger orders.

12. Cash Discount

To encourage prompt payment for goods bought, cash discount may be allowed provided that payment is made within a specified period of time, for example 28 days. Net Monthly Account on an invoice means that no cash discount is given.

13. Trade and Cash Discount Example

ABC Co Ltd bought £1000 worth of goods which were delivered on 1 August 19. .
Terms are 20% trade discount and 5% within 30 days.

Total cost	=	£1000 less 20% trade discount
	=	£1000 less £200
	=	£800
Cash discount	=	5% of £800
	=	£40

Therefore amount paid = £760

14. Estimates

An estimate differs from a quotation because it is used for items where no price list exists. It therefore deals with enquiries for special items that must be made instead of supplied from normal stock. It will be based on the cost of materials and labour, and the other expenses involved in making the item. Estimates are often used for building work where each job is different and therefore no standard price applies.

15. Order

From the quotations or estimates received the best terms will be selected and an order placed for the goods. The best terms are dependent not only on price, but also factors such as trade discount, cash discount, quality and delivery time.

16. Goods should be described in detail usually repeating the wording of the quotations or estimate to avoid any confusion. The quantity, price, discounts, sizes, place and date of delivery and all relevant information should be included.

17.

ORDER

R FISHER & COMPANY
'Pet Place'
Martin Street
SHEFFIELD   S30 5AP

TO: The Albion Supply Co Ltd   ORDER NO A245
Ashfield Avenue
West Street Corner
MIDDLESBROUGH
M16 3AL

Please supply: Date: 24 July 199

QUANTITY	DESCRIPTION	SIZE	COST
100 Cases	'Happy Pet' Dog Food	400 gm	£5.45 per case
25 Cases	'Contented' Cat Food	400 gm	£5.75 per case
50 Cases	'Purr' Cat Food	400 gm	£6.00 per case

Delivery Instructions:

Prompt delivery   SIGNED..*P. Ward*.......
Carriage Paid   for R Fisher & Company

18. Acknowledgement of Order

Many firms will acknowledge the order in writing to say that it has been received and is being attended to. Also, if the goods are not available immediately, then a date of delivery can be given.

19. Advice Note

If goods are likely to be in transit for a while then often an advice note is sent to tell a customer that the goods ordered are on their way. It gives details of the date of despatch, quantity and description of the goods, and how they have been sent, for example British Rail or Parcel Post.

20. Delivery or Despatch Note

When goods are delivered in the suppliers *own* vehicle the driver has a delivery note which gives details of the quantity and description of the goods and states the number of packages.

21. The customer can check the items delivered against this note so that any errors can be quickly spotted. This is particularly useful when orders are delivered in several parts. When checked the delivery note, which is in duplicate, is signed and one copy kept as proof of delivery.

22. Consignment Note

These are used when a firm does not deliver goods itself but sends them by road or rail transport. Details on it include:

* Weight and description of goods
* Delivery address
* Who pays for the carriage
* Whether the goods are sent at owners risk

When the goods are delivered they must be signed for to acknowledge receipt, with a note made of any damages or shortages.

23. Invoice

An invoice is sent by the supplier to his customer when goods have been bought on credit. It includes:

* A description of the goods
* The quantity supplied
* The price charged
* The total cost

24. Special terms such as cash discount are usually shown on the invoice. Trade Discount (if any) is deducted and VAT and carriage charges (if any) are added.

25. Many invoices show the abbreviation E and OE (Errors and Omissions Excepted) on the bottom left hand corner. This indicates that if a mistake is made on the invoice, the firm is not bound by it and is able to correct it later.

N.B. British firms registered for VAT must show their VAT number on all invoices.

26. Pro-Forma Invoice

A pro-forma invoice is similar to a quotation and is used as follows:

a) For goods sent on approval or on a sale or return basis. Mail Order catalogue firms use this type of invoice.

b) Where goods must be paid for before they are despatched or when they are sold cash on delivery.

27.

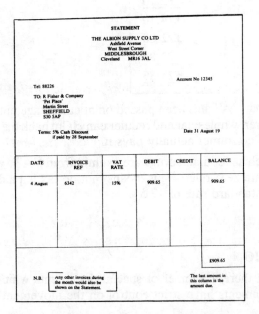

INVOICE

THE ALBION SUPPLY CO LTD
Ashfield Avenue
West Street Corner
MIDDLESBROUGH
Cleveland   MR16 3AL

INVOICE NO 6342

TO: R Fisher & Company
'Pet Place'
Martin Street
SHEFFIELD
S30 5AP

Date -4 August 199

VAT REGISTRATION NO
112 5965 85

Quantity	Description		Price	VAT Amount	VAT Rate
100 Cases	'Happy Pet' Dog Food	400 gm	£5.45	£545.00	
25 Cases	'Contented' Cat Food	400 gm	£5.75	£143.75	
50 Cases	'Purr' Cat Food	400 gm	£6.00	£300.00	
				£988.75	
	Less Trade Discount 20%			£197.75	
				£791.00	£118.65	15%
	Plus VAT			£118.65	
	Total			£909.65	

Terms: 5% Cash Discount for payment by 14th of month following month of delivery

Your Order No A/245

Delivery: Carriage paid

Dated: 24 July 198

E & OE.

28. Statement of Account

Several invoices may be received during the month from the same supplier and therefore each invoice is not paid as it arrives, but one cheque is made out to settle the account.

29. This is done when the Monthly Statement comes. It shows the balance outstanding (amount owed) at the beginning of the month, adding any invoices or debit notes, and deducting any payments received, cash discount or credit notes. The balance at the end of the month is the amount owed and the statement is really a *request for payment* of the account.

30.

STATEMENT

THE ALBION SUPPLY CO LTD
Ashfield Avenue
West Street Corner
MIDDLESBROUGH
Cleveland   MR16 3AL

Account No 12345

Tel: 88226

TO: R Fisher & Company
'Pet Place'
Martin Street
SHEFFIELD
S30 5AP

Terms: 5% Cash Discount
if paid by 28 September

Date 31 August 19

DATE	INVOICE REF	VAT RATE	DEBIT	CREDIT	BALANCE
4 August	6342	15%	909.65		909.65
					£909.65

N.B. Any other invoices during the month would also be shown on the Statement.

The last amount in this column is the amount due.

31. **Credit Note**

A credit note is sent by a supplier to a customer to make an allowance which is deducted from the original invoice. This might happen where:

a) There is an overcharge on an invoice

b) Goods are lost in transit

c) Goods are returned as damaged, faulty, incorrect or short.

d) Empty packing cases or delivery pallets etc, which have been charged on the invoice, are returned.

Credit notes are usually printed in red to distinguish them from other documents.

32. **Debit Note**

Debit notes are sent to customers to notify them of an increase in the amount owed, since it is easier to send a separate document rather than alter the invoices and accounts. For example, a debit note may be sent to correct a mistake on an invoice or to charge for packing cases or delivery pallets which have not been returned.

VALUE ADDED TAX (VAT)

33. VAT is a tax on sales and is added to the selling price of most goods and services.

34. As the name suggests, it is a tax on the value added to items at all stages of manufacturing and distribution. For example, when a manufacturer sells goods to a wholesaler, VAT is added to the invoice. When the wholesaler sells the goods to retailers, he also adds VAT to his invoice. Finally, the retailer includes VAT in the selling price so it is the final consumer who actually pays it.

35. **Example**

Manufacturer sells a stool for	£8.00
Plus VAT at 17.5%	£1.40
Total selling price	£9.40
Wholesaler sells stool for	£12.00
Plus VAT at 17.5%	£2.10
Total selling price	£14.10
Retailer sells stool for	£22.00
Plus VAT at 17.5%	£3.85
Final price to customer	£25.85

36. Therefore it can be seen that VAT has been passed on at each stage until the stool is bought by the final customer. The manufacturer, wholesaler and retailer can claim back the VAT paid from the government. Therefore only the final consumer actually pays it.

37. Some 'essential' goods such as food and drugs are exempt from VAT, whilst others such as books, newspapers and heating fuels are zero-rated. This means that no tax is paid. However, the majority of goods sold carry VAT at the standard rate of 17.5%.

EXPORT DOCUMENTATION

38. When goods are exported there a number of special documents which must be used. These are important because most governments have strict control on the movement of goods and finance.

39. The main documents are:

   a) **The Bill of Lading**   This is used when goods are sent by sea. The shipping company provides a printed form which the cargo owner completes giving details of the:
   i)   Name of the ship and port of loading
   ii) Description of the cargo and its destination
   iii) Charges payable
   At the destination a copy of the Bill of Lading is presented by the importer to claim the goods at the dockside. It provides a 'document of title' (ie proof of ownership) which is important because the goods may have been sold whilst at sea.

   b) **The Air Consignment Note or Air Waybill**   This is used as a receipt for goods sent by air. However, it is not a 'document of title' like a Bill of Lading.

   c) **The Customs Declaration**   This is used for statistical purposes. It gives details of the type and value of the goods. This information is used in compiling the monthly trade figures.

   d) **The Shipping Note**   This document is sent to the Port Authorities when goods are delivered to the docks. It gives details of the goods, name of ship and destination port, and acts as a docks receipt.

   e) **The Certificate of Origin**   This provides evidence of where the goods were made. It is important because goods from some countries (for example outside the EC) will be subject to customs duties.

   f) **The Insurance Certificate**   This provides proof that goods have been insured against loss or damage during transit.

   g) **Consular Invoice**   Some countries require a copy of an export invoice which must be signed by the Consul in the importing country (see Chapter 3). This helps to speed up the customs procedures.

   h) **Import Licence**   Often this is required from the importing government before goods are allowed into the country. It can be used to enforce quotas.

   i) **Export Licence**   This must be obtained before certain types of goods are allowed out of the country, for example works of art or firearms.

SUMMARY

40. a)   In a typical business transaction any or all of the following special documents could be used to make it as quick and efficient as possible.
   i)   Enquiry – a request for information about goods
   ii)   Quotation – which will include details of any trade or cash discount
   iii) Estimate – used where no price list exists
   iv)   Order – a request for goods
   v)   Acknowledgement of the order – to say that it has been received
   vi)   Advice Note – stating when the goods are likely to be delivered
   vii) Delivery or Despatch Note – used when goods are sent by the supplier's own vehicle
   viii) Consignment Note – used when goods are sent by road or rail
   ix)   Invoice – which will take account of any debit or credit notes
   x)   Pro-forma Invoice – similar to an invoice but not charged to a customers account
   xi)   Statement of Account – a request for payment

   b)   VAT may well be added to an invoice, thus increasing the cost of the goods purchased. However, this is then added to the selling price so that in effect it is paid by the final consumer.

   c)   Special documents must be used for exported goods.

REVIEW QUESTIONS

Answers can be found in the paragraphs shown.

1.   List and briefly describe all the business documents which would be passed between a manufacturer (or wholesaler) and a retailer buying goods on credit, from the time the order is placed to when the account is settled. (2-28)

2.   What is the difference between a quotation and an estimate? (6-9, 14)

3.   Does discount increase or decrease the amount owed? (11)

4.   What is the meaning of Nett Monthly Account? (12)

5.   Explain the difference between an invoice and a pro-forma invoice. (23-27)

6.   What is the purpose of the Statement? (28-30)

7.   In what situations are credit notes used and what effect do they have on a customers account? (31)

8.   Which document would be made out to correct an undercharge on an invoice? (32)

9.   Briefly explain what you understand by VAT. (34-37)

10. What is the difference between goods which are exempt and those which are zero-rated? (34)

11. Why are special export documents needed? (38)

12. List 6 documents which are used when goods are exported. (39)

EXAMINATION PRACTICE QUESTIONS

Marks

1.   Name and explain the purpose of any 3 business documents. — 6

2.   The document sent in reply to an enquiry is called a . . . . — 1

3.   a)   How does trade discount differ from cash discount? — 2

    b)   If goods on an invoice totalling £200 were subject to 20% trade discount, what would be the actual cost? — 2

4.   If goods purchased for £300 were subject to 17.5% VAT, what would be the total cost? — 2

5.   If a retailer pays his supplier by cheque, is he entitled to receive cash discount? Give reasons for your answer. — 3

6.   Briefly describe the main differences between a Bill of Lading and an Air Consignment Note. — 2

MULTIPLE CHOICE/COMPLETION

1.   On which of the following items will VAT *not* be paid?
   a)   Petrol
   b)   Newspapers
   c)   Takeaway food
   d)   Alcohol

2.   If a trader buys goods for £1500 and receives 20% trade discount and 5% cash discount. The price he pays is:
   a)   £1140
   b)   £1200
   c)   £1425
   d)   £1125

3. A credit note might be sent:
   a) To persuade traders to buy in bulk
   b) If goods are undercharged
   c) If goods are damaged
   d) To encourage prompt payment

4. Trade discount is offered by sellers:
   a) To encourage prompt payment
   b) To encourage bulk buying
   c) As compensation for goods damaged during delivery
   d) To traders when goods are to be re-sold

5. To correct an undercharge on an invoice a firm would use a:
   a) Credit Transfer
   b) Statement
   c) Debit Note
   d) Credit Note

In the following question, one or more of the responses is/are correct. Choose the appropriate letter which indicates the correct version.

   A   if 1 only is correct
   B   if 3 only is correct
   C   if 1 and 2 only are correct
   D   if 1, 2 and 3 are correct

6. Which of the following items of information would be shown on an invoice?
   1) Terms
   2) Order Number
   3) Date

RECENT EXAMINATION QUESTIONS

	Marks

LEAG 1988 GCSE BUSINESS STUDIES SPECIMEN PAPER 2B SECTION A

1. A document used to notify the buyer of the amount due is an . . . .   ½

WJEC 1988 GCSE BUSINESS STUDIES SPECIMEN PAPER I

2. On 1 August a manufacturer sold 100 cases of biscuits to a wholesaler at £8 per case less 15% discount and an invoice was forwarded to the wholesaler together with the goods. A cash discount of 5% is allowed if payment is made within 7 days. The wholesaler paid the manufacturer on the 6 August by crossed cheque drawn on Barclays Bank plc, Llandudno.

   a) What is trade discount?   3
   b) Why does the manufacturer offer cash discount to the wholesaler?   2
   c) What is the total amount due to the manufacturer as shown on the invoice?   2
   d) How much did the wholesaler pay to settle the amount due on the 6 August?   2
   e) The wholesaler paid by crossed cheque. What is a "crossing"? Why is it important?   3
   f) On what type of banking account would the cheque have been drawn?   1
   g) Suggest 2 other means of payment offered by a commercial bank   2

ASSIGNMENT

1.   Imagine that you are working in the sales office of Trade Furnishing Ltd, 24 Mansfield Road, Worksop when a retail customer telephones to make an enquiry about some goods which she might order. She asks you to send a quotation giving any trade discount and terms.

    a)   What information should be included in the quotation?

    b)   Explain, using examples, what is meant by trade discount and terms.

2.   Why might a retailer decide to buy from a manufacturer whose quotation is not the lowest he has received? Give examples of the factors which he would consider besides the actual figure quoted?

3.   The customer decides to buy from Trades Furnishing Ltd. Copy and complete the invoice below using the following information:

K Richards & Co Ltd, 51 Nottingham Road, Mansfield supplied today with 5 wooden stools (catalogue No 421) at £10 each less 25% trade discount, and 10 padded chairs (catalogue No 135) at £15 each less 25% trade discount. The order number is X275. The terms are 5% 7 days, 2½% 14 days and net thereafter.

```
                         INVOICE              No _____

To: ...................        Date ...................
    ...................        VAT Registration No 143271
    ...................        Your Order No ...........
    ...................

| Cat No | Quantity | Description | £ Unit Price | £ Total Price |

                                        .................
                                        .................
                 17.5% VAT             .................
 Terms:                                 £
```

214

17. Business Finance

1.   This chapter is about the need for capital in a business, how it is obtained and how it is used. Later we look at the financial records which a business needs to keep and how these can be analysed to judge the efficiency and profitability of its affairs.

CAPITAL

2.   Capital is vital to the running of a business. It includes everything that is used in a business from the money invested to set it up to the equipment purchased to help run it.

NEED FOR FINANCE

3.   Most people who start up in business need capital, for example a window cleaner needs to buy a ladder, bucket and wash leather. A retailer needs shop premises and a stock of goods to sell, whilst a manufacturer needs a factory, machinery and raw materials as well as money to pay for wages, advertising, heat, light, transport etc before he can make and sell anything.

4.   If the business is successful more capital may be needed for a variety of reasons. For example it may be expanding and therefore needs to buy new premises or equipment. Or it may need to modernise its equipment and perhaps introduce computers or other forms of new technology in order to increase efficiency.

5.   **Factoring**

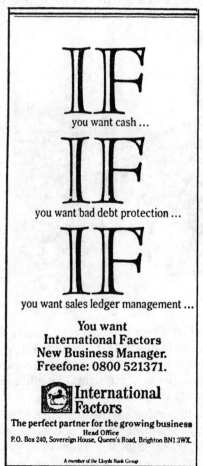

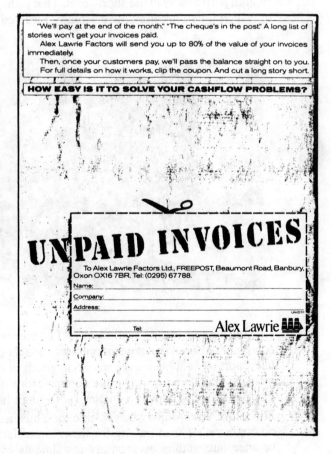

SOURCES OF CAPITAL

6. If a business wishes to raise finance there are a number of sources from which this might come.

   a) **The public**   As we saw in Chapter 6, in a small firm most of the capital required is provided by the businessman himself, possibly with the help of his family and friends or by borrowing from a bank. Whilst in companies finance can be obtained by issuing shares or borrowing.

   b) **'Ploughed back' or retained profits**   An existing business might be able to make sufficient profits to enable it to provide its own additional finance.

   c) **The Government**   Frequently it is possible for a business to obtain grants or loans from the government particularly in areas where unemployment is high.

   d) **Institutions**   Capital may also be obtained by borrowing from banks, insurance companies and other financial institutions, for example hire purchase companies.

   e) **Factoring**   When a firm sells goods it will invoice the customer and may have to wait several weeks or even months before it is paid. An alternative to this is to sell the invoices to a factor for less than the full amount. This service has developed in recent years and is usually provided by banks or finance companies. A factor purchases the invoiced debts of a business, usually paying up to 90% of the value depending on the risk involved. The firm therefore gets its money immediately leaving the factor to collect the amount outstanding and deal with any possible bad debts. For example a business has invoices outstanding for £1,000. It sells these to a factor and receives £900 for them.

   f) **Trade Credit**   Some traders build up credit with their suppliers in order to give them additional capital, particularly in the short-term. That is they buy goods and pay for them some weeks later by which time they may have already received the money for selling them.

   g) **Leasing or renting of equipment**   Leasing enables firms to acquire expensive up-to-date equipment without the large amounts of capital needed to buy it. Just as your family might rent a television set so a business can obtain goods in this way by paying an annual rental fee which includes maintenance. It is quite common for firms to lease major items like office equipment, machinery and company vehicles rather than buying them outright.

   h) **Hire Purchase**   It may be possible for a business to purchase some items like office furniture on credit rather than paying for them immediately. The firm will pay a deposit and pay the balance outstanding by monthly instalments over a period of 2-5 years thus spreading the cost.

7.   *N.B.*   Trade Credit, leasing and hire purchase do not actually increase the amount of money coming into a business. Instead they enable a firm to have the use of additional capital without needing to lay out large amounts of cash.

OVERHEADS

8.   There are many expenses involved in running a business for example rent, rates, light, heat, insurance, telephone, postage, stationery, advertising, transport, packing and bank charges. Together these expenses are referred to as the *overhead* costs or revenue expenditure of a firm.

PROFIT

9.   As seen in Chapter 8, the main aim of most businesses is to make as much profit as possible. A business receives income by supplying goods and services. But in order to do this it has to pay the various expenses involved. The difference between the income and the expenses is called profit. It is, in fact, the money that is left over. Profit then represents the return (reward) to a businessman for the risks which he has taken in setting up and running his business.

MARK-UP

10.   In order to make a profit a firm may make or buy goods at one price and sell them at a higher price. It will need to estimate its expenses to enable it to decide upon its *mark-up* or profit margin.

11.   Usually a firm will try to achieve a fixed mark-up calculated as a percentage of the cost price, for example 25%, 33%, or 50% averaged out over the full range of its products. That is, where a firm decides on an average mark-up of 25%, some goods might have a profit margin as high as 50% whilst others only 10%. Out of this profit margin the firm must pay its overheads.

COST PRICE + MARK-UP = SELLING PRICE
                    (Profit)

Examples

Cost Price	Mark-up	Selling Price	Mark-up as % cost price
£5	£2.50	£7.50	50%
£10	£2.50	£12.50	25%

12.   In some businesses mark-up is given as a percentage of the selling price, rather than the cost price.

Examples

Cost Price	Mark-up	Selling Price	Mark-up as % cost price	selling price
£20	£5	£25	25%	20%
£20	£10	£30	50%	33.3%

13.   *N.B.*

  a)   The mark-up on particular goods will vary depending upon the type of business, type of merchandise, price range, competitors, prices and pricing psychology, for example £1.99 sound a lot cheaper than say £2.01.

  b)   The right price is always the one at which goods sell most readily.

FINAL ACCOUNTS

14. At the end of each financial year any business needs to know whether or not it has made a profit or a loss, i.e. whether it has earned more than it has spent. In addition, the Government requires firms to keep proper accounts for tax purposes (see Chapter 26) and also, in the case of a company, to meet the provisions of the Companies Acts (see Chapter 6). To provide this information, accounting records are kept from which final accounts are prepared, one of which is the Trading and Profit and Loss Account which shows the gross and net profit (or loss) for the year.

GROSS PROFIT

15. The mark-up, the difference between the cost price and selling price of goods, is known as the gross profit. For example, if a business buys £50,000 worth of goods and during the year sells them for £84,000 then the gross profit = selling price – cost price

$$= £84,000 \quad – £50,000$$
$$= £34,000$$

NET PROFIT

16. A firm must also take account of the many business expenses and by deducting these from the gross profit we arrive at the net profit. For example, if the gross profit is £34,000 and the business overheads £27,000, then the net profit = gross profit – expenses

$$= £34,000 \quad – £27,000$$
$$= £7,000$$

17.

A Retailer

Trading and Profit and Loss Account for the year ended 31 December 19 . .

Opening stock (1 Jan)	2000	Sales	8600
Purchases of goods	3240	Closing stock (31 Dec)	1540
Gross profit	4900		
	£10140		£10140
Wages	1800	Gross Profit b/f	4900
Advertising	100		
Light and heating	450		
Transport	250		
Rates	204		
Insurance	25		
Stationery	20		
Net profit	2051		
	£4900		£4900

N.B. The closing stock figure is obtained from the annual stock-taking.

BALANCE SHEET – "Statement of Affairs"

18. In addition to calculating the gross and net profit, a Balance Sheet must also be prepared which shows the financial position of the business at that particular time. A balance sheet consists of two lists – one of the ASSETS (things possessed or owned by a business) and the other the LIABILITIES (anything owed by a business).

Assets are of two main types:

19. a) **Fixed Assets** (or fixed capital) which remain the same over a period of time, for example land and buildings, fixtures and fittings, office furniture and equipment and motor vehicles.

    b) **Current Assets** (or circulating capital) which are constantly changing from day-to-day for example stock of goods, cash and bank balances.

Liabilities are also of two main types:

20. a) **Fixed Liabilities** such as capital and long-term loans which remain the same over long periods.

    b) **Current Liabilities** such as creditors, bank overdrafts, and short-term loans which change from day-to-day.

21. A simplified Balance Sheet might look as follows:

G Cull Retail Supplies Ltd

Balance Sheet as at 31 March 19 . .

	£	£
Capital at start	28,000	
Add Net Profit	5,000	33,000
Current Liabilities		
Bank Overdraft	4,000	
Trade Creditors	2,000	
Unpaid Expenses	1,000	7,000
		40,000
Fixed Assets		
Shop Premises	14,800	
Fixtures and Fittings	7,200	
(8,000 less depreciation 800)		
Motor Vehicles	5,000	27,000
(6,000 less depreciation 1000)		
Current Assets		
Stock of goods	7,000	
Debtors	3,500	
Cash at bank	2,000	
Cash in hand	500	13,000
		40,000

---

22. *N.B.*

    a) **Debtor** – someone who owes money to a business, for example for goods which they have bought.

    b) **Creditor** – someone to whom a business owes money, for example a supplier from whom raw materials have been bought.

    c) On a balance sheet the assets must always be equal to the liabilities.

    d) The final accounts and balance sheet of a large organisation are much more complex than this simple example, but the basic information and presentation is the same.

DEPRECIATION

23. The balance sheet shows the value of a business's assets at a particular point in time, i.e. how much each asset would be worth if it was sold for cash. Each year some assets lose value due to wear and tear, for example a two year old car will be worth less than a new one. Therefore in its accounts a business will make an allowance for this called depreciation. In G Cull's balance sheet the fixtures and fittings are estimated to depreciate (lose value) by £800 each year, whilst the motor vehicles depreciate by £1,000 each year. Eventually these will need to be replaced. The depreciation allowance saved each year can therefore be used to purchase new items.

TYPES OF CAPITAL

24. The assets shown in the Balance Sheet of a firm represent its capital. Since capital is basically the money used in a business, the assets show how this money has been spent. For example to buy premises, stock, vehicles etc.

CAPITAL = ASSETS – LIABILITIES

25. Capital Owned and Capital Employed

The net value of the assets belonging to the owner of a business is called the *capital owned*.

> CAPITAL OWNED = TOTAL ASSETS – CURRENT LIABILITIES

26. But this may not be all the capital used in a business since a trader may borrow money from a bank or buy goods on credit i.e. use someone elses capital. On the other hand, a business may also be owed money by its debtors. Therefore the actual *capital employed* may be slightly different from what is owned.

> CAPITAL EMPLOYED = TOTAL ASSETS – DEBTORS

27. This can be seen in a simple example by looking at the figures in the balance sheet of G Cull:

> CAPITAL OWNED = £40,000 – £7,000 = £33,000
> CAPITAL EMPLOYED = £40,000 – £3,500 = £36,500

28. Working Capital

Working capital is the money which a business must have available to meet its day-to-day expenses such as staff wages, purchasing of stock and other overheads.

> WORKING CAPITAL = CURRENT ASSETS – CURRENT LIABILITIES
> In our example of G Cull £13,000 – £7,000 = £6,000

29. Working capital is essential to ensure that a firm can operate efficiently and remain *solvent*, i.e. in a position to pay its expenses. If a business is *insolvent* it means that the current assets are less than the current liabilities and thus it cannot pay its debts in full. For example, if current assets were £10,000 and current liabilities £12,000, then the firm would not have sufficient working capital to carry on the business.

30. In the short-term it may be possible to solve this problem but if it continues for any length of time the business may be forced to close down. In the case of an individual this is called *bankruptcy* or in the case of a company *liquidation*.

31. Liquidity Ratios

Sometimes working capital is a misleading measure of a firm's ability to meet its immediate debts and liquid capital is used instead. Liquidity refers to those assets which are available as cash or can be easily converted into cash, for example bank balances and debtors. Two liquidity ratios are frequently used:

    a)   Current Ratio = Current Assets: Current Liabilities
          A ratio of 2:1 is generally considered as ideal.

    b)   Acid Test Ratio = Liquid Assets: Current Liabilities

This measures whether a business can meet its short-term liabilities without reducing its stock levels. Some assets are usually financed by borrowing which incurs interest charges. Consequently if sales (and therefore revenue) fall this may affect a firm's liquidity position.

A measure of how assets are financed is the **Capital Gearing Ratio** i.e. long term borrowing: net assets (capital) employed.

32. In our example G Cull has a current ratio of almost 2:1 but an acid test ratio of 6:7. Thus he would have a problem if everyone demanded to be paid at the same time.

SIMPLE INTERPRETATION OF FINAL ACCOUNTS

33. By examining the figures in the Trading Profit and Loss Account, and in particular the Balance Sheet, it is possible to discover the financial strengths and weaknesses of a business. They provide a summary of all the important financial facts of a business and thus it is possible to see, for example, how much capital is in the business, the net profit and how much is owed to the bank and other creditors.

34. Further analysis can also take place via the different types of capital in the business (owned, employed, working, liquid), by calculating the average stock, rate of turnover, return on capital and by comparing one year's figures with another.

35. Average Stock

There are several ways of calculating this, but one of the most popular is as follows:

$$\text{Average stock} = \frac{\text{Stock at the beginning of the year} + \text{stock at the end of the year}}{2}$$

Thus if we have £20,000 of stock at the beginning of the year and £16,000 at the end then our

$$\text{average stock} = \frac{20,000 + 16,000}{2} = £18,000$$

That is, at any particular time in the year the business would probably have about £18,000 worth of goods in stock.

36. Turnover and Rate of Turnover

The main aim of any business is to sell its goods in order to make a profit. Generally, the more it sells the more profit it is likely to make. Every day some goods are sold and further stock must be bought to replace them. In time, all stock is replaced or 'turned over', hence the total sales during a trading period are referred to as the **turnover** of a business.

37. The **rate of turnover or stockturn** is the number of times that the average stock is sold (turned over) during a trading period. This rate depends very much upon the type of business, since where fresh food is sold such as meat, fish, and meat and vegetables, stock must be turned over and replaced quickly. As a result the business will have a high rate of stock turn, whereas a television, carpet or furniture trader might have goods in stock for several weeks or even months and therefore have a low rate of stockturn.

38. Example

$$\text{Rate of Turnover} = \frac{\text{Total Sales}}{\text{Average Stock}}$$

Thus if a business has sales of £20,000 and the average stock is valued at £5,000, then the rate of turnover is 4.

N.B. Rate of turnover can be calculated using the average stock at cost or selling price and is important because it provides an indication of how 'busy' a firm is.

39. The rate of turnover in a business can usually be increased in two ways:
   a) By cutting prices so that customers will buy more or,
   b) By increasing the amount of advertising and sales promotion to attract more customers.

40. Profit on Turnover

In order to compare a firm's profits with both previous years and those of other businesses, it is usual to calculate it in percentage terms. Both the gross profit and the net profit can be calculated as a percentage of turnover. Turnover is simply another word for sales.

41. Example 1

Turnover = £12,000   Gross Profit = £3,000   Net Profit = £1,200

% Profit = $\dfrac{\text{Gross Profit}}{\text{Turnover}} \times 100 = \dfrac{£3,000}{£12,000} \times 100 = 25\%$

That is for every £100 of sales £25 has been earned as gross profit.
OR

% Profit = $\dfrac{\text{Net Profit}}{\text{Turnover}} \times 100 = \dfrac{£1,200}{£12,000} \times 100 = 10\%$

42. Example 2

	Year 1	Year 2
	£	£
Turnover	40,000	60,000
Gross Profit	10,000	12,000
Net Profit	5,000	6,600

If we compare the 2 years, at first glance it would seem that most profit was made in year 2 but this does not take account of inflation or the quantity of goods sold and therefore we use a percentage comparison.

Gross Profit to Turnover

Year 1 = $\dfrac{£10,000}{£40,000} \times 100 = 25\%$

Year 2 = $\dfrac{£12,000}{£60,000} \times 100 = 20\%$

Thus the firm actually made less profit in year 2.

Net Profit to Turnover

Year 1 = $\dfrac{£5,000}{£40,000} \times 100 = 12\frac{1}{2}\%$

Year 2 = $\dfrac{£6,600}{£60,000} \times 100 = 11\%$

From these calculations it can be seen that in year 1 for every £100 worth of goods sold the cost was £75, the overheads £12.50 leaving £12.50 profit. Whilst in year 2 the cost was £80, the overheads £9 leaving £11 profit.

43. By calculating the percentage profit on turnover a business can compare its trading results with previous years to see what progress is being made and to take action where needed. For example, they may indicate improved efficiency and better buying or inefficiency, higher overheads and overmanning (i.e. too many staff employed).

RETURN ON CAPITAL

44. Normally the more capital which is invested in a business, then the higher would be the expected profit.

The percentage return on capital is calculated as follows:

$$\frac{\text{Net profit}}{\text{Capital employed}} \times 100$$

Thus if we use the above example and assume that the firm's capital was £30,000 then the percentage return is:

Year 1	$\frac{£5,000}{£30,000}$	x 100 = 19% (approx)
Year 2	$\frac{£6,600}{£30,000}$	x 100 = 22%

So for every £100 invested in the business in Year 1 £19 was earned in profit, whilst in Year 2 £22 was earned.

45. These would probably be considered as satisfactory returns on capital, but if the return was less than about 10% then it would not be very good because it would be possible to invest money elsewhere, say in a building society and earn a similar rate of return but without the risks involved by investing in a business.

SUMMARY

46. a) Capital is vital in any business whether it is needed for starting-up or to finance later expansion or modernisation

b) A business can obtain capital by borrowing from the public, using retained profits, government grants and loans, borrowing from the financial institutions, factoring, extended trade credit, leasing of equipment or by buying items on hire purchase.

c) There are many expenses, called overheads, involved in running a business.

d) The price charged for a firm's products must cover the cost of the goods, the overheads and leave a margin of profit.

e) Many firms try to achieve a fixed profit margin or mark-up averaged out over the full range of their products.

f) The mark-up on any particular item will vary considerably depending on what it is, competitors prices and pricing psychology.

g) Final accounts are prepared at the end of each financial year to calculate the gross and net profits for the business.

h) In addition, a Balance Sheet is drawn up to show the assets and liabilities of the firm. That is, what it owns and what it owes.

i) The money invested in a business is called its capital and this is used to purchase various assets. A firm must also ensure that it always has sufficient working capital to meet its day-to-day expenses.

j) The turnover of a business is another name for its sales. The rate of turnover measures how quickly its stock sells.

k) In order to compare its performance with previous years and with other businesses, a firm will calculate its profit for the year as a percentage of both its turnover and its capital.

REVIEW QUESTIONS

Answers can be found in the paragraphs shown.

1. List the main sources of capital available to a business. (5)

2. Define profit. (7)

3. Give 4 examples of the overheads which a business faces. (8)

4. A retail firm buys some light fittings which cost £1.50 each. It wishes to sell them at a mark-up of 50%. Calculate the selling price. (9, 10)

5. When and why does a firm need to prepare final accounts? (14)

6. Explain the difference between gross and net profit. (15, 16, 17)

7. What is a balance sheet? (18-21)

8. Explain briefly why there can be a difference between the capital owned and capital employed in a business. (24-27)

9. Why is working capital important to a firm? (28-30)

10. What is the rate of turnover? (36-38)

11. Goods bought for £1,000 were sold for £1,250. What was the percentage of gross profit to sales? (40-42)

12. A firm with a capital of £45,000 has a net profit for the year of £9,000. What was the return on capital? (44)

EXAMINATION PRACTICE QUESTIONS

Marks

1. Would a fish and chip show owner need to use a bank's factoring service? Give reasons for your answer. 2

2. Turnover is another name for 1

3. Is it possible for a retailer to make a gross profit on sales and still make a loss in the business? YES/NO. Explain your answer. 2

4. List 3 items of fixed capital and 3 items of circulating capital which you would need if you decided to start up in business as a painter and decorator. 6

5. When a company cannot meet its debts it is said to be in liquidation. What is the term used when a sole trader is in this position? 2

MULTIPLE CHOICE/COMPLETION

1. From the following information calculate the annual rate of stockturn:
Net sales for the year £32,500. Average stock held £6,500.
   a) 6.5
   b) 5
   c) 4
   d) 32.5

2. A businessman wishing to increase his firm's liquid assets might:
   a) Purchase a new motor vehicle
   b) Sell off surplus machinery
   c) Move to larger premises
   d) Increase the stock of finished goods

224

3. Using some or all of the following information relating to a small trader, calculate the gross profit for the year. Turnover £5,000. Stock £1,000. Overheads £700. Cost of goods sold £2,800. Closing stock £900.
    a) £2,100
    b) £2,800
    c) £1,400
    d) £5,000

4. The following is the simplified balance sheet of a self-employed plumber as at 30 June 19 . .

	£	
Capital and profits	8,500	
Current liabilities	1,200	9,700
Fixed assets	7,500	
Current assets	2,200	9,700

The working capital of the business is:
    a) +£1,000
    b) +£1,200
    c) – £1,000
    d) +£8,500

5. A firm's gross profit is £12,140. What will be the net profit if it has the following expenses? Wages £3,200. Rent £450. Light and Heat £990. Depreciation £250.
    a) £17,030
    b) £7,250
    c) £7,750
    d) £8,940

6. The summary of a firm's assets and liabilities at a particular point in time is called a:
    a) Trading Account
    b) Profit and Loss Account
    c) Trade Balance
    d) Balance Sheet

In each of the following questions, one or more of the responses is/are correct. Choose the appropriate letter which indicates the correct version.
    A   if 1 only is correct
    B   if 3 only is correct
    C   if 1 and 2 only are correct
    D   if 1, 2 and 3 are correct

7. Which of the following is/are current liabilities of a firm:
    1) Share capital
    2) Creditors
    3) Stock of goods

8. Which of the following would represent a company's fixed assets?
    1) Furniture and fittings
    2) Delivery Van
    3) Debtors

RECENT EXAMINATION QUESTIONS

LEAG MAY 1988 GCSE BUSINESS STUDIES PAPER I

Marks

1. Data Information is a public limited company with a large number of individual shareholders. The balance sheet shown below was presented to shareholders at their annual general meeting.

Data Information plc. Balance sheet as at 31.12.87

	£m.	£m.	£m.
Fixed assets			
Land & building		80	
Machinery		70	
			150
Current assets			
Stock	110		
Debtors	5		
Cash	5		
		120	
Current liabilities			
Creditors	10		
Overdraft	10		
		20	
			100
Net assets employed			250
Financed by			
Ordinary shares		100	
Long term bank loan		100	
Reserves		50	
			250

a) Explain what is meant by the terms

    i)   fixed asset

    ii) debtor

    iii) creditors

    iv) reserves   4

b) i)   What is working capital?   1

    ii) Calculate Data Information's working capital.   1

c) Analyse the business performance of Data Information by calculating and commenting on TWO relevant ratios.   4

LEAG 1988 GCSE BUSINESS STUDIES SPECIMEN PAPER 2A SECTION B

2. Patrick McNab, who owns a manufacturing business, decides to acquire his own fleet of delivery vehicles instead of using independent road haulage contractors. He also decides to lease, rather than buy, the vehicles.

a) Why do you think he chose to acquire his own fleet?   6

b) How does leasing help to reduce the initial cost of the vehicles?   3

c) What other advantages are there for Patrick in leasing rather than purchasing outright for cash?   6

SEG 1988 GCSE BUSINESS STUDIES SPECIMEN PAPER I   **Marks**

3.   Carol Roach owns and runs a small manufacturing business making children's toys. She always plans ahead and often makes monthly estimates. From past experience Carol makes the following estimates for one month: raw materials £1500, rent and rates £360, wages and salaries £3,500, other running costs £540. The average price of the toys is £14 and she hopes to sell 530 each month.

a)   Show the firm's financial position for the month.   8

b)   During the month of December Carol estimates that sales will increase by 20%.
  i)   How would this change Carol's revenue?   2
  ii)   How could Carol meet the increase in sales?   6
  iii)   Explain what the possible effects might be on profit.   10

c)   After the rush during December, Carol decides that she should try to sell her toys to Japan.
  i)   What problems could Carol's firm face when selling toys to Japan?   5
  ii)   Explain how these problems might be overcome.   9

ASSIGNMENT

R Barber is in business as a retail jeweller. In the year ended 31 December 19 . . he purchased goods for £7,000 and had a turnover of £100,000. His overheads were £20,480. Stock (1 Jan) £10,000. Stock (31 Dec) £12,000

1.   Calculate:
  a)   His gross profit
  b)   His net profit

The following is R Barber's Balance Sheet as at 31 December 19 . .

Capital	?	34,520
Plus Net Profit	?	
Fixed Liabilities		
Mortgage	12,080	12,080
Current liabilities		
Creditors	2,500	
Bank Overdraft	2,000	4,500
		£51,100
Fixed Assets		34,200
Current Assets		
Stock	12,000	
Debtors	2,700	
Bank	2,000	
Cash	200	16,900
		£51,100

2.   Using your answer to question 1 complete the balance sheet with the figure for net profit and calculate R Barber's capital.

3. Explain the following terms which appear in R Barber's Balance Sheet:
   a) Capital
   b) Creditors
   c) Bank overdraft
   d) Fixed liabilities

4. Give 2 examples of fixed assets and 2 examples of current assets which R Barber is likely to have in his business.

5. From the information given, calculate the following and explain why R Barber may wish to know each of these figures:
   a) Capital owned
   b) Capital employed
   c) Working capital
   d) Liquid capital

6. R Barber would like to compare the trading figures in his business over the last 3 years. Using the information from the earlier tasks:
   a) complete the table with the missing figures for the current year
   b) calculate the percentage net profit on turnover and percentage return on capital employed.
   c) state in which year you consider that the business was most successful and give reasons for your answer.

Capital employed		Turnover	Net Profit
Year 1	12,000	80,000	8,000
Year 2	16,000	90,000	10,000
Current year	?	?	?

7. From the information available to you, suggest 2 ways in which R Barber could increase his net profit.

18. Controlling Business Costs

1. This chapter looks at fixed and variable business costs, budgetary control, break-even charts and stock control.

INTRODUCTION

2. In Chapter 17 we saw that a firm's gross profit is the difference between the total value of goods or services sold (turnover) and the cost of buying, making or supplying these goods or services. However, a firm also has many other expenses (its overheads) which must be deducted from the gross profit to discover the net profit. For example rent, rates, telephone, postage and insurance.

FIXED AND VARIABLE COSTS

3. The above costs when associated with a manufacturing business are either fixed or variable.

4. **Fixed costs** or overheads are those costs which *do not* vary in direct proportion to a firm's output. They have to be paid regardless of the level of output. Even if there is no output at all, a firm will still have fixed costs which it must meet. For example rent of premises, rates, heating, lighting, insurance, postage and telephone.

5. **Variable costs** or the cost of production, on the other hand, vary directly with output. For example if a firm produces more goods it will need additional raw materials, labour and transport.

6. *N.B.* Although costs are usually classified as fixed or variable over a period of time, all costs are likely to vary.

CASH FLOW

7. Money flows both into and out of a business. When it sells goods or services it receives income but it also has a flow of money out in order to meet its fixed and variable costs.

8. It is essential for success that there is a regular **cash flow** into a business. Therefore a system of control is important to ensure that a firm is able to pay its expenses and earn sufficient additional income to make a profit.

BUDGETARY CONTROL

9. In order to monitor and control their activities many firms set targets of achievement and limits on spending for the various aspects of the business.

10. The most common form of financial regulation is called budgetary control and this is now very widely used in both public and private sector businesses.

11. Targets will be set, for example, in terms of output, sales volume and profits. Then on the basis of these targets, budgets are calculated for purchasing, production, distribution, personnel, administration and capital expenditure etc. For example a firm may have an output and sales target of 100,000 units and a budget for capital spending (on machinery etc) of £25,000. Thus budgetary control involves the planning of expenditure on the basis of a business's expected income.

12. Regular reviews can be made to check whether or not these performance measures are being met and that spending is within the limits set. Any problems can then be identified and action taken to correct the situation.

13. In a large business organisation these targets will be sub-divided so that there is an individual target to achieve for each factory, office, branch, geographical area or product.

BREAK-EVEN POINT

14. Linked with the concept of planning through budgetary control is the use of break-even charts. These enable firms to analyse changes in sales volume, prices and costs.

15. Example

A	B	C	D	E	F	G
Output (no. of units) (produced)	Fixed Costs £	Variable Costs £	(B+C) Total Costs £	Sales Revenue £	(E–D) Profit £	(E–D) Loss £
0	2000	0	2000	0		2000
100	2000	500	2500	1000		1500
200	2000	1000	3000	2000		1000
300	2000	1500	3500	3000		500
400	2000	2000	4000	4000	NIL	NIL
500	2000	2500	4500	5000	500	
600	2000	3000	5000	6000	1000	
700	2000	3500	5500	7000	1500	

16. The above information shows a firm with variable costs of £5 per unit and a selling price of £10 per unit. In this situation the firm would need to sell 400 units before it reaches break-even point i.e. where total costs = total sales revenue. Beyond this point a profit can be made. However, if the firm sells less than 400 units it will be operating at a loss.

17. The break-even point can be calculated using the following formula:

$$\text{Break-even} = \frac{F}{S-V}$$

Where F = Total fixed costs   S = Selling price per unit   V = Variable costs per unit
Thus in the example above we know that F = £2,000   S = £10   V = £5

$$\text{Therefore break-even} = \frac{2,000}{10-5} = \frac{2,000}{5} = 400 \text{ units}$$

Variable costs at break-even point = 400 x £5 = £2,000

18. This information can also be shown graphically on a break-even chart.

Break Even Chart

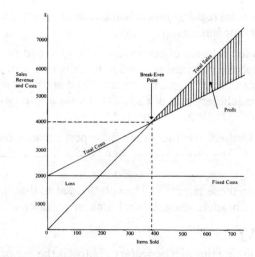

A break-even chart illustrates the profit or loss at different levels of a firm's output.

19.   In the illustrations the sales revenue of £6,000 would represent the sale of 600 items sold for £10 each. From the chart we can also see that it would cost £5,000 to make this number of items. Thus the cost of producing each item would be £5,000 divided by 600=£8.33. Thus the profit per item sold was £1.67 (£10−£8.33).

20. On the other hand, if sales were only £3,000, i.e. 300 items, we can see that the total cost would be £3,500. Thus to produce each item it would cost £11.67 (£3,500 divided by 300). At this level of sale the firm would be making a loss of £1.67 per item.

21. *N.B.* As the firm sells more so the *average cost* of producing each unit will fall. This is because the fixed costs do not change and therefore these costs are spread over a larger output.

$$\text{Average cost} = \frac{\text{Total Cost}}{\text{Output}}$$

22. **Example**

Using the figures in paragraph 15

a)	At an output of 100 Average cost =	$\dfrac{2,500}{100}$	= £25 per unit
b)	At an output of 500 Average cost =	$\dfrac{4,500}{500}$	= £9 per unit

Thus, although the variable cost per unit is still £5, the fixed cost per unit has fallen from £20 (£25 − £5) to £4 per unit (£9 − £5).

STOCK CONTROL

23. Most organisations need to carry stocks whether it be raw materials, components, finished goods or stationery. If too much stock is held this takes up storage space and ties up cash, whilst a shortage of stock can cause delays in production and possible loss of sales.

24. Therefore stock records need to be kept which monitor the movement of stock into and out of an organisation. It is also necessary to set maximum and minimum stock levels and a re-order level at which an order will be placed with a supplier. These levels will depend upon how frequently the item is used or sold, and how quickly stock can be replaced.

25.

Midland Auto Spares Ltd STOCK CARD						
ITEM:	WHEEL TRIMS (Speciality)			MAX STOCK:		50
REF NO:	4721			MIN STOCK:		20
LOCATION:	ROW 4A			RE-ORDER LEVEL:		30
DATE	RECEIPTS		ISSUES			BALANCE
19 ..	QUANTITY	SUPPLIER	QUANTITY	CUSTOMER		
1 Sept						20
2 Sept	30	Car Distributors Ltd				50
3 Sept			10	A1 Garages		40
10 Sept			10	Fenchurch Garage		30

26. Proper stock control should ensure that stock is always available when needed. Many businesses now use computerised record systems which automatically control stock.

SUMMARY

27. a) There are two basic types of business costs – fixed which remain the same regardless of the level of output, and variable which vary directly with output.

b) Many firms use budgets to monitor and control their business.

c) Budgetary control involves the planning of expenditure on the basis of a business's expected income.

d) Break-even point is the level of sales at which total costs are equal to total revenue.

e) This information can be shown graphically on a break-even chart.

f) Stock control is important to ensure that stock is available when needed and also to prevent 'tying up' too much cash.

REVIEW QUESTIONS

Answers can be found in the paragraphs shown.

1. Give 2 examples of fixed costs. (4)
2. Explain the difference between fixed and variable costs. (4, 5)
3. How does a system of budgetary control help a firm to monitor its activities? (9-13)
4. At what point does a firm reach break-even? (14-17)
5. What is illustrated on a break-even chart? (18-20)
6. How is a firm's average cost calculated? (21, 22)
7. Why is stock control important in an organisation? (23-25)
8. What is the main advantage of using a computerised stock control system? (26)

EXAMINATION PRACTICE QUESTIONS

Marks

1. A firm has fixed costs of £15,000 pa and its variable costs are £10,000. If 500 articles are produced what is the average cost? 2

2. Explain and give one example for each of the following:
   a) Fixed cost
   b) Variable cost
   c) Total cost 6

3. Revenue minus cost equals 1

4. The overheads of a firm are also referred to as its . . . . costs. 1

5. A manufacturing firm's variable costs may also be referred to as its costs of 1

6. Study the graph opposite and then answer the following questions.

The firm uses 100 units of stock each week. Delivery time from despatch of order is 1½ weeks.

   a) What are the minimum and maximum stock levels? 2
   b) What is the stock level at week 5? 1
   c) Which letters indicate the points at which the firm orders its stock? 2
   d) Which letters indicate the points when stock deliveries are received? 2
   e) What do the distances vw and yz represent? 2
   f) Give 2 reasons why v and y are above the minimum stock level. 3

232

Marks

g) Give 2 reasons why w and z are below the maximum stock level.   3
h) Name and briefly describe the document used for the purchasing of stock.   4
i) Give 3 reasons why firms need a system of stock control.   6

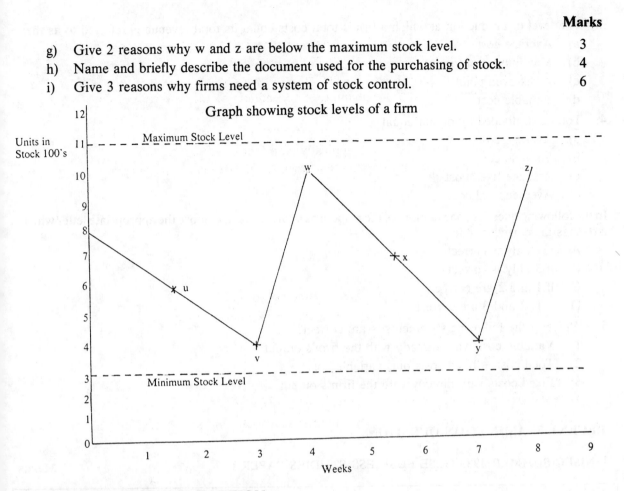

Graph showing stock levels of a firm

MULTIPLE CHOICE/COMPLETION

1. The following table shows part of the costs incurred by a manufacturing company:

Output	Fixed Cost £	Variable Cost £	Total Cost £
0	10	15	25
1	10	25	35
2			46

What is the total variable cost if 2 units are produced?
a) £12.50
b) £22.50
c) £36.00
d) £45.00

2. A firm which produces video recorders has fixed costs of £30,000. If the selling price is £350 each and variable costs are £100 per unit, the break-even point will be at an output of:
a) 80
b) 120
c) 250
d) 300

3. The level of production at which a firm's total costs equal its total revenue is referred to as the:
   a) Average cost
   b) Maximum profit point
   c) Break-even point
   d) Variable cost

4. Total cost divided by output equals:
   a) Average cost
   b) Variable cost
   c) Average fixed cost
   d) Average total cost

In the following question, one or more of the responses is/are correct. Choose the appropriate letter which indicates the correct version.

   A   if 1 only is correct
   B   if 3 only is correct
   C   if 1 and 2 are correct
   D   if 1, 2 and 3 are correct

5. Which of the following statements is/are correct?
   1) Variable costs vary directly with the firm's output
   2) Total cost = fixed costs plus variable cost
   3) Fixed costs vary directly with the firm's output

RECENT EXAMINATION QUESTIONS

1. NISEC SUMMER 1989 GCSE BUSINESS STUDIES PAPER I   **Marks**

Ivan Breen owns a garage where he services vehicles. He pays out £200 in fixed costs each week and, on average, £30 per customer on variable costs. He charges, on average, £50 per customer and usually has 30 customers each week.

   a) In relation to Ivan's business:
      i) Give *one* possible fixed cost,   1
      ii) Give *one* possible variable cost.   1
   b) Using the above data, construct a Break-Even Chart for Ivan's business, labelling it correctly   6

Ivan is considering diversifying his business. He is thinking of buying a franchise from a Fast Food Company but estimates that he will need additional capital of £40,000, which he hopes to obtain from his bank.

   c) Explain, in detail, what is meant by franchising.   5
   d) List *two* benefits Ivan would enjoy by owning a franchise.   2
   e) Advise Ivan on the information he will need to have available when he approaches his bank for the loan.   6
   f) Why do you think Ivan requires this large amount of extra capital?   6
   g) What may be the main reasons for Ivan deciding to diversify?   6

2. WJEC MAY 1989 GCSE BUSINESS STUDIES PAPER I

Ali Singh sells jeans in a local outdoor market. The graph below shows data on the business for a week in May.

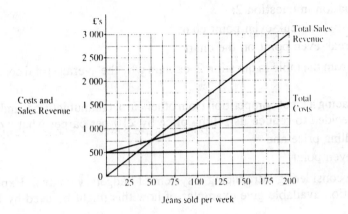

Jeans sold per week

a) Use the above graph to find the following:

    i) the value of fixed costs;   1

    ii) the value of the variable costs when 200 pairs of jeans are sold;   1

    iii) the total revenue when 200 pairs of jeans are sold;   1

    iv) the average price of a pair of jeans.   1

b) How is the graph useful to Ali Singh?   7

c) How and why would you expect the total sales revenue on the graph to change if it showed data for a week in January?   4

ASSIGNMENT

The following information relates to K Weaver Ltd, a small carpet manufacturer in the West Midlands. Complete the 7 tasks which are based on it.

1. Identify the variable costs from the following list:

Wages, packaging, rates, rent, maintenance, wool and other raw materials, heating and lighting, power, managing director's salary, delivery vans, petrol, insurance.

2. Copy and *complete* the missing figures in the following table which is based on the company's daily costs of production:

Output Carpets	Fixed Costs	Variable Costs	Total Costs	Average Total Costs	Sales Revenue
	£	£	£	£	£
0	180	0	180	180	0
1	180	50			110
2	180				220
3	180	150			330
4	180	200			440
5					550
6	180	300			660

3. From the table in question 2 identify the following:
   a) Break-even point
   b) Selling price per carpet
   c) Variable cost per carpet

4. Using the information in question 2:
   a) Draw and label a break-even point chart
   b) Mark the break-even point on the chart

5. Using examples from the table in question 2, explain why the average total cost falls as more carpets are made.

6. The company is facing a lot of competition from other carpet manufacturers and is examining ways to increase sales. If it decided to reduce its selling price by £10 per carpet what would be:
   a) The new selling price and
   b) The break-even point

7. The directors are considering introducing a system of budgetary control. Explain what this means and from the information available give examples of how this might be used by K Weaver Ltd.

19. Insurance

1.   Insurance provides protection against loss by paying compensation. This chapter is about the risks which are faced in life by individuals and businesses. It explains the need for insurance, types of insurance cover, the insurance market, the principles on which insurance is based and its importance to the economy.

INTRODUCTION

2.   Can you think of some insurance companies who have offices in a nearby town? Commercial Union, General Accident, Prudential and Sun Alliance are some examples which you might find. At some time in our life we all need insurance.

THE NEED FOR INSURANCE

3.   Many years ago if your house was burnt down or your possessions stolen, then that was just too bad. You simply lost everything. If a trader lost goods in a shipwreck or a fire, again it was just bad luck. This had the effect of discouraging businesses from taking risks and slowed down the growth of trade. Therefore insurance developed to help overcome these problems.

HOW INSURANCE WORKS

4.   Nobody knows who is going to have bad luck, so insurance companies collect small amounts of money called *premiums* from a lot of people. This enables them to pay out larger amounts of compensation to the unlucky people who suffer a misfortune. This is known as the *'pooling of risks'*.

5.

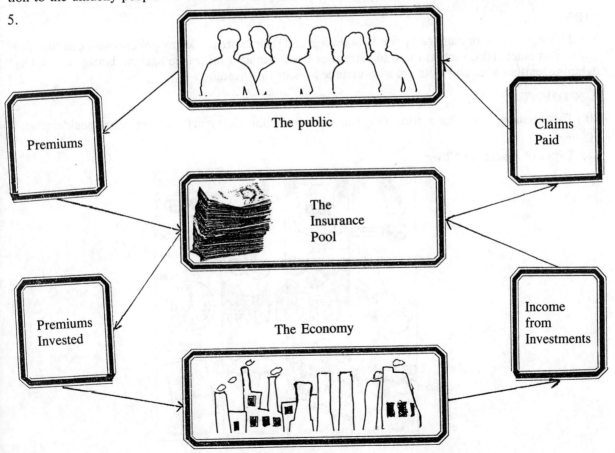

237

PREMIUMS AND RISKS

6. a) Insurance companies are in business to make a profit. Therefore they aim to collect more money in premiums than they have to pay out in claims.

   b) Premiums are related to the risk, the bigger the risk, the higher the premium. This is based on past statistics from which the insurance company can calculate how often a particular risk is likely to occur. For example, teenage drivers pay higher car insurance premiums because they are more likely to have accidents.

   c) Statisticians who calculate insurance risks and premiums are called actuaries.

TYPES OF INSURANCE COVER

7. The main risks which can be insured against are grouped under the headings Marine, Fire, Accident and Life.

MARINE

8. This is the oldest form of insurance which deals with all the risks connected with the sea. There are four main types of marine insurance most of which is conducted at Lloyd's of London.

   * *Hull* insurance which covers damage to vessels
   * *Cargo* insurance which covers the goods which ships carry
   * *Freight* insurance which offers compensation should a shipowner not be paid for delivering a cargo.
   * *Shipowners' Liability* covers the others risks which a shipowner may face including damage to other vessels or harbours, and injury to passengers or crew.

FIRE

9. This covers loss or damage by fire to buildings and their contents. Many policies also combine fire cover with other risks, such as theft and storm or flood damage. Insurance against damage caused by lightning, earthquakes and riots are also included under this heading.

ACCIDENT

10. This includes cover for a wide range of risks including motor vehicles, personal accidents and holidays.

11. Types of Insurance Cover

LIFE ASSURANCE

12. Marine, Fire and Accident are all called *insurance* because they offer protection against risks which may or may not happen. The word *assurance* is used here because it refers to cover for risks which will happen – death.

13. The two main types of life assurance are:

a) **Whole life** – premiums are usually paid until the insured person dies. A lump sum is then paid out to the dependents.

b) **Endowment** – premiums are paid for an agreed number of years, for example 20. The sum assured is payable at the end of the period or when the person dies if this is earlier. Therefore this is also a form of savings.

HOW TO TAKE OUT INSURANCE

14. **Proposal Form**   Everyone who wishes to take out insurance cover must first fill in a proposal form (application form) which gives details about themselves and the risk involved. This then forms the basis of the insurance contract.

15. **Policy**   Once the risk has been accepted and the premium paid, the company will issue a policy. This is a contract which sets out the terms and conditions of the insurance.

16. **Cover Note**   Sometimes while the policy is being prepared, the company will confirm that the risk has been accepted by issuing a temporary document called a cover note. This is common where car insurance is concerned.

17. **Certificate**   This is issued with the policy and provides proof that an insurance policy exists.

18. **Claim**   When an insured risk happens the insurance company should be informed as soon as possible. The insured person will then be sent a form which is used to provide details of the claim. The compensation will be calculated from this information.

19. **Example of a Proposal Form**

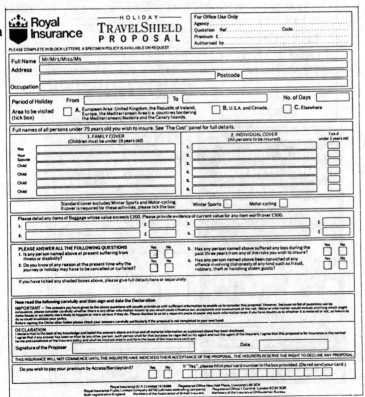

THE INSURANCE MARKET

20. Anyone wanting to take out insurance can either buy it direct from an insurance company or through brokers and agents.

INSURANCE COMPANIES

21. You can deal with an insurance company direct by:
    a) Using a local office
    b) Writing to a local or head office
    c) Answering an advertisement

INSURANCE BROKERS

22. A broker usually works full-time on behalf of a number of insurance companies. Brokers offer clients a choice of policies from the different companies which they represent. The broker acts as a 'middleman' and is paid commission by the insurance companies. The customer is able to use the brokers advice in selecting a policy best suited to their needs.

INSURANCE AGENTS

23. Agents often sell certain types of insurance, usually on a part-time basis in addition to their normal business. For example, banks, estate agents and travel agents often offer insurance services. Agents usually work for just one or two companies and receive commission on policies sold.

24.

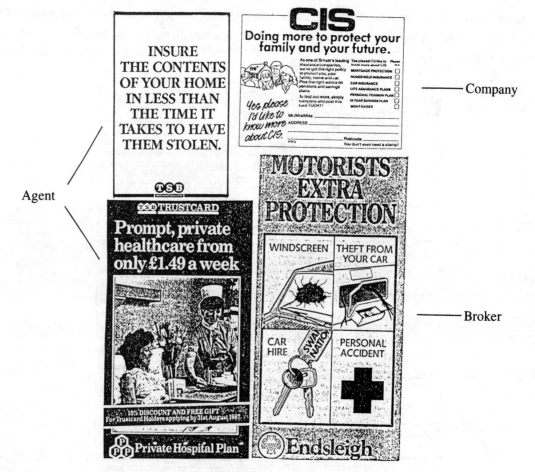

LLOYDS OF LONDON

25. Lloyd's is an international insurance market which began in London in the seventeenth century. Originally it dealt only in marine insurance but now includes everything except life assurance.

26. Lloyd's consist of two types of *members* called *underwriters* and *brokers*. Underwriters sell insurance and brokers buy insurance on behalf of the general public.

UNDERWRITERS

27. These are very wealthy people who accept insurance risks in the hope of making a profit. They are so called because they write their names under the amount of risk which they are prepared to take. Each operates on their own account. They have to deposit a minimum amount of capital and accept unlimited liability. Therefore they are personally responsible for paying insurance claims which they underwrite.

BROKERS

28. The public cannot deal direct with underwriters. Anyone requiring insurance must go through a Lloyd's *broker*. The broker approaches several underwriters to obtain the best premium quotation. Brokers are paid a commission for their work based on the amount of the premium.

SYNDICATES

29. Although an underwriter acts as an individual, they are grouped into *'syndicates'*. This is because of the complexity of many risks and also the large amounts of money involved. Each syndicate is represented at Lloyd's by an underwriting agent who actually carries out the insurance business. There are over 14,000 underwriters formed into about 400 syndicates. Big insurance risks are often shared by a number of different syndicates each of whom underwrites part of the total.

REINSURANCE

30. Much of Lloyd's business comes from overseas and a lot involves *reinsurance*. This is when one insurer agrees to share a risk accepted by another insurer. This is usually necessary where the sum involved is very large, for example a ship or large building.

31.

PRINCIPLES OF INSURANCE

32. Insurance can only work because it is based upon a number of basic principles – insurable interest, indemnity (including subrogation and contribution), utmost good faith and proximate cause – which are all explained below. If these were not followed the system of pooling risks would collapse.

INSURABLE INTEREST

33. Anyone wishing to take out insurance must personally be in a position to suffer loss. That is, they must own or be responsible for whatever is insured. This principle is necessary to stop people using insurance for their own gain.

34. **Example**

> I cannot insure my neighbours house against fire. If I could it might be to my advantage to burn it down and claim the insurance money. Likewise, you can only insure a person's life if their death would mean a financial loss for you, for example your wife or business partner.

INDEMNITY

35. The aim of insurance is to compensate (indemnify) the insured so that they are placed in the same financial position as before a misfortune occurs. That is, you cannot make a profit out of a loss.

36. **Example**

> If my 6 month old car is destroyed in a crash the insurance company would not buy me a new car as this would put me in a better position than before. Instead they would indemnify me to the value of a 6 month old car.

The principle of 'indemnity' is supported by two others – subrogation and contribution.

37. **Subrogation**   Once an insurance claim is settled the insured has no further rights over the item insured.

38. **Example**

> If I receive compensation for my car written-off in a crash then the damaged car and its scrap value belongs to the insurance company.

39. **Contribution**   If a risk is insured with more than one company then any loss would be shared between them. That is, each company would make a contribution.

40. **Example**

> A handbag stolen from a car might be covered by both motor vehicle and house contents insurance policies.

UTMOST GOOD FAITH

41. Anyone wanting insurance must complete the proposal form truthfully and disclose all relevant facts. The insurance company for its part must state the terms of the cover being offered in a clear, understandable way.

42. **Example**

> If someone, who knew he was dying of cancer, took out a life assurance policy without disclosing this fact then the contract would be invalid.

PROXIMATE CAUSE

43. This principle states that any claim will only be paid if the loss suffered was a direct result of the insured risk happening.

44. **Example**

> If my home was destroyed by fire the insurance company would pay compensation for the loss. However, if what happened made me ill and lose time off work, I could not claim for this because it was not the risk insured.

INSURANCE FOR BUSINESSES

45. Anyone who starts or runs a business takes certain risks. It may be the risks of damage by fire to the premises or goods being stolen. Another risk is that goods or services do not sell and therefore the business makes a loss. Some of these risks can be protected by insurance.

46. **Employers Liability** insurance is compulsory by law. This provides protection against claims for compensation from their staff who have accidents at work.

47. **Public Liability** insurance is also needed to compensate anyone else who may have an accident whilst visiting a firm's premises.

48. Other important types of business insurance include:

Buildings/Stock – against fire or other damage

Goods in transit – to cover the risks of theft or damage whilst goods are being delivered

Machinery and Equipment – against fire, theft or damage

Fidelity Guarantee – to protect businesses against the possible dishonesty of employees. For example the stealing of money and goods.

Bad Debt – the risks of losses due to customers not paying for goods bought on credit.

Consequential loss – covers any loss of earnings following a fire or other damage. For example, the loss of profit while a shop is closed following a fire. It can also include the cost of renting alternative premises and other expenses which the business faces until it is working normally again.

Motor Vehicle – all vehicles must, by law, have third party insurance. This covers passengers or pedestrians injured in accidents. The two most common forms of motor insurance are:

    a)   Third Party, Fire, Theft, (TPFT). This is the minimum cover which most car owners choose. It includes third party insurance plus the risks of loss or damage due to fire or theft.

    b)   Comprehensive – includes TPFT and also provides compensation if the driver is injured or his vehicle damaged in an accident.

UNINSURABLE RISKS

50. Not all risks can be insured against. For example, a business cannot insure against making a trading loss, shoplifting or going out of business.

51. This is because these may be caused by inefficiency, out-of-date stock, changes in fashion or even how hard someone works. These are factors which it is impossible for an Insurance Company to calculate and are therefore uninsurable risks.

THE IMPORTANCE OF INSURANCE TO THE ECONOMY

52. a)   **Development of Business**

       Insurance provides protection against many of the risks involved in trade and thereby encourages the setting-up and growth of business.

    b)   **Funds for Investment**

       Every year hundreds of millions of pounds are collected in premiums by insurance companies. Much of this money (especially life assurance premiums) is invested in stocks and shares. This both provides important capital for British industry and also raises income which helps to keep down the cost of insurance.

    c)   **Balance of Payments**

       The insurance industry earns Britain over £4000 million from overseas business. Therefore it is a very important 'invisible' export which helps our balance of payments (see Chapter 3).

    d)   **Protection for Individuals**

       Insurance provides protection for people and their property against the many risks in life including fire, theft and accidents.

SUMMARY

53. a) Insurance is a way of protecting people against unexpected losses.

b) Insurance companies collect money (premiums) from persons and businesses and distribute it to those who suffer a loss.

c) The four broad categories of insurance are marine, fire, accident and life.

d) The main documents used in insurance are the proposal form, policy, cover note, certificate and claim form.

e) The insurance market consists of companies, brokers, agents and Lloyd's of London.

f) Insurance is based on the principles of insurable interest, indemnity (supported by subrogation and contribution), utmost good faith and proximate cause.

g) Businesses can insure against many of the risks involved in trading including employers liability, public liability, consequential loss and motor vehicle.

h) Insurance aids the economy by reducing the risks of business, providing funds for investment, helping the balance of payments and protecting individuals and their property.

REVIEW QUESTIONS

Answers can be found in the paragraphs shown.

1. Why did insurance develop? (3)

2. Explain the 'pooling of risks'. (4, 5)

3. Name the 4 main types of insurance. (7-13)

4. Explain the difference between insurance and assurance. (12)

5. Briefly explain the purpose of a proposal form, policy, certificate, cover note and claim form. (14-19)

6. What is the difference between an insurance agent and an insurance broker? (22-23)

7. What is Lloyd's of London? (25-30)

8. Name the principles of insurance. (32)

9. Explain why each of these principles is important. (32-44)

10. Why should a business take out a consequential loss policy? (48)

11. Name 4 other types of insurance which a business might need. (46-48)

12. In what ways is insurance important to Britain's economy? (52)

EXAMINATION PRACTICE QUESTIONS

Marks

1. Choose the correct word(s) from the following list to fill the gaps in the sentences.

fidelity guarantee   premium   brokers   agents   uninsurable   policy
insurable interest   contribution   proximate cause   indemnity

a) If 2 insurance policies cover the same loss each company would make a . . . . towards it.   1

b) The . . . . is the sum of money paid for insurance.   1

c) Insurance against dishonest employees is called   1

d) When an insurance company is unable to calculate the extent of future claims the risk is usually   1

e) . . . . are independent professional insurance experts who advise clients on all companies and policies.   1

244

2.   A business takes out insurance against fire and loss of trade due to the fire. What is the insurance against loss of trade known as?   2

3.   Mr Patel wants to insure his new car which he recently purchased for £6000. From your knowledge of insurance can you help him with the following:
   a)   What is the minimum cover which he requires by law?   1
   b)   Explain the difference between comprehensive and third party fire and theft insurance.   2
   c)   Which of these would you recommend him to take out and why?   2

4.   A catering business, which employs 80 people, owns a number of restaurants and a delivery van.
   a)   What are the main risks which it should be insured against in respect of:
      i)   its restaurants, employees and customers?   10
      ii)   the delivery van?   6
   b)   State, with reasons, at least two risks in the business which could *not* be covered by insurance.   4

MULTIPLE CHOICE/COMPLETION

1.   Insurance risks at Lloyd's are accepted by:
   a)   Brokers
   b)   Underwriters
   c)   Agents
   d)   Companies

2.   The principle whereby all relevant facts must be given on an insurance policy form is called:
   a)   Insurable interest
   b)   Contribution
   c)   Subrogation
   d)   Utmost good faith

3.   The insurance principle of indemnity means that:
   a)   A profit cannot be made out of a loss
   b)   You can only insure something in which you have a direct interest
   c)   The risk is uninsurable
   d)   The risk carries a high premium

4.   Which of the following risks would a retailer *not* be able to insure against?
   a)   An employee stealing from the tills
   b)   Damage from a burst water pipe
   c)   The business being unsuccessful
   d)   Breaking of a shop window

5.   A manufacturer is insuring his factory for £40,000 and its contents for £20,000. If the premium for the building is £4.00 per £1,000 and for the contents £5.00 per £1,000 he will pay a total of:
   a)   £200
   b)   £480
   c)   £540
   d)   £260

In the following question, one or more of the responses is/are correct. Choose the appropriate letter which indicates the correct version.

A   if 1 only is correct
B   if 3 only is correct
C   if 1 and 2 are correct
D   if 1, 2 and 3 are correct

6. Which of the following types of business insurance are compulsory by law?
   1) Employers' liability
   2) Third party motor insurance
   3) Fidelity guarantee

RECENT EXAMINATION QUESTIONS   Marks

LCCI JUNE 1990 PSC STRUCTURE OF BUSINESS

1. What are the benefits of insurance to:
   a) the business world   10
   b) private individuals?   8

RSA JUNE 1989 BACKGROUND TO BUSINESS STAGE I PART II

2. a) Why are some risks uninsurable? Give an example of an uninsurable risk.   4
   b) What steps should be taken by a newly formed small business wishing to take out motor insurance?   8
   c) Explain the insurance principles:-
      i) the pooling of risks
      ii) indemnity   8

ASSIGNMENT

Working in small groups complete the following tasks. Each member of the group should produce an individual piece of written work.

1. Visit your nearest town and make a list of:
   a) All the insurance companies which have branches in the town
   b) The names of any insurance brokers
   c) The names of any insurance agents

2. Visit one or more of the companies or brokers and ask for leaflets on the main types of insurance for householders and businesses.

3. a) Explain how insurance companies make a profit
   b) Why do they regard some risks as uninsurable?
   c) Give 2 examples of such risks

4. Find out from a relative or friend:
   a) What insurance cover they currently have or have taken out in the past year and why
   b) Whether they used an insurance company, broker or agent
   c) Comment on your findings

5. Finally state with reasons what you consider to be the 4 most important types of insurance for each of the following:
   a) A married man, with 2 children, who is buying his house on a mortgage. He owns a small car.
   b) A town centre furniture store which employs 6 staff. It offers a delivery service to local customers.

20. The Stock Exchange

1.   In Chapter 6 we referred to shares as being a major source of capital for companies. In this chapter we consider the different types of shares, how public companies issue new shares and the role of the Stock Exchange in providing a market for them.

INTRODUCTION

2.   When a limited company is formed, the Board of Directors must decide how much capital is needed to finance the trading operations. This capital is then divided up into smaller equal parts called shares. Each share therefore represents a small part of the business and these are then sold to raise the money required to trade. Shares normally carry some voting rights which enables their holders to have a say in how the company is run, but this varies according to the type of share.

SECURITIES

3.   A security is simply a written or printed document acknowledging the investment of money. People who purchase securities are called *investors* and they can put their money into either stocks or shares. Generally speaking stocks are loans which carry a fixed rate of interest, whilst the return of shares varies.

4.   Investors who purchase shares in a company receive a share of the profits called a *dividend*. Most companies pay a dividend twice a year, an *interim* (for the first 6 months of their financial year) and a *final* (at the end).

5.   A dividend is declared as a percentage of the face value of a share, for example, a 5% dividend would pay 5p on every £1 share in the company. Thus a shareholder with 1,000 shares would receive £50.

N.B. Shareholders will only usually receive a dividend if the Company makes a profit.

6.
A Dividend Voucher

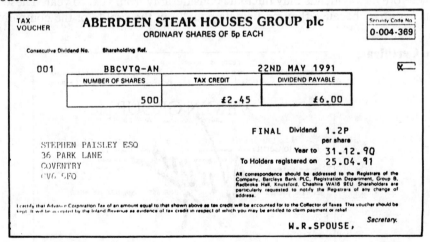

A dividend voucher is sent to shareholders showing the dividend which is being paid.

TYPES OF SECURITIES

7.   There are a number of different types of securities, the most common being preference shares, ordinary shares, debentures, and government and local authority bonds.

PREFERENCE SHARES

8.   These are so called because they receive a fixed dividend which is paid *before* all other classes of shareholders. The dividend is expressed as a fixed % on the nominal (original) value of the share, for example 8% £1 Preference Shares, means that the dividend is 8p per share p.a. Preference shareholders do not usually have any voting rights. There are several types of preference shares which are as follows:

a)   **Cumulative Preference Shares**

If there is insufficient profit to pay the dividend in one year then this will be made up in later years, for example 1989 no profit, therefore no dividend on 8% £1 Preference Shares, then in 1990 if there is sufficient profit the dividend will be 16p per share.

b)   **Non-cumulative Preference Shares**

These are exactly the same as cumulative, but without the right to receive any arrears of dividend. Dividends are paid out of current year profits only, therefore no profit means no dividend.

c)   **Redeemable Preference Shares**

These shares are issued for a specified period and the company agrees to repay the capital at some future date, for example 10,000 £1 Preference Shares, Redeemable 1998 means that the company must repay this capital in 1998.

d)   **Participating Preference Shares**

In addition to the fixed dividend, these shares receive an additional dividend depending on the company's profits.

ORDINARY SHARES

9.   These are by far the most common type of share. Once the preference shareholders have been paid then the directors of the company decide how much of the profits to keep in reserve (i.e. money which is kept for future expansion or against a 'rainy day') and how much to pay as a dividend on the ordinary shares. Ordinary shareholders usually have voting rights and they also carry the greatest risk because profits and therefore the dividends may fluctuate considerably from year to year. These shares are often referred to as *'equities'* because they participate equally in the profits of the company.

10. **A Share Certificate**

DEBENTURES

11. These are not shares in a company but long-term loans. They are issued in £100 units and secured against property or other assets. Debenture holders receive a fixed rate of interest, which must be paid whether the company makes a profit or not, and usually have a guaranteed repayment date.

GILT EDGED (GOVERNMENT) SECURITIES

12. The government borrows money from the public to pay for capital expenditure on roads, hospitals, housing and other projects. It issues securities, variously called 'Treasury' stock, 'Exchequer' stock, 'Funding' and 'Tap' stock in £100 units. They are called gilt-edged because they are a very safe investment. A fixed rate of interest is paid and they usually have a fixed date for repayment, for example 10% Treasury 1994.

13. They appear in newspapers as below:

1994	Exchequer	12.25	96.62	99.50	95.0
Date of Repayment	Name of Bill	Rate of Interest	Current Price	Highest Price During Year	Lowest Price During Year

LOCAL AUTHORITY LOANS

14. These are issued by Local Councils to finance their long term expenditure, for example city centre developments. These bonds carry a fixed rate of interest for a fixed number of years and are another very safe form of investment.

THE ISSUE OF SHARES

15. Public limited companies can issue shares to raise capital by a public issue, offer for sale, placing or rights issue, as explained below.

PUBLIC ISSUE

16. This is a direct approach to the public which is usually handled on behalf of the company by a specialist issuing house. Merchant banks, clearing banks, or a firm of issuing brokers will do this in return for a commission.

17. The issuing house prepares a *prospectus* which must be advertised in at least two national newspapers inviting the public to buy the shares. It must also be lodged with the Registrar of Companies before any shares can be sold. The prospectus gives information about the company including:

* Financial position
* Recent profits record
* Trading prospects
* Number of shares to be sold
* Price per share
* Closing date for applications

The issue price may be at *par* (the face value of the shares, for example £1) or at a *premium* (more than the face value, for example £1 shares offered at £1.25).

18.

An Advertisement offering Shares for Sale

19. After the applications have been received the shares will be allotted to purchasers. If the issue is *over-subscribed* the issuing house will allot some proportion of the shares applied for to each applicant.

20.

Issue of 1 million 10p Ordinary Shares @ £1.45 each	Applications received for 3 million Shares OVERSUBSCRIBED 3/4 million Shares UNDERSUBSCRIBED

21. If the issue is *undersubscribed* the issuing house will be left with unsold shares. This problem is overcome by the use of *underwriters* (usually merchant banks). They agree a price before a sale at which they will buy any unsold shares.

22. Sometimes shares are issued not at a fixed price but by *tender*. Applicants are invited to state a price at which they are prepared to buy shares, subject usually to a set minimum.

23.

Issue of 2 million Ordinary Shares at a minimum tender price of £1.30 each	Applications received 5 million Shares at a price of £1.30 and above	Sale of 2 million Shares at an issue price of £1.80

24. In the above illustration anyone who tendered for shares at a price of £1.80 or above would receive the full amount applied for at the issue price of £1.80. Anyone offering less than £1.80 would receive no shares at all.

OFFERS FOR SALE

25. Sometimes a company will sell its entire share issue to an issuing house. The issuing house will then offer the shares to the public as outlined above.

PLACINGS

26. A large number of share issues are 'placed' by the issuing house with its own clients, usually large financial institutions. Thus the shares are not offered directly to the public.

RIGHTS ISSUE

27. This is a cheap way for a public company to raise additional capital. Existing shareholders are offered the 'right' to buy some more shares in the company at a discount to the market price. For example, if the current market price is £3.50, for each ten shares held, shareholders may be given the right to buy one at a price of £3.00 each.

THE STOCK EXCHANGE

28. A company is not like a bank or building society and therefore it cannot give shareholders their money back when they ask for it because it has already been spent – on buildings, machinery, materials, wages, and all the other needs of the business. However, before buying securities investors naturally want to know that they can sell them again if they need their money back. This problem is overcome by having a Stock Market.

29. The Stock Exchange is a highly organised financial market based in London, where over 7,000 different securities can be bought and sold, including shares in over 500 leading overseas companies.

HOW THE STOCK EXCHANGE WORKS

30. In a sense the Stock Exchange is no different to any other market place selling consumer goods, except that:

    a)   It only deals in second hand securities.

    b)   The 'goods' for sale are in fact the shares of companies which represent the value of part ownership of that business.

    c)   It is not open to the public, only members may do business. Members are of two types, market makers and brokers (also called stockbrokers or broker dealers).

    d)   The 'Trading Floor' is a SEAQ (Stock Exchange Automated Quotation System) television screen located in brokers offices – anywhere in the UK or overseas – connected to the Exchanges central computers in London.

MEMBERS OF THE STOCK EXCHANGE

31. **Market makers** are specialist firms who arrange the purchase and sale of securities on behalf of brokers. They are like wholesalers buying shares at one price and selling them at a higher price to make a profit. Because some 7,000 different securities are listed on the Stock Exchange, market makers specialise in particular categories, for example banking, building, engineering, oils etc.

32. **Brokers** act on behalf of members of the public (called clients) who want to buy or sell shares. They charge a percentage commission on the value of the deal, for example 500 shares bought at £2 each, total cost £3,000, commission at 1.65% = £49.50. Brokers will also give advice to clients on their investments.

DEALING IN SHARES

33. The client instructs his broker to buy or sell some shares. Using SEAQ, the broker will check a list of all prices to try and get the best deal for his client. Prices are adjusted in response to changes in *supply* and *demand*.

34. Two prices are shown, a higher one at which they will sell shares (offer price) and a lower one at which they will buy (bid price), for example £1.25 and £1.20. When he has found the best price of the share being traded, the broker will complete the transaction through computer systems or over the telephone.

35. **SHARE DEALING**

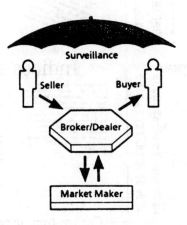

UNLISTED SECURITIES MARKET (USM)

36. Often young companies going public will seek admission to the USM as a first step towards acceptance to the full Stock Exchange official list because it is cheaper and easier to do. This 'second tier' market was started in 1980 and shares are traded in exactly the same way as outlined above.
The Stock Exchange considers that the USM no longer fulfils its role of providing capital for smaller companies and therefore it is to close at the end of 1995. In its place the official list will include a 'smaller companies sector'.

QUOTED OR LISTED COMPANIES

37. A quoted or listed company is one whose shares and/or debentures can be bought and sold on the stock market. The *Stock Exchange Daily Official List* is a list of all quoted companies and gives particular details including the latest prices and dividend payments.

38. Details of the share prices of most companies quoted on the Stock Exchange can be found in the Financial Times, but many other daily newspapers such as The Express, Mail and Telegraph include shorter lists restricted to the more important and well known companies.

39. **A selection of share prices as they appear in the Daily Mail.**

		1993 High	Low
Vodafone	441	+1	471	367
Volex	429		441	368
WholesaleF	253		255	223

ELECTRICITY

Eastern El	501	-½	506	399
East Midlands	477		487	389
London Elec	498	-1	501	404
Manweb	551	-4	559	458
Midlands	512	+4	514	424½
Nat Power	362		372	273
Northern El	544	-2	554	440
Nth Ireland	141	+1	141	100
Norweb	531	+4	544	439
PowerGen	384		392	273
Scot Hydro	343	+6	356	304
Scot Power	319	+2	337	285
Seeboard	527*	+2	535	436
Souther El	502	-2	506	406
South Wales	561	-1	571	469
Sth West Elec	509	+1	532	426
Yrkshire El	538	-3	552	455

ENGINEERING

APV	98	+1½	132	88
Adwest	176		176	124
Alumasc	545		545	415
Alvis	43*		48	17
Babcock	35½		41½	31
Bespak	530		707	461
Bimec	5¼		11¾	3¼
Br Aero	420	+15	429	165
Bridon	103		119	64
Bromsgrove	104		109	78
Bullough	120		120	91
Carclo	244	+2	244	178
Control Tc	321	-3	356	225
Concentric	216		246	186½
Cook (Wm)	198	+1	209	120
Dobson Prk	72		77	50
Domino Prt	426	-2	620	419
EIS	395		421	367
ERF	250*	+5	264	155
Elliott (B)	59		66	45
Expamet	76	-1	87	47
FR Group	262	+1	290	226
Fairey Grp	667		668	499
GEI	74*		85	71
GKN	453		489	434
Glynwed	295		311	245
Haden Mac	54		57	30½
Hall Eng	228		235	115
Hill & Smith	152		152	112½
Hopkinsons	43½		49	30
Howden	76		82	54½
Johnson&F	51½		64	51
Laird	296		303	266

		1993 High	Low
Ivory&Sime	152		153	125
M&G Group	824	-1	829	633
MAI	212½		213	154
Manakin	61		61	47
MAM	536	+6	536	389
Prov Fincl	368		397	270
Rutland	22		23½	17
Singer F	67		70	48
Smith N Ct	269		285	115
Trio Hldgs	72*		81	55

FOOD MANUFACTURING

Acatos & H	249	+4	255	170
Albt Fisher	63		76	55
Ass Br Fd	472	-5	515	461
Berisford	130		141	112½
Bibby (J)	76		133	75
Booker	407	+3	455	357
Borthwick	48½	+½	52	35
Brake Bros	502		505	430
Cadbury-S	450	-2	511	413
Dalepak	193	-12	384	168
Dalgety	453	-2	491	424
Finlay J	70		94	64
Geest	381	-1	483	328
Greggs	708		710	430
Hazlewood	195		203	147
Hillsdown	142		171	131
Matthews B	57		58	41
Nthn Foods	251	-5	290	242
Perkins Fd	87	-1	115	83
Tate&Lyle	385	-2	439	357
Unigate	350	+1	375	300
Unt Bisc	368	+4	437	340½
Watson & P	298		337	248

INDUSTRIALS

AAH	485 *		616	478
ADT	613		675	463
ASW	200		233	81
AlexandraW	143		147	113
Anglo Utd	2¾		7	2¾
Arjo Wiggins	169	-1	195	144
Attwoods	115		142	108
Avon Rbr	488		541½	434
BBA	162		172	147
BM Gp	16½		77	13
BSS	429		487	353
BTR	362	-6	380	318
Barlow Rand	662	+12	1062	556
BarryWehm	170	-1	221	170
Benson Grp	16¾		27½	15½
Black P	179		183	136
Blockleys	57		63	36
Blue Circ	241	-3	265	189
Bodycote	278		293½	247
Boustead	20		22	15

Equities hit by profit-taking

BTR bid talk fires engineering shares

SHARES ended a traumatic week yesterday on a firm note, but still showed the considerable damage caused by the jump in bank lending and the poor trade figures.
The feature of the day was renewed speculation that BTR could be planning a mega bid for the ...

Sudden interest rate rise sends shares tumbling

Indices shape up for new highs

SHARES pushed ahead at the end of the Account yesterday as impetus was provided by expectations of a rising oil price after the Opec meeting.
Oil shares were prominent, while properties ended an excellent week with renewed strength. Speculators were still talking about a possible mega takeover bid from BTH for GKN.

Profit-taking absorbed

STOCK MARKETS yesterday celebrated the Conservatives victory with yet another record-breaking performance by equities. The announcement quickly sent shares soaring to fresh peaks, and a mid-morning bout of profit-taking proved easy to absorb.

— Change from previous day's price

SHARE PRICES

40. The price of stocks and shares varies from day to day according to the supply and demand, ie. the number of people who want to sell shares and the number who want to buy. Thus if the demand for shares exceeds the supply the price will rise. If the supply exceeds demand the price will fall. So although you might buy a share for £1 it could go up in value if the company does well, to say £1.50. Prices may also be affected by some of the following factors.

SOME REASONS WHY SHARE PRICES FLUCTUATE

41. a) The recent company profit record and rate of dividend paid and the growth prospects of the company's market.

b) Rumours and announcements of proposed take-overs and mergers or trading difficulties.

c) Changes in Government policy, for example restriction on consumer spending will probably cause a fall in the share price of companies making consumer durable goods.

d) World political and economic events will have some effect on the shares of companies which have a large export trade, for example a recession or boom in another country.

e) Changes in the rate of interest on government securities will sometimes affect share prices. A rise in the market rate of interest might cause some 'switching' from shares to government securities.

f) Major events such as a General Election, the Budget, or something affecting a particular company like the discovery of a new drug can all influence share prices.

g) Views of experts. Articles by well-known financial writers can persuade people to buy or sell certain classes of shares.

h) Industrial disputes or settlements.

STOCK EXCHANGE INVESTORS

42. There are two main reasons why investors may put their money into securities (as an alternative to a bank or building society).

a) They receive a regular *income* in the form of a dividend payment on shares or interest on stocks like debenture and gilts.

b) They may make a *'capital gain'* if the securities increase in price and thus can be sold at a profit. Investors who buy shares for 'capital gain' are called speculators.

43. There are three main types of speculators, although they could be the same person operating at different times.

a) **Bulls** – who buy shares in the hope that their price will rise so that they can sell them at a profit. For example 1,000 shares bought for £1 each (cost £1,000) sold 6 months later at £1.50 each (sold for £1,500) gives a capital gain of £500.

b) **Bears** – who sell shares in the belief that their price will fall so that they can buy them back again later at a lower price. For example 1,000 shares sold for £1.50 each (sold for £1,500), bought again three months later at a price of £1.00 each (cost £1,000) gives a profit of £500.

c) **Stags** – who buy new share issues in the hope of selling them immediately at a profit.

UNIT TRUSTS

44. Instead of buying shares themselves, investors can purchase through a unit trust. This helps to spread the risks of investment because a unit trust is supervised by trustees (usually banks or other reputable institutions) and managed by professional investment managers. They invest in a wide range of companies or government securities.

45. The fund is divided into units so that each unit represents a fraction of all the investments of the fund. The units are sold to the public who may, if they wish, sell them back to the managers at some future date. Unit holders receive dividends in much the same way as shareholders.

46. A selection of Unit Trust prices as they appear in the Daily Telegraph

EQUITABLE UNIT TRUST MNGRS LTD
Walton St, Aylesbury, 0296 431480

Cancellation Price	Name	Bid	Offer	Change on Day
94.67	Equitable Pelican	97.04	102.15	+1.69
144.32	Far Eastern	147.37	155.13	+1.68
47.83	Gilt & Fixed Int.	48.17	*50.71	+0.41
98.25	High Income	100.85	106.16	+2.03
60.67	North American	62.24	65.52	+0.54
84.36	Special St	87.63	92.24	+1.5
93.31	Trust of Inv Tst	96.73	*101.82	+1.23
65.95	Intl Gwth	67.8	71.37	+0.75
51.54	European Tst	52.33	55.08	+0.57
44.0	Smaller Co's	46.82	49.28	+0.87

EQUITY & LAW TST MNGRS LTD
St George's House, Corporation St,
Coventry CV1 1GD. 0203 553231

Cancellation Price	Name	Bid	Offer	Change on Day
226.0	UK Growth Tst. Acc.	229.9	244.6	+2.9
172.5	UK Growth Tst. Inc.	175.4	186.7	+2.1
398.0	Higher Inc. Tst. Acc.	405.9	431.9	+4.8
269.5	Higher Inc. Tst. Inc.	274.8	292.4	+3.3
82.08	Gilts/Fxd Int Tst Inc.	82.46	86.8	+0.08
132.2	Gilt & Fix Acc	132.7	139.7	+0.2
124.7	North Am Tr	128.4	136.6	+2.2
193.6	Far East Tst	195.3	207.8	+2.4
187.7	Europe Tst	189.8	202.0	+1.4
321.7	General Tst	324.2	344.9	+4.1
47.95	British Exell	47.95	51.01	+0.69
61.24	Brit Fndmtls Tst Acc	61.24	65.15	+0.37
53.25	Brit Fndmtls Tst Inc	53.25	56.65	+0.32
47.61	Global Opp Tst	48.75	51.87	+0.59

EXETER FUND MNGT LTD
23 Cathedral Yard, Exeter EX1 1HD
0392 412144

Cancellation Price	Name	Bid	Offer	Change on Day
21.07	Exeter Fund Inv Tst	21.32	*22.75	+0.34
45.41	High Income Trust	46.55	*49.66	+0.14
41.43	Capital Growth	43.83	47.01	+0.56

HALIFAX STANDARD TRUST MANAGEMENT LTD
PO Box 600, Edinburgh, EH15 1EW
0800 838 868

Cancellation Price	Name	Bid	Offer	Change on Day
25.38	Global Advantage Inc	25.8	*27.35	+0.01
25.2	Global Advantage Ac	25.62	*27.16	+0.01

HENDERSON UNIT TRST MNGMT LTD
PO Box 2003, Brentwood, Essex CM13 1XT
Enqrs: 0277 227300 Dealing: 0277 690370

Cancellation Price	Name	Bid	Offer	Change on Day
99.36	American Recovery	99.36	106.03	+1.31
42.3	American Small Co's	42.3	45.73	+0.26
61.96	Asian Enterprise Tst	61.96	66.41	+0.42
94.0	Australian	94.0	101.05	-0.02
44.96	Best of British Tst	44.96	48.13	+0.93
282.18	European	282.18	299.34	+2.58
53.67	European Inc	53.67	*56.8	+0.39
99.54	European Small Co's	99.54	105.57	+1.06
223.12	Extra Income	223.12	238.03	+3.02
48.91	Fixed Interest	48.91	52.09	+0.06
56.8	Global Inc & Growth	56.8	60.97	+0.84
60.42	Global Resources	60.42	*64.47	-0.14
241.99	High Income	241.99	*259.24	+5.03
138.07	Income & Assets	138.07	148.13	+2.28
191.75	Income & Growth	191.75	205.14	+4.35
439.27	Income & Gth Acc	439.27	469.95	+9.94
164.72	International	164.72	175.07	+1.68
155.07	Japan	155.07	*164.61	+1.38
164.68	Japan Special Sits	164.68	174.76	+1.86
138.92	Nth American	138.92	*147.72	+0.89
104.7	Pacific Smaller Co's	104.7	112.27	+0.18
36.09	Preference & Gilt	36.09	*39.59	+0.44
112.65	Smaller Co's Div	112.65	*124.28	+1.59
183.49	Special Sits Inc	183.49	196.66	+4.13
270.56	Special Sits Acc	270.56	289.98	+6.1
35.84	Spirit of the East	35.84	38.31	+0.21
124.71	European Exmpt	124.71	128.61	+1.14
73.89	Global Tech Exmpt	73.89	76.62	+1.4
47.95	Pension Managed Fd	47.95	49.82	+0.54

THE MANULIFE GROUP PLC
St. George's Way, Stevenage
Dealing: 071-256 5858

Cancellation Price	Name	Bid	Offer	Change on Day
142.9	Gilt & Fixed Int.	142.9	150.2	+0.3
122.3	Growth Units	123.6	131.5	+1.9
141.5	High Income Units	142.9	152.1	+2.0
127.9	Int. Growth Units	129.0	137.3	+1.4
77.1	Nth. American Units	79.28	84.34	+1.14
101.8	Far East Units	102.4	109.0	+1.1
91.87	U.K. Smaller Comp's	91.87	97.73	+1.1
61.31	High Yield Gilt	61.31	*64.59	+0.04
50.56	European	51.86	54.02	+0.39
44.37	Managed Port	44.6	47.45	+0.64
34.12	Japanese Gr	34.12	36.33	

MARKS & SPENCER UNIT TST MNGT LTD
P.O. Box 410, Chester X, CH99 9QG
0244 680066

Cancellation Price	Name	Bid	Offer	Change on Day
102.8	M & S Inv Portfolio	103.2	*110.3	+1.7
108.7	M & S Inv Port Acc	109.1	*116.6	+1.8
91.99	UK Select Port Inc	92.94	99.4	+2.92
96.18	UK Selection Port	97.15	103.9	+3.1

MARTIN CURRIE UT LTD
48 Melville St, Edinburgh EH3 7HF
031-226 4372

Cancellation Price	Name	Bid	Offer	Change on Day
85.23	MC Far East (ScPac)	85.23	90.47	+0.75
54.53	MC Incme & Gwth Fd	55.06	*58.44	+1.16
31.95	MC Nth American	31.95	33.91	+0.15
50.7	MC European	51.21	*54.36	+0.83
54.46	MC Int Gwth	54.46	58.88	+0.25
47.69	MC UK Growth Fund	47.69	50.62	+0.47
35.92	Japan	35.92	38.13	+0.23
44.16	Intl Inc Fd	44.71	47.46	+0.37
42.26	High Yield Fd	42.91	*45.55	+0.31
84.13	Charities	85.41	*90.66	+0.59

The cancellation price is the minimum redemption price for the units.

INSTITUTIONAL INVESTORS

47. It is estimated that 15-20% of the UK's population are direct investors owning securities which they have purchased. However, about 90% are indirect investors via the *institutional investors*. These include insurance companies, trade unions, pension funds and unit trusts who all invest large sums of money in securities.

'BIG BANG'

48. This is the name given to the important changes which took place in the Stock Exchange on 27 October 1986. These can be summarised as follows:

a) The system of *fixed commissions* for buying and selling shares was *abolished*. Brokers can now charge what they like thus making the market more competitive.

b) The old distinctions between stockjobbers (who make a market in shares) and stockbrokers (who buy and sell for investors) were removed and *all members became broker dealers*. Firms are now able to operate in a 'dual capacity' as both market makers and brokers, although they usually operate separately to avoid conflicts of interest.

c) The new *electronic price display network* SEAQ was introduced. An electronic dealing system SAEF followed in 1989. SAEF (SEAQ Automatic Execution Facility) operates for small orders of 1000 shares or less (estimated to be about 40% of all bargains). These orders are entered directly into the computer and executed automatically at the touch of a button. SAEF provides a quicker and cheaper service for investors.

d) The setting up of a *'third tier' market* for smaller, less well-established companies. This began in 1987 but was abolished in December 1990.

e) In March 1986 prior to the 'Big Bang', another important change allowed *outside institutions* to take over and control existing stock exchange member firms. This has already resulted in increased competition from foreign securities firms namely the two largest from Japan and USA – Nomura Securities and Merrill Lynch.

CONTROL OF THE STOCK EXCHANGE

49. The Stock Exchange is controlled by the provisions of the 1986 *Financial Services Act*. This Act was introduced to increase the protection for investors by making it an offence for any person or firm to carry out investment business unless they are authorised to do so.

50. It set up the *Securities and Investments Board* (SIB), directly accountable to Parliament, to supervise the whole operation and five *Self-Regulatory Organisations* (SRO's). Each SRO sets stringent rules which member firms must follow. Investment businesses seeking authorisation can either apply direct to SIB or the appropriate SRO. They have to prove that they are 'fit and proper persons' to conduct such businesses. Investment business must also be conducted through a Recognised Investment Exchange (for example The Stock Exchange, London Metal Exchange), and each Exchange must settle its business through a Recognised Clearing House. The Settlement Service Division of The Stock Exchange is the recognised Clearing House for Stock Market transactions.

51.

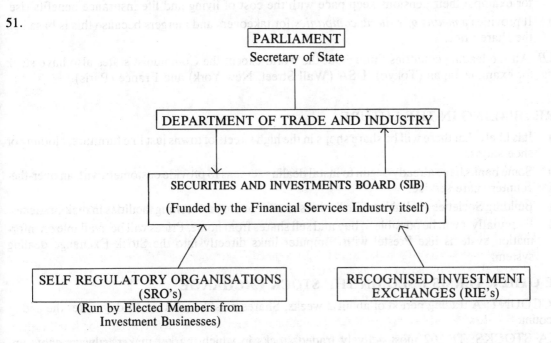

52. The SRO which regulates the Stock Exchange is called the **Securities Association**. It has the following main functions:
* To control the admission of new member firms
* To set rules for the conduct of the Exchange
* To discipline and sometimes expel members who break the rules
* To maintain a compensation fund to pay the clients of any member firm which fails to meet its obligations

*   To handle applications from companies wanting their shares traded on the Exchange.

53. *N.B.* The Stock Exchange Quotation Committee makes a detailed investigation of a company's profits record, shares offered and directors background before allowing its shares to be traded on the Exchange.

IMPORTANCE OF THE STOCK EXCHANGE TO THE BRITISH ECONOMY

54. a)   It *encourages people to invest* in securities because it provides a market where they can get their money back.

    b)   *Companies can raise large amounts of money* on the Stock Exchange for investment in new machinery, buildings etc. Firms cannot expand unless they can raise the necessary finance. Mass production could not take place, goods could not be produced as cheaply, leading to higher unemployment and a lower standard of living. Therefore ultimately our standard of living and way of life are affected by the Stock Exchange.

    c)   The *Government can raise finance* for the nationalised industries and various essential projects by selling government bonds on the Stock Exchange. Obviously without the Stock Exchange this could not be done. There would be fewer and more costly state services and taxation would have to be increased to provide the funds. In recent years over 75% of new issues have been in gilt-edged securities.

    d)   *Most people will gain from successful stock market investments* by the institutional investors, for example their pensions keep pace with the cost of living and life insurance benefits rise.

    e)   It provides a *means of valuing companies* for takeovers and mergers because this is based on the share price.

55. *N.B.* All the leading countries throughout the world except the Communist states also have stock markets, for example Japan (Tokyo), USA (Wall Street, New York) and France (Paris).

SHARE DEALING IN THE FUTURE

56. a)   It is likely that there will be share shops in the high streets of towns just like furniture, clothing or shoe shops.

    b)   Some banks have already begun to instal dealing screens to provide customers with an over-the-counter share service.

    c)   Building Societies are linking with brokers to offer buying and selling facilities in their branches.

    d)   Eventually it will be possible to buy and sell shares from home. Prices will be available on information systems like Prestel with computer links directly into the Stock Exchange dealing system.

SOME OTHER TERMS USED ON THE STOCK EXCHANGE

57. ACCOUNT: A trading period of about 2 weeks, Shares must be paid for 10 days after the end of the account.

ALPHA STOCKS: The 62 most actively traded stocks in which market makers always show up-to-date prices.

APPLICATION FORM: Used to apply for new issues and found at the back of the prospectus.

BARGAIN: Any Stock Exchange transaction.

BETA STOCKS: Actively traded stocks which market makers always show. They are up-dated regularly.

BLUE CHIP: A description applied to the shares of large and highly regarded companies, for example Marks & Spencer, ICI, BT.

CALL: A demand for payment of an instalment due on shares. Sometimes only part of the money is paid on allotment and the balance due in one or more future calls.

CONTRACT NOTE: A written confirmation from a broker that a bargain (buying or selling) has been carried out.

DELTA STOCKS: Little traded stocks for which market makers do not show prices, but merely indicate that they are prepared to trade in them.

EARNINGS: A company's net profits after tax.

EARNINGS PER SHARE: A company's total earnings divided by the number of its shares.

F T INDEX: Financial Times Industrial Ordinary Share Index based on the shares of 30 leading UK companies, for example ICI, GKN, Glaxo. It is used to measure the overall movement of stock market prices. There is also an FT All Share Index.

FT/SE 100: Known as the 'Footsie', this is the Financial Times/Stock Exchange 100 Share Index based on 100 of the largest companies listed on the Stock Exchange. In January 1984 a base of 1000 was set. It reached 2500 in 1991.

FLOTATION: When a company goes public offering its shares to the market for the first time.

FUTURES: Contracts which give the holder the right to buy securities for an agreed price at a future date.

GAMMA STOCKS: Relatively inactive stocks in which market makers display quotes, ie only give an indication of the likely price.

INVESTMENT TRUST: A company formed specifically to invest in the shares of other companies.

JOBBER: Before the 'Big Bang' a jobber was a wholesaler in stocks and shares, who traded with brokers. This function is now performed by market makers.

PENNY SHARES: Shares worth less than 60p.

PERSONAL EQUITY PLANS (PEP's): Government scheme to encourage investment in shares by allowing income and capital gains tax benefits.

PORTFOLIO: The total of an individual's share holdings.

PRICE/EARNINGS RATIO (P/E): The share price divided by earnings per share. A useful guide to the value placed on a company. A share selling at 75p with a P/E ratio of 10 would be less profitable than one selling at 75p with a P/E ratio of 5.

SETTLEMENT DAY: The day when share purchases must be paid for.

SHARE CERTIFICATE: An official document issued to confirm ownership. The Stock Exchange plans, eventually, to stop using these.

SHARE REGISTER: A company's list of its shareholders.

TALISMAN: The Stock Exchange computerised settlement system.

TAURUS: Electronic system for transferring shares without a share certificate.

TRADED OPTIONS: Transferable contracts giving the right to buy and sell securities at a set price within a set period.

TRANSFER FORM: A form signed by the seller of a security authorising the company to remove his name from the register and substitute that of the buyer.

TURN: The difference between a market makers buying and selling price ie profit.

YIELD: The annual return on money invested based on the current price of the

security = $\dfrac{\text{Par value of share} \times \% \text{ rate dividend}}{\text{current price}}$

for example a £1 share bought for £2. If the dividend declared is 10% then the

yield = $\dfrac{£1 \times 10\%}{£2}$ = 5%

Generally lower yields reflect a secure business with growth potential, higher yields suggest riskier investments.

SUMMARY

58. a) Public Limited Companies, the Government and Local Authorities all issue securities in order to raise capital from investors.

b) The main types of securities are preference shares, ordinary shares, debentures and government and local authority bonds.

c) A company can issue shares via a public issue, offer for sale, placing or rights issue.

d) A public issue is usually handled by an issuing house which prepares a prospectus and advertises the shares to the public.

e) The Stock Exchange provides a market where second-hand securities can be bought and sold.

f) Market makers operate like wholesalers with a supply of shares which they buy from and sell to brokers.

g) Brokers act on behalf of clients who want to buy or sell shares.

h) The price of shares varies from day-to-day according to supply and demand.

i) Investors including 'institutions' may seek to receive income from securities or to make a capital gain.

j) Bulls, bears and stags are Stock Market speculators.

k) The Stock Exchange is controlled by the Securities Association which is a Self Regulatory Organisation.

l) The 'Big Bang' brought about important changes in the operation of the Stock Exchange.

m) The Stock Exchange is very important to the economy because it makes it possible for companies and the Government to raise large sums of money.

REVIEW QUESTIONS

Answers can be found in the paragraphs shown.

1. Give the main features of preference shares, equities, debentures and gilt-edged securities. (7-13)

2. Distinguish between a 'public issue', 'offer for sale', 'placing' and 'rights issue'. (15-27)

3. Briefly describe the process involved if you wanted to buy 500 shares in British Gas. (30-36)

4. List 5 factors which might affect a company's share price. (40-41)

5. Explain the difference between stock market 'bulls', 'bears' and 'stags'. (42-43)

6. How do unit trusts spread the risks of investment? (44-46)

7. What are institutional investors and why are they important? (47)

8. How did the 'Big Bang' affect the operation of the stock market? (48)

9. Outline the importance of the London Stock Exchange to the UK economy. (28, 29, 54)

10. In what ways do the SIB and SRO's protect investors? (50-53)

11. In what ways is share dealing likely to become much easier in the future? (56)

12. Explain each of the following – 'Blue Chip', 'FT Index', 'Portfolio'. (57)

EXAMINATION PRACTICE QUESTIONS

1. The capital of Company X is as follows:
   100,000 5% Preference shares of £1 each
   50,000 5% Debentures of £1 each
   200,000 Ordinary shares of £1 each

If profits of £27,500 are available for distribution: **Marks**

   a)   How much must be paid in interest to the Debenture holders?   2

   b)   How much would be paid to the Preference shareholders?   2

   c)   What rate of dividend will be paid to the Ordinary shareholders?   2

   d)   If the Ordinary shares market price is £1.60 what is the current yield?   2

   e)   What is the nominal value of the equity of the Company?   2

2.   Stock Exchange members are called broker dealers. Explain how they make a profit if they operate as:

   a)   Market Makers   2

   b)   Brokers   2

3.   What is a cumulative preference share?   2

4.   The Chairman of City Electrical plc states that the amount available for distribution to debenture holders and shareholders is £35,000. The company has share capital of 200,000 Ordinary Shares of £1 each, 50,000 Preference Shares of £1 paying 8%, as well as £10,000 worth of 10% Debentures.

   a)   What are Debentures?   2

   b)   What are Preference Shares?   2

   c)   What are Ordinary Shares?   2

   d)   Calculate the amount paid to the Debenture holders.   2

   e)   Calculate the amount payable to the Preference shareholders.   2

   f)   Calculate the amount of profit now available for distribution to the Ordinary shareholders.   2

   g)   Calculate the percentage dividend payable to the Ordinary shareholders. (show your working)   3

MULTIPLE CHOICE/COMPLETION

1.   A company which issues debentures must pay the holders:

   a)   Interest

   b)   Commission

   c)   Bonuses

   d)   Dividends

2.   Details of a new share issue are given in a company's:

   a)   Articles of Association

   b)   Memorandum of Association

   c)   Prospectus

   d)   Profit and Loss Account

3.   A shareholder in a plc wishing to sell his shares would:

   a)   Ask the company to buy them back

   b)   Be unable to sell them

   c)   Advertise to find a buyer

   d)   Instruct a stock-broker to sell on his behalf

4.   A Treasury Bill is a:

   a)   Blue Chip share

   b)   Gilt-edged security

   c)   Debenture

   d)   Preference share

5. An investor owns 500 shares in a company which have a nominal value of £300 and a market value of £400. If a 10% dividend is declared the shareholder would receive:

   a) £30
   b) £40
   c) £330
   d) £440

In the following question, one or more of the responses is/are correct. Choose the appropriate letter which indicates the correct version.

   A   if 1 only is correct
   B   if 3 only is correct
   C   if 1 and 2 only are correct
   D   if 1, 2 and 3 are correct

6. Which of the following would you expect to find operating in the Stock Market?

   1) Bulls
   2) Bears
   3) Brokers

RECENT EXAMINATION QUESTIONS

Marks

LCCI DECEMBER 1989 SSC BACKGROUND TO BUSINESS

1.

High	Low	Company	Price
180	125	Comlon International plc £1 Ordinary Shares	150 +2 XD

The above information relates to the Ordinary Shares of Comlon International plc on 24 November 1989.

   a)   What is the nominal value of the shares and what is the importance of this value?
   b)   Explain the meaning of XD.
   c)   How much would an investor pay if he wishes to buy 500 shares?
   d)   What dividend would the owner of 500 shares receive if the Company declared a dividend of 10%?
   e)   What was the price of 1 share on the previous day?
   f)   Explain the purpose of the columns headed **High** and **Low**.

18

ASSIGNMENT THE STOCK MARKET

The trading results of public limited companies are often reported in the financial press, ie the Financial Times and business section of the Daily Telegraph, Guardian, Times and other newspapers. Look carefully at the following article which gives a report of the results of Jones Industries and then answer the 10 questions which apply to it.

JONES FIGHTING RECOVERY

By Henry Goodstaff

A much improved performance from computer supplies group Jones Industries caught City pessimists by surprise yesterday and sent the shares soaring 35p to 235p.

The dividend cut and poor trading figures announced by UK competitor Mitchem on Wednesday had led everyone to expect another set of poor results.

But Jones has managed to maintain its unbroken profits record by the narrowest of margins and delighted shareholders by increasing the dividend for the year ending December 1993.. Profits are up from £15.6 million to £16.2 million against expectations of around £14 million.

A final dividend of 5p brings the total payment for the 12 months to 8p. The group has pulled back losses in the microchip division from £1.8 million to almost break-even despite continuing competition from the Far East. Rental profits have improved slightly to £7.5 million and would have been better but for the recent cancellation of a large French order.

Expansion in Europe has helped the maintenance division to achieve another good performance whilst profits from commercial software have moved ahead due mainly to last year's takeover of the Swedish company Talcos Systems.

---

1. Name the 4 trading divisions of the company.

2. Which of the 4 divisions showed a loss in the year ending December 1993?

3. a) What is the name of the company's main UK competitor?
   b) How did it perform for the year?

4. What was the previous day's price of Jones Industries shares?

5. a) Explain what you understand by the dividend.
   b) What has happened to the dividends for the year ending December 1993?

6. a) How is profit calculated?
   b) Did Jones Industries profits increase or decrease in 1993, and by how much?

7. Explain why the shareholders of Jones Industries are delighted with the results.

8. What do you understand by the 'City pessimists' and why were they caught by surprise?

9. The article states that the company has managed to maintain its unbroken profits record. Explain this comment.

10. What information, if any, is there in the article to suggest that the company could make even higher profits in 1994?

21. Recruitment, Selection and Training

1. This chapter looks at the process of employing staff which involves recruitment, selection and interviewing. It also considers employment legislation and the different types of training in a business. It ends with a look at TEC's and Government training schemes including YT and ET.

2. A business's success very often depends upon the quality of the staff it employs. Their efficiency, loyalty, attitude and enthusiasm can make the difference between a firm making a profit or a loss. Therefore, many firms have a Personnel Officer or Staff Supervisor with the responsibility to find the right person for a particular job and to help staff to work efficiently and happily. The main function of the Personnel department therefore is to recruit staff.

RECRUITMENT

3. Before recruiting staff an employer must first of all decide:

   a) What staff are needed and

   b) How to attract suitable applicants.

JOB DESCRIPTION

4. When considering appointing staff an employer usually prepares a simple description of the job concerned. This will give the title of the job, an outline of the main purpose followed by a more detailed list of the duties which it involves.

5.

Example 1

TITLE:	TRAINEE SALES ASSISTANT
PURPOSE:	To perform a range of general duties as specified by the store manager
DUTIES: will include	Dealing with customers Selling Taking money Checking Stock Filling Shelves Moving Stock

Example 2

TITLE:	JUNIOR OFFICE CLERK
PURPOSE:	To undertake general clerical duties Responsible to the Office Manager
DUTIES:	Completing relevant paperwork Filing Answering the telephone Some Word Processing General Reception Duties

JOB SPECIFICATION

6. From the job description an employer can draw up a job specification. This is a check-list of the personal qualities, experience and skills which are needed in order to be able to do the job.

7. **Example 1**

JOB TITLE:	TRAINEE SALES ASSISTANT
QUALITIES/SKILLS:	Good appearance Ability to get on with people Good general education Honest Numerate Physically strong Age 16-17

Example 2

JOB TITLE:	JUNIOR CLERK
QUALITIES/SKILLS:	RSA I Typewriting/Word Processing 3 GCSE's Grade C including English Good appearance Good telephone manner Reliable Age 16-18

FINDING SUITABLE APPLICANTS

8.   The employers next task is to attract suitable applicants for the job. As you will probably know there are a number of ways of finding out about job vacancies including the following:

*   Local Careers Officers
*   Newspaper Advertisements
*   Trade Magazines
*   Job Centres
*   Private Employment Agencies
*   Friends and Relatives
*   Local Radio or Television

9.   Many firms use advertisements like the one shown below in the national or local newspapers to fill job vacancies. The advertisement gives details about the job itself and information on how to apply.

JOB ADVERTISEMENT

10.

SCHOOL LEAVER WANTED

for

General Office in City Centre

Duties include

Filing, Word Processing, Photocopying
and Reception Work

Training given. Good pay and prospects.

Apply in writing only, to:
Personnel Manager
Mr N Selby
Crompton & Co
57 High Street
Leicester

---

11.   Usually an advertisement asks people to reply in writing either by *letter*, by requesting an *application form* or by sending in a *curriculum vitae* (CV). The following examples illustrate the main features of each.

LETTER OF APPLICATION

12.

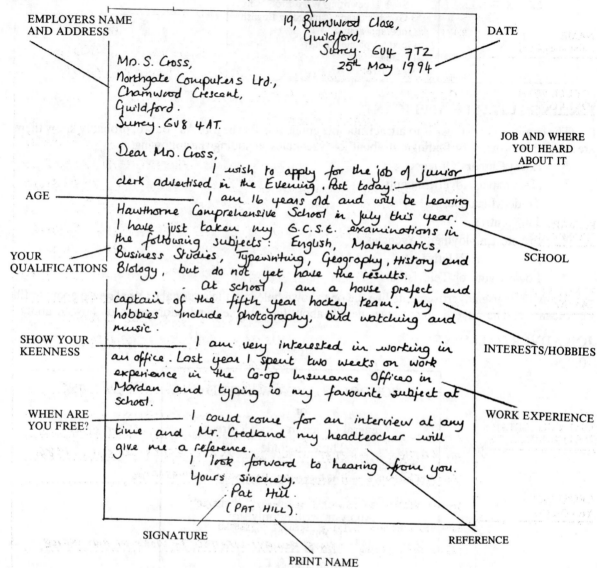

YOUR ADDRESS & TELEPHONE NUMBER (IF APPLICABLE)

EMPLOYERS NAME AND ADDRESS

DATE

19, Burnwood Close,
Guildford,
Surrey. GU4 7TZ
25th May 1994

Mr. S. Cross,
Northgate Computers Ltd.,
Charnwood Crescent,
Guildford.
Surrey. GV8 4AT.

Dear Mr. Cross,

JOB AND WHERE YOU HEARD ABOUT IT

I wish to apply for the job of junior clerk advertised in the Evening Post today.

AGE

I am 16 years old and will be leaving Hawthorne Comprehensive School in July this year.

SCHOOL

I have just taken my G.C.S.E. examinations in the following subjects: English, Mathematics, Business Studies, Typewriting, Geography, History and Biology, but do not yet have the results.

YOUR QUALIFICATIONS

At school I am a house prefect and captain of the fifth year hockey team. My hobbies include photography, bird watching and music.

INTERESTS/HOBBIES

SHOW YOUR KEENNESS

I am very interested in working in an office. Last year I spent two weeks on work experience in the Co-op Insurance Offices in Morden and typing is my favourite subject at school.

WORK EXPERIENCE

WHEN ARE YOU FREE?

I could come for an interview at any time and Mr. Credland my headteacher will give me a reference.

I look forward to hearing from you.
Yours sincerely,
Pat Hill.
(PAT HILL).

REFERENCE

SIGNATURE

PRINT NAME

APPLICATION FORM

13.

NAME (print in capitals)	HENLEY ENGINEERING LTD APPLICATION FORM

Surname ...HUSSAIN.........   Christian Name(s)... SAJID ......

Home Address ...19, EDGWICK CLOSE..., BINLEY WOOD

IN FULL WITH POST CODE

COVENTRY CV6 4ED ....

Telephone No ..(0203) 616477 ...

Nationality ....BRITISH ....   Date and place of birth 12 : 8 : '72

...BIRMINGHAM.......

Name and address of parent or guardian ...MR. K. HUSSAIN, 19 EDGWICK

CLOSE, BINLEY WOOD, COVENTRY CV6 4ED...

PRIMARY AND SECONDARY

Schools attended and dates   COUNDON COMPREHENSIVE SCHOOL

COVENTRY   1983 - 1988

BINLEY PRIMARY SCHOOL 1977 - 1983

IF NOT YET TAKEN, SAY SO

Exams taken and passes   G.C.S.E. ENGLISH LANGUAGE ....

MATHEMATICS, BUSINESS STUDIES

HISTORY, BIOLOGY, SPANISH ART +

DESIGN.

Other   E.S.B. SENIOR GRADE ONE ...

GIVE FULL DETAILS INCLUDING DATES

Previous employment (including part-time and holiday jobs) SATURDAY JOB...

ON FATHER'S MARKET STALL SELLING CARPETS — SINCE 1986

YOUTH TRAINING — HARGREAVES ENGINEERING 1988 ~ '1990

CROSS OUT YES OR NO

Are you willing to travel if necessary? YES/~~NO~~

Have you a current Driving Licence? ~~YES~~/NO

Reason for applying I HAVE ALWAYS WANTED TO WORK IN AN OFFICE...

Name and address of 2 referees:

MR. J. SMITH (HEADMASTER)   MR. T. JONES (YOUTH LEADER)

COUNDON COMPREHENSIVE   30 WESTVIEW

CAVENTRY CV6 3LJ.   FITTON HILL COVENTRY

ARE YOU FIT TO DO THE JOB?

Details of serious illnesses ...CHICKEN POX 1980...

SPARE TIME ACTIVITIES

Any special skills ....

Interests SPORT CRICKET RUGBY YOUTH CLUB CYCLING.....

Signature ...Sajid Hussain.......   Date .24TH MAY 1991......

CURRICULUM VITAE

14.

NAME:	MALCOLM O'CONNER
ADDRESS:	15 Eaton Grove BUXTON Derbyshire
TELEPHONE:	(0298) 47321
DATE OF BIRTH:	14 August 1975
EDUCATION:	High Peak School Long Road Buxton September 1986 – July 1991
QUALIFICATIONS:	**GCSE June 1991** Mathematics (Grade A) French (Grade B) Biology (Grade B) Business Studies (Grade C) English Language (Grade A) Chemistry (Grade E) Physics (Grade D)
INTERESTS/HOBBIES:	Tennis Camping Stamp collecting Reading
WORK EXPERIENCE:	2 weeks Office work at Dunstons, Buxton Saturday Sales Assistant at BJ Menswear, Buxton Jan. '90 – July '91
OTHER INFORMATION:	April 1990 Team Captain for Tennis November 1986-91 Member Eastwood Common Youth Club
REFEREES:	Head Teacher High Peak School Long Road BUXTON Tel: (0298) 611021 Mr B Salmon Manager BJ Menswear Manchester Road BUXTON Tel: (0298) 46274

15. Whichever method is used the employer wants to find out as much as possible about the people who are applying for the job. This information is then used (by the Personnel Department if there is one) to select a *short list* of suitable candidates for interview.

16. *N.B.*

    a) **References** Most employers will require anyone applying for a job to give the names of two people who know them well to act as referees. For example teacher, youth leader, vicar or former employer. The firm will then ask them for a confidential opinion on the character, attendance, punctuality and suitability of the applicant for the job.

    b) Some employers also accept **testimonials**. These are not confidential, and are usually headed 'To whom it may concern'. Copies can be given to any employer when applying for a job.

INTERVIEW

17. An interview is the last stage before getting a job. Many people may apply for a job, but only a small number will be interviewed. Many employers also ask candidates to take an aptitude test so that they can assess whether or not someone is suitable for the type of work, for example police cadets, nurses, engineering apprentices.

18. The interview is important for the employer who wants to find the best person for the job. It is also an opportunity for the candidate to find out more about the job and whether it is what they want. Therefore it is very important to prepare for it.

19.

HOW TO PREPARE FOR AN INTERVIEW

20. Before You Go

    * Find out as much as possible about the firm

    * Be prepared to answer questions – know everything about yourself

    * Make sure that you know the time and place of the interview

    * Work out what you need to ask the employer

21. **The Big Day**
    * Dress sensibly – look neat and tidy
    * Be punctual
    * Take your interview letter with you
    * Remember *and* use the interviewer's name
    * Be pleasant and polite – shake hands, wait to be asked to sit down, say thank you
    * Don't smoke, unless invited to
    * Speak clearly and answer questions fully, not just 'yes and no'
    * Show that you are interested in the job – be enthusiastic
    * Have some questions to ask – take a list if you wish

22. **Some Questions You Could Ask**

If an employer has not already told you, the following are examples of possible questions:
    * What training will I be given?
    * Will I be paid weekly or monthly?
    * What are the prospects for promotion?
    * Who will I be working with?
    * When will I be expected to start?

23. **What Questions Might You Be Asked?**
    * Why do you want to work here?
    * How did you hear about the job?
    * What are your interests and hobbies?
    * How did you like school?
    * What type of work does your family do?
    * What kind of books or newspapers do you read?

STARTING WORK – LEGISLATION AFFECTING EMPLOYMENT

24. When an employer makes an *offer* of a job and the employee *accepts* it in return for a *consideration* (payment of wages/salary), then a legal agreement called a *contract* exists.

25. The *Contract of Employment Acts* 1972-1982 state that an employee must be given a written state-ment of the main terms and conditions of their employment within 13 weeks of starting a new job. This should include details of the following:
    * Job Title
    * Date the job started
    * Rate of pay
    * Frequency of payment, for example weekly, monthly
    * Hours of work and holidays
    * Sickness benefits
    * Grievance procedure i.e. dealing with problems at work
    * Rights concerning Trade Union Membership
    * Disciplinary rules
    * Period of notice required to leave

Sometimes not all this information is given directly to employees but instead is kept in a 'conditions of service' booklet to which they must be able to refer at any time.

26. Other legislation which has been introduced to protect employees and improve their conditions of employment includes the Health and Safety at Work Act 1974, Equal Pay Acts 1970 and 1983, Sex Discrimination Act 1975 and Race Relations Act 1976.

27. **Health and Safety at Work Act 1974**   The purpose of this Act is to protect employees or members of the public from health and safety hazards at work. The Act makes everyone concerned with work activities responsible for health and safety, including:

* Employers, the self-employed, employees
* Manufacturers, designers, suppliers and importers of articles and substances for use at work
* Those in control of premises, for example Headteacher in a school.

28. The Act requires employers to:

* Maintain safe plant, equipment and systems of work
* Provide safety training and produce a Safety Policy Statement of which all employees must be made aware.

Employees are responsible for taking reasonable care at all times and for co-operating with the employer on safety matters.

29. The **Health and Safety Commission** was set up to enforce the Act. It employs Health and Safety Inspectors who visit firms. They may make recommendations to help firms or, where hazards are found, issue improvement orders (requiring an unsafe system to be altered within a specified period of time, usually 21 days), or prohibition orders (stopping the use of unsafe practices immediately). Anyone who breaks the law may be prosecuted and could be fined up to £20,000 or face a 6 month prison sentence. In Northern Ireland the Health and Safety Agency performs a similar function.

Can you spot at least 6 hazards?

Health and Safety at Work

HEALTH & SAFETY (GENERAL REGULATIONS) 1993

30. Sweeping changes to Health & Safety legislation were introduced in January 1993 when 6 new EC Directives came into force affecting virtually all employers, employees and the self-employed.

The regulations cover:
* **Health and Safety management**
  designed to encourage a more systematic and better organised approach to dealing with health and safety.
* **Work equipment safety**
  governing the use of equipment at work which can be anything from a simple hand tool like a

hammer, to complex plant such as an oil refinery.

* **Manual handling of loads**
applying to any manual handling operations which may cause injury at work including lifting, pushing, pulling, carrying or moving loads by hand or other bodily force.

* **Workplace conditions** which define specific standards covering working environment, safety, housekeeping and facilities.

* **Display screen equipment** designed to reduce the risks to employees who use a V.D.U. as a significant part of their normal work e.g. Typists.

* **Personal protective equipment** (PPE) setting out principles for selecting, providing, maintaining and using P.P.E. including clothing and equipment.

31. **Equal Pay Acts 1970 and 1983** (and corresponding legislation in Northern Ireland). Under these Acts women are entitled to receive equal pay with men when doing the same or broadly similar work.

32. **Sex Discrimination Act 1975 and 1986.** These Acts make it unlawful to discriminate between men and women in employment, education and training, and the provision of housing, goods, facilities and services, and in advertising. Northern Ireland has similar legislation.

33. The **Equal Opportunities Commission** was set up in 1975 (1976 in Northern Ireland). It advises people of their legal rights and may give financial help when a case goes to a Court or Tribunal.

34. **Race Relations Act 1976** This Act makes it unlawful to discriminate against someone on the grounds of colour, race or ethnic or national origin in employment, education and training, and the provision of housing, goods, facilities and services and in advertising.

"An employer must not discriminate when selecting employees."

35. The Commission for Racial Equality was set up to investigate and eliminate discrimination and to promote racial harmony. It also provides advice and may assist individuals who have complaints.

36. Through a series of **Employment Protection Acts** workers are also protected against unfair dismissal. Someone who feels that they have been unfairly dismissed can appeal to an Industrial Tribunal and, if successful, get their job back or receive compensation.

37. **Industrial Tribunals** are independent legal bodies set up to deal with complaints from employees on infringements of their rights under a number of Acts. For example, Contracts of Employment, Equal Pay, Unfair Dismissal, Sex Discrimination and Redundancy Payments.

ROLE OF THE PERSONNEL DEPARTMENT

38. In addition to recruiting staff the Personnel Department also performs other important functions in a business including the following:

a) **Staff Welfare** This is anything which affects the well-being of staff, for example the provision of canteens, social facilities, sporting facilities, medical and safety matters, pensions or sickness.

b) **Recommending promotions and keeping confidential staff records** All firms need certain information about their staff for example name, age, address, date of joining company, departments worked in, wages and any changes, various jobs performed, for example assistant manager, details of any training courses attended, examinations passed or progress made, educational qualifications, sickness records etc. References for future jobs or positions will then be based on this information.

c) **Discussing staff problems**   This may be something to do with domestic problems at home such as housing, or financial worries, or it may be some personal matter which is affecting an individual's work.

d) **Industrial relations**   Many staff will probably be members of a trade union and frequently the Personnel Officer will negotiate with the union(s) on matters relating to wages, working conditions or staff problems.

e) **Staff training**   When there is not a separate training department this is often the role of the Personnel Officer.

TRAINING

39. Most training takes place *'on-the-job'*, i.e. people learn at work either from other people or by themselves, often from experience. However, *'off-the-job'* training, either inside or outside a firm, is also important. For example a course in a firm's own training school or a day release or evening class at a local college.

40. There are five main types of training which firms may carry out.

a) **Induction** – that is, *all* new staff should be introduced to the firm generally and told about the business, for example the goods which it makes and sells, the general organisation and what their particular job involves.

b) **Basic skills** – whilst all new staff should receive induction training, junior staff in particular should also undertake an organised training programme. This should be designed to teach them basic skills required in their job and thus to develop them into more efficient and effective employees.

c) **Re-training** – regular refresher or updating courses should take place for all staff. For example when new technology, Health and Safety measures or new products are introduced.

d) **Management trainees** – many larger companies run special management trainee courses, for example ICI and Marks and Spencers. Often people with a University degree or GCE 'A' levels are recruited to undertake an intensive training programme. Staff who join the firm from school at 16 can usually join the scheme after a few years basic training.

e) **Management** – regular training in the latest management techniques should form an essential part of any firm's overall training plan to ensure that its business operates efficiently.

POSSIBLE BENEFITS FROM TRAINING

41. **For the employee:**
* Opportunity to develop skills and knowledge
* May improve promotion prospects
* May improve job satisfaction

42. **For the employer:**
* Improves quality and motivation of staff
* Brings in new ideas and skills
* Better health, safety and hygiene standards

43. College courses offer another way of obtaining qualifications and improving job prospects.

TRAINING & ENTERPRISE COUNCILS (TEC's)

44. Introduced in March 1989 TECs were set up and funded by the Government to co-ordinate and develop training and enterprise in specific areas. They are private limited companies with up to 15 directors of whom at least two thirds are local business executives and the rest are from Local Authorities, Trade Unions, education and voluntary organisations.

45. 82 TECs cover England and Wales e.g. Eltec (East Lancashire), Powys Tec, Avon Tec, Letec (London East) and Tyneside Tec, whilst in Scotland there are 22 local enterprise companies (LECs).

46. TECs are responsible for researching into local labour market needs and skill shortages and then organising a range of existing and new programmes to meet the needs identified. These programmes include Youth Training, Employment Training, Business Growth Training, Small Firms Counselling and the Enterprise Allowance Scheme which TECs manage and adapt locally within broad government guidelines.

47. **Some North-West Tec's.**

Youth Training (YT)

48. Youth Training is available to anyone who has left school and offers a guaranteed place to all 16 and 17 year olds who are not in a job or full-time education. A weekly training allowance is paid which is higher than unemployment benefit. Trainees in a job receive a full wage.

49. Youth Training is run through TECs by approved training organisations (ATOs) including: employers, private training firms, local councils, voluntary organisations and further education colleges – who are responsible for arranging the trainees pay, work placement, training programme, and for looking after their general welfare.

50. All YT includes the following features:
   a) **Induction training** including health and safety.
   b) **Work Experience** because trainees are based with an employer.
   c) **Off-the-Job Training** at work or in a college or training centre.
   d) **Qualifications** all schemes provide the opportunity to obtain specific job skills and qualifications to a minimum of NVQ Level II.
   e) **New Technology Training** including the use of computers
   f) **Extended training** for those with special needs such as a disability or numeracy and literacy problems.
   g) **A National Record of Achievement (NROVA)** documenting all the skills and experience gained.

51. The length of YT will depend on the qualification being aimed at. At the end of their YT an employer may offer a trainee a job unless the trainee is unsuitable or there are no vacancies. A similar scheme in Northern Ireland is called the Youth Training Programme (YTP).

52. *N.B.*
   a) In many areas firms are now using YT to replace their apprenticeship schemes because the government pays the cost of training.
   b) An apprenticeship is a traditional method of learning a skill or craft which involves a period of training, for example five years.
   c) National Vocational Qualifications (NVQs) are based on real work standards which have been set by industry indicating what an individual is actually competent to do in a job. There are initially 4 levels ranging from basic tasks at Level I to management skills at Level IV.
   d) The Government has announced its intention to offer **Training Credits** to all school-leavers aged 16 and 17 by 1996. These operate within the broad framework of YT and give an entitlement to receive training to approved standards.

Employment Training (ET)

53. a) ET mainly offers training for adults who have been unemployed for more than six months with priority being given to 18-24 year olds.
   It also helps any unemployed adult who is going into self employment; a skill shortage area; is victim of large scale redundancy or returning to the labour market (e.g. women after having children).
   b) Like YT, ET is run through TECs by ATOs who assess each individual's needs, develop a personal action plan and arrange their training programme. This can be either to update existing skills or learn new ones, and includes opportunities for training in new technology and basic numeracy/literacy.
   c) The programme includes both work experience and 'off-the-job' training with the opportunity to obtain a vocational qualification, for example City and Guilds, RSA, BTEC, NVQ.

d)   ET is free and trainees receive a training allowance and certain travel expenses.

e)   At the end of the training period further guidance is given to assist participants to move into employment or further training.

Business Growth Training (BGT)

54.   Introduced in 1989 BGT aims to help small and medium size firms (less than 500 employees) to improve their training. Grants are available to assist with the costs of:

i)   training consultancy

ii)   developing innovative training methods

iii) business skills training for owners and managers

Small Firms Counselling

55.   The Small Firms Service provides free information for small businesses, whether established or just starting up. It also provides business counselling, a role being taken over by TECs.

Business Start-up Scheme (BSUS)

56.   The BSUS (formerly the Enterprise Allowance Scheme) helps unemployed people to start their own business. A weekly allowance is paid for between 26-66 weeks of the new enterprise as well as business training and counselling.

To qualify:

i)   individuals must be over 18 and unemployed for at least 8 weeks

ii)   have £1,000 to invest in the business, although this can be a loan or overdraft

iii) the business must be considered suitable for the scheme and should not have started trading until accepted.

Training, Education and Enterprise Directorate (TEED)

57.   Based in Sheffield with regional offices throughout the country, TEED is the Department of Employment section which liaises with and advises TECs.

SUMMARY

58.   a)   Recruitment involves deciding what staff are needed and then attracting suitable applicants.

b)   A Job Description gives details of the main duties involved in a job, whilst a Job Specification outlines the skills and experience needed to do work.

c)   Information about job vacancies can be found in many places including newspapers, careers offices, job centres and private employment agencies.

d)   Applications for jobs may be made using a letter, application form or curriculum vitae.

e)   In order to find out more about applicants for jobs, employers usually ask for a reference.

f)   Short-listed candidates are usually invited to an interview.

g)   It is important to prepare for interviews both beforehand and on the 'big day'.

h)   Everyone who starts work must be given a Contract of Employment.

i)   A number of Acts provide protection for employees covering areas which include Health and Safety, Equal Pay, Sex Discrimination, Race Relations, Unfair Dismissal and Redundancy.

j)   A firm's Personnel Department is usually responsible for recruiting staff. It also looks after staff welfare, staff records and industrial relations.

k) Staff training is important for all employers from induction for new staff, to up-dating for managers.

l) The 82 TEC's were set up to develop local training and enterprise.

m) YT, ET, Business Growth, Small Firms Counselling and the Enterprise Allowance Scheme are Government funded training schemes run by TEC's.

REVIEW QUESTIONS

Answers can be found in the paragraphs shown.

1. Why is it important that a firm recruits good staff? (2)

2. What is the difference between a job description and a job specification? (4-7)

3. List 4 ways of finding out about job vacancies. (8-10)

4. List 6 pieces of essential information which should be included in a letter of application for a job. (12)

5. How does a curriculum vitae differ from an application form? (13-14)

6. What is the difference between a reference and a testimonial and why do employers need them? (16)

7. What is the purpose of an interview? (17, 18)

8. Suggest 6 ways in which a candidate could prepare for an interview. (19-23)

9. What is a Contract of Employment? (24-25)

10. Give brief details of 3 other laws which protect employees at work. (26-37)

11. Outline the main functions of a firm's Personnel Department. (38)

12. What is training and why is it needed? (39-42)

13. Why were TEC's set up? (44)

14. Briefly outline the role of TEC's. (46-57)

EXAMINATION PRACTICE QUESTIONS

Marks

1. What are the advantages to a 16 year old school leaver of entering Youth Training?

   3

2. a) What is a curriculum vitae? — 2

   b) Why might an employer ask for a CV in preference to using an application form? — 3

3. What types of training would be given to Jane Smith who is starting work in a bookshop when she leaves school next week?

   2

4. a) Describe five functions of a personnel department in a manufacturing company with 400 employees.

   15

   b) In what ways can the personnel department contribute to the efficient working of the business?

   10

MULTIPLE CHOICE/COMPLETION

1. In a large engineering firm which department would be responsible for recruiting staff?

   a) Training
   b) Production
   c) Administration
   d) Personnel

2. The Health and Safety at Work Act 1974 requires that all employees
   a) Are trained in first aid.
   b) Always follow health and safety regulations.
   c) Are insured against accidents at work.
   d) Wear protective clothing at work.

3. 'Off-the-Job' training could take place in all except which one of the following?
   a) Further Education College
   b) Company Training School
   c) Private Training Centre
   d) Place of work

4. The Personnel department of a firm will normally carry out all except which one of the following functions?
   a) Keep staff records
   b) Interview applicants for jobs
   c) Advertise the firm's products
   d) Negotiate with Trade Unions

In each of the following questions, one or more of the responses is/are correct. Choose the appropriate letter which indicates the correct version.
   A if 1 only is correct
   B if 3 only is correct
   C if 1 and 2 are correct
   D if 1, 2 and 3 are correct

5. By law which of the following must be written into a Contract of Employment?
   1. Hours of work and holidays
   2. Period of notice
   3. Rate of National Insurance Contributions

6. Job Centres
   1. Cannot be used by school leavers
   2. Provide information about job vacancies
   3. Pay unemployment benefit

RECENT EXAMINATION QUESTIONS

Marks

LEAG 1988 GCSE BUSINESS STUDIES SPECIMEN PAPER 2B **SECTION B**

1. Barbara Green has been left £10,000 in a relative's will. She would like to set up a hairdressing business and employ 3 assistants. Explain to Barbara:
   a) How a bank current account would be useful for making business payments   3
   b) TWO possible ways of recruiting staff for Barbara's business   2
   c) Brief details of 2 laws which Barbara must be aware of when appointing staff   2
   d) A form of training suitable for the school leaver appointed as an assistant for Barbara.   2
   e) How a good training programme benefits both employer and employee   3
   f) Reasons why employees are likely to be contented in their work.   3

LCCI JUNE 1989 SSC BACKGROUND TO BUSINESS

2. a) Why would a young college leaver who has secretarial qualifications still benefit from training when starting his/her first full-time job?   12

    b) What are the limits of on-the-job training?   6

ASSIGNMENT

Diana's Interview

Diana has recently taken her GCSE and RSA II Typewriting examinations and is awaiting the results. When she leaves school she wants to work in an office and has written to several firms hoping for an interview. She was really thrilled last week when the local council wrote and invited her for an interview as a Junior Typist in the Education Department. Diana had done well at school and her tutor advised her to prepare thoroughly for the interview and not to stay out too late the night before.

The interview was on the day after her 16th birthday which she planned to celebrate by going to the Youth Club Dance. At the dance she wore the new jumper and skirt, shoes and tights which her mother had bought specially for her interview.

Diana had a super time and stayed until the end, getting home at 12.30 am. Throwing her clothes onto the nearby chair, she flopped into bed, tired but happy.

Next morning her parents called her at 7.30 am as they left for work. Diana intended getting up but fell asleep again not waking until 9.00 am. Her bus left at 9.30 am so she quickly got up and started to dress. However, she noticed a ladder in her tights and her skirt was badly creased. Unable to find another pair of tights and with no time to press her skirt, she rushed out of the house to the bus stop brushing her hair as she went.

Diana arrived 5 minutes late at the Council offices and was unable to find her interview letter. She could not remember where she had to go and asked the receptionist for help. Several 'phone calls later the problem was solved and Diana was sent to the Education Department where she nervously apologised for being late.

She was asked to join 5 other girls who had already started a typewriting test. Diana felt hot and bothered and her typing was not as good as usual.

Fortunately, by the time she was interviewed Diana had calmed down and was able to answer all the questions well. The interviewer was impressed and could see that she was a bright, intelligent girl who was hopeful of achieving good examination results. She also had good references and interesting hobbies.

---

1. Identify 2 aspects of Diana's preparations which were correct for someone attending their first interview.

2. Make a list of at least 5 ways in which Diana could have prepared better for her interview.

3. Suggest 2 main factors which would be against Diana getting the job.

4. List 4 main points which could help Diana to get the job.

5. Do you think Diana is likely to be offered the job? Give reasons for your answer.

22. People and Work

1. This chapter is about people at work, the money which they earn and how it is paid to them. It also considers the 'fringe benefits' which employees may receive and why some workers are paid higher wages than others.

MOTIVATION AND JOB SATISFACTION

2. It is important in running a business to understand what motivates workers and gives them *job satisfaction*. The more people enjoy their job the more likely they are to work harder and take a pride in what they do. If workers are bored then they may be unhappy and therefore gain little job satisfaction.

3. Most people go to work because they need to earn money to pay for their food, clothing and housing. However, there are also many other non-money factors which are important in giving people job satisfaction for example:

* Good working conditions
* Prospects for promotion
* Job security
* Responsibility to make decisions
* Recognition or rewards for work done
* Social factors, for example friendship of other workers
* Status, for example Manager, Director, Senior Clerk

4. **Why people work**

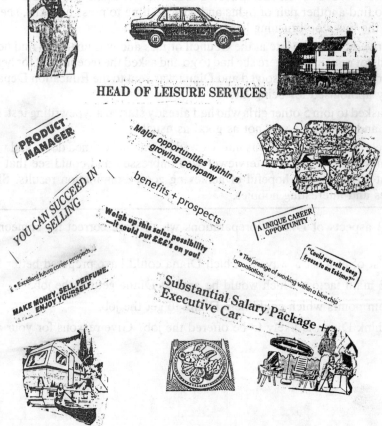

HEAD OF LEISURE SERVICES

PRODUCT MANAGER

Major opportunities within a growing company

benefits + prospects

YOU CAN SUCCEED IN SELLING

A UNIQUE CAREER OPPORTUNITY

Weigh up this sales possibility —It could put £££'s on you!

• Excellent future career prospects

"Could you sell a deep freeze to an Eskimo?"

• The prestige of working within a blue chip organisation

MAKE MONEY, SELL PERFUME ENJOY YOURSELF

Substantial Salary Package + Executive Car

WAGES AND SALARIES

5.   The money which people receive for work may be paid to them in cash, by cheque or directly into a bank or building society account. The term 'wages' is used when people are paid weekly, often in cash. A salary on the other hand is used to refer to a monthly payment, which is usually paid straight into an employees bank account.

GROSS AND NET PAY

6.   The **gross pay** of an employee is the total amount earned before any deductions are made. **Net pay** (or take home pay) is what is actually received after deductions have been made by the employer. There are two types of deductions – statutory and voluntary.

STATUTORY DEDUCTIONS

7.   These are compulsory and must be deducted by law.
   a)   **Income Tax** which is collected under Pay As You Earn (PAYE). The amount an employee pays in income tax depends upon their personal circumstances and the rates of tax fixed by the Government. (see paragraphs 34-42)
   b)   **National Insurance** Everyone earning over a certain amount also has to pay National Insurance contributions. This money is then used to provide a range of benefits including unemployment benefit, sickness benefit, state pensions and maternity sick pay.

VOLUNTARY DEDUCTIONS

8.   Many employees choose to have other deductions made straight from their wages, for example:
   *   **Superannuation** which is a contribution to an employers private pension scheme. When an employee retires this pension is paid in addition to the state pension.
   *   **Trade Union Subscriptions**
   *   **Private Medical Schemes** for example BUPA
   *   **Company Social Club**
   *   **Savings Schemes** for example the government Save As You Earn (SAYE) scheme.

PAY ADVICE AND PAYROLL

9.   Details of how much an employee has earned and any deductions are given in the form of a *pay advice* which everyone receives with their wages or salary. This is usually in the form of a slip of paper which tells an employee how their net pay has been calculated.

10.   In addition an employer needs to keep a record of the wages and deductions for all employees. This is known as the *payroll*.

11.   Frequently nowadays computers are used which can calculate and print out the payroll and individual payslips.

PAY IN ARREARS

12.   Many firms pay wages a week in arrears. This gives the wages department time to calculate the wages and make the necessary deductions. When a worker leaves the firm they will receive any money owed to them.

13. **Example of a Wages Slip**

NAME	DATE	WORKS NUMBER	TAX CODE	BASIC WAGE	OVERTIME	TAX	NI	OTHER DEDUCTIONS	NET WAGE
A VANN	28 FEB. '94	43758	260L	200.60	25.40	53.90	14.20	4.70	153.20

14. Example of a Salary Advice

EMPLOYEES NAME	PAY DATE (a)	PAYROLL NUMBER (b)	NI NUMBER (c)	TAX CODE (d)	BASIC PAY (e)	OVERTIME (f)	TOTAL GROSS PAY (g)
JONES S	28 FEB '94	04878341	YL979401B	260L	£770.94	£40.00	£810.94

NI (h)	TAX (i)	SUPERANN (j)	TRADE UNION (k)	SAYE (l)	OTHER DEDUCTIONS (m)	TOTAL DEDUCTIONS (n)	MONTH 11(r)
£31.22	£160.72	£48.66	£4.00	-	-	£244.60	NET PAY (s) £566.34

TAXABLE PAY TO DATE (o)	TAX TO DATE (p)	SUPERANNUATION TO DATE (q)	
£7597.31	£1581.37	£484.94	

A salary slip is similar to a wages slip but usually has more information on it as can be seen above.

15. The letters used on S Jones' payslip are explained below:

a) *Payment* will be made on 28th February 1994.

b) Firms usually give employees *individual reference numbers*.

c) Everyone, when they start work, is given a *National Insurance (NI) Number*.

d) A *Tax Code* is issued by the Inland Revenue and tells employers how much tax to deduct.

e) *Basic Pay* is the pay for a normal working week, say 40 hours.

f) Payments for working more than the normal working week are called *overtime*.

g) *Total Gross Pay* equals basic pay plus any overtime.

h) & i) are the *statutory deductions* from pay this month.

j), k), l) and m) are *voluntary deductions* from pay.

n) *Total deductions* includes the total of statutory and voluntary deductions.

o) *Taxable pay to date* shows how much S Jones has earned since April. His tax deductions are based on this figure.

p) *Tax to date* shows S Jones' total tax since April 1993.

q) *Superannuation to date* shows the payments into the company's pension scheme since April 1993.

r) Month of *current tax year* beginning on 6th April.

s) *Net pay* is found by taking the total deductions of *£244.60* from the total gross pay of *£810.94* leaving *£566.34*.

METHODS OF PAYMENT

16. Wages may be calculated in a number of different ways:

17. **Hourly or time rates**   Often wages are paid on the basis of so much per hour, for example £2.00. This method is often used to pay factory workers.

18. **Flat Rate**   This is a fixed amount per week or month, for example £80 per week. Most office workers are paid in this way.

19. **Overtime**   If an employee works more than the usual hours they may be paid overtime, which for example, may be paid at time-and-a-half or double-time (perhaps for working Sunday).

20. **Example**

£76.00	Basic (£2.00 per hour for 38 hours)
£9.00	3 hours at time-and-a-half (£3 per hour)
£12.00	3 hours at double-time (£4.00 per hour)
£97.00	

21. **Piece-Work rates**   This is another common method of payment in factories. The work is broken down into 'pieces' and a worker is paid for each 'piece' produced. The more they produce the more they

are paid. For example a sewing machine operator may be paid 25p for each sleeve sewn on a coat. If she sews 500 sleeves in a week she would earn £125.00.

22. **Commission**   People who work in selling are often paid only for what they sell. This is usually a percentage of the value of the total sales, for example, a person might be paid commission at 10%. If they sell £1500 worth of goods in a week they would receive £150.

23. **Fees**   Professional people like dentists, solicitors and accountants charge a fee for their services, for example, £35 per hour or per visit.

24. **Bonus**   Often employees are paid an additional amount for completing a particular job on time, for example, motorway workers. Other forms of bonus include extra payment to workers at Christmas or holiday times as a reward for hard work or loyalty (for staying with a firm).

25. **Profit Sharing**   Sometimes at the end of the financial year a firm will give employees a share of its profits. This may be given in cash or in the form of a number of the company's shares.

HOURS OF WORK

26. Most workers in the UK now work for five days a week, although the actual hours and days of work depend upon the type of job, for example, most shop workers are expected to work on Saturdays, with a day off during the week. Teachers, on the other hand, work Mondays to Fridays.

FLEXITIME

27. In recent years some firms have started to introduce a system which allows flexible hours of work. Employees, particularly those in office jobs, are allowed to vary the time at which they start and finish work. Usually everyone must work a 'core time' perhaps from 10.00 am – 4.00 pm each day with an hour for lunch. They can then choose the rest of their hours to suit themselves.

28. The great *advantage of flexitime* to firms is that it reduces absenteeism and leads to happier, better motivated workers. Employees benefit because it enables them to avoid rush hour travel and fit in appointments, for example dentists, doctors or hairdressers. Married women with children find flexitime particularly useful. However, it also means that firms must keep strict records and could have some problems, for example, it may prove difficult to arrange staff meetings at a convenient time and staying open longer hours may incur extra heating and lighting costs.

SHIFTWORK

29. To enable a firm to operate its machinery for longer periods, often 24 hours a day, it will use different groups of workers in rotation. This is known as shift work. For example workers operating a three shift system might work 2.00 pm – 10.00 pm; 10.00 pm – 6.00 am or 6.00 am – 2.00 pm. In return for this they are usually paid an extra shift allowance.

CALCULATING THE PAYMENT OF WAGES

30. Different methods of payment may be used even within the same firm. For example, factory workers may be paid a piece rate or receive a bonus, office staff may be paid a salary with possibly overtime, whilst a sales representative may receive a basic wage plus commission on sales.

31. Therefore to enable a firm to calculate the wages, records must be kept. For each employee it will need to know their attendance, hours worked and where applicable the amount of work produced or sales achieved. The two most common ways of recording attendances are by time-book and clock-card.

32. a)   **Time Book**   This is frequently used in offices. Employees sign the book each day when they start and finish work.

   b)   **Clock Card**   These are most common in factories. Each employee has their own card which is kept in a special rack near a clock. When they arrive and leave work the card is put into the clock which automatically records the time on it.

33. Clock Card

PAYE

34. The method used to collect income tax from employers is called Pay As You Earn (PAYE). Under this system employers deduct tax each week or month directly from employees wages before they are paid. How much tax a person pays depends upon how much they earn, what allowances they can claim and the current rate of tax.

35.

TAX ALLOWANCES 1991/92	
	£
Personal	3,295
Married Couple	1,720
Additional personal and widow's bereavement	1,720
Personal (65-74)	4,020
Married couple (65-74)	2,355
Personal (75 plus)	4,180
Married Couple (75 plus)	2,395
Age allowance income limit	13,500

36. Everyone who works completes a tax return (P1) which the Department of Inland Revenue uses to calculate a Tax Code. This code number indicates how much 'Free Pay' an employee can earn before they start to pay tax, for example, a single man with allowances of £4,600 would have a code of 460L. This means he would only pay tax on earnings above this amount.

37. Each week or month the employer uses the Tax Code to calculate the amount of tax to be deducted. This is based on special tax tables provided by the Inland Revenue.

38. This code number will change when someone's personal circumstances change. For example, when a single man gets married he will be given a higher code. The higher the code the more one can earn before being taxed.

39. Notice of Coding

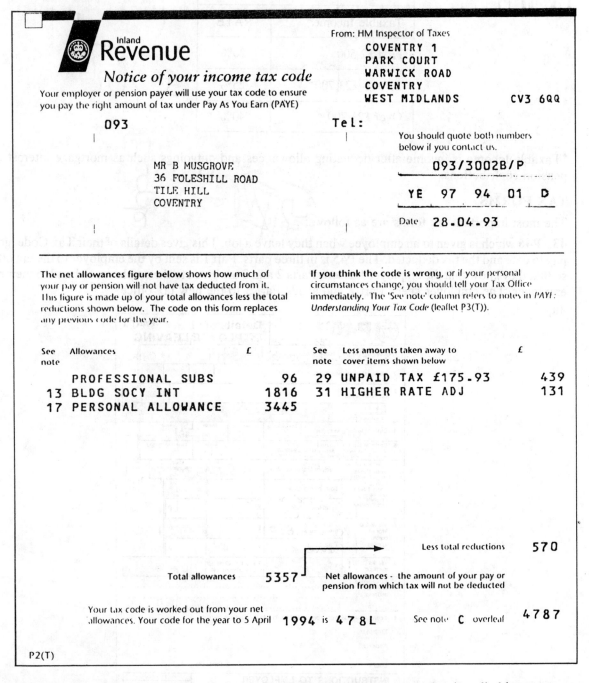

Inland **Revenue**

Notice of your income tax code

Your employer or pension payer will use your tax code to ensure you pay the right amount of tax under Pay As You Earn (PAYE)

093

MR B MUSGROVE
36 FOLESHILL ROAD
TILE HILL
COVENTRY

From: HM Inspector of Taxes

COVENTRY 1
PARK COURT
WARWICK ROAD
COVENTRY
WEST MIDLANDS   CV3 6QQ

Tel:

You should quote both numbers below if you contact us.

093/3002B/P

YE 97 94 01 D

Date 28.04.93

The net allowances figure below shows how much of your pay or pension will not have tax deducted from it. This figure is made up of your total allowances less the total reductions shown below. The code on this form replaces any previous code for the year.

If you think the code is wrong, or if your personal circumstances change, you should tell your Tax Office immediately. The 'See note' column refers to notes in *PAYE: Understanding Your Tax Code* (leaflet P3(T)).

See note	Allowances	£	See note	Less amounts taken away to cover items shown below	£
	PROFESSIONAL SUBS	96	29	UNPAID TAX £175.93	439
13	BLDG SOCY INT	1816	31	HIGHER RATE ADJ	131
17	PERSONAL ALLOWANCE	3445			

Less total reductions   570

Total allowances 5357

Net allowances - the amount of your pay or pension from which tax will not be deducted

Your tax code is worked out from your net allowances. Your code for the year to 5 April **1994** is **478L**   See note **C** overleaf   **4787**

P2(T)

40. If someone does not have a Tax Code an employer will deduct tax at what is called **'emergency code'**. This means paying a higher rate of tax because the code does not include any allowances. Any tax overpaid will be refunded when the correct code number is known.

41. The **tax year** runs from 6 April to 5 April the following year. The rate of income tax is set at so much in the £ by the Chancellor of the Exchequer. Any changes are announced in the Budget which now takes place in December each year. The rates of tax for the 1993/94 tax year are as follows:

42.

INCOME TAX 1993/94	
Taxable Income*	**RATE**
First £2,500	20%
2,501 – £23,700	25%
Over £23,700	40%

*Taxable Income is income after deducting allowances and outgoings such as mortgage interest and pension contributions.

TAX FORMS

The most important tax forms are as follows:

43. **P45** which is given to an employee when they leave a job. This gives details of their Tax Code, gross pay to date and the tax deducted. The P45 is in three parts. Part 1 is sent by the employer to the tax office so that they know that the employee has left. Parts 2 and 3 are given to the employee to hand to their new employer. The employer keeps Part 2 and sends Part 3 to the new tax office.

44.

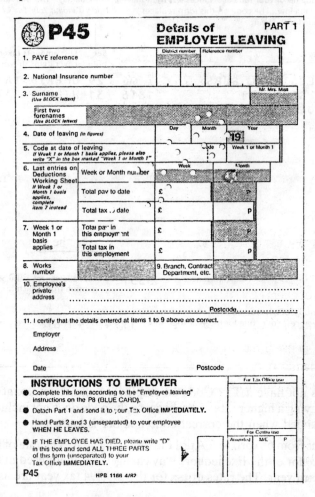

45. P60 which is given to all employees at the end of the tax year i.e. after 5 April. It shows the total pay and tax for the year.

P60 Certificate of pay, tax deducted and National Insurance contributions				Do not destroy

P60 Certificate of pay, tax deducted and National Insurance contributions   **Do not destroy**

Employee's National Insurance number — *Enter here "M" if male "F" if female*

Tax District and reference — Year to 5 April **19**

Employer's full name and address

Employee's surname *in CAPITAL LETTERS*   First two forenames

National Insurance contributions in this employment

Contribution Table letter	Total of Employee's and Employer's contributions payable 1a	Employee's contributions payable 1b	Employee's contributions at Contracted-out rate included in column 1b 1c
	£	£	£
	£	£	£
	£	£	£
	£	£	£

Employee's works/payroll number etc.

Employee's private address

Amount of Statutory Sick Pay included in the "Pay" section of the "This employment" box below   £

Total for year		Previous employment		This employment	Tax deducted or refunded "R" indicates refund
Pay	Tax deducted	Pay	Tax deducted	Pay	
£	£	£	£	£	£

I/We certify that the particulars given above include the total amount of pay for income tax purposes (including overtime, bonus, commission, etc.) paid to you by me/us in the year ended 5 April last, and the total tax and National Insurance contributions deducted by me/us (less any refunds) in that year.

To the employee. Keep this certificate. It will help you to check any Notice of Assessment which the Tax Office may send you in due course. You can also use it to check that your employer is deducting the right type of National Insurance contributions for you and using your correct National Insurance number. If he is not, you should tell him. You cannot get a duplicate form P60.

Final tax code	Employee's Widows and Orphans / life insurance contributions in this employment	Week 53 payment indicator
	£	

P60

46. P11 An employer records PAYE on this form which is sent each month to the Department of Inland Revenue.

FRINGE BENEFITS

47. In addition to money many firms offer other incentives to their workers. These are called 'fringe benefits' or 'perks of the job', some examples of which include:

* Company cars – sales staff, senior managers and directors often have the use of a car
* Luncheon Vouchers (LV's) – which can be used to help pay for meals in cafes and restaurants which accept them
* Canteens – large firms often provide subsidised low-priced meals for employees
* Transport – many firms provide free coaches or cheap transport for their employees
* Pension Schemes
* Help with house purchase, for example low interest loans
* Medical facilities, for example nurse on premises
* Life Assurance
* Sports facilities
* Good Holidays
* Discounts on firm's products or services

PAY INCREASES

48. It is usual in the UK for employees to receive a regular increase in their salary or wages. This normally happens once or twice a year.

49. **Cost of Living Increases**   Most firms give an annual pay increase to cover the rising cost of living caused by inflation. Often the amount given to workers will be negotiated between the management and the trade unions. It may be given as a flat rate, for example, £200 per worker, or as a percentage, for example, 5% of present pay.

50. **Merit Increases**   These are given by some firms as a reward to employees (often salaried staff) who have worked particularly well.

51. **Fixed Increments**   Under this system every employee receives a pay rise at a certain time, for example, in September each year. This system is also commonly used to pay salaried staff.

52. **Example**

GRADE 5	
Increment Point	£
0	4400
1	4706
2	5030
3	5520
4	5900
5	6375
6	6730

Incremental Scale

After two years service an employee on the above scale would receive an annual salary of £3030. Employees under 21 are often given wage increases on their birthday.

DETERMINATION OF WAGE RATES

53. The wages which workers receive for different jobs will vary for a number of reasons. As a general rule wage rates are determined by **supply and demand**. That is where there are a lot of workers who are able to do a particular job, wages are likely to remain low. Where there is a shortage of workers wages are likely to be higher.

54. The following examples explain this in more detail and also include other reasons for what are called **wage differentials**.

   a)   Certain types of work require *highly specialised skills* for which people may need to study or train for many years. Therefore, once qualified they receive higher rates of pay, for example, doctors, solicitors and accountants.

   b)   *Unskilled workers* receive lower rates of pay because very little knowledge or training is needed to do the job, for example cleaners and labourers.

   c)   Managers, supervisors and foremen are usually paid more than workers because they have a *responsible* job.

   d)   A *high level of unemployment* in an area like Northern Ireland or the North East of England is likely to keep wages lower because there will be more workers available for each job.

   e)   From time to time the *government* also controls wages, particularly in the public sector industries.

f)   The *power of the trade unions* in an industry can also affect the wages of workers, for example, car and print workers get higher wages because the unions are well organised, whilst in retailing and catering unions are weak and therefore wages relatively low.

SUMMARY

55. a)   Most people work for money.
    b)   A wage is usually paid weekly and a salary monthly.
    c)   Details of an employees pay is shown in their pay advice.
    d)   This includes statutory deductions i.e. PAYE and National Insurance and voluntary deductions, for example Trade Union Subscriptions.
    e)   The methods of paying workers include by hourly rates, flat rates, overtime, piece-work, commission, fees, bonus or profit-sharing.
    f)   Income Tax is deducted by PAYE and is calculated from each workers Tax Code.
    g)   Important tax forms include P45, P60 and P11.
    h)   Many firms provide fringe benefits for workers, for example cheap canteen meals or free travel.
    i)   Pay increases may be given to cover the cost of living, as a merit reward or as a regular increment.
    j)   Workers usually receive higher wages in jobs requiring greater skills or carrying more responsibility.

REVIEW QUESTIONS

Answers can be found in the paragraphs shown.

1.   What is the difference between gross and net pay? (5, 6)
2.   Name 2 compulsory and 2 voluntary deductions from wages. (7, 8)
3.   List 6 items of information which are usually given on a pay advice. (9, 13–15)
4.   Name 4 methods of paying wages to employees. (16-25)
5.   What is flexitime and how does it operate? (27)
6.   What is PAYE and how is it calculated? (7, 34-42)
7.   Which tax form does an employee receive at the end of the tax year? (44, 45)
8.   Use examples to explain the meaning of fringe benefits. (47)
9.   Explain the difference between cost of living, merit and incremental pay increases. (48-52)
10. Why are some workers paid higher wages than others? (53, 54)

EXAMINATION PRACTICE QUESTIONS

Marks

1.   A bank clerk earns £900 per month (gross) but receives £730 per month (net). Why is there a difference between gross and net pay?

2

2. Match the following terms with the appropriate definition from the list a-j.
   i)   Basic pay . . . .
   ii)   Pay advice . . . .
   iii) Overtime pay . . . .
   iv)   Statutory deductions . . . .
   v)   Net pay . . . .
   vi)   Salary . . . .
   vii) Flexitime . . . .
   viii) Earnings . . . .
   ix)   Voluntary deductions . . . .
   x)   Bonus pay   10

   a)   monthly pay usually for executive and clerical workers
   b)   income tax, National Insurance contributions
   c)   superannuation, trade union subscriptions, social clubs etc
   d)   payment for working more than the normal working day or week
   e)   employees can vary the time at which they start and finish work
   f)   addition to normal wage as reward for loyalty, or higher productivity
   g)   basic wage plus additional payments such as overtime or bonus pay
   h)   pay received after all deductions
   i)   wages slip giving details of how net pay has been calculated
   j)   payment for working minimum number of hours required

3. Which tax form does an employee receive when he leaves his employment?   1

4. Name 2 of the main benefits provided by the National Insurance Scheme.   2

5. a)   What is the difference between time rate and piece rate methods of calculating wage payments?   2
   b)   A firm pays its employees by piece rates. Give *one* advantage and *one* disadvantage to:
        i)   the firm   1
        ii) the employees   1

6. Apart from Income Tax, name three other deductions which might be made from an employees gross pay.   3

MULTIPLE CHOICE/COMPLETION

1. When workers are paid according to the amount they produce it is known as
   a)   Payment by results
   b)   Profit sharing
   c)   A fringe benefit
   d)   A bonus

2. Which of the following items is a statutory deduction from an employees wages?
   a)   Social club
   b)   Superannuation
   c)   Trade Union subscription
   d)   National Insurance

3. At the end of the tax year an employee is given a:
   a) P11
   b) P45
   c) P60
   d) Bonus

4. Flexitime allows workers to
   a) work overtime for extra pay
   b) work at times to suit themselves
   c) choose which days they want to work
   d) vary their start and finish times

5. PAYE is deducted by an employer from employees and sent monthly to the
   a) Local Authority
   b) Inland Revenue
   c) Department of Health and Social Security
   d) HM Customs and Excise

6. The Income Tax year ends on
   a) 5 April
   b) 6 April
   c) 31 July
   d) 31 December

7. Nita Chouan is paid a basic wage of £2 per hour for a 40 hour week. Last Sunday she worked 3 hours overtime at double-time and on Wednesday 2 hours overtime at time-and-a-half. How much did she earn for the week?
   a) £80
   b) £102
   c) £98
   d) £88

In the following question, one or more of the responses is/are correct. Choose the appropriate letter which indicates the correct version.
   A   if 1 only is correct
   B   if 3 only is correct
   C   if 1 and 2 are correct
   D   if 1, 2 and 3 are correct

8. Which of the following items must be shown on an employees pay slip?
   1. Gross pay
   2. Income Tax deductions
   3. Trade Union subscriptions

RECENT EXAMINATION QUESTIONS

NISEC SUMMER 1989 GCSE BUSINESS STUDIES PAPER 2

OFFICE COORDINATOR

We represent major overseas manufacturers and specialise in facsimile and photocopier sales and service.

Due to continued expansion we require a lady to take responsibility for the day-to-day running of our office.

Experience in typing, book-keeping, PAYE and VAT essential, a driving licence an advantage.

Applicants under 21 need not apply.

Apply for an application form and job description to ANSOM Ltd, 3 Raphael Street, Belfast BT5 4AQ.

---

a) Name TWO places where you would be likely to see advertisements such as this. 2

b) i) What is a job description? 2

    ii) Give TWO items which should be included in a job description. 2

c) Of what use would this information be to a person considering applying for the job? 4

d) i) What is illegal about the advertisement? 2

    ii) What additional information would be useful? 4

e) Job satisfaction is just as important as wages. Suggest TWO ways in which an employer might increase the job satisfaction of his workforce. 4

LEAG MAY 1989 GCSE BUSINESS STUDIES PAPER I

2. Arthur Lee is a part-time student taking a Business Studies course at a local technical college. He also has two part-time jobs:

on market days and Saturdays he works in a record shop:

on other days he sells cleaning materials door-to-door in the area.

Arthur's payslip for April from the record shop contains the following information:

SURNAME AND INITIALS	CODE	BASIC PAY	OVERTIME	OTHER	TAXABLE GROSS PAY
LEE A.	242				223·75

REF	PAY DATE	TAX DEDUCTED	NATIONAL INSURANCE	OTHER DEDUCTIONS	NET PAY
	30 APRIL	5·94	1·15		216·66

a)   i)   Explain the meaning of the following items on the payslip.

      Code

      National Insurance

      Net Pay

    ii)   State the amount that Arthur can earn in a year without paying tax.   2

b)   Name TWO items that may be found in the 'OTHER DEDUCTIONS'
section of the payslip   1

c)   i)   Describe the type of income normally earned by door-to-door salespeople.   1

    ii)   Give ONE reason why salespeople are paid in this way.   1

d)   Explain whether Arthur is likely to be better or worse off than a full-time student living
on a fixed grant, when inflation is at a high rate.   2

e)   In April, Arthur's hourly rate of pay at the record shop was increased from £2.00
to £2.50. During the month he worked a total of 98.5 hours of which 45 hours were at
the old rate per hour. Check whether he has been paid the correct gross pay.
Show your workings.   3

ASSIGNMENT

RATCLIFF ELECTRICAL COMPANY LTD

School Leaver required for
GENERAL OFFICE WORK
Starting wage £60.00 pw gross + profit sharing
Flexitime scheme in operation
LV's, 40 hour week, annual increments
Apply giving details of personal interests
and examinations (to be) taken.

Mr K Shields
Personnel Manager
Ratcliff Electrical Co Ltd
4 Grant Street
SKIPTON

Study the advertisement shown above and answer the following:

1. What do the following abbreviations stand for?

    a)   pw

    b)   LV's

2. What do you understand by the following?

    a)   gross

    b)   profit sharing

    c)   annual increments

3.   a)   Explain how flexitime works

    b)   Give one advantage to Ratcliffe Electrical and one advantage to its employees of operating
flexitime.

4. Assume that you are successful in getting this job, how many hours per week will you be working?

5. How much per hour will you be paid?

6. At the end of the first week you receive the following pay slip:

Name	Gross Pay	Tax	NI	Other Deductions	Total Deductions	Net Pay
	£160.00	£27.25	£6.00	£6.50	£ ?	£ ?

a) What do the letters NI stand for?

b) Give one example of 'other deductions'

7. Calculate the following from the information given in the pay slip.
   a) Total deductions
   b) Net pay

8. State 2 points, *NOT* mentioned in the advertisement which you would consider before accepting the job.

23. Communication

1. This chapter looks at the need for effective communication in the business world. It gives details of the main methods of internal and external communications which are used today including the important impact of new computerised technology.

DEFINITION

2. Communication is a two-way process to enable information to be passed from one person or organisation to another, or in the case of automatic systems, from one process to another. To be effective, communication must be understood and acceptable by all parties, both those giving the information and those receiving it. Unfortunately, it is often very easy to misunderstand or mis-interpret what is meant.

TYPES OF COMMUNICATION

3. Communication in a business may take place in many different ways. It may be:
    a) **Verbal** i.e. spoken by someone, for example face to face or on the telephone *or*
    b) **Non-verbal** i.e. written, for example letters, memos, reports, diagrams etc.
    c) **Formal** i.e. following correct laid down procedures of which records are usually kept, for example committees, recruitment interviews, safety notices *or*
    d) **Informal** i.e. as and when appropriate without the need to follow procedures or keep records, for example meeting or telephoning someone to discuss a particular problem as it arises.
    e) **Internal** i.e. takes place within a business organisation, for example between the sales and personnel departments *or*
    f) **External** i.e. outside an organisation or between organisations, for example with a customer or supplier.

All of these forms of communication are important to a business.

NEED FOR EFFECTIVE COMMUNICATION

4. A business organisation is unlikely to be successful without effective communication because a firm must:

   a) be able to issue instructions to its staff to tell them what to do and thus enable the business to operate.

   b) communicate with its suppliers, customers, banks and other contacts in carrying out its business. It must send information about its products, receive orders, supply goods, deal with documents and arrange payments.

   c) keep staff informed of what is going on so that they are able to perform their work better and enjoy what they are doing. It must transmit information about the firm's organisation, products, safety regulations and training.

   d) provide essential information to staff on pay, pensions, holidays, other benefits and general working conditions.

5. **Effective Communication** involves four elements:

   a) **The Transmitter** i.e. the sender or source of the communication

   b) **The Message** or content of what is being communicated

   c) **The Medium** or method through which the communication travels, for example letter, telephone etc.

   d) **The Receiver** i.e. the audience or people to whom the communication is being sent.

6. **The Elements of Communication**

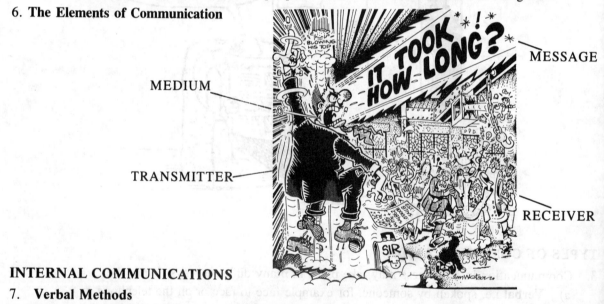

MEDIUM

TRANSMITTER

MESSAGE

RECEIVER

INTERNAL COMMUNICATIONS

7. **Verbal Methods**

Spoken communications are the most common way of passing information within an organisation. This involves seeing people face to face, for example the holding of meetings or contacting them by telephone.

Telephone extensions are frequently used in an organisation to enable communications to take place between various sections or departments. This saves time if it is not possible to meet someone to speak to them personally.

Interviews or individual discussions with staff are common in all organisations. They are used not only to select staff but also, for example, to deal with particular problems or disciplinary matters or to assess staff performance.

Business meetings may take place where a number of people need to be involved in discussions. These may be formal or informal.

BUSINESS MEETINGS

8. **Informal meetings** may be called at short notice to discuss matters which arise suddenly. Usually there is no agenda and often no record is kept of what happened.

9. **Formal meetings** are usually held after the people involved have been notified in advance, usually in writing and often with an accompanying **Agenda**. This lists the items to be discussed.

10. **Example of an Agenda:**

A B C ELECTRICAL SUPPLIERS LTD

MEETING OF MARKETING CO-ORDINATION COMMITTEE
ON FRIDAY 13th NOVEMBER 1994 at 10 AM
TO BE HELD IN THE BOARDROOM

AGENDA

1. Apologies for absence.
2. Minutes of previous Meeting
3. Matters arising:
    - 21   Sales Training
    - 22   Promotion of New Products
    - 25   Advertising Budget
4. Marketing Department staffing.
5. Report on Sales Enquiry Forms.
6. Exhibition Plan.
7. Any other business.
8. Date and time of next meeting.

---

11. Most organisations, whether a Youth Club, School, College or Company have committees which meet to discuss and make policy decisions. Often these consist of people elected to represent the views of members. Formal bodies usually have an Annual General Meeting (AGM) held once a year to elect officials, receive reports and to give members an opportunity to speak; for example, a limited company will hold an Annual General Meeting to which all its shareholders are invited.

12. A formal meeting is controlled by a chairman and minutes are taken by a secretary. **Minutes** are a record of a meeting and serve as a reminder of the issues discussed and decisions taken. All members of the committee will receive a copy of the minutes and any matters arising will be discussed at the next meeting.

INTERNAL COMMUNICATIONS

13. Non-Verbal (Written) Methods

Memoranda (memos) are the method of written communication most commonly used within an organisation. They can be sent in a firm's internal post, are usually short and deal with only one or two specific points.

14. **Example of a memoranda:**

INTERNAL MEMORANDUM	
From: Personnel Manager	To: Mr J Hall cc G Morris
Subject: Staff	Date: 10 November 1994
Bill Haworth has 'flu and will be absent from work until next week.	

15. **Minutes** are used to provide a summary of the main points which are discussed at a meeting.

16. **Letters** are not normally used within a business. However, they are sent in some formal situations, for example, to confirm the promotion of staff or to accept their resignation.

17. **Notices** are often used to display matters of interest to staff. However, unfortunately there is no way of ensuring that these are either read or understood.

18. **Example of a Notice Board**

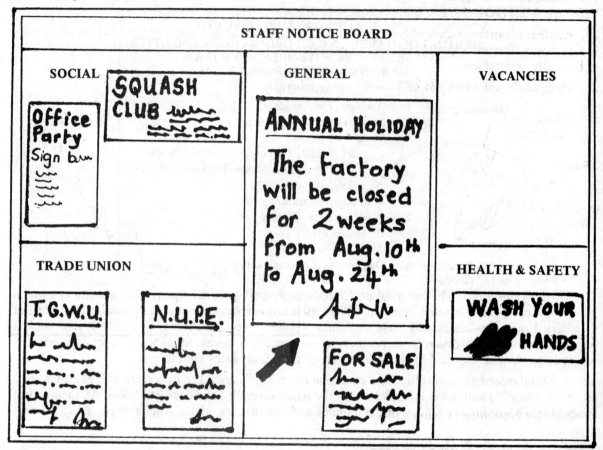

19. **House Bulletins/House Journals** In some organisations notices are circulated by means of a weekly or monthly staff bulletin. Some larger organisations also have a glossy house magazine or journal which includes information on a wide range of work-related and social topics, for example new products, new employees, births, deaths and marriages, or sports activities.

20. **Reports** are formal written communications required to cover a certain business topic. They may be provided for a number of reasons. For example many firms have a standard accident or sickness report form. Periodic reports may be needed to assess a firm's budget or sales performance. Technical reports may be prepared on new products and processes of production.

OTHER INFORMAL METHODS OF COMMUNICATION

21. Communication may also take place in other ways in particular via the 'grapevine', over lunch and on social occasions.

22. The **'grapevine'** or jungle telegraph is the term used to describe the rumours and general gossip which staff often use as a source of information in an organisation.

23. Informal **lunchtime** conversations are often used for both internal and external communication. They may involve casual discussion between staff or be working lunches often with visitors to an organisation.

24. **Social occasions** of all types provide a further opportunity for both internal and external communication to take place. Examples might include a Christmas Dinner, cricket match or annual outing where a number of staff will mix and talk together.

VISUAL METHODS OF COMMUNICATION

25. Another important means of communication, both internal and external is the use of charts, graphs and diagrams. The use of visual presentation enables complicated information, particular statistical data, to be easily understood.

26. **Four Different Methods of Visual Communication**

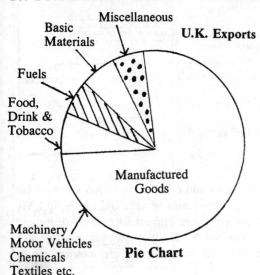

Pie Chart

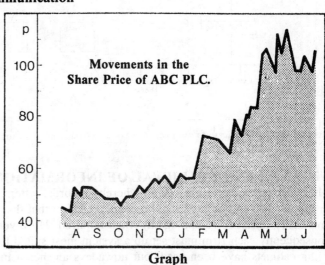

Graph

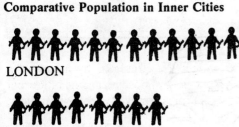

Comparative Population in Inner Cities

LONDON

MANCHESTER

LIVERPOOL   Pictograph

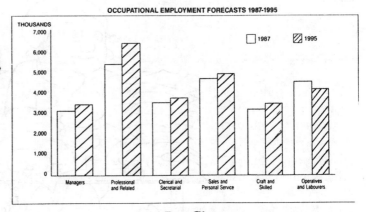

Bar Chart

EXTERNAL COMMUNICATIONS

27. The most common forms of external communication are letters and the telephone. In the UK the major suppliers of these and other external communication services are the Post Office and British Telecom (see Chapter 24). These organisations provide a wide range of national and international

communication systems which are becoming increasingly sophisticated with the introduction of new computerised technology.

28. *N.B.* **Compliment slips** are often used when a letter is not needed; for example when a firm sends out leaflets or other information which has been requested by potential customers.

29. Advertising and sales promotion is also an important means by which a firm communicates with its customers and this is dealt with fully in Chapter 11.

30. **A Summary of the Main Methods of Business Communications**

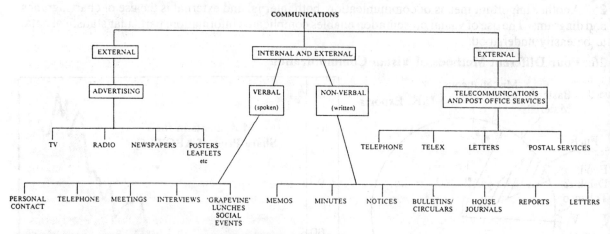

STORAGE AND RETRIEVAL OF INFORMATION

31. All businesses need a system whereby records, letters, documents and other information can be filed or stored. It is important for good communication that this data is kept clean and safe and can be quickly and easily retrieved (found again) when required. However, there is no one correct method of filing and consequently each firm must set up a system most suited to its own needs. Traditionally various types of filing cabinets have been used, but nowadays an increasing number of organisations are making use of computerised systems.

32.

"Now where did I put it?"

33. **Computers** are able to store, retrieve and sort data at great speed. Information can be retrieved either directly onto a screen, printing out a hard copy on paper or on *microfilm*. Many firms need a lot of space for filing and this problem is reduced by microfilming, which involves taking miniature photographs of data. A special 'microfiche' viewer or reader is then used which enlarges the film so that it can be read easily. An example of the use of microfilm or microfiche can probably be seen in your local library which may store book lists or telephone directories in this way.

34. *N.B.* Microfilm uses a roll of film usually 16 mm, whereas microfiche is a sheet of film say 10½ cm x 15 cm on which many pages of data can be recorded.

35. Many organisations now use computers to prepare the payroll, keep stock records and control the accounts. This can be seen if you visit a travel agency to book a holiday where the details, for example, place, dates, hotel, costs etc are entered directly into a computer. Most building societies now enter data directly into a computer and bank statements, gas, electricity and telephone bills are also prepared by computers. Companies usually keep a register of their shareholders on computer so that it can be kept up-to-date as shares are bought and sold.

36. **Word processing** is now used by many firms instead of typewriters. A word processor consists of an electronic keyboard with a built-in computer memory linked to a visual display unit (VDU). This is a screen rather like a television on which the typed information appears. Material can be quickly and easily corrected or altered on the screen before it is printed. When completed the information can be filed (stored) away on magnetic tape or on a floppy or hard disc until it is needed again.

37. Word processors have many uses and can produce a vast range of material including letters, graphs, charts and diagrams. They are particularly useful for repetitive typewriting tasks such as standard letters which only require the name and address, date and time, or other simple information to be changed. Other uses might include the preparation of invoices, accounts, memos and reports.

38. **Computer Technology**

39. **Data Protection Act 1984**

This Act controls the type of information which can be recorded and processed electronically and how it can be used. All organisations and individuals who hold personal records on computer must register with the Data Protection Registrar. Individuals have the right to know what information is kept about them (and request a copy) and can claim compensation if it is used unlawfully.

SUMMARY

40. a) Communication is a two way process to enable the exchange of information to take place.

    b) It may be verbal, non-verbal, formal or informal and may take place inside an organisation (internal) or between organisations (external).

    c) Effective communication is essential if a firm is to be successful. Staff need clear instructions whilst customers and other business contacts require a flow of information.

    d) The main verbal (spoken) methods of communication are personal contact with people either face to face, in interviews, or in meetings or by telephone. The 'grapevine', working lunches and social events are others.

    e) The main non-verbal (written) methods of communication include memos, minutes, notices, staff bulletins, house journals and reports. Visual communication may take place via the use of charts and diagrams.

    f) Letters are not usually sent within an organisation but are the main method of external communication. The telephone, other telecommunications and postal services are also important, as are the various forms of advertising and sales promotion.

    g) Increasingly firms are now using computers for preparing and storing (filing) data.

    h) Word processing is one major application of computer technology.

REVIEW QUESTIONS

Answers can be found in the paragraphs shown.

1. Briefly define 'communication'. (2)
2. Explain the need for effective communication in a business. (4)
3. List the main verbal and non-verbal methods of internal communication. (3, 7, 13-24)
4. What information is given in an Agenda? (9, 10)
5. Why are minutes taken in a meeting? (12, 15)
6. Give 2 examples of visual means of communication. (25, 26)
7. List the 4 main methods of external communication. (27-30)
8. What is filing and why is it important? (31-33)
9. Give 2 examples of the use of computers in business. (34-36)
10. What is word processing? (37, 38)

EXAMINATION PRACTICE QUESTIONS

Marks

1. The most common form of written communication used within a business is called a . . .   1

2. a) Underline the external methods of communication in the following list:
newspaper advertisement, letter post, managers meeting, price list, memorandum   3

    b) Which of the above methods of communication would be most appropriate in each of the following situations:
      i) To confirm an offer of a job to a new employee.
      ii) To inform all staff that the hours of work are to be altered.   2

3. State 2 methods of external communication and 2 methods of internal communication which a soap powder manufacturer might use.   2

4. Give 2 possible advantages of preparing the minutes of a meeting using a word processor.   2

5. A firm's Directors are anxious to keep their employers and customers better informed.
   a) What methods of communication could be used within the firm to ensure that staff are kept up-to-date with developments in their own job and the firm as a whole?   10
   b) i) What are the main methods of communication a firm would have with its customers?
      ii) What problems might occur with each method?   10

MULTIPLE CHOICE/COMPLETION

1. To send a written message to all workers within a company, it is usual to:
   a) Telephone each individual
   b) See everyone personally
   c) Send a letter to each person
   d) Send a memorandum to each person

2. The Data Protection Act 1984 allows an individual to:
   a) Register for data protection
   b) Have access to personal information
   c) Use a computer at work
   d) Use a computer at home

3.

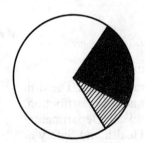

The diagram above is an example of:
   a) A pie chart
   b) A bar chart
   c) A flow chart
   d) A line graph

4. The Agenda for a meeting is:
   a) A record of what has been discussed
   b) A record of who has attended
   c) A list of items to be discussed
   d) Only used for an Annual General Meeting

5. A VDU is:
   a) A screen used to display information
   b) A computer
   c) An electronic typewriter
   d) A word processor

6. Which of the following is a non-verbal method of communication:
   a) Business meeting
   b) House Journal
   c) Telephone
   d) Interview

In each of the following questions, one or more of the responses is/are correct. Choose the appropriate letter which indicates the correct version.

   A   if 1 only is correct
   B   if 3 only is correct
   C   if 1 and 2 only are correct
   D   if 1, 2 and 3 are correct

7. Which of the following can be used for the storage of micro-computer data?
   1) Floppy disks
   2) Microfiche
   3) Cassettes

8. Which of the following is/are informal methods of communication?
   1) Social Events
   2) Staff Notice Boards
   3) Reports

RECENT EXAMINATION QUESTIONS

Marks

MEG 1988 GCSE BUSINESS STUDIES SPECIMEN PAPER I

1. Read the following paragraph carefully and answer the questions printed below.

J Hamilton Ltd is a medium sized textile manufacturer with two plants 5 miles apart. The firm has five departments concerned with marketing, production, finance, personnel and distribution. There has been a serious accident and the Board of Directors have told all Departmental Managers to remind employees of their duties and obligations under the Health and Safety at Work Act.

   a) State what you understand by the following terms used above.
      i)   Board of Directors.   2
      ii) Departmental Managers   2
   b) State THREE suitable methods of communicating these 'duties and obligations' to all employees.   3
   c) To which Departmental Manager would you expect the following employees to report?
      i)   salesman
      ii) lorry driver
      iii) accounts clerk
      iv) machinist   4
   d) Give TWO reasons why operating on two sites might lead to communications problems.   4
   e) State THREE methods by which J Hamilton Ltd could communicate changes in their product range to customers?   3

f)   At the end of the financial year, J Hamilton Ltd's shareholders would normally expect
to receive a dividend.
    i)   What is a dividend?   2
    ii) Why do shareholders expect to receive dividends?   2

2. LEAG MAY 1988 GCSE BUSINESS STUDIES PAPER 2A

a)   i)   Name ONE method of communication.

     ii) Suggest ONE situation in which this method of communication would be useful.

b)   Give ONE reason why communication is important in the business world.   2

ASSIGNMENT

1.   You have recently started work in the offices of Barnard's Engineering plc. During your first few
weeks training you are asked to complete a number of tasks including the following:

> It is 0915 and you have just answered the telephone. "Hello my name is Trevor Lloyd of
> Alexander Harris Computers Ltd. I would like to speak to Mr Williams your Sales Director".

You explain to the caller that Mr Williams is out of the office at the moment, so he asks you to
take a message.

The following passage records the rest of the conversation.

> "I had arranged to see him on Monday next. I was going to talk about the possibility of running a
> joint stand at the Olympia Exhibition in 3 months time. I can still keep the appointment, but if it
> was delayed until next week then I could show him our new model. I am away on business for
> the rest of the week but will be in contact with the office for any messages. Could he let me know
> if it is convenient to change the date. At the moment I am free most of next week. Perhaps he
> could ring my secretary on Derby 50792?
>
> If he wants to speak to me personally my home number is 061-797-6821, but I am not usually in
> before 1830. Thank you."

a)   Underline or make a list of all the important details of the conversation.

b)   Leave a message for Mr Williams using the company's standard telephone message pad
     shown below.

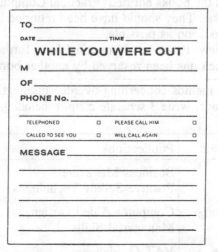

2.   Look at the graph below of the company profits and then fill in the missing words in the following sentences.

Barnard's Engineering plc Profits Record 1981-1991

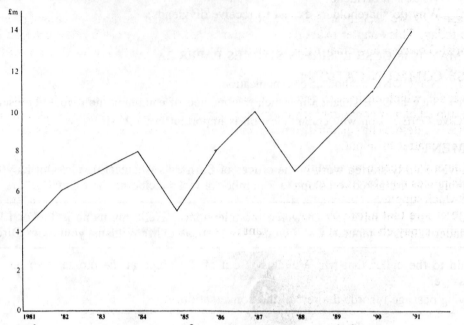

This chart shows the . . . . of . . . . plc from . . . . to . . . .
From the . . . . it can be seen that the lowest profits figure was . . . . in . . . . whilst the highest profits of . . . . were achieved in . . . . With the exception of . . . . and . . . . the profits have . . . . steadily over the . . . . year period.

3.

MEMORANDUM			
TO:	E Redhead Computer Services	DATE:	28 August 199 .
FROM:	Assistant Librarian	REF:	LIB/AWD/SD
SUBJECT:	Overdue Publications		

According to our records the books entitled 'Practical Computing' and 'Advanced Computer Research' are now overdue. They should have been returned by Monday 19 August. Would you please return them as soon as possible.
If required you may re-new 'Practical Computing' for a further 2 weeks but not 'Advanced Computer Research' which has been reserved by another borrower.

You are asked to write some memos concerning overdue publications borrowed from the company's library. Using the example above, write 3 separate memos including all the information contained in the following list:

Name	Department	Publications	Date Due	Reserved
A Harris	Sales	Business Magazine	20 August	No
		Positive Selling Techniques	22 August	Yes
P Farmer	Engineering	Computer Aided Design	17 August	No
		Managerial Skills	19 August	No
J Glover	Accounts	VAT Guidelines	21 August	Yes

24. Postal Services and Telecommunications

1.   In Chapter 23 we looked at the main internal and external methods of communication used in businesses today. This chapter examines in greater detail the range of services provided by the Post Office, British Telecom and other firms to enable businesses to communicate quickly and effectively.

BUSINESS COMMUNICATION

2.   The ways in which businesses communicate with each other have changed dramatically in recent years. The impact of new computer technology has greatly increased the speed of communications in the UK. The use of satellites has enabled communication, by both sound and vision, to be made throughout the world in a matter of minutes.

3.   Nowadays we receive news almost as soon as it happens via television, radio and newspapers. Modern businesses therefore also expect their methods of communication to be fast and effective. The speed with which suppliers, customers, staff and other business providers, such as banks, are contacted is important to ensure that a firm operates efficiently. There are many different forms of communication which a business may choose and it is important to select the most effective in any particular situation.

4.

THE POST OFFICE

5.   Postal Services in the UK are provided by the Post Office which is a Public Corporation owned and controlled by the Government. Every working day it delivers over 50 million letters and 600,000 parcels. Details of its main services are summarised below. Up-to-date information about all services can be found in the Post Office Guide which is published annually.

LETTER SERVICES

6.   Britain has a two tier postal system whereby letters, postcards and newspapers can be sent either first or second class. **First class post** is slightly more expensive but the Post Office aims to deliver it the day after posting. **Second class post** is cheaper but may take several days to deliver.

7.   *N.B.* To speed up the letter service an automated system has been introduced to enable mail to be sorted faster. Every address has now been given a 'Post Code' and this is used for electronic sorting.

8.   Recorded Delivery

Gives proof that a letter has been delivered. A fee on top of the normal postage ensures that letters/packages must be signed for when they are delivered. This service is useful for sending legal documents, final demands for debt, certificates and other important material.

9.   Registered Post

Any first class letter can be registered, but usually a special envelope is purchased from the Post Office. This service is used to send money or items of value through the post. On payment of a fee they can be insured so that compensation is paid if the item is lost or damaged.

10.   Freepost

Allows people to reply to firms without a stamp. The cost of the postage is paid by the firm. A special licence is required to use this service.

11.

12.   Business Reply Service

Businesses can also obtain a licence which allows them to pay the cost of postage by issuing pre-printed envelopes, postcards or folded advertisements to potential customers. These can be used at no cost to the customer. Both Freepost and the Business Reply Service are widely used to encourage people to respond to advertisements.

13.   First and Second Class Business Reply

PARCEL SERVICES

14.   The Post Office accepts parcels up to a certain size and weight. However it does not have a monopoly (complete control) of parcel delivery, and faces competition from many other firms who run courier parcel services, for example TNT and Securicor.

15. The Postage Forward Parcel Service

Allows a package to be sent and paid for on delivery by the person receiving it. Mail Order companies often use this service for returned goods.

16. Compensation Fee (CF) Parcel

If CF is paid on a parcel when it is posted compensation can be claimed if it gets lost or damaged.

17. Cash on Delivery (COD)

Mail Order firms will often send goods to customers and arrange for the payment to be made on delivery. For a small charge the postman collects the amount due which is then forwarded to the company. This helps a firm because it ensures prompt payment for the goods.

EXPRESS SERVICES

18. These are available for the urgent delivery of mail, for example Express Post, Datapost and Special Delivery.

    a) **Express Post** This is a special same day messenger collection and delivery service which is available in London and other large cities. Charges are based on the distance and weight of the letter or parcel and therefore the service is generally used for short distances.

    b) **Datapost** is a door-to-door overnight collection and delivery service intended mainly for sending computer data, although it can be used for other items. Arrangements are made with the Post Office to operate this service on a daily, weekly or monthly basis and charges made accordingly. However items can also be handed in at main Post Offices. **Datapost International** provides the same service for overseas packages.

    c) **Special Delivery** can be arranged for items posted first class. For an additional fee messengers deliver mail as soon as it is received at the destination Post Office. Items must be marked 'Special Delivery' and have a broad blue stripe marked on them for easy identification.

    d) **Railex** Where Post Office messengers take letters to the nearest railway station. At their destination other messengers collect and deliver them.

19. **An overseas Express Delivery Service**

20. *N.B.*

   a) **Red Star** is a same day parcel service provided together with British Rail. For an additional fee, parcels with first class postage can be taken to the nearest station and travel on the next train. They can then be collected at their destination or delivered by first class post.

   b) **Night Star** provides a similar service but it operates overnight. Parcels can be collected and delivered by special messenger if required.

OVERSEAS MAIL

21. The Post Office also provides a letters and parcels service to countries throughout the world. For more rapid delivery **Airmail** can be used which costs more.

22. **Swiftair** is a service which is available for the speedy delivery of letters to Europe and for Airmail letters to other countries. An additional fee is paid at the Post Office when the item is handed in.

OTHER MAIL SERVICES

23. Certificate of Posting

Letters or packages can be taken to a Post Office and for payment of a small fee a receipt is issued to prove they have been posted. However it does not provide proof of delivery.

24. Bulk Postage Rebate

If a firm is sending a lot of second class mail it can make special arrangements with the Post Office to receive a discount on the cost of the postage.

25. Post Restante

Allows letters to be addressed to any main town Post Office for collection when convenient. This service can be particularly useful for someone who does a lot of travelling.

26. Franking Machines

Are used instead of stamps by organisations who send large quantities of mail. They frank (print) the postage on an envelope and automatically record the number of units used. Some firms also include an advertising message on franked mail, examples can be seen below:

27.

28. Private Post Box Service
This allows a customer to have their mail delivered to a private box number instead of their usual address.
29.

Fairfield Pottery Ltd.,
P.O. Box 29,
LEEK,
Staffordshire.

30. Intelpost
Is a high speed service available at over 100 Post Offices for sending exact photocopies (facsimiles) of documents and other urgent items. It is possible, within minutes, to send copies to major cities within the UK for delivery or collection the same day. The service is also available to more than 2000 overseas centres.

OTHER POST OFFICE SERVICES
31. In addition to the many methods of communication discussed so far, the Post Office also provides many other services on behalf of the Government. These include:
   a)   Payment of pensions and social security benefits, for example unemployment.
   b)   Issuing licences for example television, and road fund tax.
   c)   Sale of National Insurance stamps. (see Chapter 26)
   d)   Sale of National Savings Certificates, Premium Bonds and other securities.
   e)   Girobank. (see Chapter 5)

32. Post Office Services

Get more out of your post office

33. *N.B.* The Post Office Users National Council (POUNC)

Will deal with any complaint or queries related to Post Office services. The Post Office must also consult POUNC about any major proposals affecting its services.

TELECOMMUNICATIONS

34. The main telecommunications services summarised below are run in the UK by B.T. which was government owned until 1986. It has now been privatised and operates in the private sector as a public limited company. In the 1990's, Mercury, run by Cable and Wireless plc, has developed as a competitor to B.T.

TELEPHONE

35. This is the main method of communication used by businesses because it is very quick and relatively cheap. The most expensive time for telephone calls is before 1.00 pm and the cheapest is after 6.00 pm and at weekends. Anyone who has a telephone is called a subscriber and is able to make use of a wide variety of services offered by B.T.

MAIN TELEPHONE SERVICES (in alphabetical order)

36. a) **Alarm Calls**
For a small charge you can arrange for the operator to ring you at an agreed time.

b) **Advice of Duration and Charge (ADC)**
It is possible when making calls via the operator to arrange to be informed of how long the call took and how much it cost.

c) **Call Cards**
Can be bought at Post Offices and in some newsagents. They are used in special public telephone boxes instead of coins.

d) **Fixed-time Calls**
These are calls which for an extra charge can be booked in advance. At the agreed time(s) the operator will connect the call and ring you.

e) **Freephone**
Calls are made through the operator. A firm can offer this facility whereby they pay for the cost of calls made by customers.

f) **Information Services**
Are available by dialling the appropriate number, for example time, weather forecasts, motoring information and stock exchange prices.

g) **Personal Calls (person-to-person)**
If someone is difficult to contact, for example an overseas businessman, it is possible, for a small fee, to ask the operator for a personal call. If the person you want to speak to is not available then there is no charge for the call.

h) **Radio Phones**
Are mobile telephones which enable calls to be made from cars and other vehicles anywhere in the UK.

i) **Subscriber Trunk Dialling (STD)**
This system automatically connects calls in Britain, and through **International Direct Dialling (IDD)**, to many parts of the world without the use of an operator.

j) **Telephone Credit Cards**
Enable calls to be made from any telephone (except your own) via the operator without payment at that time. Charges are added to the subscribers regular telephone account.

k) **Transferred Charge Calls (reversed charge)**
These calls are made through the operator. Provided that the call is accepted it is possible to ring someone and they will pay the cost.

TELEPHONE DIRECTORIES

37. Directories list the telephone numbers of subscribers. Each local subscriber is given a free copy and is able to buy directories for other areas.

38. The two main directories are:

a) **'The Phone Book'**
Which lists the subscribers in a particular area and also provides information on B.T. Services. This book can also be obtained on microfiche.

b) **Yellow Pages**
Is a directory of local business addresses and telephone numbers which are classified for easy reference. For example, it contains lists of banks, plumbers and suppliers of telecommunications equipment.

OTHER B.T. SERVICES

39. Telex

This service uses a special teleprinter machine which can send and receive messages from similar machines in the UK and throughout the world. Providing the machine is switched on it will automatically receive messages at any time of the day or night. This is very useful when contacting businesses overseas.

40. The system is very similar to using the telephone except that the message is typed in and is then printed out at the other end. Each subscriber has a telex number and is issued with a UK Telex Directory. The cost of telex messages is based on the time it takes to transmit (send) the message and the distance involved.

41. A Telex Machine

42. Telemessage(s)

These are accepted by telephone or telex and are delivered the next day by first class post. Telemessages replaced inland telegrams but **International telegrams** still exist.

43.

> ## Offices rush for facsimile machines and mobile phones
>
> MORE small companies are joining the communications revolution.
>
> About one in three now have facsimile machines, while 22 p.c. are equipped with mobile telephones, 13 p.c. have telex facilities and 11 p.c. have pagers.
>
> The new figures emerge from the latest quarterly small business survey produced by the Small Business Research Trust which underlines growing worries about high interest rates.
>
> The report says the biggest expansion in business telecommunications over the next year will be in facsimile.
>
> Only 3 p.c. of companies have electronic mail links and 5 p.c. on-line database services.

44. Facsimile Transmission (FAX)

Paragraph 30 described the Post Office's **Intelpost** system for sending facsimile (exact) copies of letters, documents and other information.

45. British Telecom also has a facsimile service called **Bureaufax**. This enables firms with their own facsimile machine to send copies to other firms with similar machines either in the UK or overseas. The machines are linked by telephone and operate automatically once the contact is made.

46. Contravision

This service links individuals or groups of people in different places by sound and vision. This can be quicker and cheaper than trying to get a group of people together. For example, sales staff throughout the country can be linked in this way for a conference thus saving travelling costs and hotel bills. Contravision links can be made, via satellites, to many countries throughout the world.

47.

312

48. *N.B.* **Office of Telecommunications (OFTEL)**

OFTEL is an independent body which was set up in 1986 when B.T. was privatised. It monitors and regulates the services provided and gives advice and assistance to telecommunication users.

OTHER TELECOMMUNICATION SERVICES

49. **Teletex**

Is used to describe any computerised information displayed on a television screen which is broadcast by a TV company. It includes **Ceefax** the teletex system provided by the BBC and **Teletext** (formerly Oracle) the IBA system.

50. Where telephone lines are used to transmit data it is called **Viewdata**, examples of which are British Telecom's Prestel and Datel Services.

51. **Share Prices on Teletex**

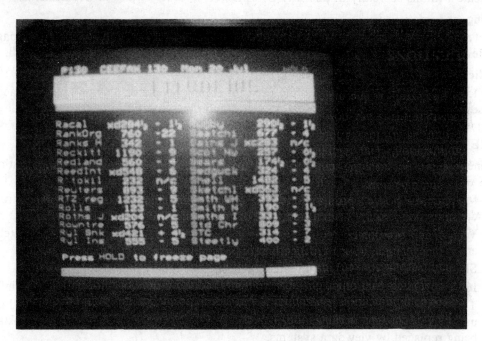

52. **Prestel**

This is a computerised system which provides a data base of both general and business information on a wide variety of topics, for example share prices, financial statistics and sports results. To use the system a specially adapted television set is needed which is connected to a telephone line linked to the Prestel computer.

53. Prestel is what is referred to as an interactive or two-way system because as well as receiving information users can also send messages both to each other and to information providers. The system can be used to order goods from a supermarket, book a holiday or hotel room or reserve a theatre seat.

54. **Datel**

This telecommunication service operates using the telephone lines and can link a computer in one place with computers in other parts of the country and in many overseas countries.

55. This service is particularly useful, for example, where a firm has a number of branches but needs to process orders centrally. It can have its main computer at Head Office with links in each branch.

OTHER INTERNAL COMMUNICATIONS EQUIPMENT

56. Telephone Switchboard

Most businesses have a telephone switchboard which, depending on the size of the firm, can vary from one main line with use of a few extensions to hundreds of lines and thousands of extensions.

57. Telephone Answering Machines

These make it possible to leave messages for people when they are out. A tape recorder is attached to the telephone receiver which automatically switches itself on to receive incoming calls. This enables messages of all kinds to be left after business hours.

58. Intercom

In addition to telephone extensions many firms also use an intercom system. This is a small microphone and loudspeaker which enables two or more people to speak to each other. For example a manager may communicate with his secretary in this way or with staff in other offices or departments.

59. Paging

The use of a pager enables businessmen to be contacted when they are out of the office. The pager bleeps to indicate when people are required who then go to the nearest telephone to take the call.

60. Public Address Systems (Tannoy)

This is a loudspeaker system which is often used for calling people or playing music in factories and warehouses. They are also used at football matches and other sporting events.

FUTURE DEVELOPMENTS IN COMMUNICATIONS

61. Businesses will continue to make use of new and improved methods of communication. A few examples of how this might affect all of us in the future include:

   a) More people **working from home**, contacting their offices and other businesses through view-data and other links.

   b) **Videophone** This is a facility being developed which links a small TV screen to a telephone to enable two people to see each other as they talk.

   c) **Shopping from home** using Prestel could become quite common.

   d) It will soon be possible to **talk to computers** instead of operating them by keying in information.

   e) The use of **electronic mail** systems like Prestel, Datel and Fax could develop so that they are used not just by businesses but by all of us. This might result in newspapers and postal services being replaced by viewdata systems.

SUMMARY

62. a) The Post Office and B.T. provide most of the UK's communication services.

   b) Letter services include first and second class post, recorded delivery, registered post, freepost and the business reply service.

   c) Parcels can also be sent either first or second class. COD, Postage Forward, and CF are other services.

   d) Express services include Expresspost, Datapost and Special Delivery.

   e) Red Star, Night Star and Railex are operated by the Post Office together with British Rail.

   f) Overseas mail can be sent by ordinary post, or using Airmail, or Swiftair if faster delivery is needed.

   g) Other mail services include certificates of posting, bulk postage rebate, post restante, franking machines, private post boxes and intelpost.

   h) The telephone is the main method of telecommunication.

i) Telephone services include alarm calls, ADC, call cards, fixed time calls, freephone, information, personal calls, credit cards, STD, radio phone and reverse charges.

j) Other B.T. services include telex, telemessages, FAX and contravision.

k) Teletex is provided by Ceefax and Oracle whilst Prestel and Datel are forms of viewdata.

l) Other internal communication equipment includes telephone switchboards and answering machines, intercoms, paging and public address systems.

REVIEW QUESTIONS

Answers can be found in the paragraphs shown.

1. What is the Post Office Guide? (5)

2. List the main means of communication which the Post Office provides for business use. (5, 6)

3. What is the difference between Recorded Delivery and Registered Post? (8, 9)

4. Name 2 ways in which firms can receive postal replies from their clients without them paying postage. (10-13)

5. What do the initials COD and CF represent? (16, 17)

6. Describe 3 express mail services. (18-20)

7. Which postal service would a firm use to send a very urgent letter to Europe? (21, 22)

8. How does a franking machine help a firm with its mail? (26, 27)

9. Which B.T. service is now the main means of business communication? (35)

10. Describe 3 different types of telephone calls connected by the operator. (36)

11. What do the initials STD, IDD and ADC represent? (36)

12. Who pays the cost of a reverse charge call? (36)

13. Give an example of a classified telephone directory. (38)

14. Briefly describe a facsimile transmission service. (30, 44)

15. How might contravision help an international company? (46, 47)

16. What are Ceefax and Oracle examples of? (49)

17. Explain why Prestel is described as 'inter-active'. (50-52)

18. Briefly explain Datel. (50, 54)

19. How can a telephone answering machine assist a business? (57)

20. List some of the possible effects resulting from future developments in communications. (61)

EXAMINATION PRACTICE QUESTIONS

Marks

1. The method whereby the cost of the contents is collected on delivery by the Post Office is known as   1

2. Give one advantage and one disadvantage of using the telephone for business communication.   2

3. a) Explain the function of the Datapost Service.   2
   b) Give one example to illustrate how a business might use it.   1

4. Briefly explain the difference between teletext and viewdata, and give one example of each.   4

Marks

5. a) **Name** and describe 2 ways in which a firm could arrange to pay the postage costs of letters received from its customers.   4

   b) Why do firms offer these services to customers?   2

6. a) Explain the main differences between the telephone and telex services as a means of communication.   6

   b) Give an example of a communication:
      i) for which telex would be more suitable than telephone
      ii) for which neither telephone nor telex would be suitable
      iii) for which a personal meeting would be essential   6

   c) i) Distinguish between 'recorded delivery' and delivery by 'registered post'
      ii) Illustrate the distinction by giving, in each case, an appropriate example of a communication sent   8

   d) Describe the Intelpost Facsimile Service offered by the Post Office   5

MULTIPLE CHOICE/COMPLETION

1. Before a business can operate a reply paid service it must:
   a) Inform all its customers
   b) Print special envelopes or postcards
   c) Obtain a licence from the Post Office
   d) Already operate a 'Freepost' service

2. Insurance against the loss of goods in the post is provided by which one of the following Post Office services?
   a) Registered Post
   b) First class post
   c) Freepost
   d) Telex

3. Which of the following would be used to find the name and telephone number of a local insurance broker?
   a) Post Office Guide
   b) The Phone Book
   c) Local street map
   d) Yellow Pages

4. Which of the following Post Office services provides proof of delivery?
   a) Business Reply Service
   b) Franking
   c) Certificate of Postage
   d) Recorded Delivery

5. The UK telephone system to which most subscribers are linked is called:
   a) OFTEL
   b) BBC
   c) STD
   d) CBI

6. When answering the telephone a firm's telephonist should say:
    a) The name of the firm
    b) "Yes, what do you want?"
    c) "Hello, who are you?"
    d) "Wait a minute please"

In the following questions, one or more of the responses is/are correct. Choose the appropriate letter which indicates the correct version.
    A   if 1 only is correct
    B   if 3 only is correct
    C   if 1 and 2 are correct
    D   if 1, 2 and 3 are correct

7. Which of the following statements about Telex is/are correct?
    1. Teleprinters must be hired from the Post Office.
    2. It provides the sender with a written record of the message.
    3. Overseas calls can be made through an International Telex Exchange.

8. Which of the following communication services is/are 'inter-active'?
    1) Ceefax
    2) Oracle
    3) Prestel

RECENT EXAMINATION QUESTIONS

Marks

LEAG 1988 GCSE BUSINESS STUDIES SPECIMEN PAPER 2B SECTION A
In the following questions 1-5 there is one group of responses A, B, C and D. Each letter in the group may be used once, more than once or not at all. For each question select the best response.

A   Telephone   B   Postal Service
C   Contravision   D   Intelpost

1. is a means of holding face-to-face meetings between people working in different areas of the country.   ½

2. is used to acknowledge receipt of a routine order from another firm.   ½

3. is a means of transmitting facsimiles of documents and drawings at high speed.   ½

4. is used to discuss a business problem with a colleague at a branch in another town.   ½

5. is used to link individuals or groups of people in different cities by sound and vision.   ½

LCCI DECEMBER 1989 SSC BACKGROUND TO BUSINESS
2. Organisations use many different methods of communication depending on the type of information to be conveyed.
    a) Describe 4 methods of communication which may be used to convey information to all employees. Give examples of the type of information appropriate for use with each method.   12
    b) Describe 2 methods of communication which may be used to convey information as quickly as possible to an overseas customer with examples of the type of information appropriate for use with each method.   6

ASSIGNMENT

> J Harris Ltd is a clothing manufacturer with its Head Office and main factory in Preston where it employs 200 staff. It also has two smaller factories and distribution depots, one employing 75 staff in Dundee to cover Scotland. The other is in Dover for deliveries in the South of England, where 80 people are employed.
>
> The firm manufacturers ladies and gents coats ranging from short light-weight types for summer wear to heavy overcoats for the winter. Much of its business comes from newspaper advertising, although it does supply a number of wholesalers and larger retailers. It delivers approximately half of its orders through its own depots, and the rest are sent through the post.
>
> Mail order customers are invited to send in their orders or place them by telephone. The company is keen to increase the number of telephone orders.

Working in groups complete the following tasks related to the above case study:

1. Describe the main services available to enable a business to communicate with its customers.

2. Explain the ways in which the Post Office can assist Harris's with its mail order trading.

3. Give examples of situations when the firm might decide to use the following services:
   a) Send a parcel COD
   b) Send a letter by 'recorded delivery'
   c) Send a parcel CF

4. Suggest reasons for the firm wanting to increase the number of telephone orders.

5. Complaints have been received about the telephone manners of some of the firm's junior staff.
   a) State what you think should be done about this.
   b) Give 3 important points to follow when answering the telephone.

6. In what ways could business firms suffer as a result of poor communications?

7. The firm is planning to hold a major staff conference in the near future. However, travelling is a problem and the management is concerned that it might need to virtually close down its depots for a week if this event took place in one location. Briefly describe any alternative ways of tackling this problem and advise the firm on what it should do to achieve the most cost effective means of communication.

8. Finally your group should make a brief verbal presentation of the answers to tasks 1-7.

25. Industrial Relations

1.   This chapter deals with the problems of industrial relations in a firm. It considers the influence of trade unions, employers associations and the government within a working situation.

DEFINITION

2.   The term 'Industrial Relations' covers every aspect of the relationship between a firm's management and its workers. People are crucial to the successful running of any business and therefore it is important that workers are happy in their job.

3.   Industrial Relations then is about preventing conflict (disagreements) at work. It is largely concerned with employees conditions of service, working environment and pay.

TRADE UNIONS

4.   A trade union is a group of workers who have joined together to bargain with their employers about pay and conditions of work. If one man in a firm tries to negotiate his own wages he will have little power, and if he goes on strike it will have little effect on the firm. However, if 1,000 workers join together in a union then they are in a much stronger bargaining position.

5.   There are about 280 trade unions in Britain today, with a total membership of about 9 million people. In 1979 trade union membership reached a peak of 13.2 million.

6.   In recent years the number of trade unions has been declining mainly because a lot of smaller unions have joined with others to form larger unions. The number of union members has also fallen because of the increase in unemployment.

7.   **Trade Union Membership 1900 – 1990**

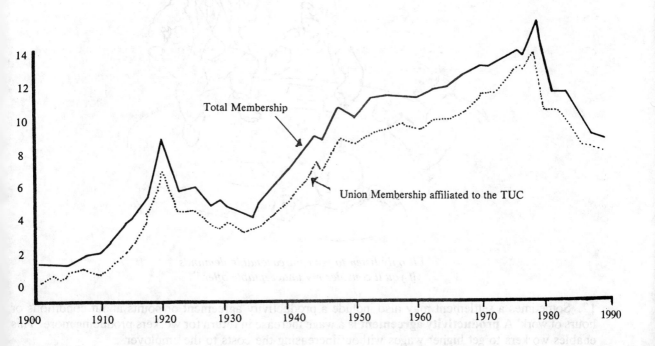

319

Aims of Trade Unions

8. The following is a list of some of the *main aims* which unions work to achieve for their members:
    *   Better pay and working conditions
    *   Shorter working hours
    *   Longer holidays
    *   Improved Health and Safety at work
    *   Better Education and Training
    *   Job security
    *   Worker involvement in decision making
    *   Equal pay and equal opportunities

COLLECTIVE BARGAINING

9. To achieve these aims trade unions negotiate with employers by a process known as collective bargaining. Each side seeks to get the best deal and reach a collective agreement which they both find acceptable.

10. **Example**

> a) The trade union demands a wage increase of £20 per week for all members.
> b) The employers offer £10 per week.
> c) Further bargaining takes place between the two sides.
> d) Both the trade union and the employers agree to an increase of £15 per week.

11.

*"I'll only listen to your unreasonable demands
if you'll consider my unacceptable offer."*

12. Sometimes a settlement may also include a productivity agreement or points about conditions or hours of work. A **productivity agreement** is a wage increase in return for workers producing more. This enables workers to get higher wages without increasing the costs to the employer.

TYPES OF TRADE UNIONS

13. The four main types of trade unions are craft, industrial, general and white collar.

14. Craft Unions

These are the oldest type of union and tend to be quite small. They represent workers in particular skilled crafts or trades, for example. Society of Shuttlemakers, National Graphical Association (NGA) and Associated Society of Locomotive Engineers and Firemen (ASLEF). As traditional skills have been replaced by new technology the number of craft unions has declined.

15. Industrial Unions

These unions represent any workers in a particular industry, for example National Union of Mineworkers (NUM) and National Union of Seamen. Because they frequently represent all workers in an industry, these unions can often be very powerful.

16. General Unions

These are the largest type of union and represent groups of unskilled and semi-skilled workers in many different jobs and industries, for example TGWU (Transport and General Workers Union) which has over 1 million members and GMB with 860,000 members. In 1993 Public Sector Unions NUPE (National Union of Public Employees), NALGO (National and Local Government Officers' Association) and COHSE (Confederation of Health Service Employees) merged to form UNISON with nearly 1½ million members.

17. White Collar Workers

This is the most recent and rapidly growing type of union. They represent professional and clerical workers in a wide range of commercial and service industries, for example, National Union of Teachers (NUT) and National Union of Journalists (NUJ).

18.

19. A trade union gets its money from its members who pay a subscription, for example £1.25 per week. This is used to pay the running costs of the union and also to provide various benefits for members, for example, strike pay, pensions.

TRADE UNION ORGANISATION

20. The basic structure of a typical trade union can be summarised as follows:

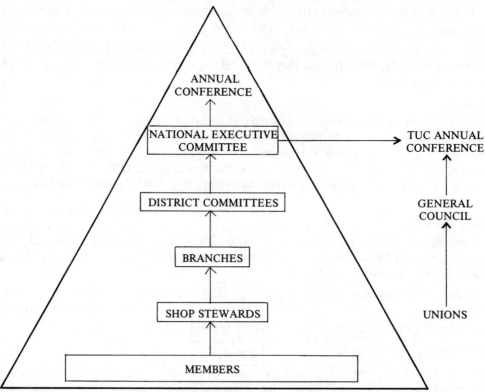

21. **Branches**   All union members belong to a branch which is either organised where they work or in the town where they live. It is usually run by a small committee including a chairman, treasurer and secretary who are unpaid volunteers elected by the members. Regular branch meetings are held to which all union members are invited to discuss union policy.

22. **Shop Stewards**   These are unpaid union officials who are elected by the members to represent them at work. Some larger firms will have several shop stewards.

23. Shop stewards carry out a number of important duties which may include:
    *   Recruiting new members
    *   Representing the union on committees, for example Health and Safety
    *   Collecting union subscriptions
    *   Dealing with problems on 'the spot'
    *   Negotiating with management

24. **District Committees**   Groups of local branches belong to geographical areas called 'districts'. These are usually run by a few full-time officials whose job is to help and advise members.

25. **National Executive Committee**   Most unions are actually run by their executive committee. It is responsible for day-to-day union affairs and also negotiates with employers and the government. Members of this committee are frequently full-time officials headed by a General Secretary.

26. **Annual Conference** Each district or branch elects representatives (called delegates) who meet once a year with the Executive Committee. The Conference considers a report on the unions affairs and this is followed by a debate to decide on union policy for the coming year.

TRADES UNION CONGRESS (TUC)

27. At the top of the trade union movement is the TUC to which most unions belong. It acts as a pressure group on matters which affect trade unions generally and speaks for the common interests of all its members. In particular, it tries to influence government policies on economic, social and industrial issues, for example, unemployment, social security benefits and taxation. The TUC holds an annual conference to which member unions send representatives. The Conference decides general policy and elects a General Council to organise its affairs for the following year.

Trades Union Congress

28. *N.B.*   Trade Unions in Northern Ireland are represented by the Northern Ireland Committee of the Irish Congress of Trade Unions (ICTU), although the majority of members belong to unions based in Great Britain.

CLOSED SHOP

29. In some firms the union(s) and the employer come to an agreement that all employees should be union members to work there. However, under the 1990 Employment Act this cannot be enforced and anyone refused a job for not joining a 'closed shop' can complain to an Industrial Tribunal.

EMPLOYERS ASSOCIATIONS

30. Just as workers may be members of trade unions so employers can belong to an employers association. These are formed by firms in the same industry and represent them in negotiations with trade unions.

31. They also provide other services for members, for example statistical information, and advice or help with recruitment, training, health, safety and industrial relations problems.

32. **Examples**

Engineering Employers Federation	British Decorators Association
Road Haulage Association	Building Employers Confederation

33.

CONFEDERATION OF BRITISH INDUSTRY (CBI)

34. The employers equivalent of the TUC is the CBI whose members include both industrial companies and employers associations. The CBI represents the interests of its members and aims to encourage greater efficiency and competition in British industry. It is run by a full-time staff headed by the Director General. Members can also get a wide range of help and advice including industrial relations, technical and export problems.

35.

36. *N.B.* Both the TUC and CBI are very powerful organisations representing millions of people, therefore they are frequently consulted by the government particularly when changes in wages, salaries and prices are being considered.

INDUSTRIAL ACTION

37. If trade unions and employers cannot reach an agreement, either side can take industrial action to put pressure on the other. The main types of industrial action are outlined below.

38. **Work-To-Rule** This involves following every single rule and regulation in such a way as to slow down work and add to the employers costs, for example, a bus driver may cause problems by refusing to drive a bus with a faulty petrol gauge.

39. **Go-Slow** This occurs when workers deliberately work slowly.

40.

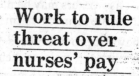

41. **Overtime Ban** Workers may also refuse to work more than their normal hours which may delay an urgent order.

42. **Sabotage** Sometimes workers will deliberately damage machinery and equipment thus delaying work.

43. **Sit-Ins** This happens when workers refuse to leave their place of work in protest at some action by their employer. Sit-ins are often used to delay or stop a firm selling or closing down a factory.

44. **Boycott**   This occurs when union members refuse to handle certain goods or materials or refuse to work with other employees.

45. **Strikes**   If everything else fails then as a 'last resort' workers may strike, i.e. withdraw their labour and refuse to work.

46. An **official** strike is called by a union which sometimes also provides strike pay for workers. However, some strikes are **unofficial** because they take place without the backing of the union. Unions can be liable for damages if an industrial dispute is deemed unlawful.

47. A 'lightning' or 'wild cat' strike is a sudden walk-out as an expression of workers anger. Union members who refuse to join a strike are known as **'scabs'**.

48. **UK Working Days Lost Through Industrial Disputes 1980 – 1993**

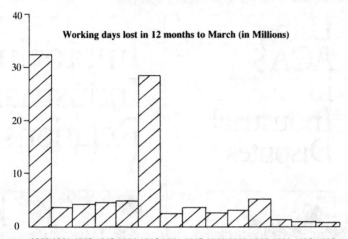

Source: Employment Gazette, Department of Employment

49. Workers on strike usually picket their firm which means that they stand outside the gates trying to persuade people, not in the union, from going to work. By law only 6 persons may picket at any one entrance to a work place.

50. **Lock-Out**   This is the employers version of a strike. A firm may literally lock the gates to prevent its employees from getting to work.

REASONS FOR DISPUTES

51. Some of the main reasons why workers take industrial action are summarised below:
   * Pay and working conditions
   * Demarcation — these are disputes between unions over which workers should do which jobs. For example, if a plumber fills a hole in a wall the union may be annoyed because it is a plasterer's job.. The problem is often caused because there are different rates of pay for different jobs and unions want to protect the jobs and wage rates of their members.
   * Victimisation – when a worker feels that they are being 'got at' by the firm.
   * Threat of redundancy – where employees may lose their jobs because there is no work for them.
   * New technology and how it is introduced, for example computers, robots – particularly where this may result in the loss of jobs.

ADVISORY, CONCILIATION AND ARBITRATION SERVICE (ACAS)

52. Where unions and employers cannot agree in a dispute they may request the help of ACAS. This is an independent body set up by the government to help improve industrial relations and encourage collec-

tive bargaining. ACAS is run by a council consisting of a chairman and nine members – three nominated by the TUC, three by the CBI and three independent members.

53. ACAS provides four main services:

    a)   It gives free **advice** to unions and employers on any industrial relations issues.

    b)   It offers a **conciliation** service. This involves trying to persuade the two sides in a dispute to start talking to each other again.

    c)   If both sides agree ACAS can offer **arbitration**. An independent third party listens to all the arguments and then makes a decision which both sides agree to accept.

    d)   If both sides do not want a binding agreement ACAS can arrange **mediation**. This involves getting the two sides together with a third party who puts forward proposals for a solution. It is then up to the two sides to decide whether to accept or ignore it.

54. **ACAS Leaflets**

ROLE OF THE GOVERNMENT

55. The government also plays an important part in industrial relations.

    a)   It is a **large employer of labour**. The government pays the wages of workers in the public sector and in recent years it has issued 'guidelines' saying that their pay increases should not be in excess of a certain percentage, for example 5%.

    b)   **Wages Councils** have been set up to decide minimum wages and working conditions in some areas of work where unions are weak, for example, catering, retailing, clothing and agriculture. These are being abolished under the 1992 Employment Rights Bill.

    c)   It can introduce **prices and incomes policies** which attempt to limit price increases and prevent large pay increases. The present Conservative government has not used this policy.

d) It may pass **new laws** which affect both workers and employers. For example the Employment Protection Act 1975 which set up ACAS, the Health and Safety at Work Act 1974, and the Trade Union Act 1984 which states that before taking industrial action, a union must first obtain the support of its members through a secret ballot (vote).

56. Modern governments have tended to get more involved in the whole structure of industrial relations. No government wants industrial disputes which slow down production thus damaging the economy. Equally, workers do not want to lose wages, whilst employers do not want to lose profits. As consumers we do not want to suffer the inconvenience of a bus or electricity strike or of not being able to buy goods because of industrial action. Therefore peaceful, industrial relations are of benefit to everyone.

SUMMARY

57. a) A trade union is a group of workers who have joined together to protect and improve their pay and other working conditions.

b) Negotiations between unions and employers are known as collective bargaining.

c) The four main types of union are craft, industrial, general and white collar.

d) Trade union members elect shop stewards to represent them in their place of work.

e) The usual organisation consists of branches, districts and a national executive committee.

f) Most unions belong to the TUC which puts forward union views to the government.

g) Employers may also join together by becoming members of an employers association.

h) The employers equivalent of the TUC is the CBI.

i) Industrial action by workers may include a work-to-rule, go-slow, overtime ban, sabotage, sit-in, boycott or strikes.

j) Employers may lock-out their workers in a dispute.

k) The main reasons for disputes include pay, working conditions and demarcation issues.

l) ACAS is an independent body which can offer help when unions and employers cannot agree in a dispute.

m) The government also influences industrial relations through its policies and legislation.

REVIEW QUESTIONS

Answers can be found in the paragraphs shown.

1. Explain the term 'industrial relations'. (2, 3)

2. What is a trade union? (4)

3. List the main aims of trade unions. (8)

4. Who takes part in collective bargaining? (9, 10)

5. List the 4 main types of union and give an example of each. (13-17)

6. Briefly explain how most trade unions are organised. (20-26)

7. What is the employers equivalent of a trade union? (31-33)

8. What are the TUC and CBI and who do they represent? (27, 28, 34-36)

9. List 6 different types of industrial action. (37-50)

10. List 4 main reasons for industrial disputes. (51)

11. Briefly describe the functions of ACAS. (52, 53)

12. Explain the role of the government in industrial relations. (55)

EXAMINATION PRACTICE QUESTIONS

Marks

1. Give 2 advantages for an employee being a member of a trade union. 2

2. Name 3 types of industrial action which workers may take in support of a claim for higher wages.

3

3. a) Name 2 of the main aims of trade unions. 2

   b) What is the Trades Union Congress? 2

4. Why do coal miners have greater bargaining power than hotel workers? 2

5. Name the term which is used to describe the situation where you cannot get a job with a particular firm without joining a trade union.

1

MULTIPLE CHOICE/COMPLETION

1. An official strike is one that is:
   a) Approved by the Government
   b) Recognised by a Union's Executive Committee
   c) Supported by the TUC
   d) Usually called by a shop steward

2. In an industrial dispute workers may take all but one of the following forms of action:
   a) Go slow
   b) Work to rule
   c) Strike
   d) Lock out

3. ASLEF is an example of:
   a) A white collar union
   b) A craft union
   c) A general union
   d) An industrial union

4. A shop steward's main role is to:
   a) Collect union dues
   b) Monitor Health and Safety standards
   c) Represent members at their place of work
   d) Try to increase union membership

5. Demarcation disputes are concerned with:
   a) Which union members should do which job
   b) The hours per week which people work
   c) Which union workers should join
   d) Workers' fringe benefits

6. Collective bargaining usually takes place between:
   a) The Government and the employers
   b) Union Officials and employers
   c) Shop Stewards and their members
   d) Trade Unions and the TUC

In each of the following questions, one or more of the response(s) is/are correct. Choose the appropriate letter which indicates the correct version.

    A   if 1 only is correct

    B   if 3 only is correct

    C   if 1 and 2 only are correct

    D   if 1, 2 and 3 are correct

7. Which of the following are provided by ACAS?

    1) Free industrial relations advice to employers and unions

    2) A conciliation service to persuade parties in dispute to negotiate

    3) Mediation resulting in proposals for settling a dispute

8. The number of trade unions is decreasing because:

    1) Many unions have merged together

    2) Unemployment has resulted in fewer members

    3) Government legislation

RECENT EXAMINATION QUESTIONS

LEAG MAY 1989 GCSE BUSINESS STUDIES PAPER 2B

Marks

1. A large firm, selling household goods, has retail stores in most towns in Britain. It employs over 10,000 people, many of whom are members of one trade union. Officials of the trade union meet with management on a regular basis to discuss rates of pay.

    a) i) Name a trade union to which most of this firm's employees could belong.   1

          ii) What type of trade union is this?   1

    b) Suggest TWO reasons, other than improving rates of pay, why this firm's employees might wish to belong to a trade union.   2

    c) Explain TWO differences between a full time union official and a shop steward.   2

    d) i) When officials of this trade union and management of the firm discuss rates of pay, this is known as   1

          ii) What action, other than strike action, can this trade union take to encourage the firm's management to improve rates of pay?   2

          iii) What action taken by the trade union is most likely to be successful? Explain your answer.   2

    e) i) What is a closed shop?   1

          ii) What would this trade union have to do if it wanted to introduce a closed shop?   1

NEA 1988 GCSE BUSINESS STUDIES SPECIMEN PAPER **SECTION B**　　　　　　**Marks**

2.　The following news item appeared in the Daily News.

THREATENED STRIKE AT ROLLFLEX

Shopfloor workers at Rollflex Engineering are threatening industrial action over management's *plans to reduce manning levels*.

"Productivity just has to be improved", said Managing Director, Bob Smith, "Our competitors are already undercutting us and we are struggling to keep up orders". Despite management assurances that there will be no *compulsory redundancies*, the *union shop steward*, Arthur Jones, stated, "We are determined to fight these plans, even if it means calling the workers out on strike".

---

a)　Which trade union is it likely that the workers at Rollflex belong to?　　　　1

b)　Explain what is meant by the phrases underlined in the passage:
　　i)　plans to reduce manning levels;
　　ii)　compulsory redundancies;
　　iii)　union shop steward.　　　　6

c)　Apart from reducing manning levels explain how else Mr Smith might improve productivity.　　　　6

d)　What other forms of industrial action might the workers at Rollflex take, apart from strike action?　　　　3

e)　If direct negotiation between management and workforce fails, what other ways are open to them to settle the dispute, apart from industrial action?　　　　4

MEG 1988 GCSE BUSINESS STUDIES SPECIMEN PAPER I

3.　Read the following information and answer the questions below. An engineering firm wants to increase its scale of production and decides to build a second factory in the Midlands. The company has been attracted to the area for the following reasons:

A　a record of good employer/trade union relations

B　grants for the training of employees in the use of new technology

C　good motorway links with the rest of the country.

a)　GIVE TWO advantages to the firm of increasing its 'scale of production'.　　　　4

b)　Explain why each of the reasons for the firm moving to the new area are important.
　　i)　good employer/trade union relations　　　　3
　　ii)　grants for the training of employees in the use of new technology　　　　3
　　iii)　good motorway links with the rest of the country　　　　3

c)　Suggest TWO ways the firm could recruit new employees.　　　　2

d)　i)　Give an example of 'new technology'.　　　　1
　　ii)　Why might employees need to be 'trained in the use of new technology'?　　　　2

e)　Name TWO trade unions whose members might work for this firm.　　　　2

f)　Give TWO advantages of membership of a trade union.　　　　2

ASSIGNMENT

The scene is set in the canteen of a printing company in Manchester. Two young workers are talking noisily in the corner – when they are joined by an older man with grey hair and a lined face.

JOHN:	"Hello Bill. This is Mary I was telling you about. She's just joined the company. She's been blowing her top because she's been told she must join the union. This is Bill Arnold, our shop steward. Mary, you can tell him what you think now."
MARY:	"Nothing personal Bill. I've nothing against unions, but I don't like being told I've got to join one".
BILL:	"Well, you see Mary, it's a closed shop".
MARY:	"I know that, but I thought this was a free country".
BILL:	"Listen Mary. A few years ago there used to be some of us who paid our subscriptions – and quite a few people who didn't. They were happy enough to accept the increases in pay our union got for them, but it was a different story when it was time to pay the union subscriptions".
JOHN:	"Yes, and when we took industrial action last year, it meant that we were all in it together".

Answer the following questions which are based on the above conversation.

1. Bill is a shop steward. What does this mean and what are his duties?

2. The union has a closed shop agreement with the company.
    a) Explain what this means
    b) From the conversation give one advantage and one disadvantage of a closed shop agreement
    c) Now give one further advantage and one further disadvantage of a closed shop.

3. What does Mary mean when she says "I thought this was a free country"? What legal rights has she got in this situation?

4. Bill refers to 'the union subscriptions'. Use an example to explain what these are and why they are needed.

5. A strike is one form of industrial action. What is meant by a strike?

6. Apart from going on strike, name 3 other forms of industrial action.

7. What do you think Mary should do if her work-mates ever decided to take industrial action? Give reasons for your answer.

8. If Mary's work-mates went on strike and Mary decided not to join them, what term would be used to describe her action?

26. The Government and Business

1. In many of the earlier chapters reference has been made to the influence of the Government on business. This chapter draws together some of these influences in terms of state ownership, legal and other controls, and the use of taxation and monetary measures to control the economy.

STATE OWNERSHIP

2. As discussed in Chapters 6 and 7, Britain has a 'mixed economy'. This means that some businesses are privately owned by individuals, whilst others like British Rail and British Coal are owned and controlled by the Government.

STATE ASSISTANCE TO AND REGULATION OF BUSINESS

3. Other examples of the influences of the Government on industry and commerce are found throughout this text including: International Trade, Company Legislation, Location of Industry, Employment, Training, Industrial Relations, Marketing, Consumer Protection, Monetary Policy and, in this chapter, Fiscal Policy (Taxation and Public Expenditure).

4. International Trade

Chapter 3 examined the assistance given to exporters through the BOTB and ECGD. The Government also influences overseas trade through its foreign exchange and balance of payments policies, customs duties and export documentation.

5. Company Legislation

Chapter 6 outlined the Government's control on both private and public limited companies through the Companies Acts.

6. Location of Industry

Chapter 9 discussed the assistance given to firms to influence the location of industry. In particular, the Government provides grants, tax relief and other benefits to encourage businesses to move into or expand in the Development Areas.

7. Employment and Training

Chapters 21 and 25 outlined some important legislation which affects the employment of people. The Government has introduced several laws, both to protect employees and also to improve their working conditions. Training is encouraged through Government funded schemes co-ordinated by TEC's.

8. Industrial Relations

In Chapter 25 the role of ACAS was discussed. This is a body which seeks to improve industrial relations and settle disputes quickly. The Government has also passed laws like the Trade Union Act 1984 which states that a trade union must hold a secret ballot before taking industrial action.

9. Marketing and Consumer Protection

Chapters 11 and 15 referred to the various laws which exist to protect consumers. The Office of Fair Trading is responsible for consumer affairs and consumer credit, whilst the Monopolies and Mergers Commission investigates proposed mergers which may not be in the public interest (see Chapter 9).

10. Economic Policy Measures

The amount of Government intervention in the economy has increased enormously during the present century. This has come about in order to raise the nations standard of living by seeking to achieve five main economic aims.

* **FULL EMPLOYMENT** – Britain has some 3 million people unemployed which is 11% of the working population. The Government therefore must be aware of the effect of its policies on the creation of jobs.

* **BALANCE OF PAYMENTS STABILITY** – In order to pay for the goods which we import we need to export and 'balance' the nations account with the rest of the world (see Chapter 3).

* **CONTROL OF INFLATION** – In the UK inflation in 1993 was about 2%. That is, the general level of prices is rising by about 2% per annum. If prices are rising, money loses value which affects business confidence and the level of investment. Therefore all Governments want to reduce inflation although there is no policy which will definitely achieve this. In the past, a Prices and Incomes Policy has often been used, whereby the Government controls the level of price and wage increases.

* **ECONOMIC GROWTH** – If a country is to enjoy a higher standard of living with an increasing amount of goods and services, then it needs a growing economy. To achieve economic growth requires capital investment in order to create extra wealth. Government policies can have an important influence on the level of investment.

* **FAIR DISTRIBUTION OF INCOME AND WEALTH** – Some people have much more than others in society. Therefore the Government tries to assist the less well-off, for example, sick, disabled, and the unemployed through 'taxation' and other policy measures.

11. Inflation 1978 – 1992

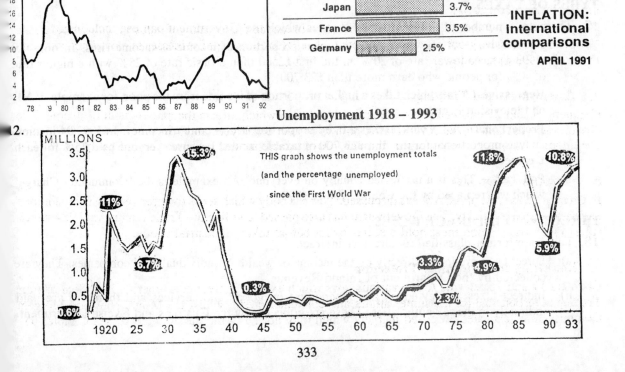

INFLATION: International comparisons
APRIL 1991

UK	8.2%
United States	5.3%
Japan	3.7%
France	3.5%
Germany	2.5%

Unemployment 1918 – 1993

12.

THIS graph shows the unemployment totals (and the percentage unemployed) since the First World War

13. Trying to achieve these aims may cause certain conflicts. For example, a policy for growth may lead to balance of payments difficulties, whilst measures to reduce inflation may lead to unemployment. Also, the Government must consider its social objectives. That is, issues which affect the community such as:

* Noise and pollution
* The protection of individual's rights, for example, employment protection
* Democratic decision making, for example election of MP's and local councillors
* Freedom of opportunity and choice
* Conservation

14. In seeking to achieve its economic aims, the Government makes use of both **Monetary Policy** and **Fiscal Policy** (Taxation and Public Expenditure).

15. **Monetary Policy**

Chapter 5 outlined the Governments monetary policy as operated by the Bank of England. Essentially monetary policy involves the control of the supply of money circulating the economy by altering interest rates, exchange rates and the availability of credit. Monetary policy can be used to encourage or discourage spending which in turn affects investment, the demand for goods and services, prices, employment and foreign trade. For example, if people have more money to spend (from increased wages and extra credit), then unless output increases, prices are likely to rise i.e. inflation.

16. **Fiscal Policy**

The Government uses fiscal policy for a number of reasons including:

* To finance expenditure, for example on health, education and roads.
* To control the economy and influence the level of demand, investment, inflation, employment and economic growth.
* To redistribute National Income and help the less well-off.
* To give incentives to industry to influence location and encourage production and investment.
* To discourage smoking, drinking and gambling.
* To control the import of certain goods either for Balance of Payments or other reasons.

TYPES OF TAXES

17. There are a number of different types of taxes which the Government can use including:

* **Progressive** – A tax which takes a higher proportion of income as income rises. Income tax (1993-4) has a lower rate of 20% on the first £2500 then a basic rate of 25% with a higher rate of 40% for people who earn more than £23,700.
* **Regressive** – A tax which takes a higher proportion of income from the poor, for example, VAT and television licences.
* **Proportional** – A tax which takes a fixed proportion of someone's income. In 1993/94 income tax was proportional for the first £23,700 of taxable income because everyone paid 25% for each £ earned.
* **Poll Tax** – This is a tax levied equally on everyone. An example is the 'Community Charge' which was replaced by the Council Tax in 1993.

DIRECT AND INDIRECT TAXES

18. Taxes are further classified as direct or indirect:

a) Direct taxes are levied directly on the income or wealth of individuals and companies. They are collected by the Department of Inland Revenue.

b) Indirect taxes are levied on the expenditure on goods and services and therefore are paid indirectly to the tax authorities. These are collected by the Customs and Excise Department.

DIRECT TAXES

19. The main direct taxes are income tax, corporation tax, petroleum revenue tax, inheritance tax and capital gains tax.

20. Income Tax

This is a progressive tax on people's income. A number of personal allowances reduce the amount of a person's taxable income. Most people pay their income tax under PAYE, whereby tax is deducted by their employer (see Chapter 22).

21. The Government can alter the level of personal taxation by changing the rate of tax, for example, reducing the basic rate from 25% to 20% in the £ or by altering the allowances.

22. Corporation Tax

This is a proportional tax on company profits. Companies are allowed to deduct certain expenditure as tax-free allowances from their gross profit. Tax must then be paid on the net profit remaining. The main rate is 33% with a reduced rate of 25% for small companies (those with profits below £250,000 pa). A high level of corporation tax could affect economic growth because it would leave firms with less money for investment.

23. Petroleum Revenue Tax (PRT)

Companies like BP and Shell who make profits from the production of North Sea Oil and Gas are also charged PRT at 50% but only on profits from existing fields.

24. Capital Gains Tax

When people sell assets such as shares, works of art or land, they are liable to pay 30% capital gains tax on any profits which they make in excess of £5,800. Exemptions are granted for the sale of certain assets, such as the sale of a person's home. Tax is charged at an individual's top rate i.e. 25% or 40%.

25. Inheritance Tax

This tax applies to transfers of personal wealth from one person to another when they die or within seven years of their death. The rate of tax is nil below a certain threshold (£150,000 in 1993/94) and 40% on anything more. Some transfers are exempt, for example those between husband and wife or involving small businesses.

INDIRECT TAXES

26. Indirect taxes may be *specific* ie consisting of a fixed sum regardless of the value of the goods, for example, 80p per packet or pint on tobacco or alcohol or *ad valorum* ie a percentage of the value of the goods, for example, 10%. The main indirect taxes are Value Added Tax and Customs and Excise Duties.

27. Value Added Tax (VAT)

As discussed in Chapter 16 VAT is levied at each stage in the production and distribution of goods and services. The final tax is paid by the consumer. The basic rate is 17½% but some items are *exempt* (for example insurance, education and postal services) whilst others are *zero rated*, for example, most food, books, drugs and exports. The effect of VAT is to increase prices which generally reduces demand.

28.

29. Customs and Excise Duties

Customs duties are charged on all *imported* goods except those from the EC. They provide income for the Government and a measure of protection from foreign competition by increasing the price of imports.

30. Excise duties are levied mainly on *home* provided goods and services including beer, wine, spirits, cigarettes, fuel and gambling.

31. Planned Receipts and Expenditure of Central Government 1992-93

Pence in every pound

Receipts				Expenditure
			9	Defence
Income tax	26		1	Foreign and Commonwealth Office
			1	Agriculture, Fisheries and Food
			1	Trade and Industry
Corporation tax	7		1	Employment
			3	Transport
Capital gains tax	1		3	Environment – housing
Inheritance tax	1		1	Environment – other environmental services
			12	Environment – local government
Value added tax	17		3	Home Office and legal departments
			3	Education and Science
Community charge and local authority rates	10		11	Health and OPCS
Duties on petrol, alcoholic drinks and tobacco	10		26	Social Security
			2	Scotland
Social security receipts	17		1	Wales
			3	Northern Ireland
			2	Chancellor of the Exchequer's departments
Interest and dividends	2		3	Other departments and European Community
Gross trading surpluses and rent	2		4	Local authority self–financed expenditure
Other duties, taxes, levies and royalties	4		2	Reserve
			7	Central government debt interest
Other receipts	2		2	Accounting adjustments
General government borrowing	12		−3	Privatisation proceeds
Total	**100**	**100**		**Total**

Cash totals £258,500 million

Sources: *Financial Statement and Budget Report 1992-93* and *Autumn Statement 1991*.

Note: Differences between totals and the sum of their component parts are due to rounding.

OTHER FORMS OF TAXATION

32. These include Car Tax, Stamp Duty, National Insurance, Licence Duties and Local Authority Rates.

33. Stamp Duty

This is charged at 1% on the total price of any property sold above a value of £60,000. (1993/94)

34. National Insurance

This is a form of direct taxation collected specifically to help finance the National Health Service and to contribute to the funds needed to provide unemployment and sickness benefits. There are four classes of National Insurance contribution:

- Class 1 – paid by employees and their employers;
- Class 2 – paid by the self-employed;
- Class 3 – paid voluntarily for pension purposes; and
- Class 4 – paid by the self-employed on their taxable profits between certain upper and lower limits. This is in addition to their Class 2 contribution.

35. The Class 1 rate paid varies with the size of a person's income, the higher the income the bigger the deduction. Employers must also pay National Insurance for every person employed and they contribute over 50% of the total amount.

36. Licence Duties

Television, driving and gun licences are all forms of taxation. A licence duty is also charged on all motor vehicles including cars, motor cycles, lorries and buses.

37. Community Charge (Poll Tax)

This is the only major tax which is not paid to the central Government. (See Chapter 7).

THE BUDGET

38. Each year, the Chancellor of the Exchequer presents a Budget to Parliament. In 1993 this was moved from March/April to November/December. This is a Financial Statement which gives the Government's estimated revenue and expenditure of the last financial year, and forecasts for the next year. It also gives details of any proposed tax changes. Sometimes 'mini' budgets are used at other times of the year.

39. The Budget has two main functions. It enables the Government to:
   a)   Regulate the economy by controlling the demand for goods and services
   b)   Redistribute income and wealth among the various sections of the community

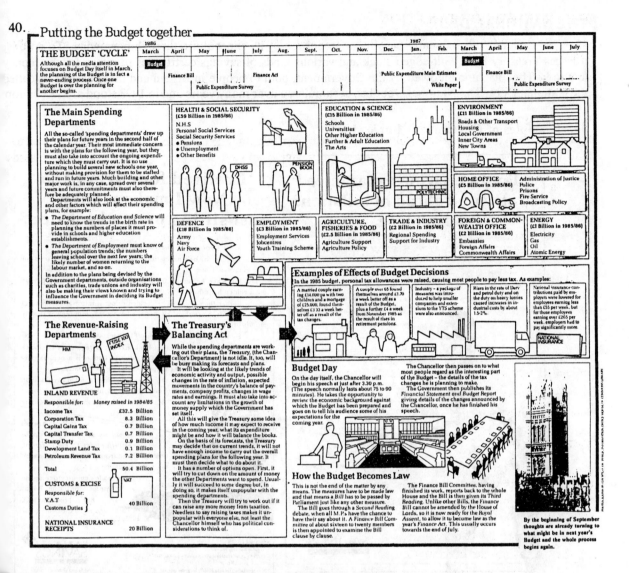

40. Putting the Budget together

THE BUDGET 'CYCLE'

Although all the media attention focuses on Budget Day itself in March, the planning of the Budget is in fact a never-ending process. Once one Budget is over the planning for another begins.

The Main Spending Departments

All the so-called 'spending departments' draw up their plans for future years in the second half of the calendar year. Their most immediate concern is with the plans for the following year, but they must also take into account the ongoing expenditure which they must carry out. It is no use planning to build several new schools one year, without making provision for them to be staffed and run in future years. Much building and other major work is, in any case, spread over several years and future commitments must also therefore be adequately planned.

Departments will also look at the economic and other factors which will affect their spending plans, for example:

- The Department of Education and Science will need to know the trends in the birth rate in planning the numbers of places it must provide in schools and higher education establishments.
- The Department of Employment must know of general population trends; the numbers leaving school over the next few years; the likely number of women returning to the labour market, and so on.

In addition to the plans being devised by the Government departments, outside organisations such as charities, trade unions and industry will also be making their views known and trying to influence the Government in deciding its Budget measures.

HEALTH & SOCIAL SECURITY
(£59 Billion in 1985/86)
N.H.S
Personal Social Services
Social Security Services
- Pensions
- Unemployment
- Other Benefits

EDUCATION & SCIENCE
(£15 Billion in 1985/86)
Schools
Universities
Other Higher Education
Further & Adult Education
The Arts

ENVIRONMENT
(£11 Billion in 1985/86)
Roads & Other Transport
Housing
Local Government
Inner City Areas
New Towns

HOME OFFICE
(£5 Billion in 1985/86)
Administration of Justice
Police
Prisons
Fire Service
Broadcasting Policy

DEFENCE
(£18 Billion in 1985/86)
Army
Navy
Air Force

EMPLOYMENT
(£3 Billion in 1985/86)
Employment Services
Jobcentres
Youth Training Scheme

AGRICULTURE, FISHERIES & FOOD
(£2.5 Billion in 1985/86)
Agriculture Support
Agriculture Policy

TRADE & INDUSTRY
(£2 Billion in 1985/86)
Regional Spending
Support for Industry

FOREIGN & COMMONWEALTH OFFICE
(£2 Billion in 1985/86)
Embassies
Foreign Affairs
Commonwealth Affairs

ENERGY
(£1 Billion in 1985/86)
Electricity
Gas
Oil
Atomic Energy

Examples of Effects of Budget Decisions

In the 1985 budget, personal tax allowances were raised, causing most people to pay less tax. As examples:

A married couple earning £14,000 pa with two children and a mortgage of £25,000, found themselves £3.33 a week better off as a result of the tax changes.

A couple over 65 found themselves around £1.70 a week better off as a result of the Budget, plus a further £4 a week from November 1985 as the result of rises in retirement pensions.

Industry – a package of measures was introduced to help smaller companies and extensions to the YTS scheme were also announced.

Rises in the rate of Derv and petrol duty and on the duty on heavy lorries caused increases in industrial costs by about 1.5-2%.

National insurance contributions paid by employers were lowered for employees earning less than £55 per week, but for those employees earning over £265 per week, employers had to pay significantly more.

The Revenue-Raising Departments

INLAND REVENUE

Responsible for:	Money raised in 1984/85
Income Tax	£32.5 Billion
Corporation Tax	8.3 Billion
Capital Gains Tax	0.7 Billion
Capital Transfer Tax	0.7 Billion
Stamp Duty	0.9 Billion
Development Land Tax	0.1 Billion
Petroleum Revenue Tax	7.2 Billion
Total	50.4 Billion

CUSTOMS & EXCISE
Responsible for:
V.A.T
Customs Duties } 40 Billion

NATIONAL INSURANCE RECEIPTS 20 Billion

The Treasury's Balancing Act

While the spending departments are working out their plans, the Treasury, (the Chancellor's Department) is not idle. It, too, will be busy making its forecasts and plans.

It will be looking at the likely trends of economic activity and output, possible changes in the rate of inflation, expected movements in the country's balance of payments, company profits, changes in wage rates and earnings. It must also take into account any limitations in the growth of money supply which the Government has set itself.

All this will give the Treasury some idea of how much income it may expect to receive in the coming year, what its expenditure might be and how it will balance the books.

On the basis of its forecasts, the Treasury may decide that on current trends, it will not have enough income to carry out the overall spending plans for the following year. It must then decide what to do about it.

It has a number of options open. First, it will try to cut down on the amount of money the other Departments want to spend. Usually it will succeed to some degree but, in doing so, it makes itself unpopular with the spending departments.

Then the Treasury will try to work out if it can raise any more money from taxation. Needless to say raising taxes makes it unpopular with everyone else, not least the Chancellor himself who has political considerations to think of.

Budget Day

On the day itself, the Chancellor will begin his speech at just after 3.30 p.m. (The speech normally lasts about 75 to 90 minutes.) He takes the opportunity to review the economic background against which the Budget has been prepared and goes on to tell his audience some of his expectations for the coming year.

The Chancellor then passes on to what most people regard as the interesting part of the Budget – the details of the tax changes he is planning to make.

The Government then publishes its *Financial Statement and Budget Report* giving details of the changes announced by the Chancellor, once he has finished his speech.

How the Budget Becomes Law

This is not the end of the matter by any means. The measures have to be made law and that means a *Bill* has to be passed by Parliament just like any other measure.

The Bill goes through a *Second Reading* debate, when all M.P.s have the chance to have their say about it. A *Finance Bill Committee* of about sixteen to twenty members is then appointed to examine the Bill clause by clause.

The Finance Bill Committee, having finished its work, reports back to the whole House and the Bill is then given its *Third Reading*. Unlike other Bills, the *Finance Bill* cannot be amended by the House of Lords, so it is now ready for the *Royal Assent*, to allow it to become law as that year's *Finance Act*. This usually occurs towards the end of July.

By the beginning of September thoughts are already turning to what might be in next year's Budget and the whole process begins again.

PUBLIC SECTOR BORROWING REQUIREMENT (PSBR)

41. If the proposed revenue and expenditure are equal then the Budget is in balance. When revenue is greater than expenditure it is in *surplus*, if it is less than the Budget, it is in *deficit*. When the Budget is in deficit the Government must borrow in order to finance its expenditure. This is called the PSBR.

42.

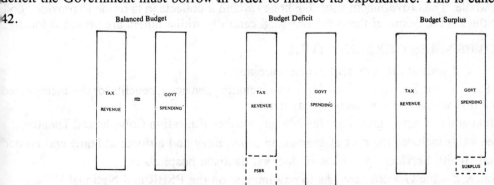

THE NATIONAL DEBT

43. The Government frequently pays for a proportion of its expenditure through borrowing. To do this, it issues Treasury Bills, Gilt-edged stock and various kinds of savings certificates in return for the money lent to it. The total amount owed by the Government, both to people in Britain and those abroad, is called the National Debt. The National Debt has accumulated over many years and in 1993 stood at £135 billion

44. Examples of Government Borrowing

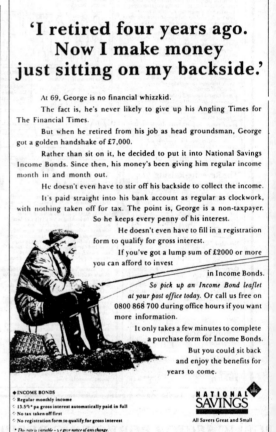

PUBLIC EXPENDITURE

45. This is the term used to describe the money which the Government spends for the benefit of the community as a whole. The Government uses the money which it collects in taxation to provide goods and services for the nation. Some of these are provided centrally whilst others are provided locally.

CENTRAL GOVERNMENT EXPENDITURE

46. The main items of central Government expenditure are:
   * Social Security and Personal Social Services – including pensions, benefits for the unemployed, sick and disabled and social security payments.
   * Education and the Arts – grants to Universities, Further Education Colleges and Theatres.
   * Defence – this includes the cost of keeping an army, navy and airforce at home and abroad
   * National Health Service – provision of doctors, dentists, hospitals etc.
   * Debt Interest – the Government has to pay interest on the PSBR and National Debt.

* Nationalised Industry – loans to public corporations for capital expenditure.
* Trade Industry and Employment – this includes grants to industry and the cost of operating Job Centres, and Training and Enterprise Councils.
* Environmental Services – spending on roads, law and order, housing etc
* Grants to Local Authorities – the Government pays a 'revenue support grant' to help finance some of the services provided by local councils and transitional relief for the new Council Tax.

LOCAL GOVERNMENT EXPENDITURE

47. The main items of Local Government expenditure are:
* Education – the provision of schools is the single most important item of local authority expenditure.
* Law and Order – police and fire services.
* Roads and transport – maintenance of minor local roads. Sometimes local transport services may be subsidised or free travel passes issued.
* Housing – provision of council houses and other accommodation.
* Social Services – for example children's homes, old people's homes, home helps and social workers for those who need help.
* Environmental services – parks, cemeteries, refuse collection, toilets etc. Also sport centres, museums, libraries and other local facilities.
* Debt interest – local councils also borrow money to finance expenditure on which interest has to be paid.

COST-BENEFIT ANALYSIS

48. When the Government is considering a major item of public expenditure, for example, developing a new motorway or coal mine, it may decide to carry out a cost-benefit analysis. Such studies attempt to evaluate all the costs and benefits which are expected to affect the community. These costs can be both private and social.

49. The *private cost* of something is essentially the price which an individual or organisation pays for it, for example, buying a car for £5,000. The *private benefits* of this purchase are difficult to estimate but will include the convenience, flexibility and saving from not using other forms of transport.

50. However, there will also be wider social costs and social benefits from this decision to buy a car. *Social costs* are those which affect the community and will include the extra traffic congestion, noise, loss of business to public or other transport, pollution from exhaust fumes and the increased wear and tear of the roads. *Social benefits* which will occur include a more flexible, mobile workforce, additional employment – in garages for parts and servicing, or road maintenance, and more Government revenue from the tax on petrol sales.

N.B. All economic activities will result in a similar mixture of costs and benefits.

51. **Social Costs and Benefits of Mining**

SUMMARY

52. a) The Government has a wide influence on business activity including some state ownership.

b) Its aim is to both encourage and regulate business activity.

c) Some areas of intervention include international trade, company legislation, location of industry, employment, training, industrial relations, marketing and consumer protection.

d) In regulating the economy the Government seeks to achieve the 5 main aims of full employment, balance of payments stability, control of inflation, economic growth and a fairer distribution of income and wealth.

e) It does this by influencing the level of demand in the economy through its monetary (controlling the supply of money) and fiscal (taxation and public expenditure) policies.

f) Direct taxes, like income tax and corporation tax, are those levied directly on the income or wealth of individuals and firms.

g) Indirect taxes are those levied on spending on goods and services and include VAT and Customs and Excise duties.

h) The Council Tax is the only major tax not paid to the central Government.

i) The Budget is a statement of how the Chancellor of the Exchequer intends to raise revenue to pay for the Governments planned public expenditure.

j) Public expenditure is the term used to describe the money which the Government spends for the benefit of the community.

k) The main items of expenditure are on Health and Social Security, Defence, Education and National Debt interest.

l) Sometimes the Government will carry out a cost-benefit analysis before embarking on major items of public expenditure.

REVIEW QUESTIONS

Answers can be found in the paragraphs shown.

1. List at least 5 ways in which the Government influences the economy. (2-9)

2. Briefly describe the Governments main economic aims. (10)

3. Name the 2 main types of policy which are used to achieve these aims. (13)

4. List the main ways in which the Government uses fiscal policy. (16)

5. Explain the differences between progressive, regressive, proportional and poll taxes. (17)

6. Using 2 examples of each, distinguish between direct and indirect taxes. (18-37)

7. In what sense is the Council Tax different from all other taxes? (37)

8. What are the 2 main functions of the Budget? (39)

9. Explain the difference between the PSBR and National Debt. (41-43)

10. Briefly explain what is meant by Public Expenditure. (31,45)

11. Give 3 examples of the main items of central Government expenditure and 3 examples of local Government expenditure. (46-47)

12. Using examples distinguish between social costs and benefits and private costs and benefits. (48-51)

EXAMINATION PRACTICE QUESTIONS

	Marks

1.   Name 2 items of public expenditure.   2

2.   The Government is considering building a new motorway. Give one example of:
   a)   A social cost
   b)   A social benefit
which might result from this development.   2

3.   a)   'Income Tax' is a progressive tax. Explain what this means.   2
   b)   'VAT' is an example of an indirect tax. What is meant by an indirect tax?   2

4.   What is the 'Budget' and why is it necessary?   3

5.   Suppose that you are thinking of buying a Japanese car on hire purchase. How would you be affected by the following Government controls?
   a)   An import quota on Japanese cars
   b)   The tightening up of hire purchase restrictions.   4

MULTIPLE CHOICE/COMPLETION

1.   Which of the following is *NOT* likely to be an objective of the Government in reforming the taxation system?
   a)   To bring it more in line with the EC countries
   b)   To make the system more regressive
   c)   To make the system more progressive
   d)   To reduce the costs of tax collection

2.   All of the following would be likely to cause an increase in Government expenditure except:
   a)   A balance of payments deficit
   b)   A Government policy aimed at reducing unemployment
   c)   An increase in the birth rate and reduction in the death rate
   d)   Raising the school leaving age

3.   Which of the following is *NOT* a source of income for local authorities:
   a)   Council Tax Revenue
   b)   Grants from the nationalised industries
   c)   Grants from the central Government
   d)   Revenue from trading activities

4.   Which of the following measures, designed to stimulate the economy, is *not* a fiscal measure:
   a)   Reduction in VAT
   b)   Budget deficit
   c)   Less hire purchase control
   d)   Lower income tax

In each of the following questions, one or more of the responses is/are correct. Choose the **appropriate** letter which indicates the correct version.

A   if 1 only is correct

B   if 3 only is correct

C   if 1 and 2 only are correct

D   if 1, 2 and 3 are correct

5.   Taxation can be used for a number of purposes. Which of the following describe uses of taxation in this country?

    1)   To raise revenue for the Government

    2)   To regulate the level of economic activity

    3)   To bring about greater equality of incomes

6.   For which of the following reasons would you expect the Government to increase its expenditure?

    1)   To increase the range of social services

    2)   To strengthen its defence policy

    3)   To raise the general level of employment

RECENT EXAMINATION QUESTIONS

Marks

SEG 1988 GCSE BUSINESS STUDIES SPECIMEN PAPER I

LOCAL AIRPORT TO BE DEVELOPED INTO A BUSINESS AREA

1000 new jobs are to be created and it is hoped that it will attract an additional 200 flights per week for small business aircraft.

Response to the news by local residents was mixed,

"I don't want another Heathrow on my doorstep".

"I've got young children who go to school in the area and the news means that there will be more traffic on the roads".

"More work for the area".

"Is it too late to stop it"?

Farncove Recorder April 1986

---

1. a)   How would the following people feel about the news?

        i)   A young couple buying a house in the area.   4

        ii)   A local hotelier.   4

        iii) A local bus company.   4

  b)   The local residents have decided to form themselves into a pressure group.

        i)   What is a pressure group?   4

        ii)   From the passage explain the points that the pressure group might use to support their case.   8

  c)   Prepare a report for the local council to:

        i)   Show the problems that the new development might create   8

        ii)   Explain how these problems might be overcome.   8

MEG 1988 GCSE BUSINESS STUDIES SPECIMEN PAPER I   **Marks**

2.   Brenda Stannard owns a business in Middlesbridge making and selling hand-thrown pottery. The District Council is redeveloping the part of the town which she thinks will not be as good for her business.

Brenda is looking at her accounts to see whether she can afford the move. She will get £66,000 for her fixed assets, and current assets are worth £20,000. She has a bank overdraft of £2,000 and creditors of £3,000.

    a)   A local councillor described Brenda's move as a social cost.
        i)   What did he mean?   2
        ii)   Give another example of a social cost.   1
    b)   State and explain TWO problems Brenda might face as a result of her move.   4
    c)   What is the difference between current assets and fixed assets?   2
    d)   Give one example of a current asset and one example of a fixed asset.   2
    e)   Brenda has estimated that she needs an extra £20,000 capital. Suggest THREE appropriate sources.   3
    f)   Brenda is worried about the success of her business in the new location. What is the importance of profit to her?   5

LCCI DECEMBER 1990 PSC STRUCTURE OF BUSINESS

3.   a)   What is the purpose of a budget?
    b)   What are the main aims of a government's economic policy?
    c)   Explain how fiscal policies may help to create more economic activity.   18

ASSIGNMENT

Working in small groups complete the following tasks:

1.   Explain what you understand by:
    a)   Monetary Policy
    b)   Fiscal Policy

2.   Discuss the advantages and disadvantages of direct and indirect taxation using examples to illustrate each point.

3.   Using the information below (or the most recent information available), devise a Budget which you think would be appropriate to our economy at the present time. List your proposals, give reasons for your decisions and outline the likely effects.

Information

Unemployment 3 million (11%) compared with 1.9 million (7%) in 1980

Inflation Less Than 3% compared with 22% in 1980.

Economic growth 3%

Balance of Payments – deficit on visible trade offset by invisibles leaving a small surplus

Distribution of income – dissatisfaction shown by run-down inner city problems and a general shift of population from North to South

4.   Present your findings in questions 1-3 above to the rest of the class.

Outline Answers

CHAPTER 1 – DEVELOPMENT OF ECONOMIC ACTIVITY

Examination Practice Questions

1. Trade

2. Barter

3. Division of labour

4. Large-scale production of a standardised product.

5. a) Primary   – extractive industries, for example coal mining.
   Secondary – conversion or construction of raw materials into finished products, for example steel, house building.
   Tertiary   – ensuring final distribution of goods to consumers. For example banking, transport. Also direct personal services not mainly concerned with goods, for example doctors.

   b) Oil company's activities:
      i)   Extraction of crude oil; prospecting and drilling
      ii) Oil refining into various products and grades for use in industry or by consumers.
      iii) Transport of crude oil or gas, or refined products. Marketing of oil products, distribution and advertising.

   c) It is limited in supply
      Seeking petrol substitutes
      Searching for new oil fields
      Making better use of by-products
      Diversifying into other energy services
      Branching out into new areas

Multiple Choice/Completion

1. D   2. B   3. B   4. A   5. D   6. C   7. C   8. C

CHAPTER 2 – POPULATION

Examination Practice Questions

1. Birth rate, migration

2. Demand, mobility, progression, dependency

3. a) Average number of years someone can expect to live
   b) Number of deaths per 1000 of the population
   c) Number of people per square mile

Multiple Choice/Completion

1. A   2. D   3. C   4. B   5. C   6. E

CHAPTER 3 – INTERNATIONAL TRADE

Examination Practice Questions

1. Tariffs – tax on imported goods
   Quotas — restrictions on quantity of imports.

2. $12,000

3. Free trade between member states, common external tariff on all imported goods.

4. Difference in value between imports and exports of services.

5. £1,000 million surplus

346

Multiple Choice/Completion

1. A   2. D   3. C   4. A   5. B   6. B   7. D   8. C

CHAPTER 4 – COMMERCIAL BANKS

Examination Practice Questions

1. a) Cash dispenser, standing orders, direct debits, bank giro, safe deposit, banker's draft etc.

   b) Night safe – used after banking hours
   Cheque Cards – guarantees payment on cheques
   Standing Orders/Direct Debits – regular payments for goods bought on credit
   Credit Cards – to increase business etc

2. a) Standing Order
   b) Crossed
   c) Overdrafts
   d) Interest
   e) Stale

3. a)

DATE	DETAILS	DEBIT	CREDIT	BALANCE	
1 June	b/f			£115.50	Cr
6 June	117594	4.50		£111.00	Cr
6 June	117597	22.95		£88.05	Cr
10 June	Cr Transfer		101.95	£190.00	Cr
11 June	Standing Order	12.00		£178.00	Cr
14 June	117596	34.00		£144.00	Cr
14 June	Cash Dispenser	50.00		£94.00	Cr
18 June	D D	25.00		£69.00	Cr
19 June	Standing Order	20.00		£49.00	Cr
22 June	Sundry Credit		13.90	£62.90	Cr
28 June	Charges	3.70		£59.20	Cr

   b) Balance 30 June = £59.20 credit.

4. Fixed amount lent by bank usually for fixed time and with a fixed rate of interest on cost.
A fluctuating amount with an agreed upper limit. Interest rate may vary and is charged on the amount outstanding.

5. Must be paid into bank account, cannot obtain cash over the counter.

Multiple Choice/Completion

1. C   2. B   3. C   4. B   5. C   6. A   7. D   8. B

CHAPTER 5 – THE GOVERNMENT AND BANKING

Examination Practice Questions

1. a) When you do not have a bank account with a cheque book, small amounts
   b) Cross it
   c) Add stamps to the value of 7p
   d) Poundage
   e) Girobank

2. Ordinary – £1 deposit, withdrawals up to £100 on demand
Investment – £5 deposit, one month's notice, higher rate of interest

3. Government's bank – keeps Government's accounts, manages national debt, implements monetary policy etc. Banker's bank – keeps accounts for all commercial banks, cheque clearing settlement etc.

Multiple Choice/Completion

1. C   2. D   3. D   4. A   5. B   6. D

CHAPTER 6 – TYPES OF BUSINESS ORGANISATION – PRIVATE ENTERPRISE
Examination Practice Questions

1. a) Own boss, job satisfaction, easy to set up, innovation etc.
   b) Bank loan, friends, trade credit, ploughed back profits.
   c) Partner who shares in the management of the business.
   d) More capital, division of labour, sharing of risks and responsibilities, cover for absence during holidays or sickness.
   e) Equally

2. a) Share = Part of the capital of a company. Shareholders supply the capital and therefore own part of the business. In return receives dividend (share of profits).
   b) Limited liability. Only stand to lose amount invested.

3. PLC or LTD, minimum share capital of £50,000 for PLC, Sale of Shares to public, restriction on transfer of shares.

4. Co-operative Wholesale Society. Manufactures and supplies goods to co-operative retail societies.

5. Certificate of Incorporation.

Multiple Choice/Completion

1. D   2. C   3. A   4. B   5. A   6. A   7. D   8. C

CHAPTER 7 – TYPES OF BUSINESS ORGANISATION – PUBLIC ENTERPRISE
Examination Practice Questions

1. Community Charge, business rates, grants, loans, trading activities.

2. a) Established by Act of Parliament. Owned and controlled by government. Monopolies. Profit making not main aim, provision of social service(s). Organisation – Minister, Chairman, Board, Areas.
   b) Provision of social service(s), profits to the nation.

3. a) Private, owned by individual shareholders.
   b) Ownership – shareholders/government
      Management/control – Board of Directors/Minister – Board
      Capital – shares, loans, profits/government, loans, profits
      Size – various/large, monopolies.

Multiple Choice/Completion

1. C   2. B   3. B   4. C   5. D   6. D   7. A   8. C

CHAPTER 8 – BUSINESS ORGANISATION AND MANAGEMENT
Examination Practice Questions

1. Directors, Managing Director

2. a) Administration – Office Services, Data Processing
      Marketing – Research, Advertising, Promotion, Sales
      Purchasing – Ordering, Storage, Stock Control
      Training – Induction, Junior, Refresher, Management
      Production – Manufacturing, Quality Control

b) Without production there is nothing to market, without marketing goods may not sell, therefore no need for production. Both must meet agreed deadlines and work together.

3. The number of subordinates who can be properly controlled by a manager/supervisor/foreman.

4. Credit.

Multiple Choice/Completion

1. A   2. A   3. D   4. C   5. B   6. C   7. D   8. C

CHAPTER 9 – LOCATION AND THE SIZE OF FIRMS

Examination Practice Questions

1. Diseconomies of scale/diminishing returns.

2. Industrial inertia.

3. 25%

4. Vertical   – acquisition of businesses at different stages of production process
   Horizontal   – acquisition of businesses at same stage of production process
   Lateral   – acquisition of business producing related products

5. Large a) and d)
   Small b), c), e)

Multiple Choice/Completion

1. D   2. B   3. C   4. C   5. A   6. D   7. B   8. D

CHAPTER 10 – MARKETING

Examination Practice Questions

1. a) Electric kettle   (v)
   b) Insurance   (i)
   c) Coffee   (iv)
   d) Sales records   (ii)
   e) Test Marketing   (iii)

2. Market Research

3. a) Cycle through which the sales of a product progress from development, introduction to growth, maturity, saturation and decline.

   b) Sales likely to decline as competitors enter the market with improved products using the very latest technology.

Multiple Choice/Completion

1. A   2. D   3. D   4. A   5. C   6. A

CHAPTER 11 – ADVERTISING AND SALES PROMOTION

Examination Practice Questions

1. a) Goods sold at near or below cost to attract customers. For example sugar and tea in supermarkets.

   b) Name applies to a particular product to distinguish it from similar products made or sold by other firms.

2. a) Higher prices due to cost of advertising being added to the price of goods.

b) Lower prices due to mass production. If firms sell more because of advertising they can produce in large quantities which is cheaper.

3. Voluntary – ASA, Broadcasting Act 1990, Radio Authority Code of Practice.
Legal – Trade Descriptions Act 1968. Consumer Credit Act 1974

4. Impulse buying

5. a) Television – reaches mass market
        Radio Luxembourg – teenagers listen to pop music in the evenings
        Teenage magazine – read by potential customers
        Cinema – visited by large number of teenagers
    b) Romance, ambition and success, hero worship, social acceptance etc.
    c) Informative advertising – provides factual information; examples
        Persuasive – attempts to influence consumer; examples
    d) Questionnaires. Interviews. Telephone enquiries. Sampling by a Panel. Test marketing.
    e) If the product not successful, a lot of money wasted. Production expensive. Market research to find target audience. To enable production of product which consumers want.

Multiple Choice/Completion

1. B   2. D   3. C   4. D   5. D   6. B   7. A   8. C

CHAPTER 12 – MARKETS AND MIDDLEMEN
Examination Practice Questions

1. a) Wholesaler   b) Middleman   c) Cost   d) Retailers
    e) Manufacturers   f) Consumers

2. a) i) Buying goods in large quantities from manufacturers and supplying them in smaller quantities to retailers.
        ii) Allowing retailers to buy goods now and pay for them at the end of the month.
    b) Turnover large enough for them to order in bulk direct from manufacturers *OR* provide their own wholesale organisations within the firm.

3. Diamonds

4. a) Buying something at today's price for delivery in the future.
    b) Commodities, for example wool, sugar, rubber, cocoa, Foreign Exchange.

5. Large organisations which use other people's money to invest in stocks and shares, for example Insurance Companies, Unit Trusts.

Multiple Choice/Completion

1. B   2. C   3. B   4. A   5. C   6. B   7. D   8. D

CHAPTER 13 – RETAILING
Examination Practice Questions

1. i) C   ii) A   iii) B   iv) H   v) G

2. a) Variety chain store — 10+ branches, own brands, range of quality goods etc.
    b) Department Store – collection of departments, additional comfort and facilities, town centre sites etc.
    c) Hypermarket – at least 50,000 sq ft. Out of town centre where land is cheaper. Stocks wide range of goods. Competitive prices. Free parking. Cheap petrol. Special offers.
    d) Discount Store – mainly electrical goods. Consumer durables. Cheaper prices due to bulk purchases. Few assistants. Edge of town centre.

3. Economies of scale – direct (bulk) buying from manufacturers, specialist staff, national advertising etc.

4. **Advantages**
    a) Small retailer – personal service, convenience
    b) Supermarket – cut prices, choice, atmosphere
    c) Department Store – comfort, selection, credit
    d) Multiple Store – standards, price, range
    e) Discount Store – low prices, car parking

    Disadvantages
    a) Small retailer – higher prices, limited stock
    b) Supermarket – impersonal, location, check-out delays
    c) Department Store – location, prices, impersonal
    d) Multiple Store – impersonal, sameness, transport costs
    e) Discount Store – location, delivery

5. Dividend – share of profit with customers.

6. a) Chocolate, milk, drinks, food, soap powder, cigarettes etc.
    b) Unsuitable for bulky items or where advice is needed, for example furniture, cars, electrical equipment.

Multiple Choice/Completion

1. A   2. B   3. D   4. B   5. D   6. B   7. C   8. C

CHAPTER 14 – TRANSPORT

Examination Practice Questions

1. Baltic Exchange
2. Environmental costs of traffic such as noise, pollution and the need for police patrols.
3. Advantages   – convenience, 'free' advertising, cheaper, quicker, assets
    Disadvantages – more capital needed, particularly if vehicles bought outright, more expensive if fleet not fully used, maintenance.

Multiple Choice/Completion

1. C   2. B   3. B   4. D   5. A   6. C   7. D   8. C

CHAPTER 15 – CONSUMER PROTECTION

Examination Practice Questions

1. Yes, unless they were made aware of the fault when purchasing the goods.
2. Apply to the Office of Fair Trading for a credit licence.
3. a) Trade Descriptions Act 1968 – made it an offence to mislead consumers be falsely describing goods or services.
        Consumer Credit Act 1974 – provides consumers with a wide range of protection when buying goods on credit.
        For example, information about the true annual percentage rate of interest, etc.
        Sale of Goods Act 1979 – updated earlier legislation. Goods sold must be:
        i)   of merchantable quality
        ii)   fit for their normal purpose
        iii) as described
        If any of these conditions are not met, then the consumer has legal rights to get the problem(s) resolved.
    b) Office of Fair Trading, Statutory Bodies, for example POUNC.

Multiple Choice/Completion

1. C   2. D   3. A   4. A   5. B   6. C

CHAPTER 16 – BUSINESS DOCUMENTS
Examination Practice Questions
1. Enquiry, quotation, order, invoice, statement, plus explanation of each.
2. Quotation
3. a) Reduction in price to trade customers. Percentage deducted if debt paid within specified period.
   b) £160
4. £352.50
5. Yes. Cash discount is given for prompt payment. Cheque is normal method used.
6. Sea/Air transport; Bill of Lading provides proof of ownership. Air consignment note receipt only.

Multiple Choice/Completion
1. B   2. A   3. C   4. B   5. C   6. D

CHAPTER 17 – BUSINESS FINANCE
Examination Practice Questions
1. Unlikely because fish and chips are sold for cash.
2. Sales.
3. Yes. If the overheads are greater than the gross profit there will be a net loss.
4. Fixed – stepladders, brushes, buckets, vehicle, blowtorch etc.
Circulating – paint, wallpaper, paste, turps etc.
5. Bankruptcy.

Multiple Choice/Completion
1. B   2. B   3. A   4. A   5. B   6. D   7. B   8. A

CHAPTER 18 – CONTROLLING BUSINESS COSTS
Examination Practice Questions
1. £50
2. a) Fixed costs do not vary with output for example rent.
   b) Variable costs vary directly with output, for example raw materials.
   c) Total cost = fixed cost + variable cost, for example finished product.
3. Profit
4. Fixed
5. Production
6. a) 300 units & 1100 b)   800 units
   c) u, x   d) v, y
   e) Quantity of stock ordered/received
   f) In case of delivery delays. More than minimum might be required to meet special orders.
   g) As maximum stock is the most a firm can afford to finance/has room for, a smaller amount may be preferred. Prompt delivery makes it unnecessary.
   h) Order form – request for goods including description and price(s).
   i) Ensures sufficient stock to meet production/customer demand. Limited storage space. Does not tie up too much finance.

Multiple Choice/Completion
1. C   2. B   3. C   4. A   5. C

CHAPTER 19 – INSURANCE
Examination Practice Questions

1. a) Contribution
   b) Premium
   c) Fidelity guarantee
   d) Uninsurable
   e) Brokers

2. Consequential loss

3. a) Third Party
   b) Third Party Fire and Theft (TPFT) – covers liability for insurers to other people including passengers and damage to their property, plus damage to the car by fire and theft.
      Comprehensive – as for TPFT but including accidental damage to the car, medical expenses and loss of radios, clothing and personal effects.
   c) Comprehensive – because new car. Mr Patel would stand to lose a lot if his car was badly damaged in a crash.

4. a) i) **Restaurants** – premises, equipment/contents, stock – against fire, damage, burglary; consequential loss
      Employees – employers liability; fidelity guarantee
      Customers – public liability – in case of accidents on premises
   ii) **Delivery Van** – motor vehicle, third party minimum by law, TPFT, comprehensive.
   b) Depreciation, trading loss, bankruptcy – such risks are dependent on quality of management of firm; therefore cannot be calculated.

Multiple Choice/Completion

1. B   2. D   3. A   4. C   5. D   6. C

CHAPTER 20 – THE STOCK EXCHANGE
Examination Practice Questions

1. a) £2,500
   b) £5,000
   c) 10%
   d) $\frac{100}{160} \times 10\% = 6.25\%$
   e) £200,000

2. a) Difference between bid and offer prices
   b) Commission on value of transaction

3. Share on which a fixed dividend is paid out of profits before Ordinary Shares. Entitled to arrears in future if profits are inadequate.

4. a) Debentures – Loans to the company. Creditors to be paid first. Fixed rate of interest. Can force company to liquidation.
   b) Preference Shares – Safe shareholding. Fixed rate of interest. First shareholders to be paid out of profits unless cumulative variety are owed money. Seldom have vote.
   c) Ordinary Shareholders – one share one vote. Last to be paid a dividend. But dividend varies according to profits of the company. Consequently could be higher than for Preference.
   d) £1,000
   e) £4,000
   f) £30,000 available
   g) 15% $\left(\frac{£30,000 \times 100}{200,000}\right)$

Multiple Choice/Completion

1. A   2. C   3. D   4. B   5. A   6. D

CHAPTER 21 – RECRUITMENT, SELECTION AND TRAINING

Examination Practice Questions

1. Training, increased chance of getting a job, pay, meeting friends etc.

2. a) Summary of career and qualifications
   b) To see how someone 'presents' themselves

3. Induction, basic skills

4. a) Recruitment and training – ensuring that all employees are in suitable jobs
   Dismissals, resignations and retirements – looking after formalities
   Personnel records – full up-dated records of all employees
   Welfare – provision of canteen, social club etc., help for individual in difficulties
   Safety – compliance with regulations, first aid
   Relations with trade unions and/or employee associations – minor and major disputes, wages negotiations
   b) Improve job satisfaction
   Safety and welfare activities may reduce absences of staff due to sickness, accident, domestic difficulties
   Industrial relations – quick and amicable settlement of disputes

Multiple Choice/Completion

1. D   2. B   3. D   4. C   5. C   6. C

CHAPTER 22 – PEOPLE AND WORK

Examination Practice Questions

1. Gross pay is what is actually earned from which statutory and voluntary deductions are made to calculate net pay.

2. i) j
   ii) i
   iii) d
   iv) b
   v) h
   vi) a
   vii) e
   viii) g
   ix) c
   x) f

3. P45

4. Unemployment, sickness, pension, medical treatment.

5. a) Payment per hour or portion of hour worked; payment per item produced
   b) i) Supervision costs are reduced
      ii) Earnings are directly related to effort

6. National Insurance, superannuation, SAYE, union subscription, sports/social club

Multiple Choice/Completion

1. A   2. D   3. C   4. D   5. B   6. A   7. C   8. C

CHAPTER 23 – COMMUNICATION

Examination Practice Questions

1. Memorandum (memo)

2. a) Newspaper advertisement, letter post, price list
   b) i) Letter   ii) Memorandum

3. External – advertising, postal, telecommunications etc.
Internal – memo, personal contact, house journal etc.

354

4. Alterations and corrections on screen, no need to re-type, sending copies of the minutes to committee members.

5. a) Written communication in form of: house magazine, memorandum on important orders won or policy developments, bulletins on staff notice board; clear job descriptions, staff assessment/appraisal. Visual communication on results, for example, break-even charts, sales or profits graphs. Verbal communication between management and staff on methods, purpose, training in new developments.

    b) i) Telephone   ii) delays in answering, difficulty in finding people, poor telephone manner

        i) Letters   ii) delays in answering, quality of content, poor presentation
        i) Documentation/Forms   ii) quality/ease of filling in firm's forms
        i) Advertising/Promotion   ii) poor sales literature, product instructions, ineffective advertisements
        i) Face-to-Face (verbal)   ii) Poor/unhelpful/badly trained staff

Multiple Choice/Completion

1. D   2. B   3. A   4. C   5. A   6. B   7. D   8. C

CHAPTER 24 – POSTAL SERVICES AND TELECOMMUNICATIONS

Examination Practice Questions

1. Cash on Delivery. (COD)

2. Advantage – immediate answer, quick and easy.
Disadvantage – no written record, may have difficulty contacting someone.

3. Datapost provides overnight door-to-door service throughout the country. Particularly suited to sending computer data.

4. Teletext – computerised information broadcast by TV company, for example Ceefax (BBC), Teletext (IBA)
Videotext – computerised information transmitted via telephone lines, for example Prestel, Datel.

5. a) Business Reply Service – specially printed cards or envelopes supplied by firm.
    Freepost – customer use own envelope (with no stamp). Licence from Post Office required for both.

    b) Encourages people to buy.

6. a) Telephone – oral, person to person, messages could be mis-understood
    Telex – printed record, machine to machine, available anytime.

    b) i) Overseas or out of hours calls
      ii) Communications accompanied by documents
         Communications needing signature(s) (for example contracts)
         Confidential messages
      iii) Interview for job (or other valid answer)

    c) i) Recorded Delivery merely provides evidence of delivery
         Registered Post also covers insurance against loss of contents
      ii) Recorded Delivery – application for job to ensure delivery
         Registered Post – valuable enclosures, covered if lost.

    d) Available at over 100 Post Offices, high speed service for sending exact copies of documents and other urgent items. Same day delivery, collection to over 2000 centres including overseas.

Multiple Choice/Completion

1. C   2. A   3. D   4. D   5. C   6. A   7. D   8. B

CHAPTER 25 – INDUSTRIAL RELATIONS

Examination Practice Questions

1. Job protection, help obtain better working conditions and pay, offer help and advice.

2. Strikes, work-to-rule, overtime ban.

3. a) Improving wages, working conditions, job security, maximise membership, achieving closed shop.
    b) Federation of Trade Unions to protect their interests.

4.   Better organised in trade unions because work in large groups. Hotel workers are less well organised because they are dispersed throughout the country.

5.   Closed shop.

Multiple Choice/Completion

1. B   2. D   3. B   4. C   5. A   6. B   7. D   8. C

CHAPTER 26 – THE GOVERNMENT AND BUSINESS

Examination Practice Questions

1.   Education, Health, Defence, Social Security etc

2.   a)   Pollution, loss of land, loss of business on existing route etc
     b)   By-pass towns and villages, faster travel, possible extra jobs etc

3.   a)   Tax that takes proportionately more from higher than lower incomes. The higher the income the greater percentage rate of tax deducted.
     b)   Tax on goods and services.
          May be a proportion or a flat rate.

4.   Government's annual financial statement giving details of proposed income and expenditure. Outlines proposed tax changes needed to control economy and achieve main economic aims.

5.   a)   Could be difficult to find a car or the model required. The price may rise because they are scarce.
     b)   If deposit raised from say 20% to 30%, would involve finding more cash.
Both of above may mean unable to buy car.

Multiple Choice/Completion

1. B   2. C   3. B   4. C   5. D   6. D

Index (By reference to chapter and paragraph)

Index *(By reference to chapter and paragraph)*

Index *(By reference to chapter and paragraph)*

A First Course in
STATISTICS
D Booth

This book provides a core text for introductory level courses in statistics. It assumes the student has no prior knowledge of statistics whatsoever and no more than an ability to handle simple arithmetic.

COURSES ON WHICH THIS BOOK IS KNOWN TO BE USED:
BTEC Business and Secretarial Studies; RSA; LCCI; AAT Certificate.

CONTENTS:

This is Statistics • Fundamental Ideas • Asking the Question • Collecting the Data • Deriving the Statistics • Communicating the Results • **Asking Questions** • Questions and Statistics • Who Asks the Questions • How to Ask Questions • How Not to Ask Questions • Questionnaire Design • When to Ask Questions • **Collection of Data** • Primary Data • Probability and Sampling • Organising the Data • Tabulation of Data • Secondary Data • Graphical Representation of Data • **Deriving the Statistics** • Single Statistics • Dispersion • Multiple Statistics • Index Numbers • Regression • Correlation • Time Series • **Communicating the Results** • The General Principles of Presentation • Demonstration Tables • Pictorial Representation • The Use of Words • Answers to Exercises.

REVIEW COMMENTS:

'The book is a breath of fresh air to those who think statistics is an essentially practical subject, as it has not only a section on the derivation of individual statistics but also three sections dealing with the practical details and problems associated with 'Asking the question', 'Collecting the data' and 'Communicating the results' which are so often given such little emphasis in introductory statistical texts ... Each chapter of each section ends with a short series of exercises, answers being provided only to alternate questions, a nice touch to cut out the "right answer/wrong calculation" effect yet still giving students some answers...'
"The Mathematical Gazette"

Free Lecturers' Supplement

ISBN: 0 905435 84 2

Extent: 304 pp

Size: 246 × 189 mm

A First Course in
MARKETING
F Jefkins

This book has been specially prepared for those with no prior knowledge of marketing and who need to get to grips with the subject in a simple and straightforward manner. It has quickly gained wide use as support material on BTEC First and National courses.

COURSES ON WHICH THIS BOOK IS KNOWN TO BE USED:
BTEC First and National; RSA; LCCI; CAM Certificate in Communication Studies.

CONTENTS:

The Nature of Marketing • What is Marketing ? • What is the Marketing Mix? • How does Competition Affect Marketing Strategy? • What is the Product Life Cycle? • Sales Forecasting, Price and Marketing Research • How are Sales Forecasts and Risks Assessed? • What Determines Price? • What is Marketing Research? • Distribution • How are Goods and Services Distributed? • How has Distribution Changed in Recent Years? • How is Direct Response Marketing Conducted? • Promotion and Public Relations • What is the Role of Advertising? • How can Public Relations Help Marketing? • What is the Role of Sales Promotion? • How can Sponsorship Help Marketing? • How are Industrial Goods and Services Marketed? • Consumerism, Legal and Voluntary Control • How does Consumerism Affect Marketing? • Legal Controls Affecting Marketing • Self-Regulatory Controls Affecting Marketing.

REVIEW COMMENTS:

'Another superb DPP book - ideal for the BTEC National Diploma Introduction to Marketing module!' '...useful on any basic marketing course...' 'Well planned - is British with British examples...' '...accessible to students ...'   Lecturers

ISBN: 1 870941 28 4

Extent: 192 pp

Size: 246 × 189 mm

Free Lecturers' Supplement

A First Course in
COST AND MANAGEMENT ACCOUNTING

T Lucey

This book provides a broad introduction to cost and management accounting for those who have not studied the subject before. It is written in a clear, straightforward fashion without technical jargon or unnecessary detail. The text includes many practical examples, diagrams, exercises and examination questions. Features include several objective tests for self-assessment and assignments for activity-based learning.

COURSES ON WHICH THIS BOOK IS KNOWN TO BE USED:

BTEC National Business and Finance; RSA; LCCI; AAT; Management and Supervisory Studies; Business Studies and Marketing courses; Access courses; Purchasing and Supply and any course requiring a broad, non-specialist treatment of cost and management accounting.

CONTENTS:

Cost Analysis and Cost Ascertainment • What is Product Costing and Cost Accounting? • Elements of Cost • Labour, Materials and Overheads • Calculating Product Costs • Job, Batch and Contract Costing • Service, Process and Joint Product Costing • Information for Planning and Control • What is Planning and Control? • Cost Behaviour • Budgetary Planning • Budgetary Control • Cash Budgeting • Standard Costing • Variance Analysis • Information for Decision Making and Performance Appraisal • What is Decision Making? • Marginal Costing • Break-even Analysis • Pricing Decisions • Investment Appraisal • Performance Appraisal of Departments and Divisions.

Free Lecturers' Supplement

ISBN: 1 870941 54 3
Extent: 300 pp
Size: 246 × 189 mm